USING BLOCKCHAIN TECHNOLOGY IN HEALTHCARE SETTINGS

'*Using Blockchain Technology in Healthcare Settings* is a game-changer. With its clear explanations and actionable insights, this book is essential reading for healthcare professionals looking to navigate the complexities of data management and privacy in the digital age.'

Habib Youssef, University of Sousse, Tunisia

This book looks at the integration of blockchain technology in healthcare settings, focusing on its potential to address security and privacy concerns of medical applications. From fragmented electronic health records (EHRs) to data breaches and interoperability issues, innovative solutions are necessary to unlock the full potential of health information and prevent the recurrence of such issues.

Blockchain offers a promising framework for addressing these challenges. Its decentralized, tamper-resistant nature holds the key to building trust and transparency in healthcare data management. By leveraging blockchain technology, secure, interoperable systems empower patients to take control of their health information while facilitating a seamless collaboration among healthcare providers. Throughout this book, the authors explore the fundamental principles of blockchain technology and its applications within the healthcare landscape. From EHRs and patient consent management to pharmaceutical supply chains and clinical research, this book examines how blockchain can drive efficiency, enhance security, and ultimately improve patient outcomes.

This book is intended for a broad audience, including healthcare professionals, patients, policymakers, and anyone interested in the intersection of technology and healthcare.

Analytics and AI for Healthcare

Artificial intelligence (AI) and analytics are increasingly being applied to various healthcare settings. AI and analytics are salient to facilitate better understanding and identifying key insights from healthcare data in many areas of practice and enquiry including the genomic, individual, hospital, community, and/or population levels. The Chapman & Hall/CRC Press Analytics and AI in Healthcare Series aims to help professionals upskill and leverage the techniques, tools, technologies, and tactics of analytics and AI to achieve better healthcare delivery, access, and outcomes. The series covers all areas of analytics and AI as applied to health care. It will look at critical areas including prevention, prediction, diagnosis, treatment, monitoring, rehabilitation, and survivorship.

About the Series Editor

Professor Nilmini Wickramasinghe is professor of digital health and the deputy director of the Iverson Health Innovation Research Institute at Swinburne University of Technology, Australia, and is inaugural professor–director of health informatics management at Epworth HealthCare, Victoria, Australia. She also holds honorary research professor positions at the Peter MacCallum Cancer Centre, Murdoch Children's Research Institute, and Northern Health. For over 20 years, Professor Wickramasinghe has been researching and teaching within the health informatics/digital health domain. She was awarded the prestigious Alexander von Humboldt award in recognition of her outstanding contribution to digital health.

Using Blockchain Technology in Healthcare Settings
Empowering Patients with Trustworthy Data
Edited by Ben Othman Soufiene, Saurav Mallik, and Abdulatif Alabdulatif

For more information about this series, please visit: https://www.routledge.com/analytics-and-ai-for-healthcare/book-series/Aforhealth

USING BLOCKCHAIN TECHNOLOGY IN HEALTHCARE SETTINGS

Empowering Patients with Trustworthy Data

*Edited by Ben Othman Soufiene, Saurav Mallik,
and Abdulatif Alabdulatif*

CRC Press

Taylor & Francis Group
Boca Raton London New York

CRC Press is an imprint of the
Taylor & Francis Group, an **informa** business

Designed cover image: Photo de stock Blocs avec serrures sur fond bleu 2040640298 | Shutterstock

First edition published 2025
by CRC Press
2385 NW Executive Center Drive, Suite 320, Boca Raton FL 33431

and by CRC Press
4 Park Square, Milton Park, Abingdon, Oxon, OX14 4RN

CRC Press is an imprint of Taylor & Francis Group, LLC

© 2025 selection and editorial matter, Ben Othman Soufiene, Saurav Mallik and Abdulatif Alabdulatif; individual chapters, the contributors

Library of Congress Cataloging-in-Publication Data
Names: Soufiene, Ben Othman, editor. | Mallik, Saurav, editor. | Alabdulatif, Abdulatif, editor.
Title: Using blockchain technology in healthcare settings : empowering patients with trustworthy data / edited by Ben Othman Soufiene, Saurav Mallik, and Abdulatif Alabdulatif.
Description: First edition. | Boca Raton, FL : CRC Press, 2025. | Series: Analytics and AI for healthcare | Includes bibliographical references and index.
Identifiers: LCCN 2024044044 (print) | LCCN 2024044045 (ebook) | ISBN 9781032774473 (hbk) | ISBN 9781032774459 (ppk) | ISBN 9781003483113 (ebk)
Subjects: LCSH: Blockchains (Databases)--Medical applications.
Classification: LCC R859.7.B56 U85 2025 (print) | LCC R859.7.B56 (ebook) | DDC 610.285/57588--dc23/eng/20241209
LC record available at https://lccn.loc.gov/2024044044
LC ebook record available at https://lccn.loc.gov/2024044045

ISBN: 978-1-032-77447-3 (hbk)
ISBN: 978-1-032-77445-9 (pbk)
ISBN: 978-1-003-48311-3 (ebk)

DOI: 10.1201/9781003483113

Typeset in Sabon
by KnowledgeWorks Global Ltd.

CONTENTS

EDITORS

Ben Othman Soufiene is an assistant professor of computer science at the University of Gabes, Tunisia. He earned a PhD in computer science at Manouba University in 2016 for his dissertation on "Secure Data Aggregation in Wireless Sensor Networks." He earned an MS degree at Monastir University in 2012. His research interests include the Internet of Medical Things, wireless body sensor networks, wireless networks, artificial intelligence, machine learning, and big data. He has coauthored more than 110 research articles with a Google H-index of 20.

Saurav Mallik (Member, IEEE) earned a PhD at Jadavpur University, Kolkata, India, in 2017. His postgraduate studies were conducted with the Machine Intelligence Unit, Indian Statistical Institute, Kolkata, India. He is a research scientist at the University of Arizona, USA. He previously held a postdoctoral fellow with Environmental Epigenetics, Harvard T. H. Chan School of Public Health, University of Texas Health Science Center, Houston, and with the Miller School of Medicine, University of Miami, USA. He has coauthored more than 150 research articles with a Google H-index of 20. His research interests include computational biology, bioinformatics, data mining, biostatistics, and pattern recognition.

Abdulatif Alabdulatif is an assistant professor at the School of Computer Science and Information Technology, Qassim University, Saudi Arabia. He earned a PhD in computer science at RMIT University, Australia, in 2018. He earned a BSc in computer science at Qassim University, Saudi Arabia, in 2008, and an MSc in computer science at RMIT University, Australia, in 2013. He has published more than 70 academic papers in prominent journals. His research interests include applied cryptography, cloud computing, and e-health.

CONTRIBUTORS

Alanoud Eisa Faraj Alfalahi, United Arab Emirates University, Al Ain, United Arab Emirates.

Shahd Rashed Abdulla Alhebsi, United Arab Emirates University, Al Ain, United Arab Emirates.

Syed Immamul Ansarullah, Govt. Degree College, Sumbal, Jammu and Kashmir, India.

R. Mohan Krishna Ayyappa, Mahatma Gandhi Institute of Technology, Hyderabad, India.

J. Balajee, Mother Theresa Institute of Engineering and Technology, Chittoor, Andhra Pradesh, India.

Syed Muzamil Basha, REVA University, Bengaluru, Karnataka, India.

C A Bindyashree, REVA University, Bengaluru, Karnataka, India.

Faten Chaabane, University of Gabes, Tunisia.

Mrinalini Choudhary, Royal University of Women, Riffa, Bahrain.

Narayanage Jayantha Dewasiri, Sabaragamuwa University of Sri Lanka, Belihuloya, Sri Lanka.

Sonia Dhiman, Chitkara University, Punjab, India.

Fayaz Ahmad Fayaz, Lovely Professional University, Punjab, India.

G. S. Pradeep Ghantasala, Alliance University, Bengaluru, India.

Sumita Gupta, Amity University, Noida, Uttar Pradesh, India.

Prabhjot Kaur, Chitkara University, Punjab, India.

Shahbaz Khan, University of Tabuk, Tabuk, Saudi Arabia.

Adyaa Khaneja, Amity University, Noida, Uttar Pradesh, India.

Mamatha Kurra, Chitkara University, Punjab, India.

Anand Muni Mishra, Chandigarh University, Mohali, Punjab, India.

Anita Mohanty, Silicon University, Bhubaneswar, Odisha, India.

Maitri Mohanty, GIET University, Gunupur, Odisha, India.

Ambarish G. Mohapatra, Silicon University, Bhubaneswar, Odisha, India.

Thangavel Murugan, United Arab Emirates University, Al Ain, United Arab Emirates.

Amar Ratnakar Naik, PES University, Bangalore, India.

Sivachandran Narayanan, Putra Business School, Serdang, Malaysia.

Sukanta Nayak, Vellore Institute of Technology, Inavolu, Amaravati, Andhra Pradesh, India.

Paresh Kumar Panigrahi, Vellore Institute of Technology, Inavolu, Amaravati, Andhra Pradesh, India.

Md Mahfujur Rahman, Universiti Utara Malaysia, Sintok, Kedah, Malaysia.

Premansu Sekhara Rath, GIET University, Gunupur, Odisha, India.

Mananage Shanika Hansini Rathnasiri, Sabaragamuwa University of Sri Lanka, Belihuloya, Sri Lanka.

Kamalesh Ravesangar, Tunku Abdul Rahman University of Management and Technology, Kuala Lumpur, Malaysia.

Anuradha Reddy, Chitkara University, Punjab, India.

Shrddha Sagar, Galgotias University, Greater Noida, Uttar Pradesh, India.

Puneeta Singh, Galgotias University, Greater Noida, Uttar Pradesh, India.

Rubee Singh, GLA University, Mathura, India.

Muzaffar Ahmad Sofi, Lovely Professional University, Punjab, India.

Ben Othman Soufiene, University of Sousse, Tunisia.

Kalyan Tadepalli, Jio Institute, Ulwe, Navi Mumbai, Maharashtra, India.

Mounira Tarhouni, University of Gabes, Tunisia.

A. Thriveni, Viswam Engineering College, Annamayya, Andhra Pradesh, India.

T. Vijaykumar, Mother Theresa Institute of Engineering and Technology, Chittoor, Andhra Pradesh, India.

Abdul Wahid Wali, Govt. Degree College, Sumbal, Jammu and Kashmir, India.

1

APPLICATIONS OF BLOCKCHAIN TECHNOLOGY IN THE GLOBAL HEALTHCARE SYSTEM

Adyaa Khaneja and Sumita Gupta

1.1 Introduction

The process of bringing a trade or exchange to a close or settlement is usually used to define the term "transaction." Regardless of the scale or complexity, all transactions, regardless of their size or type, have one thing in common: they all demand that the parties involved have faith in one another or follow a set of rules that makes this faith possible. Nearly all of the functions of regulatory bodies and specific government departments are to set enforceable rules or laws that foster trustworthy environments for stakeholders to conduct business.

A technical study [1] describing Satoshi Nakamoto's conception of a brand-new payment system known as Bitcoin was published in 2008. The paper makes the claim that conventional trust-based payment methods, which allow for reversals, raise transaction costs and the amount of intermediary work required by a "trusted third party" (in this example, a bank). Small-value transactions cannot be completed digitally due to the high transaction fees.

According to the study, trust might be added to transactions cryptographically rather than through "trust systems" or "trusted third parties."

Without the parties having to be acquainted, this would guarantee a shared order of transactions through computations. Participants would be able to perform transactions without the requirement for an intermediary party through a peer-to-peer distributed network that timestamps transactions, avoiding the inefficiencies brought on by the more conventional approach [2].

This established the basis for the blockchain technology, which is a decentralized, distributed digital ledger made up of records called blocks that are

DOI: 10.1201/9781003483113-1

securely linked together using cryptographic hashes to record transactions across many computers. As a result, any involved block cannot be changed retroactively without changing all succeeding blocks, making it tamper-proof and secure [3].

Data ownership and data security are the two main issues facing the healthcare industry today. Currently, sensitive medical records do not have a safe framework, which causes data breaches with serious repercussions. Another issue is that individuals do not now fully own their medical data, a point that is becoming more important with the emergence of wearable technology and personalized therapy. A digital healthcare ecosystem must successfully address both of these concerns [4].

Blockchain technology has the potential to transform the healthcare system. It uses the three principles of cryptography, decentralization, and consensus to create a highly secure underlying system that is nearly impossible to tamper with which can improve accessibility and security of patient information and can therefore address the two challenges of the digital healthcare ecosystem mentioned above [5].

1.1.1 Research objectives

- To look into how blockchain technology is currently being used and how it may be applied in the healthcare industry.
- To evaluate the effects of blockchain on data privacy and security in healthcare systems, especially in the context of managing electronic health records (EHRs).
- To explore the potential of blockchain in improving interoperability and data exchange among different healthcare providers and systems.
- To investigate how blockchain technology might improve the management of the supply chain for drugs and medical equipment in the healthcare sector.
- To analyze the benefits and challenges of implementing blockchain in clinical trials and research, focusing on data integrity, transparency, and participant consent.
- To evaluate the role of blockchain in facilitating efficient health insurance and claims processing, including fraud prevention and streamlined administrative processes.
- To investigate the potential of blockchain in supporting telemedicine and remote patient monitoring, enabling secure and decentralized patient–doctor interactions.
- To review real-world case studies and implementations of blockchain in health care, analyzing their outcomes and identifying key success factors and limitations.
- To assess the overall impact of blockchain on healthcare outcomes, including improved patient outcomes, reduced costs, and enhanced healthcare delivery.

- To provide recommendations for healthcare organizations, policymakers, and researchers on the adoption and future directions of blockchain technology in health care.

These research objectives will guide the study and help explore various dimensions of blockchain implementation in health care, ensuring a comprehensive analysis of its benefits, challenges, and potential impact.

1.2 Blockchain technology: Overview and key concepts

1.2.1 Definition

The distributed ledger technology (DLT) known as blockchain creates a layer of trust and does away with the necessity for a third party to verify the transactions. Distributed systems, cryptography, and other technologies are all combined in blockchain technology [6].

Blockchains contain records called blocks that contain data and transactions that are protected from tampering using cryptographic hash algorithms (as shown in Figure 1.1). Using the hash function, blocks are securely linked to one another. This results in a blockchain, a distributed ledger that is kept across different network nodes. Each block includes transaction information, the preceding block's hash, a date, etc., as shown in Figure 1.1.

At the majority of places, it is challenging for an enemy to change the stored details. In comparison to a centralized system, blockchain hence offers greater security. A Merkle tree is used to hash and encode batches of legitimate transactions into blocks. To link each block to the one before it in the blockchain, a cryptographic hash is included in each block. A chain is created

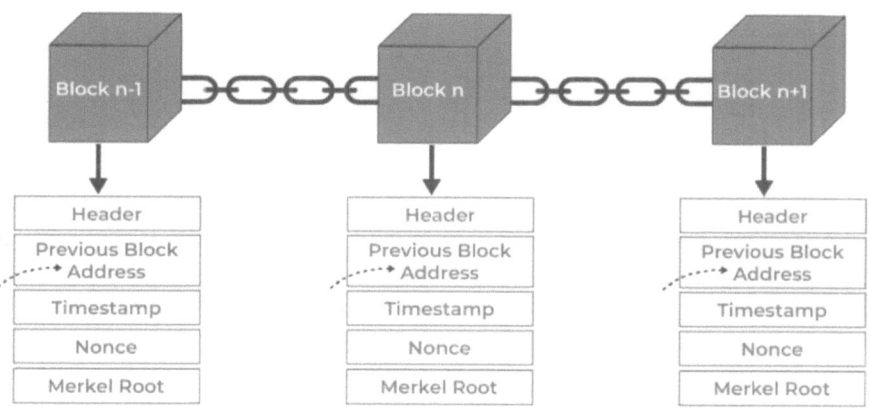

FIGURE 1.1 Block structure in a blockchain.

Source: [Original (created by authors)]

by the connected blocks. The genesis block, also known as Block 0, is the first block in an iterative process that verifies the integrity of each subsequent block. Digital transactions are entered into a shared ledger by members of the distributed network. The proposed transaction is evaluated and verified by network members before being added to the network. In the event that the transaction is accepted by the majority of the network's participants, the shared ledger is updated to reflect the new transaction. In minutes or, in some circumstances, seconds, changes to the shared ledger are reflected in every copy of the blockchain. A transaction cannot be modified or withdrawn after it has been added; it becomes immutable. No single member of the network has the ability to tamper with or change data because every member possesses a full copy of the blockchain.

1.2.2 Distributed ledger technology

Using distributed ledger technology (DLT), many locations simultaneously record asset transactions and their associated information (as shown in Figure 1.2). Distributed ledgers lack a central data store and management features in contrast to conventional databases. The nodes in a distributed ledger process and validate every item, producing a record of it and establishing a consensus as to its truthfulness [7].

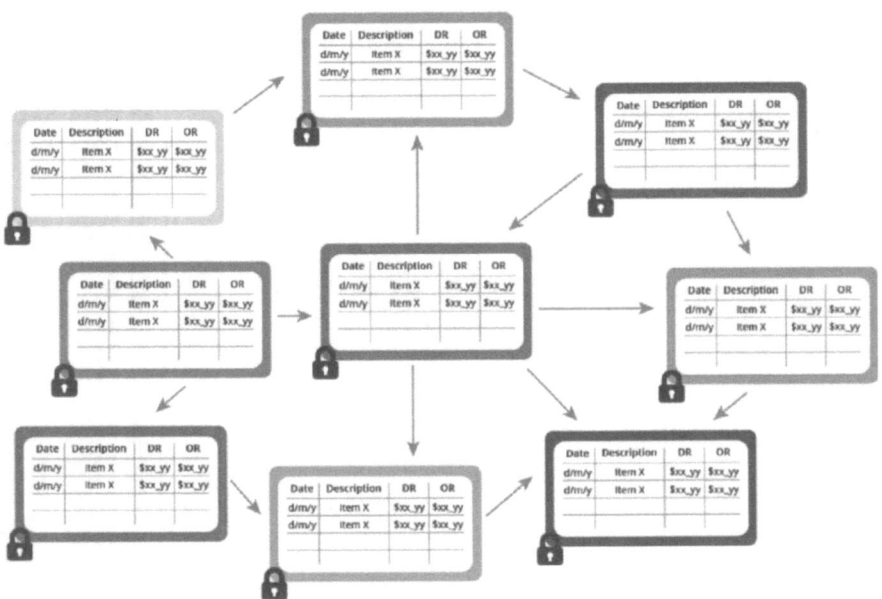

FIGURE 1.2 Recording the transactions in blocks.

[Original (created by authors)]

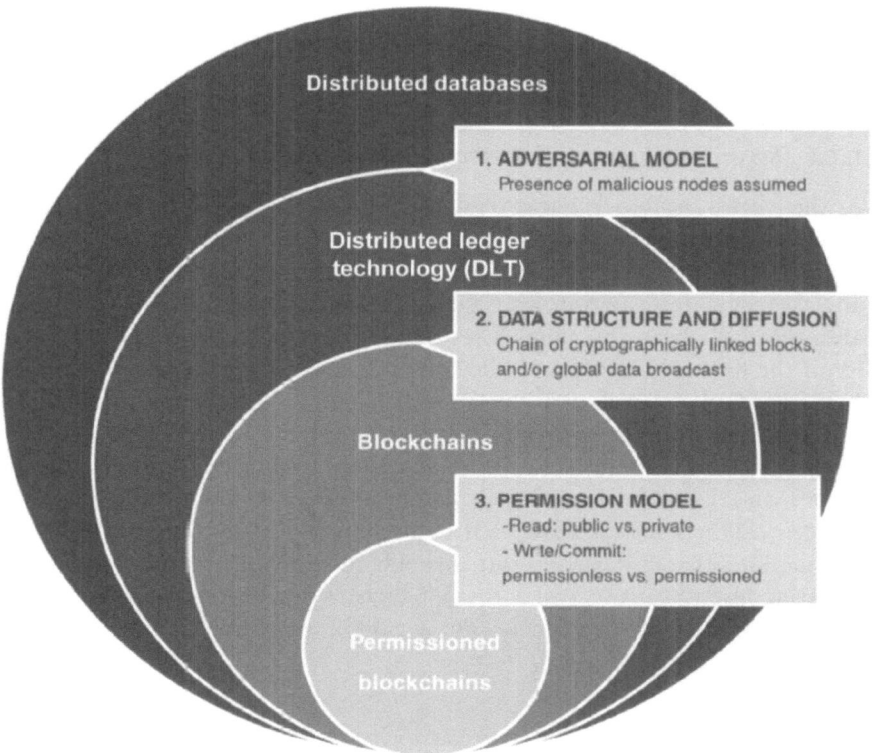

FIGURE 1.3 Distributed ledger technology.

[Original (created by authors)]

Several comparable technologies, including blockchain, are referred to together as distributed ledger technology (DLT) (as shown in Figure 1.3). Although the terms "distributed ledger technology" and "blockchain technology" are sometimes used interchangeably, they each utilize a distinct mechanism for data storage. One way to conceptualize a blockchain is as a subset of DLT in which a number of transactions are maintained in "blocks" and cryptographically linked to the previous block through a "chain."

Simply said, blockchain technology uses distributed databases to store data about transactions between parties. These databases are distinguished by the inability to change them without the consent of a majority of the distributed database's custodians (and users). The application of cryptographic functions means that transactions can be completed without the need for a central authority and that they can be verified as coming from a certain identity.

As a result, blockchain is a decentralized, irreversible ledger of peer-to-peer transactions made up of linked transaction blocks. According to Gartner, the reduction of fraud, cost reductions, and more transparency would enable distributed ledgers and blockchains to deliver USD $3.1 trillion in additional corporate value by 2030 [8].

1.2.3 Recordkeeping on a timestamped, fault-tolerant ledger

At their heart, all blockchains render it both technically and financially impractical to change a record that has already been uploaded to the blockchain. All nodes of the network keep a record of the transaction's timestamp, any associated information, and the digital signatures of the parties involved after they have been appended. These data cannot be changed unless a majority of the network's nodes collude, which is increasingly rare and expensive as the network expands.

Blockchains are the best option for keeping track of any digital asset, including money, real estate, health information, valuable collectibles, domain names, and others because they by nature preserve an audit trail.

Peer-to-peer networks are used to decentralize the storage of data and transactions that are carried out through the network in the ledger. Consensus (consensus protocols) across blockchain network nodes validates and verifies transactions. In a blockchain network, the online transaction flow is depicted in Figure 1.4.

1.2.4 Smart contracts for decentralized, corruption-proof, self-triggering applications

Up to this point in the study, blockchains have only been described as a global, peer-to-peer repository, but they can also be developed to function

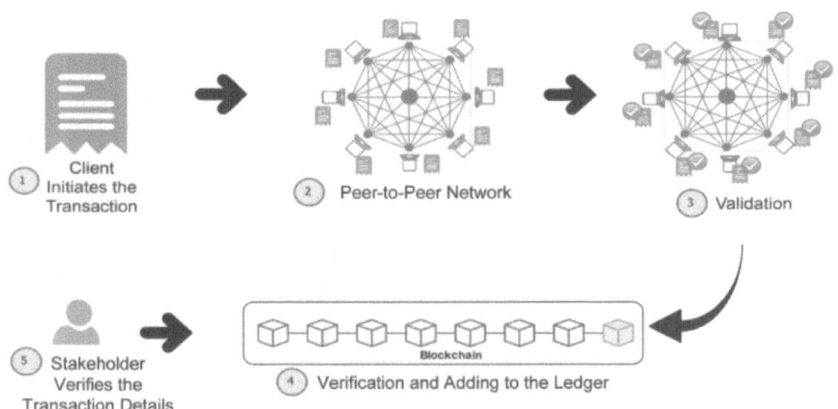

FIGURE 1.4   Blockchain network and the process of adding new transactions to a ledger.

[Original (created by authors)]

as a global, peer-to-peer processor that executes code and apps provided by developers in an unmodified manner.

A smart contract is a piece of computer code that serves as a legally binding contract on a blockchain network. Once released or turned off, the code cannot be altered. More crucially, it can automatically initiate blockchain transactions when specific criteria are met, preventing dishonest parties from interfering with the process.

The blockchain is a serverless/decentralized infrastructure where code is executed and money is transferred, preventing third parties from interfering with the transaction or intervening to divert money to their own accounts.

1.2.5 Digitization of assets and new economic models

Digital representations are possible for all types of real-world assets, including those that are movable or immovable (such as land versus cars) or fungible or nonfungible (such as gold against an IP property).

Since any asset may be represented as a token that denotes either complete or partial ownership of the underlying economic resource, blockchains are the ideal platform for asset digitization. Without the need for middlemen, blockchain tokens can be traded between parties without any friction, providing liquidity even when the underlying asset lacks it. This opens the door for novel economic models, such as smart contracts that automatically distribute dividends to partial landowners or asset consumers that automatically pay asset providers.

The identity of the token's owner can be validated, but it cannot be altered or spoofed, unlike digital assets and tokens on traditional database systems. These token transfers over blockchain systems are incorruptible, making it impossible for intermediaries to steal money or engage in double-spending.

Blockchain can influence competitiveness and innovation on digital marketplaces. Two important costs that are impacted by technology are the cost of networking and the cost of verification, according to Cataline and Gams [9].

The ability to inexpensively verify state, including details about previous transactions and their characteristics, as well as present ownership of a native digital asset, is referred to as the cost of verification.

The cost of networking depends on an organization's ability to bootstrap and manage a market, as opposed to handing control to a centralized intermediary. This is done by combining the ability to inexpensively verify state with financial incentives designed to reward state transitions that are particularly helpful from the perspective of a network, such as the gift of the resources needed to operate, scale, and secure a decentralized network.

The ensuing digital marketplaces, which are characterized by more competition, lower entry hurdles, and a lower privacy risk enables participants to make joint investments in shared infrastructure and digital public utilities without ceding market power to a platform operator.

1.2.6 Blockchain architectures

Based on a variety of various underlying technology decisions, blockchain can be divided into several groupings (as shown in Figure 1.5). The potential for the technology to significantly enhance our current procedures, as well as the criteria provided above, remain basically consistent. Below are some prominent technical options and related technology groups.

- Should transactions be made public? Blockchains are both public and private.
- Securing agreement for the inclusion of new information? Different consensus protocols.
- **Private blockchain systems:** Each node is a recognized entity in a private blockchain system and is encouraged to join the network. The system administrator may also change each network node's read/write scope. Take a huge organization that creates a blockchain for its industrial supply chain as an example. Every supply chain link will be given the option to run a node in this network. Nobody else will have the ability. Because of this, it may be claimed that the parties recognize (if not trust) one another, needing a more lenient approach to reach a decision or make database modifications. These permissioned private blockchain systems provide fine-grained access restrictions that give the system administrator control over each network node's read/write scope.
- **Public blockchain systems:** Any user may join the peer-to-peer network in a public blockchain system without needing to be invited. All nodes have the same rights, which allows them to read anything from the network and submit transactions to it.

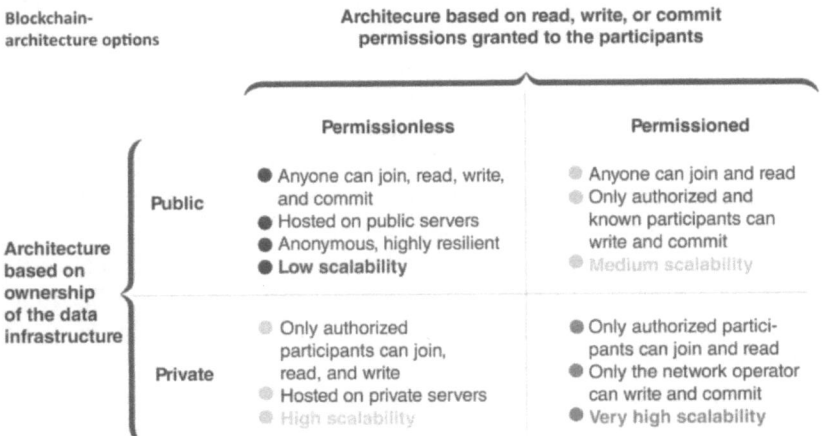

FIGURE 1.5 Blockchain architectures.

[Original (created by authors)]

These blockchains are entirely open and may include dishonest or conspiratorial players who would try, for example, to overwrite/delete prior transactions or modify a piece of data. This contrasts with private blockchains where all nodes are presumed to be trustworthy. Public blockchain systems reward moral behaviors with money and punish dishonest people with money in an attempt to deter dishonest behavior.

Legislative clarity will be necessary to permit this significant form of blockchain in India since it is anticipated that public blockchains would have the most promising use cases for a number of reasons. A token economy must be present for public blockchains to scale properly.

1.3   Applications of blockchain in health care

The healthcare landscape is evolving very quickly. Due to the improvements in genetic research and advancements in precision medicine, it is witnessing innovative approaches to disease prevention and better patient care. Simultaneously, due to advancements in IT, researchers and clinicians have access to large databases of health information that can help to further fine-tune the treatment planning for improved patient care.

Blockchain technology has the potential to solve the interoperability problems that are currently plaguing health IT systems and to establish itself as the technical norm that enables individuals, healthcare entities, providers, and researchers to safely exchange electronic health data. Additionally, this technology has the potential to significantly facilitate improved health outcomes (as shown in Figure 1.6).

A chance exists for health data management and information exchange to become more integrated and smoother across the many stakeholders thanks to blockchain-enabled interventions. In India's healthcare and other related ecosystems, this information exchange can be grouped into five key blockchain use cases. The various steps in a patient's healthcare journey over the course of their entire life span can then be matched to these use cases [10].

1.3.1   *Patient data management using electronic health records*

In the healthcare domain, the ability to securely manage and share patient health records is of utmost importance. Electronic health records (EHRs) have made significant strides in digitizing medical data, but they still face challenges related to security, interoperability, and privacy. By leveraging the unique properties of blockchain, EHR systems can be enhanced to ensure data integrity, security, and seamless sharing while maintaining patient privacy. Blockchain technology holds immense potential for revolutionizing EHR systems and patient health records. Its ability to provide enhanced

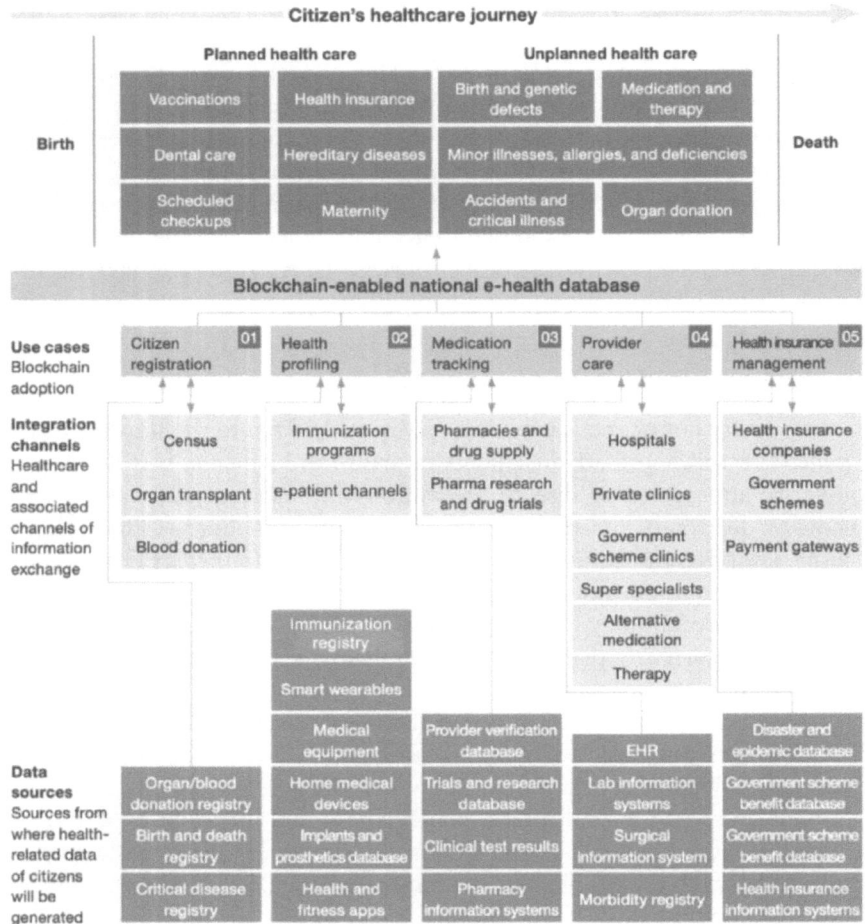

FIGURE 1.6 Major use cases of blockchain in health care.

[Original (created by authors)]

security, data integrity, interoperability, and privacy makes it an ideal solution for addressing the challenges faced by traditional EHR systems.

- **Enhanced Security and Data Integrity:** One of the fundamental features of blockchain is its ability to provide enhanced security and data integrity. Traditional EHR systems are often centralized, making them vulnerable to cyberattacks and unauthorized access. Blockchain, on the other hand, offers a decentralized architecture that is more resistant to hacking attempts due to its distributed ledger nature. In a blockchain-based EHR system, each transaction or update to a patient's record is recorded as a block and added to a chain. These blocks are cryptographically linked to previous blocks, creating an immutable and tamper-proof record. This ensures that patient health data remains secure, transparent, and unalterable. Any unauthorized attempts to modify the data are immediately detected and rejected by the network, making blockchain an ideal solution for safeguarding sensitive patient information.

- **Interoperability and Seamless Data Sharing:** Interoperability is a major challenge in health care, as different healthcare providers and organizations often use disparate systems that do not communicate effectively with each other. By offering a standardized framework for data sharing and interoperability, blockchain technology has the potential to get over this obstacle. With blockchain-based EHR systems, patient health records can be securely shared across different healthcare providers, regardless of the specific EHR software they use. The decentralized nature of blockchain eliminates the need for intermediaries and allows for direct peer-to-peer communication and data exchange. This seamless sharing of information improves care coordination, reduces medical errors, and enables a holistic view of a patient's medical history, leading to better healthcare outcomes.
- **Privacy and Patient Control:** Privacy concerns surrounding patient health records are a significant barrier to adopting digital systems. Blockchain can address these concerns by incorporating privacy-enhancing features while granting patients greater control over their own data. In a blockchain-based EHR system, patients can maintain ownership and control over their health records. They can grant permissions to healthcare providers, researchers, or other authorized entities for accessing specific portions of their data. This decentralized approach empowers patients to manage their privacy preferences and ensures that their data is not unnecessarily exposed to unauthorized parties. Furthermore, blockchain's inherent transparency enables patients to track every instance where their records are accessed, providing them with a comprehensive audit trail and enhancing trust in the system.

1.3.2 Drug traceability and supply chain management

Efficient supply chain management is vital for ensuring the availability, traceability, and safety of healthcare products and services. However, the healthcare industry faces numerous challenges in managing its complex supply chains, including counterfeit drugs, inefficient inventory management, and limited transparency. Blockchain technology presents a promising solution to address these issues and revolutionize healthcare supply chain management. The use of blockchain can enhance transparency, traceability, and security, ultimately improving patient safety and operational efficiency in the healthcare supply chain.

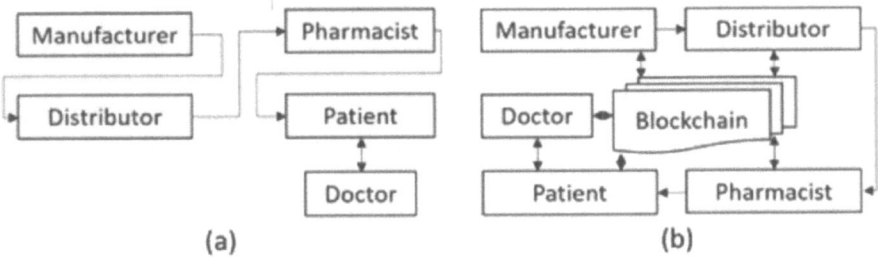

FIGURE 1.7 Solving the drug counterfeiting problem using blockchain.
[Original (created by authors)]

Figure 1.7 demonstrates how blockchain can be used to address the issue of drug fraud. In (a), there is a chance that the original drug could be tampered with at any point in the drug's journey from the manufacturer to the patient through the distributor and pharmacist by altering the labels, the expiration date, etc. Any modification cannot be recognized without a feedback system. Similarly, there is no way for the pharmacist to verify that the prescription that the doctor gave the patient was not changed. To close these possible gaps, the blockchain is utilized in (b). Every medicine is logged to the blockchain, and since everyone involved is connected to it, they can verify the veracity of any information or product they get [11].

- **Enhancing Transparency and Availability:** Transparency and traceability are critical in the healthcare supply chain to track the movement of products, identify potential issues, and ensure compliance with regulatory requirements. Blockchain technology provides a decentralized and immutable ledger that enables real-time visibility and transparency across the supply chain. By utilizing blockchain, each transaction or movement of a product is recorded as a block, forming an unalterable chain of information. This allows stakeholders to trace the entire journey of a product, from its origin to its final destination, including information on manufacturers, distributors, and retailers. The transparency provided by blockchain reduces the risk of counterfeit drugs entering the supply chain, as every step can be audited and verified, ensuring the authenticity and integrity of the products.
- **Improving Inventory Management and Efficiency:** Inefficient inventory management often leads to supply shortages, delays in patient care, and increased costs. Blockchain technology can address these challenges by streamlining inventory management processes and enhancing supply chain efficiency. With blockchain-based systems, all stakeholders in the supply chain, including manufacturers, distributors, and healthcare providers, can have access to a shared, synchronized ledger of inventory data. This

real-time view of inventory levels, demand, and distribution enables accurate forecasting, efficient stock management, and proactive replenishment. By optimizing inventory levels and minimizing stockouts, blockchain-driven supply chain management ensures timely access to healthcare products and reduces waste, ultimately improving patient care.

- **Ensuring Product Authenticity and Preventing Counterfeits:** Counterfeit drugs pose a significant threat to patient safety and public health. Blockchain technology can play a crucial role in combating this issue by ensuring product authenticity and preventing the circulation of counterfeit or substandard medications. Blockchain-based solutions enable the implementation of unique product identifiers, such as serial numbers or barcodes, that can be securely stored on the blockchain. These identifiers, coupled with smart contracts, allow for the verification of product authenticity throughout the supply chain. Patients, healthcare providers, and regulators can scan the unique identifier and instantly access information about the product's origin, manufacturing process, and distribution history. This transparency helps identify and eliminate counterfeit products, safeguarding patient health and trust in the healthcare system.

- **Enhancing Regulatory Compliance and Auditing:** A crucial component of managing the healthcare supply chain is regulatory compliance. By providing a secure and auditable record of transactions, paperwork, and quality control procedures, blockchain technology helps streamline compliance operations. By leveraging blockchain, regulatory authorities can access real-time information on the movement of healthcare products, ensuring adherence to safety standards, licensing requirements, and quality certifications. Additionally, audits can be conducted more efficiently and accurately, as the blockchain serves as an immutable source of information. This streamlines regulatory processes, reduces administrative burdens, and promotes trust between stakeholders in the supply chain.

1.3.3 Clinical trials and research

Clinical research and innovation are vital for advancing medical knowledge, developing new treatments, and improving patient care. However, the traditional clinical research process often faces challenges such as data fragmentation, lack of transparency, and concerns over data privacy and integrity. Blockchain technology presents a transformative solution by offering a decentralized and secure framework that can revolutionize clinical research and innovation in health care.

- **Security and Data Integrity:** Clinical research generates vast amounts of sensitive and valuable data, including patient health records, genomic data, and research findings. By utilizing blockchain, researchers can create an immutable and tamper-proof record of every transaction or update made to the data. Each piece of data is cryptographically linked and stored in blocks across a distributed network of computers. This decentralized nature of blockchain prevents unauthorized modifications, ensuring that research data remains transparent, trustworthy, and traceable. By eliminating the risk of data tampering, blockchain enhances the confidence in the research findings, enhances reproducibility, and establishes a foundation for evidence-based medicine, thus advancing medical knowledge and accelerating the development of new treatments and therapies.

- **Streamlined Data Sharing and Interoperability:** Efficient data sharing and interoperability are critical for accelerating medical research and fostering collaboration among researchers, institutions, and pharmaceutical companies. However, the current research landscape often suffers from siloed data repositories and fragmented systems that hinder data exchange. Blockchain technology provides a standardized and secure framework for sharing research data across different entities. With blockchain-based platforms, researchers can securely share data while maintaining control over their intellectual property rights. Smart contracts, a feature of blockchain, can automate data sharing agreements and enable selective access to specific data sets based on predefined permissions. This streamlined data sharing not only facilitates multidisciplinary collaboration but also promotes data reuse, reducing redundancy and optimizing research efforts.

- **Facilitating Tokenized Incentives and Funding:** Blockchain's inherent ability to create digital tokens and execute smart contracts opens up innovative avenues for incentivizing participation in clinical research and streamlining funding mechanisms. Tokenization enables the creation of digital assets that can represent research contributions, intellectual property, or even financial rewards. Blockchain-based platforms can incentivize researchers, patients, and other stakeholders by rewarding them with tokens for their contributions to the research ecosystem. These tokens can be exchanged for access to research data, publication credits, or even financial compensation. Furthermore, blockchain's transparent and auditable nature enhances accountability, ensuring that funds allocated for research are used appropriately and can be effectively traced throughout the research life cycle.

- **Patient Empowerment and Enhanced Consent Management:** Blockchain technology can enhance the consent process by providing patients with greater control and transparency over their data. By utilizing blockchain, researchers can securely record and manage patient consent information in an immutable and auditable manner. Patients can grant, revoke, or modify their consent preferences at any time, giving them more agency in determining how their data is used for research purposes. Blockchain-based consent frameworks enable patients to track and monitor how their data is being utilized, fostering trust and ethical transparency in the research process [12].

1.3.4 Health insurance and claims processing

The health insurance industry plays a vital role in providing financial protection and access to healthcare services for individuals and families. However, the industry faces significant challenges, including complex claims processing, fraudulent activities, and lack of transparency. Blockchain technology has emerged as a powerful tool to address these issues and revolutionize health insurance by streamlining claims processing, enhancing data security, and improving operational efficiency [13].

- **Streamlining Claims Processing:** Traditional health insurance claims processing is a complex and time-consuming procedure, involving multiple intermediaries and manual verification processes. Blockchain technology has the potential to streamline this process, reducing administrative costs and improving the efficiency of claims management. By leveraging blockchain, health insurance claims can be recorded as transactions on a decentralized ledger. Smart contracts, self-executing agreements triggered by predefined conditions, can be utilized to automate claims processing. When specific conditions, such as diagnosis codes or treatment eligibility, are met, the smart contract can automatically execute the payment, eliminating the need for manual intervention and reducing processing time. This automation not only expedites claims settlement but also minimizes errors and enhances accuracy, leading to faster reimbursement for healthcare providers and improved customer satisfaction.
- **Preventing Fraud and Improving Compliance:** Fraudulent activities, such as false claims and identity theft, pose significant challenges to the health insurance industry. Blockchain technology can mitigate these risks by providing a transparent and immutable record of transactions, making it easier to detect and prevent fraud. With blockchain, every transaction is recorded and timestamped, creating an auditable trail of activities. This allows for real-time monitoring and analysis, enabling insurers to identify suspicious patterns and detect fraudulent behavior more efficiently. By integrating data from various sources, such as healthcare providers, pharmacies, and claims processors, blockchain can provide a comprehensive view of an individual's medical history, ensuring that claims are accurate and in compliance with policy terms. This transparency and real-time monitoring enable proactive fraud prevention measures, protecting insurers and policyholders from financial losses.
- **Improving Provide–Insurer Collaboration:** Collaboration between healthcare providers and insurers is crucial for efficient claims processing and seamless coordination of care. Blockchain technology fosters this collaboration by creating a shared platform for secure and efficient data exchange. Blockchain-based systems enable real-time sharing of

information between healthcare providers and insurers, eliminating the need for manual data reconciliation and reducing administrative burdens. Providers can securely submit claims-related information, such as medical records and treatment details, directly to insurers through the blockchain network. This streamlined communication accelerates claims processing, reduces errors, and ensures timely reimbursement. Additionally, blockchain facilitates transparent communication and dispute resolution between providers and insurers, improving operational efficiency and fostering trust in the system.

1.3.5 Medical credentialing and verification

Medical credentialing and verification are crucial processes in the healthcare industry, ensuring that healthcare providers meet the necessary qualifications and standards to deliver quality care. However, traditional methods of credentialing are often time-consuming, prone to errors, and lack transparency. Blockchain technology offers a promising solution to revolutionize medical credentialing and verification processes by transforming these processes and improving efficiency, accuracy, and trust in health care.

- **Streamlining the Credentialing Process:** Blockchain technology streamlines the complex and manual processes involved in medical credentialing. By leveraging blockchain's decentralized and immutable ledger, healthcare organizations can securely store and share provider credentials, licenses, certifications, and other relevant information. Blockchain eliminates the need for intermediaries and central authorities in credentialing processes. Instead, healthcare providers can maintain their credentials on the blockchain, ensuring data integrity and eliminating the risk of falsified or outdated information. Verification of credentials becomes faster and more efficient as healthcare organizations can access the blockchain directly, rather than relying on time-consuming manual verification methods.
- **Enhanced Accuracy and Trust:** Blockchain enhances the accuracy and reliability of medical credentialing by providing a transparent and auditable record of a provider's qualifications. Each credentialing event, such as completing medical school, obtaining a license, or completing a residency program, is recorded as a transaction on the blockchain. These transactions form an immutable chain of information that can be accessed and verified by authorized parties. This transparency and immutability significantly reduce the chances of fraudulent claims and misrepresentations in provider credentials. Medical organizations, insurers, and regulatory bodies can confidently rely on the blockchain to verify a provider's qualifications, ensuring that only qualified professionals are granted privileges and reducing the risk of substandard care.

- **Providing Cross-Border Credentialing:** Blockchain has the potential to revolutionize cross-border credentialing, enabling healthcare professionals to practice internationally with greater ease. In the traditional credentialing process, providers often face significant challenges and delays when seeking to practice in different countries due to varying regulatory requirements and verification processes. Blockchain simplifies cross-border credentialing by providing a standardized platform for storing and verifying credentials. International organizations can access the blockchain to verify a provider's qualifications and streamline the credentialing process. This facilitates global mobility for healthcare professionals, promotes workforce diversity, and improves access to healthcare services worldwide.

1.4 Challenges of blockchain implementation in the healthcare domain

1.4.1 Regulatory and legal uncertainty

The introduction of blockchain technology makes the already complex legal and regulatory environment for the healthcare industry even more complex. Blockchain implementation makes it difficult to comply with data privacy rules, such as the Health Insurance Portability and Accountability Act (HIPAA) in the United States. Meeting these regulatory obligations may be difficult due to blockchain's decentralized and unchangeable nature. The right to be forgotten, data portability, and consent management may be challenging to reconcile with the permanent nature of data stored on the blockchain.

Blockchain implementation in health care may require explicit patient consent to share or access their medical data. Determining how consent is obtained, recorded, and managed on the blockchain while complying with existing legal frameworks can be complex. Consent and authorization mechanisms must be designed to address legal requirements and ensure patient autonomy and control over their data.

Blockchain technology operates across borders, and healthcare data regulations can vary significantly between jurisdictions. This presents challenges in maintaining compliance when sharing data internationally. Navigating the legal and regulatory landscape to ensure cross-border data transfers are conducted in accordance with applicable laws can be a complex and time-consuming task.

Existing regulations were not designed specifically for blockchain technology. Regulatory bodies and policymakers may need to adapt and update regulations to account for the unique characteristics and challenges posed by blockchain in health care. The lack of clear guidelines and standards for blockchain implementation can create uncertainty and hesitation among healthcare organizations.

1.4.2 Interoperability and standardization challenges

Healthcare data is generated and stored in various formats, ranging from text-based medical records to medical imaging files. The absence of standardized data formats and protocols hinders interoperability between different healthcare providers and blockchain networks. Establishing common data standards that define how healthcare data is structured, classified, and shared can enable effective integration with blockchain platforms. Healthcare terminologies and vocabularies, such as SNOMED CT or LOINC, are used for coding and classifying medical data. However, discrepancies and variations in terminologies across different healthcare organizations can impede data interoperability. Achieving semantic interoperability requires aligning and harmonizing terminologies to ensure consistent interpretation and understanding of data shared on the blockchain. Health information exchanges (HIEs) play a vital role in facilitating the exchange of patient information between healthcare providers. Integrating blockchain with existing HIEs poses challenges in terms of data synchronization, authentication, and maintaining a consistent and up-to-date patient record across multiple organizations. Collaboration between blockchain networks and HIEs is crucial to achieve seamless interoperability. Blockchain networks are built on different platforms and technologies, such as Ethereum, Hyperledger Fabric, or Corda. Ensuring interoperability between these different blockchain platforms and enabling data exchange across them is a significant challenge. Standardizing protocols and interfaces that enable cross-platform compatibility can enhance interoperability and allow healthcare organizations to leverage multiple blockchain networks. Collaborative efforts among healthcare organizations, standard development organizations, and regulatory bodies are necessary to establish common data standards, terminology frameworks, and interoperability protocols specific to blockchain in health care. These standards should be widely adopted and implemented to ensure consistency and seamless data exchange. It is also important to conduct interoperability testing and certification programs as these can validate the compatibility and compliance of blockchain implementations with established standards. These programs help healthcare organizations select interoperable blockchain solutions and provide assurance to stakeholders about the system's ability to exchange data effectively.

1.4.3 Scalability challenges

Blockchain networks often face limitations in processing transactions quickly. In health care, where real-time data exchange is crucial, scalability becomes a major concern. As the number of participants and transactions increases, the blockchain network may experience delays and reduced performance.

As the blockchain is expanded with new data, the size of the network increases, resulting in higher storage requirements and slower network performance. Storing large volumes of healthcare data, such as medical records and imaging files, on the blockchain can strain the network's capacity and impact its scalability.

Consensus algorithms, such as proof-of-work (PoW) or proof-of-stake (PoS), ensure the validity of transactions on the blockchain. However, these mechanisms may limit scalability, as they often require extensive computational resources or have limitations on the number of transactions that can be processed concurrently.

Implementing off-chain solutions, such as sidechains or state channels, can alleviate the burden on the main blockchain network, improving scalability. These solutions enable faster and more efficient transaction processing while maintaining the benefits of blockchain technology. Exploring alternative consensus algorithms that require less computational power, such as proof-of-authority (PoA) or practical Byzantine fault tolerance (PBFT), can enhance performance and scalability in healthcare blockchain applications.

1.4.4   Performance challenges

Some blockchain networks, especially those using PoW consensus, consume substantial amounts of energy. In health care, where sustainability and environmental considerations are important, the energy-intensive nature of certain blockchain implementations poses performance challenges and raises concerns about the ecological impact.

While blockchain offers immutability and transparency, maintaining patient privacy and data confidentiality is crucial in health care. Balancing the need for data privacy with the transparent nature of blockchain can be challenging, and inefficient encryption methods may impact the overall performance of the system.

Integrating blockchain technology into existing healthcare systems and infrastructure can present performance challenges. Legacy systems and interoperability issues can hinder the seamless flow of data between blockchain networks and traditional databases, potentially affecting overall system performance. Breaking down large data sets into smaller partitions and utilizing data compression techniques can optimize storage requirements and improve network performance. Storing only essential metadata on the blockchain while keeping the bulk of the data off-chain can also enhance scalability.

1.5   Blockchain ecosystem for health care and some real-world implementations

The healthcare ecosystem will gain from a patient-centric blockchain-based approach to clinical care improvement, which will also ensure that patients' trust is upheld. The advantages of such a blockchain-based ecosystem can be divided into two categories: those for the provider and those for the patient. Blockchain will act as the interface in the redesigned hospitalization scenario, allowing a clinician to change a patient's profile directly after obtaining the necessary authorization in a secure and authorized manner. The new hospitalization record will make use of the patient's medical background as well as any related health data, such as insurance plans. The patient's experience will be improved by integrating the interchange of medical information with claim and payment information [12]. A detailed flow structure of a reimagined healthcare ecosystem using blockchain is shown in Figure 1.8.

1.5.1 Blockchain use cases in health care worldwide

There are several real-world implementations of blockchain technology in the healthcare sector worldwide. Here are some notable examples:

- *MedRec (United States):* MedRec is a blockchain-based electronic medical record (EMR) system developed by researchers at MIT. It allows patients to have ownership and control over their medical data while enabling secure sharing with healthcare providers. Patients can grant access to specific parts of their medical records, improving care coordination and reducing duplication of tests.
- *Medicalchain (United Kingdom):* Medicalchain is a blockchain platform that aims to provide secure and accessible health records. It allows patients to store their medical data on the blockchain, granting access to healthcare providers and researchers as needed. Medicalchain also facilitates telemedicine consultations, prescription management, and insurance claims.
- *Guardtime (Estonia):* Guardtime is a company that has partnered with the Estonian government to implement blockchain in their national health records system. The blockchain-based system ensures the integrity and security of health records, preventing unauthorized modifications and providing an auditable trail of data changes. Every patient in Estonia has online access to a single record thanks to a national system called the Electronic Health Record (e-Health Record), which combines data from the country's many healthcare providers. The e-Health Record operates very much like a centralized, national database, but it really retrieves data as needed from multiple providers who may be using different systems and provides it in a common format via the e-Patient interface. Doctors can now readily retrieve a patient's records from a single electronic file thanks to this effective tool. Medical professionals can view test results as they are entered, including image files like x-rays from distant facilities. The retrieval of electronic medical records and the integrity of system access logs are both guaranteed by blockchain technology.

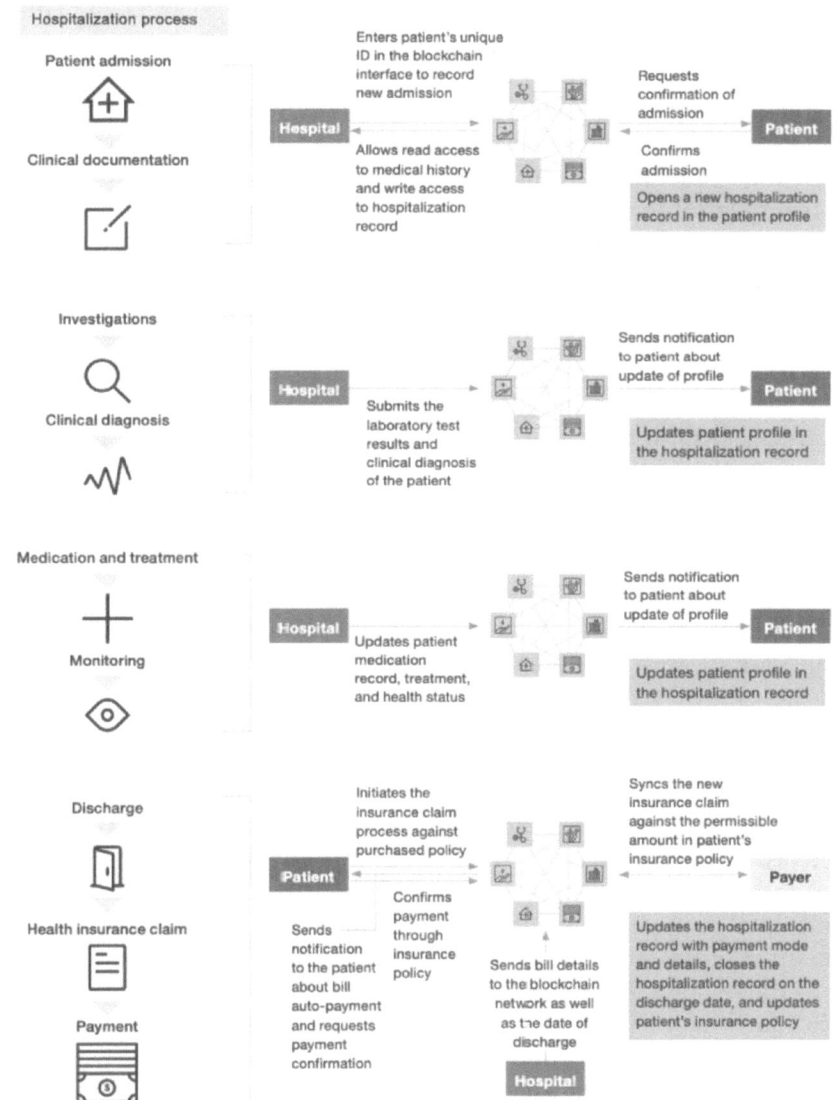

FIGURE 1.8 A reimagined healthcare ecosystem using blockchain.

[Original (created by authors)]

- *Gem and Philips Blockchain Lab (United States):* Gem, a blockchain platform provider, partnered with Philips Blockchain Lab to develop a blockchain-based data sharing and management platform for clinical trials. The platform aims to streamline the trial process; improve data integrity; and enhance collaboration among researchers, sponsors, and participants.

- *MyClinic.com (Australia):* MyClinic.com is a blockchain-based platform that allows patients to access and control their health records. It enables patients to securely store their medical data, share it with healthcare providers, and receive telemedicine services. The platform also incorporates smart contracts for insurance claims and automated payments.
- *Shivom (Global):* Shivom is a genomics and healthcare-focused blockchain platform. It aims to securely store and share genomic data while ensuring privacy and control for patients. The platform facilitates research collaborations, empowers patients to monetize their genomic data, and supports the development of personalized medicine.
- *BitMED (United States):* BitMED is a blockchain-powered telemedicine platform that connects patients with healthcare providers. The platform enables secure video consultations, medical data sharing, and prescription management. It also incorporates a cryptocurrency-based rewards system to incentivize healthy behaviors.

1.5.2 Blockchain use in the Indian healthcare system

The Indian healthcare system is a massive and complex network of both public and commercial providers. Its goal is to provide inexpensive and accessible healthcare services. Seven important parties are involved: the patient, the provider, the payer, the pharmaceutical industry, the medical technology industry, technology vendors and suppliers, and the government and healthcare regulator. To produce actionable health information, these stakeholders engage in complex networks of interconnected and data-intensive activities. India has started the process of achieving Universal Health Coverage (UHC) and has matched its National Health Policy (NHP) 2017 with this objective [14].

A technological answer that enables all participants to produce and transmit helpful health information in a secure and timely manner is necessary for initiatives of this scale. It will be important to deploy technology that connects the multiple Health and Wellness Centers (HWCs) scattered around the country in order to execute Pradhan Mantri Jan Arogya Yojana (PMJAY) and attain UHC. The Ayushman Bharat Digital Mission (ABDM) [15] aims to build the necessary infrastructure for the nation's integrated digital health system. It will close the current gap between the various stakeholders of the healthcare ecosystem through digital highways and serve as the basis for developing a national-level IT platform and to make beneficiary identification, strategic purchasing of care services, disbursal of provider payments, fraud detection, and scheme monitoring easier.

This is where the three tenets of blockchain, cryptography, decentralization, and consensus, can provide a solution to create a highly secure underlying system that is reliable and scalable. Apart from the initiatives of the government of India [16], there are several start-ups that are using the blockchain technology to provide innovative solutions in the healthcare domain.

These examples demonstrate the diverse applications of blockchain in health care, ranging from patient-controlled health records to clinical trials and telemedicine. While these implementations showcase the potential benefits of blockchain technology, it is important to note that they are still relatively early stage and ongoing research and development continue to explore the full potential of blockchain in health care.

1.6   Future directions and recommendations

While there are many ways to use the blockchain idea in the context of exchanging healthcare information in India, it is critical to pinpoint the most useful and persuasive ones that will convince providers to choose blockchain over competing technologies that are already on the market [17].

Blockchain, a relatively new technology, has the potential to increase openness and accountability in the administration of electronic data. Every user of a computer network can view an exact duplicate of a ledger of interactions known as a blockchain.

- Blockchain works most effectively for transactions that benefit from visibility and immutability, have a limited digital footprint, and are transparent. Blockchains may be particularly useful in the healthcare sector for handling dynamic consent from patients, data sharing and access authorizations, managing the supply chain for pharmaceuticals and medical devices, and identity verification.
- Blockchain technology's promise in the healthcare industry is overhyped and its value may be exaggerated. The majority of published research on blockchain's application in the healthcare industry includes theoretical frameworks, designs, or models with little technical details. Rarely can lessons be learned from prototypes or pilot projects. National blockchain technology adoption in the healthcare sector is uncommon.
- In a well-managed health information system, blockchain should be implemented where it is most appropriate and in conjunction with other technologies to meet information needs and policy objectives.
- Most significantly, blockchain is not well suited to storing huge volumes of data due to the requirement that each network participant replicate the blockchain. It would be costly and inefficient to store large records on the blockchain, such as comprehensive electronic medical files or collections of genetic data. The use of data for numerical, medical, and scientific purposes is also limited by the difficulty of querying data stored in a blockchain.
- Furthermore, storing private data "on chain," which is by definition accessible to other network users, violates data privacy. The rights granted by the European Union General Data Protection Regulation and the immutability of blocks in a chain cannot coexist. This is particularly accurate of the right to be forgotten.

1.7 Conclusion

Blockchain technology holds immense potential for revolutionizing EHR systems and patient health records to provide enhanced security, data integrity, interoperability, and privacy, making it an ideal solution for addressing the challenges faced by traditional EHR systems. Blockchain technology can revolutionize clinical research and innovation in health care by addressing key challenges such as data integrity, transparency, and collaboration. By leveraging blockchain's decentralized architecture, enhanced security, and streamlined data sharing capabilities, researchers can unlock new opportunities for multidisciplinary collaboration, accelerate the discovery of novel therapies, and improve patient outcomes. For the medical insurance sector, blockchain technology holds immense promise for transforming the health insurance industry by revolutionizing claims processing, enhancing data security, and improving operational efficiency. By leveraging blockchain's decentralized ledger, smart contracts, and enhanced data transparency, insurers can streamline claims management, prevent fraud, and provide better services to policyholders. Blockchain's immutable records ensure that all transactions are securely logged and easily auditable, minimizing disputes and errors. Smart contracts can automate claim verification and payment processes, reducing administrative overhead and speeding up claim settlements. Additionally, enhanced data transparency fosters trust among stakeholders by enabling real-time access to accurate information while maintaining data privacy through cryptographic security measures. This integration ultimately improves efficiency, reduces costs, and enhances the customer experience in the insurance sector.

Blockchain technology is transforming medical credentialing and verification processes, bringing efficiency, accuracy, and transparency to the healthcare industry. Instilling more confidence in their patients' capacity to trust that their health information is secure and ensuring interoperability by enabling easy access to patients' health records across providers are two areas of attention for healthcare providers in India and around the world. Blockchain technology will play a crucial role in each of these sectors. Collaboration among industry stakeholders, standardization efforts, regulatory frameworks, and continuous innovation are essential to navigate these challenges and create a robust and effective blockchain ecosystem in the healthcare sector.

REFERENCES

1. S. Nakamoto, "Bitcoin: A Peer-to-Peer Electronic Cash System," 2008. [Online]. Available: https://bitcoin.org/bitcoin.pdf.
2. H. S. Chen, J. T. Juliet, K. A. Carpenter, D. S. Cohen and X. Huang, "Blockchain in Healthcare: A Patient-Centered Model," Massachusetts General Hospital and Harvard Medical School, 2019. [Online]. Available: https://www.ncbi.nlm.nih.gov/pmc/articles/PMC6764776/.

3. MeitY, "National Strategy on Blockchain – Towards Enabling Trusted Digital Platforms," December 2021. [Online]. Available: https://www.meity.gov.in/writereaddata/files/National_BCT_Strategy.pdf.

4. L. A. Linn and M. B. Koo, "Blockchain for Health Data and Its Potential Use in Health IT and Health Care Related Research," 2016 [Online]. Available: https://www.healthit.gov/sites/default/files/11-74-ablockchainforhealthcare.pdf.

5. R. Kandaswamy, D. Furlonger and A. Stevens, "Digital Disruption Profile: Blockchain's Radical Promise Spans Business and Society," Gartner, 2022[Online]. Available: https://www.gartner.com/en/doc/3855708-digital-disruption-profile-blockchains-radical-promise-spans-business-and-society#:~:text=Gartner%20forecasts%20that%20the%20business,and%20%243.1%20trillion%20by%202030…

6. W. J. Gordon and C. Catalini, "Some Simple Economics of the Blockchain. National Bureau of Economic Research," 2016. [Online]. Available: http://www.nber.org/papers/w22952.

7. A. Basu and A. Majumder, "Reimagining health information exchange in India using blockchain," 2019. [Online]. Available: https://www.pwc.com/gx/en/healthcare/pdf/reimagining-health-information-exchange-in-india-using-blockchain.pdf.

8. C. Chidubem and Q. Mahmoud, "Blockchain in Healthcare: Opportunities, Challenges, and Possible Solutions," International Journal of Healthcare Information Systems And Informatics, 15(3), 2020. [Online]. Available: https://www.researchgate.net/publication/342602958_Blockchain_in_Healthcare_Opportunities_Challenges_and_Possible_Solutions.

9. W. Y. Ng, T. E. Tan, P. V. Movva and A. H. Se, "Blockchain Applications in Health Care for COVID-19 and Beyond: a Systematic Review," The Lancet, 3(1) 2021[Online]. Available: https://www.thelancet.com/action/showPdf?pii=S2589-7500%2821%2900210-7.

10. L. Hertz, "Blockchain Insurance - Streamlining Insurance Process," 2024 [Online]. Available: https://www.leewayhertz.com/blockchain-insurance-streamlining-insurance-process/.

11. M. o. H. a. F. Welfare, "National Health Policy," 2017. [Online]. Available: Available: https://www.moh.gov.bt/wp-content/uploads/moh-files/2015/11/National-Health-Policy.pdf.

12. N. H. Authority, "yushman Bharat Digital Mission," 2023 [Online]. Available: https://abdm.gov.in.

13. N. Ayog, "Blockchain: The India Strategy," 2020. [Online]. Available: https://www.niti.gov.in/sites/default/files/2020-01/Blockchain_The_India_Strategy_Part_I.pdf.

14. B. P. S. b. OECD, "Opportunities and Challenges of Blockchain Technologies in Health Care," December 2020. [Online]. Available: https://www.oecd.org/finance/Opportunities-and-Challenges-of-Blockchain-Technologies-in-Health-Care.pdf.

15. S. B. Othman, F. A. Almalki and H. Sakli. Internet of Things in the Healthcare Applications: Overview of Security and Privacy Issues. In: Chakraborty, C. and Khosravi, M. R. (eds) Intelligent Healthcare. Springer, Singapore, 2022. https://doi.org/10.1007/978-981-16-8150-9_9

16. K. S. Alqarni, F. A. Almalki, B. O. Soufiene, O. Ali and F. Albalwy, "Authenticated Wireless Links between a Drone and Sensors Using a Blockchain: Case of Smart Farming," Wireless Communications and Mobile Computing, 2022, 4389729, 13 pages, 2022. https://doi.org/10.1155/2022/4389729

17. S. Gupta, F. Alharbi, R. Alshahrani, P. Kumar Arya, S. Vyas, D. H. Elkamchouchi and B. O. Soufiene, "Secure and Lightweight Authentication Protocol for Privacy Preserving Communications in Smart City Applications," Sustainability, 15, 5346, 2023. https://doi.org/10.3390/su15065346

2

BLOCKCHAIN TECHNOLOGY IN HEALTH CARE

C A Bindyashree and Syed Muzamil Basha

2.1 Introduction

The growing importance of secure and interoperable healthcare records and introduces blockchain as a promising solution. It highlights the motivation for the review and outlines the scope of challenges to be addressed. In the contemporary landscape of health care, electronic health records (EHRs) stand as the linchpin of patient-centric information management, enabling efficient healthcare delivery and informed decision-making. However, the path to seamless EHR management is riddled with intricate challenges that encompass data security, privacy, interoperability, and patient agency. Enter blockchain technology, a decentralized and cryptographic innovation that offers a potential paradigm shift in how EHRs are designed, stored, and managed. However, before delving into the potential synergy, it is essential to comprehend the challenges posed by conventional EHR systems. Traditional systems are plagued by data silos, where patient information remains fragmented across disparate entities, leading to inefficiencies, errors, and compromised patient care. Additionally, concerns surrounding data security, especially in the wake of frequent cyberattacks targeting healthcare institutions, underscore the urgency for a more robust solution. Interoperability woes further exacerbate the situation, hindering the seamless exchange of patient data among diverse healthcare providers. Moreover, as patients increasingly demand control over their health information, issues related to data ownership and privacy have taken center stage [1].

The promise of blockchain lies in its ability to address these challenges by providing a decentralized ledger that ensures data integrity, transparency, and privacy. However, the journey from conceptualization to implementation

DOI: 10.1201/9781003483113-2

is a complex one, fraught with intricate design considerations, technological hurdles, and regulatory intricacies. Striking the balance between transparency and privacy is a pivotal concern, as blockchain's innate transparency might clash with the sensitive nature of health data. Scalability emerges as another vital aspect, given the data-intensive nature of healthcare records and the necessity for swift transaction validation. Moreover, the legal and regulatory landscape surrounding healthcare data is intricate and subject to stringent compliance requirements, adding another layer of complexity to blockchain integration. Against this backdrop, this chapter embarks on a meticulous exploration of the amalgamation of blockchain technology and EHR frameworks. It navigates through the foundational principles of blockchain [2], examines the shortcomings of conventional EHR systems, delves into the intricacies of blockchain integration, analyzes real-world case studies, and speculates on the future landscape of blockchain-enabled healthcare ecosystems.

In recent years, blockchain technology has transcended its origins as the underlying framework for cryptocurrencies and has gained recognition for its transformative potential across various industries. One such arena where blockchain's innovative capabilities hold promise is health care, specifically in the realm of securing and managing EHRs. At its core, blockchain is a decentralized, distributed ledger that ensures the secure and transparent recording of transactions. Unlike traditional central databases, blockchain operates on a network of computers, or nodes, where each node maintains an identical copy of the ledger. This decentralized nature brings inherent advantages, such as data immutability, enhanced security, and reduced reliance on intermediaries. These attributes, when harnessed within the healthcare landscape, have the potential to revolutionize EHR management. The conventional approach to EHRs often involves centralized databases managed by healthcare providers or institutions. However, this centralized structure poses challenges, including vulnerability to cyberattacks, potential data breaches, and concerns regarding data ownership and access. Blockchain, with its cryptographic foundations and decentralized architecture, can address these challenges in profound ways [3].

One of the most compelling aspects of blockchain's application in health care is its potential to establish an immutable and auditable record of patient data. Each transaction, or data entry in this context, is encrypted and linked to the previous entry through a cryptographic hash, forming a chain of data blocks. Once recorded, these blocks cannot be altered retroactively without consensus from the entire network, ensuring data integrity. This feature holds immense promise in ensuring the accuracy and authenticity of medical records, which is crucial for informed medical decisions, research, and legal proceedings. Furthermore, blockchain can empower patients by giving them greater control over their health data. Patients could grant temporary access to their records for specific purposes, ensuring their data is shared only with authorized parties. This feature aligns with the growing demand for patient-centric health care, where individuals have a say in how their data is used and shared.

In the context of healthcare interoperability, a significant challenge that plagues the industry, blockchain's decentralized nature can facilitate secure data exchange between disparate systems. It can create a standardized format for data sharing while maintaining privacy and security protocols, bridging the gap between various healthcare providers and institutions. The emergence of blockchain technology presents a promising avenue for addressing critical issues in health care, especially concerning EHR security and management. Its ability to establish trust, transparency, and data control holds the potential to revolutionize how patient records are managed and shared. As we delve deeper into the exploration of blockchain-enabled frameworks for EHRs, a thorough understanding of its potential applications and associated challenges becomes pivotal for a healthcare landscape poised for transformation. This knowledge will empower researchers, healthcare practitioners, and policymakers to engage in informed discussions and decisions regarding the transformative potential of blockchain technology in revolutionizing EHR management.

The primary objective of this chapter is to delve into the intricate landscape surrounding the design and implementation of blockchain-enabled frameworks for EHRs. The focus is centered on a comprehensive exploration of the myriad issues and challenges that emerge in this innovative intersection of blockchain technology and health care. By dissecting the complexities inherent to this integration, this chapter aims to offer a nuanced understanding of the hurdles faced and opportunities presented in the pursuit of secure, transparent, and interoperable EHR systems powered by blockchain. Through a systematic examination of these challenges, this chapter seeks to provide valuable insights for researchers, practitioners, and policymakers to navigate the complexities of deploying blockchain solutions in the healthcare domain and contribute to the advancement of efficient and patient-centric EHR management.

2.2 Blockchain technology in health care

Blockchain technology, initially recognized for its role in enabling secure and transparent transactions within the realm of cryptocurrencies, has emerged as a transformative force across a spectrum of industries. Among these domains, the healthcare sector stands poised to reap significant benefits from the integration of blockchain technology. At its core, blockchain offers a decentralized, tamper-resistant, and immutable data management framework, qualities that resonate profoundly with the healthcare industry's fundamental demands for data security, interoperability, and patient privacy. Within the context of health care, where the accurate and secure management of sensitive patient information is paramount, the application of blockchain introduces novel avenues for solving long-standing challenges. By employing cryptographic techniques and a decentralized architecture, blockchain ensures that data integrity is maintained while mitigating vulnerabilities to unauthorized access and tampering. This aspect becomes particularly pertinent when addressing EHRs, a critical repository of patient health information that demands heightened security and accessibility standards.

The integration of blockchain in health care holds the potential to revolutionize the way EHRs are managed and shared. As patients engage more actively in their healthcare journeys and demand greater control over their health data, blockchain's patient-centric approach allows for granular control over data access permissions. This shift aligns with the evolving paradigm of health care, where patients are rightful custodians of their medical information. Furthermore, blockchain's capacity to enhance interoperability cannot be understated. The current landscape of health care is marked by fragmented data silos, where patient information is scattered across different providers, leading to inefficiencies in care delivery. Blockchain's decentralized structure, coupled with standardized data formats, has the potential to break down these barriers and facilitate seamless data exchange among healthcare entities [4].

The following key features underscore the attractiveness of blockchain for healthcare applications:

- **Decentralization:** Blockchain operates as a decentralized network of nodes, eliminating the need for a central authority or intermediary. This decentralization not only enhances data security by reducing single points of failure but also aligns with the principles of patient-centered care, empowering individuals to control and share their health data on their terms.
- **Immutability:** Data once recorded on the blockchain is virtually impossible to alter retroactively. Each data entry is linked to the previous one through cryptographic hashes, creating an unbroken chain. This feature ensures the integrity of patient records, which is crucial for maintaining an accurate medical history and supporting legal and research activities.
- **Transparency and Auditability:** Blockchain's transparent and auditable nature enables participants to trace and verify each transaction or data modification. This transparency can improve trust among healthcare stakeholders, as it allows for the traceability of data access, changes, and sharing permissions.
- **Data Security:** Blockchain's cryptographic encryption ensures that data stored on the chain is highly secure. This is particularly significant in health care, where patient confidentiality and protection against data breaches are paramount. By employing advanced encryption techniques, blockchain safeguards sensitive health information from unauthorized access.

- **Interoperability:** Interoperability has been a challenge in health care, as diverse systems struggle to communicate and exchange data seamlessly. Blockchain can serve as a universal platform that standardizes data formats and protocols, facilitating data exchange among different healthcare providers, institutions, and systems.
- **Smart Contracts:** Smart contracts are self-executing agreements with predefined rules and conditions. In health care, these contracts could automate processes such as insurance claims, consent management, and medical billing. By reducing manual intervention and minimizing administrative errors, smart contracts enhance efficiency and accuracy.
- **Data Ownership and Control:** Blockchain empowers patients with greater control over their health data. Patients can grant and revoke access to their records, enhancing their agency in sharing information with healthcare providers and researchers. This shift towards patient-centric data control aligns with evolving privacy regulations and patient expectations.
- **Reliability and Trust:** The consensus mechanism in blockchain ensures that transactions are validated by network participants, enhancing the overall reliability of the system. This instills trust among stakeholders, making blockchain a suitable candidate for critical healthcare applications that demand high levels of reliability and data accuracy.
- **Reduced Fraud:** The transparent and tamper-proof nature of blockchain can deter fraudulent activities, such as insurance fraud and counterfeit drug distribution. By creating a trustworthy audit trail, blockchain can enhance the verification of medical supplies and streamline insurance claim processes.

Blockchain's key features align remarkably well with the intricate demands of the healthcare sector, making it an attractive candidate for revolutionizing EHR management and healthcare data systems. The integration of these features into the healthcare ecosystem can lead to improved data security, enhanced patient engagement, streamlined processes, and ultimately better healthcare outcomes. Beyond its application in EHRs [5], blockchain technology has found its way into various facets of the healthcare industry, presenting innovative solutions to address critical challenges. These use cases not only highlight the technology's potential in improving data security, interoperability, and patient control but also underscore its versatility across healthcare operations:

- **Supply Chain Management:** Blockchain's transparency and traceability are leveraged to enhance the integrity of the pharmaceutical supply chain. It ensures the authenticity of drugs by enabling real-time tracking of each step in the supply chain, from manufacturing to distribution. This guards against counterfeit drugs and ensures patient safety.
- **Clinical Trials and Research:** Blockchain can streamline the clinical trial process by securely recording trial data, ensuring its integrity, and

providing auditable records of participant consent. This enhances transparency and trust in research findings while addressing issues of data manipulation and selective reporting.

- **Medical Billing and Claims Processing:** Smart contracts on the blockchain can automate the complex processes of medical billing and insurance claims. These contracts execute predefined rules, ensuring accurate and timely payment transactions, reducing administrative overhead, and minimizing disputes.
- **Medical Credentialing:** Verifying medical credentials is a time-consuming process, prone to errors. Blockchain's decentralized nature can create a secure, easily accessible repository of verified medical credentials. Healthcare providers can readily validate each other's qualifications, expediting the credentialing process.
- **Health Data Exchange:** Blockchain's interoperability capabilities extend to health data exchange. It allows for secure sharing of patient records across different healthcare providers while ensuring data privacy and consent management. Patients have control over who accesses their data, enhancing trust in the exchange process.
- **Telemedicine and Remote Patient Monitoring:** Blockchain can enhance security and privacy in telemedicine by encrypting communication and securely storing patient data. In remote patient monitoring scenarios, blockchain ensures the authenticity and integrity of transmitted data, mitigating the risks of tampering or unauthorized access.
- **Personalized Medicine:** Blockchain can facilitate the secure sharing of genetic and medical data for personalized medicine research. Patients can securely contribute their data to research projects while maintaining control over access, potentially accelerating advancements in personalized treatment approaches.
- **Healthcare IoT Data:** The Internet of Things (IoT) devices in health care generate vast amounts of data. Blockchain can secure and authenticate this data, allowing for more reliable and transparent data aggregation, analysis, and sharing between devices, patients, and providers.
- **Donor Organ Matching:** Blockchain can optimize the process of matching organ donors with recipients. By creating a decentralized, immutable record of organ availability and patient needs, it can improve the speed and accuracy of organ transplantation coordination.
- **Public Health Surveillance:** Blockchain can aid in real-time monitoring of infectious disease outbreaks by securely collecting, sharing, and analysing health data across geographical regions. This timely data sharing enhances global health response efforts.

These parameters cases collectively illustrate blockchain's potential to revolutionize healthcare operations beyond EHR management. By addressing data security, interoperability, and patient control, blockchain technology presents itself as a versatile tool that can enhance transparency, efficiency, and trust within the healthcare ecosystem. As these parameters mature and pave the way for further innovations, blockchain's transformative impact on health care becomes increasingly evident.

2.3   Electronic health records

In the rapidly evolving landscape of health care, the digitization of patient information has ushered in a new era of medical recordkeeping and patient care. At the forefront of this transformation are EHRs, digital repositories that encapsulate a patient's complete medical history, diagnoses, treatments, prescriptions, and other pertinent healthcare information. EHRs are the culmination of technology's fusion with health care, revolutionizing the way medical data is collected, stored, and accessed. EHRs replace traditional paper-based records, eliminating the constraints of physical storage and manual data retrieval. By centralizing patient data in digital form, healthcare providers gain streamlined access to comprehensive patient histories, enabling informed decision-making, efficient care coordination, and improved patient outcomes. Moreover, EHRs transcend geographical boundaries, allowing authorized medical professionals to access patient records, regardless of location, fostering continuity of care and reducing duplication of tests and treatments.

The significance of EHRs extends beyond the immediate benefits to patient care. These digital records contribute to medical research, population health management, and the efficient analysis of healthcare trends. The aggregated data can empower healthcare institutions, policymakers, and researchers to make evidence-based decisions, optimize healthcare delivery, and contribute to medical advancements. However, the transition to EHRs has introduced a host of challenges that demand innovative solutions. Data security, patient privacy, interoperability, data standardization, and usability have emerged as complex issues that require careful consideration and strategic approaches. The sensitive nature of patient data necessitates robust security measures to safeguard against unauthorized access, breaches, and data loss. Privacy concerns underline the need to balance accessibility with patient consent and control over their health information. Achieving interoperability across various healthcare systems and platforms is vital to ensuring seamless data exchange and continuity of care. As the healthcare industry continues to adapt to the digital age, the integration of cutting-edge technologies holds immense potential to address these challenges. Blockchain technology, with its attributes of security, immutability, transparency, and patient-centricity, has garnered attention as a potential solution to enhance EHR management and data integrity [6].

This embarks on a comprehensive exploration of the challenges, opportunities, and emerging solutions in the realm of EHRs. It navigates the intricate terrain of data security, patient empowerment, interoperability, and privacy concerns. Additionally, it investigates the integration of blockchain technology as a novel approach to address these challenges, paving the way for a future where EHRs are not only efficiently managed but also secured and utilized to their fullest potential. By delving into these critical aspects, this survey aims to contribute to the discourse surrounding the evolution of EHRs in an era defined by technological advancement and patient-centric health care. While traditional paper-based medical record systems served as the foundation of patient data management for decades, they inherently suffered from limitations that hindered efficient healthcare delivery and data utilization. The transition to EHRs was intended to overcome these limitations, but even EHR systems themselves have encountered a set of complex challenges that must be addressed for optimal patient care and data management. This section explores the multifaceted challenges associated with traditional EHR systems, including data security, privacy concerns, data fragmentation, and lack of interoperability.

- **Data Security:** EHRs contain sensitive patient information, ranging from medical histories and diagnoses to Social Security numbers and payment details. This wealth of personal data makes EHR systems an attractive target for cyberattacks and data breaches. Traditional EHR systems often lack robust security measures, leaving patient data vulnerable to unauthorized access and potential misuse. High-profile breaches have underscored the critical importance of robust cybersecurity in protecting patient privacy and maintaining the integrity of medical records.
- **Privacy Concerns:** Privacy concerns stem from the digital nature of EHRs and the potential for unauthorized data access. Patients worry about the mishandling of their sensitive health information, potential exposure of conditions they wish to keep confidential, and the potential for their data to be used without their consent. The transition from paper-based records to digital ones has raised questions about who has access to the data and how it is protected, necessitating stringent privacy safeguards.
- **Data Fragmentation:** In the absence of a standardized data-sharing framework, healthcare institutions often maintain disparate EHR systems that do not easily communicate with each other. This fragmentation of data across different systems results in incomplete patient profiles, making it difficult for medical professionals to obtain a comprehensive view of a patient's medical history. The lack of a unified data structure hampers efficient care coordination and can lead to delayed diagnoses and treatments.
- **Lack of Interoperability:** Interoperability refers to the ability of different EHR systems to exchange and use data seamlessly. Traditional EHR

systems often lack standardized data formats and communication protocols, leading to challenges in sharing patient data between different healthcare providers, hospitals, and clinics. This lack of interoperability can hinder care coordination, increase administrative burden, and lead to duplication of tests and procedures.

The culmination of these challenges highlights the urgent need for innovative solutions that enhance the efficiency, security, and patient-centricity of EHR systems. As the healthcare industry advances, technologies like blockchain emerge as potential remedies to address these challenges, promising to redefine how patient data is managed, secured, and shared across healthcare networks. By tackling the limitations of traditional EHR systems, healthcare stakeholders can pave the way for a more interconnected, secure, and patient-centered healthcare ecosystem [7].

2.4 Benefits of blockchain-enabled electronic health records

In the ever-evolving landscape of healthcare technology, the integration of blockchain technology with EHRs presents a transformative paradigm shift. The inherent attributes of blockchain, decentralization, immutability, transparency, and security, converge to offer a novel approach to EHR management that promises to address long-standing challenges and unlock a plethora of benefits. By the precision of digital recordkeeping with the innovations of blockchain, healthcare systems stand poised to achieve enhanced data integrity, improved patient engagement, streamlined interoperability, and heightened security. This section explores the compelling benefits that arise from the integration of blockchain technology within the realm of EHRs, underlining the potential to revolutionize how patient data is collected, stored, and utilized.

2.4.1 Potential benefits of integrating blockchain technology into EHR systems

The integration of blockchain technology into EHR systems holds immense promise, offering a range of transformative benefits that address critical challenges in healthcare data management. These benefits, driven by blockchain's unique characteristics, have the potential to revolutionize EHR systems and elevate patient care to new levels. This section explores the multifaceted advantages of adopting blockchain technology in EHR systems, encompassing data integrity, immutability, auditability, patient control, and improved interoperability.

- **Data Integrity:** One of the fundamental advantages of blockchain-enabled EHR systems is the assurance of data integrity. Each piece of information added to the blockchain is cryptographically linked to the previous entry, forming an unbroken chain of data. This tamper-resistant architecture ensures that once data is recorded, it cannot be altered without consensus from the network. Consequently, the integrity of patient records is upheld, reducing the risk of errors, omissions, and unauthorized modifications.

- **Immutability:** Blockchain's immutability ensures that records entered into the system cannot be retrospectively altered, deleted, or tampered with. This permanence eliminates the potential for data manipulation or falsification, a crucial feature in health care where accurate and unalterable medical histories are essential for proper diagnosis, treatment, and legal compliance.
- **Auditability:** The transparent and traceable nature of blockchain empowers EHR systems with robust auditability. Every transaction, modification, or access to patient data is recorded on the blockchain, creating an unalterable audit trail. This feature enhances accountability and transparency, allowing healthcare providers to trace the lineage of data changes and access permissions, which is particularly valuable for compliance, legal, and quality assurance purposes.
- **Patient Control:** Blockchain technology provides patients with unprecedented control over their own health data. Through cryptographic keys and smart contracts, patients can grant or revoke access to their EHRs on a need-to-know basis. This shift empowers patients to actively participate in their healthcare journey, ensuring that their data is shared only with authorized individuals or entities, thus mitigating privacy concerns.
- **Improved Interoperability:** Interoperability challenges have long hindered the seamless exchange of patient data across disparate healthcare systems. Blockchain's standardized protocols and decentralized architecture can bridge these interoperability gaps. It enables secure and efficient data exchange between different healthcare providers, ensuring that patient records are accurately and swiftly shared while maintaining data privacy and security.

The potential benefits of integrating blockchain technology into EHR systems present a compelling vision for the future of healthcare data management. By addressing the core challenges of data integrity, immutability, auditability, patient control, and interoperability, blockchain-enabled EHRs offer the potential to reshape the healthcare landscape.

2.5 Design considerations for blockchain-enabled EHRs

The integration of blockchain technology into EHRs introduces a dynamic shift in how healthcare data is managed and secured. However, this transformation necessitates careful design considerations to harness the full potential of blockchain while addressing the unique challenges posed by healthcare data. From architectural choices to data standardization and privacy concerns, the design process for blockchain-enabled EHRs demands strategic decisions that ensure data integrity, patient privacy, and efficient interoperability. This section delves into the key design considerations that healthcare stakeholders must navigate to create a successful and impactful blockchain-enabled EHR framework.

- **Architectural Models:** The selection of the appropriate blockchain architecture is pivotal. Factors such as private versus public blockchains, permissioned versus permissionless networks, and hybrid models need to be evaluated. In health care, where data security and privacy are paramount, private and permissioned blockchains might be favored due to their controlled access and centralized governance, ensuring compliance with regulatory standards.
- **Data Standardization:** Achieving data consistency and standardization across different healthcare entities is essential. Blockchain-enabled EHRs require predefined data formats and coding standards to facilitate seamless data exchange. Establishing common data standards enhances interoperability, reduces data fragmentation, and enables a unified understanding of patient information across systems.
- **Smart Contracts:** Smart contracts are self-executing agreements that automate processes based on predefined conditions. Designing efficient and secure smart contracts can optimize healthcare operations, such as insurance claims processing, appointment scheduling, and consent management. Ensuring that these contracts accurately reflect real-world healthcare scenarios and adhere to privacy regulations is crucial.
- **Encryption and Access Control:** Privacy-preserving mechanisms, such as encryption, play a pivotal role in blockchain-enabled EHRs. Patient data must be encrypted both at rest and during transmission to ensure that only authorized individuals can access sensitive information. Access controls need to be meticulously designed to grant varying levels of access to different stakeholders, ensuring data security and patient privacy.
- **Integration with Existing Systems:** Healthcare systems often encompass a variety of legacy technologies and infrastructure. Seamless integration of blockchain-enabled EHRs with existing systems is essential to minimize disruptions and transition challenges. The design should account for compatibility, data migration, and potential data transformation requirements.
- **Scalability:** Blockchain's inherent limitations in terms of scalability and transaction throughput need to be addressed, especially in health care where data volumes are substantial. Solutions such as sharding, sidechains, and off-chain data storage can be explored to optimize performance without compromising data integrity.

- **Regulatory Compliance:** Health care is subject to stringent regulatory standards, such as the Health Insurance Portability and Accountability Act (HIPAA) in the United States. Designing blockchain-enabled EHRs that adhere to these regulations and ensure patient consent mechanisms is critical for legal and ethical data handling. The design considerations for blockchain-enabled EHRs encompass a complex array of decisions that extend beyond the technological realm. Balancing data security, privacy, interoperability, and regulatory compliance requires a comprehensive approach that involves technology experts, healthcare practitioners, legal professionals, and patients. Successfully navigating these considerations is pivotal to unlocking the full potential of blockchain in health care, paving the way for a secure, transparent, and patient-centric future of EHR management.

The architecture of blockchain-enabled EHRs, as shown in Figure 2.1, is designed to leverage the unique features of blockchain technology while addressing the complex challenges of healthcare data management. At its core, this architecture encompasses layers that work cohesively to create a secure, transparent, and interoperable ecosystem for managing patient

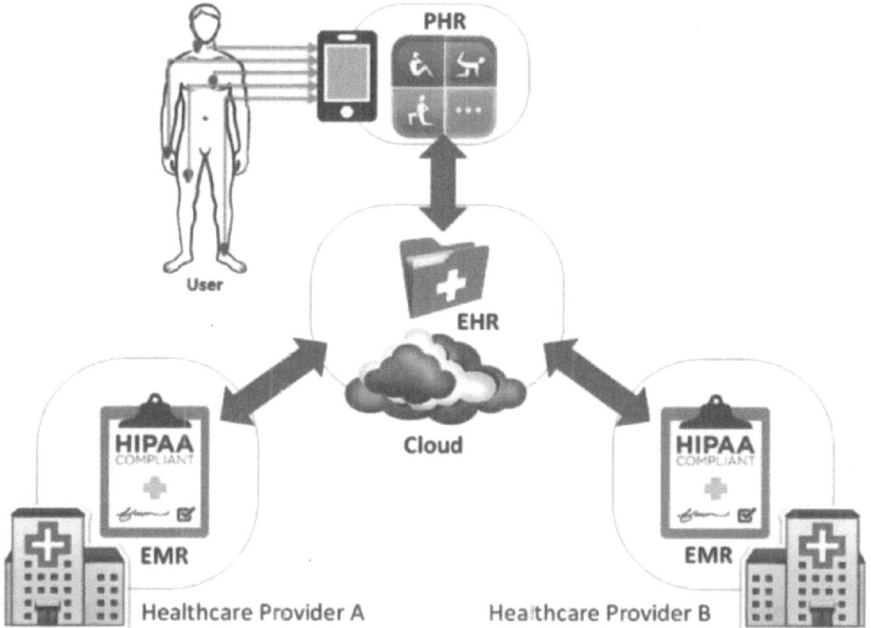

FIGURE 2.1 The architectural workflow of using blockchain technology to maintain EHR data.

[Original (created by authors)]

health information. The blockchain layer forms the foundation of this architecture. It consists of the consensus mechanism, which determines how transactions are validated and added to the blockchain. Depending on the use case, the consensus mechanism could be proof-of-work (PoW), proof-of-stake (PoS), or other methods that ensure data accuracy and security. Smart contracts, self-executing agreements triggered by predefined conditions, automate various processes such as data sharing and consent management. These contracts are securely stored on the blockchain, enhancing transparency and efficiency. The immutable ledger, composed of linked and encrypted blocks, ensures that once data is recorded, it remains tamper-proof and unalterable over time. Sitting atop the blockchain layer is the data layer, containing patient-specific health information. This includes comprehensive medical records, diagnoses, treatment histories, and other relevant data. Metadata accompanies each data entry, providing information like timestamps and transaction details, crucial for auditability and traceability [8].

Identity and access management play a pivotal role in maintaining the privacy and security of patient data. Decentralized identity solutions assign unique identifiers to patients and healthcare providers, facilitating secure interactions within the ecosystem. Access control mechanisms are established through cryptographic keys, ensuring that only authorized individuals can access specific patient records. The interoperability layer addresses the long-standing challenge of data fragmentation in health care. Standardized data formats and terminologies ensure consistency and compatibility across diverse systems. Data mapping translates existing data into these standardized formats, enabling seamless data exchange and improving care coordination. Security and privacy are paramount in blockchain-enabled EHRs. Encryption safeguards patient data both when it is at rest and during transmission, ensuring confidentiality. Consent management is facilitated through smart contracts, granting patients the ability to control who can access their data and for what purposes.

2.5.1 Private versus public blockchains

- **Private Blockchains:** Private blockchains are restricted networks where only authorized participants can join and participate in the consensus process. These networks are favored for health care due to their enhanced control over data access, increased privacy, and compliance with industry regulations. Healthcare institutions can collaborate within a controlled environment, ensuring that only trusted entities can validate transactions and access sensitive patient data. This architecture suits scenarios where consortiums of healthcare providers, insurers, and regulatory bodies collaborate while maintaining data privacy.
- **Public Blockchains:** Public blockchains, like the well-known Bitcoin and Ethereum networks, are open to anyone and rely on decentralized

consensus mechanisms. While public blockchains offer unparalleled transparency and immutability, they might not be well suited for health care due to privacy concerns and data security regulations. Patient confidentiality and regulatory compliance often require greater control over data access, which private blockchains can provide.

2.5.2 Permissioned versus permissionless networks

- **Permissioned Networks:** In permissioned networks, participants require explicit permission to join and validate transactions. This architecture aligns well with the collaborative nature of healthcare consortia and regulatory requirements. Healthcare institutions can establish trust among known participants, maintaining a controlled environment for data exchange. Permissioned networks offer enhanced scalability compared to permissionless networks, making them suitable for scenarios where a limited number of stakeholders need to interact while ensuring data privacy.
- **Permissionless Networks:** Permissionless networks, as seen in public blockchains, allow any participant to join and validate transactions. While permissionless networks offer high levels of decentralization and censorship resistance, they might not be optimal for health care due to the sensitive nature of patient data and the need for compliance with strict data protection regulations. Health care requires a higher degree of control over data access and validation, making permissioned networks a more viable option.

2.5.3 Hybrid approaches

Hybrid Blockchains: Hybrid architectures combine elements of both public and private blockchains. They offer the flexibility of public blockchains for certain transactions or data sharing while maintaining the control and privacy of private blockchains for sensitive information. Hybrid approaches can cater to scenarios where some data needs to be accessible to a broader ecosystem while ensuring that confidential patient data remains secure and compliant within a restricted network.

The choice of architectural model depends on a careful analysis of factors such as data sensitivity, regulatory requirements, collaboration needs, and the desired level of decentralization. Healthcare institutions must strike a balance between data security and accessibility, aligning their architectural decisions with their specific use cases and compliance obligations. As the integration of blockchain and EHR systems evolves, selecting the appropriate architectural model becomes pivotal in creating a resilient and effective solution that enhances healthcare data management while ensuring patient privacy and regulatory compliance.

2.6 Challenges and issues

While the integration of blockchain technology with EHR systems holds significant promise for revolutionizing healthcare data management, it is not without its challenges and issues. The implementation of blockchain in the healthcare domain introduces a range of complexities that demand careful consideration and strategic solutions. This section delves into the multifaceted landscape of challenges and issues that arise when attempting to harmonize the transformative potential of blockchain technology with the intricacies of healthcare data management. By acknowledging and dissecting these challenges, stakeholders can better navigate the path towards harnessing the benefits of blockchain-enabled EHRs while proactively addressing the hurdles that lie ahead. Maintaining the delicate balance between patient privacy, data confidentiality, and the inherent transparency of blockchain poses intricate challenges that require meticulous attention. While blockchain's immutability and transparency offer enhanced data security, addressing data privacy concerns within healthcare settings introduces complexities that demand comprehensive solutions.

2.6.1 Pseudonymous data

Pseudonymous data refers to a type of information that is associated with a pseudonym or a unique identifier rather than a person's real identity. In the context of blockchain-enabled EHRs and other data management systems, pseudonymous data is used to enhance privacy while allowing authorized parties to access and interact with the data. The pseudonym acts as a placeholder for the actual identity of an individual, reducing the direct link between the data and the person's real-world information. The concept of pseudonymous data is particularly relevant in situations where data transparency, integrity, and security are essential, as in health care. Pseudonymity aims to provide a level of privacy protection by allowing users to interact with systems and share data without necessarily revealing their full identities. Instead, a cryptographic identifier or token, known as a pseudonym, is used to represent the individual in transactions and interactions [9].

For instance, in a blockchain-enabled EHR system, patient health records could be associated with pseudonyms rather than the patients' names. This way, medical data remains confidential while still allowing healthcare providers, researchers, or authorized parties to access the information they need for treatment or analysis. The pseudonymous link can be managed through encryption techniques, access controls, and smart contracts to ensure that only those with the necessary permissions can decrypt or access the data associated with a specific pseudonym. Pseudonymous data management offers a balance between data privacy and data utility. It enables patients to share information while protecting their personal identities, which is especially critical in contexts where sensitive information is involved, such as health care. However, it also introduces challenges in managing access, ensuring data integrity, and synchronizing pseudonyms with real identities when necessary. As a result, various research efforts and methods are being explored to enhance the effectiveness of pseudonymous data management within blockchain and other secure data systems. Below are the works explained about the pseudonymous data with its advantages and disadvantages.

Samanthula et al. [10] propose an innovative approach to pseudonymous data: In their study, the authors explore the application of zero-knowledge proofs in healthcare blockchains to enhance pseudonymity while maintaining data utility. Zero-knowledge proofs allow parties to prove the validity of a statement without revealing any specific information. By employing this cryptographic method, they achieve a higher level of data privacy, enabling patients to grant access to their records without divulging sensitive details. The advantage lies in striking a balance between transparency and confidentiality; authorized participants can validate data authenticity without compromising individual identities. However, implementing zero-knowledge proofs introduces computational overhead and complexity, potentially affecting system performance and increasing the difficulty of development and auditability.

Du et al. [11] propose a hybrid approach that combines cryptographic techniques with access control mechanisms. Their method involves assigning unique identifiers to patients that can be pseudonymously linked to their real identities. Smart contracts manage access to patient data, granting authorized parties the ability to request access using the pseudonym while a trusted authority validates their identity off-chain. This approach balances transparency and privacy, allowing authorized access while minimizing the risk of exposing patient identities. However, this hybrid model requires careful synchronization between on-chain and off-chain data and introduces an additional layer of complexity in managing access.

Haddad and Aziz [12] propose a patient-controlled pseudonymity framework that leverages blockchain to provide granular consent management. Patients use cryptographic keys to control access to their health records. Access requests are validated by the blockchain network using zero-knowledge proofs. This approach empowers patients to pseudonymously grant access based on specific conditions. The advantage of this method lies in the patient's active role in data-sharing decisions. However, the decentralized nature of blockchain might lead to challenges in efficiently processing a large volume of access requests, potentially impacting system responsiveness.

Othman et al.'s [13] research focuses on enhancing pseudonymity through consensus mechanisms. They propose a privacy-preserving consensus protocol that encrypts transactions while maintaining the pseudonymous identities of patients. This approach ensures that only authorized participants can decrypt and validate transactions, enhancing both data security and patient privacy. The advantage of this method is its direct integration into the consensus process, reducing the risk of unauthorized access at the protocol level. However, encryption and decryption processes could introduce computational overhead, potentially affecting the scalability of the blockchain network. The advocate for data minimization as a pseudonymity-enhancing measure. By storing minimal patient data directly on the blockchain and utilizing off-chain storage for more detailed records, the method reduces the exposure of sensitive information. This approach aligns with the principles of privacy by design. The advantage of data minimization lies in reducing the risk associated with unauthorized access to sensitive data. However, ensuring the synchronization, security, and integrity of off-chain data poses challenges, and the trade-off between data granularity and accessibility must be carefully managed.

These research contributions underscore the complexity of pseudonymous data management in blockchain-enabled EHRs. While various methods offer promising solutions to enhance patient privacy, each approach comes with its own set of advantages and disadvantages. Striking the right balance between transparency and confidentiality remains a critical consideration in the development of blockchain-based healthcare systems.

2.6.2 Granularity of consent

Managing consent granularity presents a multifaceted challenge in blockchain-enabled EHRs, particularly when striving to align patient autonomy with data access needs. The conventional patient consent model, often binary in nature, lacks the sophistication needed to accommodate the diverse scenarios encountered in health care. To address this, Dagher et al. (2019) propose a hybrid approach that combines cryptographic techniques with access control mechanisms. This method involves assigning unique identifiers to patients, allowing pseudonymous linkage to real identities. Smart contracts then facilitate access to patient data based on these identifiers, enabling a granular approach to consent management. The advantage lies in granting patients the capacity to provide fine-grained access to their records while mitigating the risks of exposing individual identities. However, this approach introduces the challenge of maintaining synchronization between on-chain and off-chain data, requiring careful consideration to ensure consistent access controls. Furthermore, Zhang et al. [14] advocate for a dynamic consent mechanism powered by blockchain smart contracts. They propose an adaptive model where patients can specify different levels of data sharing consent for distinct aspects of their records. By embedding these preferences in smart contracts, patients retain control over their data access on a case-by-case basis. This approach enhances patient agency and aligns with the principle of informed consent. The advantage is in empowering patients to tailor their consent choices, but the potential complexity of managing a multitude of contracts requires a well-designed user interface to facilitate usability.

In a complementary vein, Ekblaw et al. [15] introduce the concept of "proxy keys" as a means to regulate data access granularity. Proxy keys allow patients to delegate access rights to different parties using predefined conditions. This method ensures that specific aspects of a patient's record can be accessed by designated entities, enhancing data granularity. The strength of this approach is in its flexibility, enabling patients to compartmentalize their data-sharing preferences. However, the challenge lies in striking the right balance between ease of delegation and the risk of overly complex access structures. Moreover, Yin et al. [16] propose a comprehensive framework where data-sharing agreements are managed through smart contracts, allowing patients to define the scope and duration of consent. Smart contracts enforce access restrictions and automatically revoke permissions after a predefined period, ensuring temporal granularity. The advantage is in enhancing data control for patients while minimizing the risk of prolonged unauthorized access. However, ensuring the synchronization of smart contracts with evolving regulations and patient preferences presents an ongoing challenge.

Lastly, Roehrs et al. [17] advocate for a patient-centered approach, emphasizing the importance of educational tools and interfaces that empower patients to comprehend and manage their consent choices effectively. They propose a consent dashboard where patients can modify their preferences and view access history. This approach prioritizes patient engagement and aligns with the ethos of shared decision-making. The advantage lies in fostering a transparent and participatory consent process. However, the challenge remains in designing interfaces that are intuitive, informative, and accessible to patients of varying digital literacy levels. In the realm of blockchain-enabled EHRs, tackling the granularity of consent is pivotal to respecting patient autonomy and data privacy. The convergence of cryptographic techniques, smart contracts, and user-friendly interfaces offers promising solutions, but careful attention is required to strike the right balance between granular access control and usability.

2.6.3 Encryption and key management

In the landscape of blockchain-enabled EHRs, ensuring the confidentiality and security of patient data is of paramount importance. Encryption and key management emerge as critical components in achieving this objective. Encryption involves the transformation of sensitive information into an unreadable format that can only be deciphered with the appropriate decryption key. The effective integration of encryption techniques with blockchain technology not only safeguards patient privacy but also addresses concerns related to unauthorized access and data breaches. Accompanying encryption, key management strategies are essential to securely generate, store, distribute, and revoke encryption keys. The coordination of encryption and key management within the blockchain context presents a complex yet essential challenge that requires careful consideration to strike the delicate balance between data security and accessibility.

Yin et al. [18] propose a data-sharing framework. They employ attribute-based encryption (ABE) and smart contracts to manage access permissions. Patient data is encrypted with attributes and smart contracts enforce access control. The advantage lies in fine-grained control and confidentiality, but ABE's computational overhead and smart contract complexity might impact system performance. Azaria et al. [1] introduce MedRec. Encrypted data is stored off-chain, and Ethereum smart contracts manage access. Off-chain storage reduces blockchain bloat, while smart contracts ensure precise control. However, synchronization challenges and scalability limitations of smart contracts are disadvantages. Dagher et al. [19] present MedChain. They use ABE for data encryption and blockchain for key distribution. Patients provide consent through smart contracts. ABE ensures privacy and transparency, and patients maintain control. However, key management complexity and ABE's computational overhead can pose challenges.

Ekblaw et al. [15] propose MedRec 2.0. They introduce "proxy keys" for access delegation. Patients maintain data control, allowing specific access to authorized parties. While flexible, managing a complex hierarchy of proxy keys can be challenging. Xu and Zhu [20] present an EHR system. They use blockchain and hierarchical attribute structures for data access control. Blockchain ensures data integrity and secure key distribution. Hierarchical attributes offer flexibility but managing them and blockchain's computational overhead may impact system usability. These authors collectively highlight the significance of encryption and key management in blockchain-based EHRs. While their proposed methods provide advantages in data privacy and access control, challenges such as complexity, computational overhead, and scalability must be navigated to create effective and secure healthcare data systems.

2.6.4 Off-chain data

In the intricate landscape of blockchain-enabled EHRs, the challenge of managing off-chain data arises as a critical consideration. Off-chain data encompasses information that, due to its volume or sensitivity, is stored outside the blockchain to address scalability limitations and ensure efficient data management. This introduces the need to strike a delicate balance between maintaining data integrity, security, and accessibility while optimizing the advantages of blockchain technology. As such, exploring methodologies and solutions for incorporating off-chain data within blockchain-based EHR systems becomes pivotal in addressing these complex considerations [21].

Zohrevand and Beznosov [22] present a hybrid data storage approach. They propose a hybrid solution where critical patient data is stored off-chain using IPFS, while essential metadata is stored on-chain. This ensures that large files do not bloat the blockchain while maintaining data integrity and traceability. The advantage lies in efficient data management, but challenges include ensuring consistent data synchronization between on-chain and off-chain storage. Ekblaw et al. [15] introduce MedRec 2.0. They leverage off-chain storage for patient records, enhancing scalability. MedRec 2.0's approach allows medical data to be referenced on-chain, while actual files are stored off-chain. This minimizes the blockchain's storage burden while maintaining data availability. However, managing data synchronization and access control between on-chain references and off-chain storage introduces complexities. Kuo et al. [23] present blockchain hybrid architecture. Their system employs off-chain storage for medical records, improving scalability. Patient data is encrypted and stored off-chain, while access control and permissions are managed via blockchain smart contracts. This approach addresses blockchain scalability concerns while ensuring data confidentiality. Nevertheless, the potential challenge of ensuring synchronized access control and data availability warrants careful consideration.

Mohsin et al. [24] propose a privacy-preserving EHR system. They utilize off-chain storage for encrypted patient data, ensuring that only authorized parties can access it. Off-chain storage supports efficient data management while maintaining patient privacy. However, the potential disadvantage of this method lies in addressing synchronization issues between encrypted off-chain data and access control mechanisms on the blockchain. Chen et al. [25] explore privacy and scalability. They highlight off-chain solutions like secure multiparty computation (SMPC) to enhance privacy while addressing scalability issues. SMPC allows computation on encrypted data without exposing the actual data, enhancing both confidentiality and scalability. This approach's advantage is the potential for preserving privacy in computations, but integrating SMPC with blockchain might introduce integration complexities. The incorporation of off-chain data in blockchain-enabled EHR systems emerges as a crucial consideration in optimizing scalability, privacy, and data accessibility. While off-chain storage offers significant advantages, challenges associated with data synchronization, access control, and system complexity necessitate meticulous planning to ensure that the advantages of blockchain are harmoniously aligned with the complexities of managing sensitive and voluminous patient information.

2.6.5 Regulatory compliance

In the evolving landscape of blockchain-enabled EHRs, adhering to stringent regulatory frameworks while harnessing the benefits of decentralized technology introduces the challenge of regulatory compliance. The intersection of blockchain's transparency and immutability with healthcare data's sensitive and regulated nature demands meticulous consideration to ensure that patient privacy, data security, and legal requirements are effectively balanced.

Pilkington et al. [26] examine blockchain and GDPR compatibility. Pilkington explores the compatibility of blockchain with the European General Data Protection Regulation (GDPR). While blockchain's transparency aligns with GDPR's principles, challenges emerge due to the permanence of data and the "right to be forgotten." The advantage lies in fostering transparency, but addressing GDPR's nuances in a blockchain context can pose challenges. Shaikh et al. [27] analyze blockchain and health data sharing. They discuss blockchain's potential to enable controlled health data sharing while addressing HIPAA compliance. Blockchain's data-sharing model can align with patient-centered control and privacy requirements. However, challenges include integrating blockchain within complex regulatory environments and ensuring that decentralization does not compromise data security. Ouaddah et al. [28] explore blockchain in EHRs and GDPR. They propose a blockchain-based EHR system that adheres to GDPR principles. Patients control data access through smart contracts, ensuring transparency and user consent. The advantage is in enabling patient-centric data sharing, but integrating GDPR principles within smart contract logic and ensuring compliance across different jurisdictions remain challenges.

Yin et al. [16] emphasize patient consent and compliance. Their approach integrates patient consent with blockchain, ensuring compliance with HIPAA and GDPR. Smart contracts manage consent and access, enhancing patient control. The advantage lies in empowering patients, but challenges include translating complex regulations into executable smart contracts and addressing potential conflicts between regulations. Yin et al. [29] present MedChain's privacy framework. They propose MedChain as a solution to privacy concerns and regulatory compliance. MedChain employs attribute-based encryption to align with data protection regulations. The advantage is in ensuring data privacy while maintaining transparency, but potential challenges include educating users about the compliance mechanisms and addressing the intricacies of various regulations.

The use case diagram in Figure 2.2 gives an overview of how patient registration takes place in a secure manner and how the block creation process takes place.

- **Actor Initialization:** The sequence starts with an authorized actor, such as a healthcare provider or an authenticated user, initiating the process to update the patient's EHR data.
- **Authentication and Authorization:** The actor interacts with the system to authenticate their identity and obtain the necessary permissions and access rights to modify EHR data.
- **Data Preparation:** Before updating the EHR, the actor prepares the new data to be incorporated. This could include medical reports, treatment records, or any other relevant patient information.

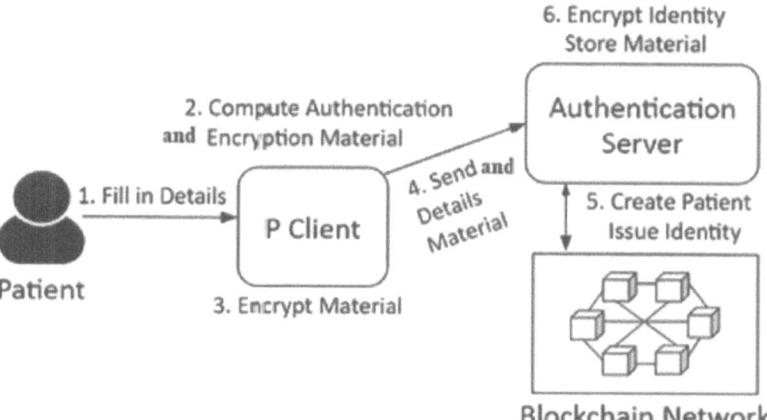

FIGURE 2.2 Patient registration with secure creation of block.

[Original (created by authors)]

- **Data Verification:** The new data undergoes a verification process to ensure its accuracy, legitimacy, and conformity with healthcare standards. Verification methods may include digital signatures, consensus mechanisms, or validation by medical professionals.
- **Data Hashing:** Once verified, the new data is transformed into a unique cryptographic hash. This hash serves as a secure representation of the data.
- **Blockchain Update Request:** The actor submits a request to the blockchain component, indicating their intent to update the patient's EHR data.
- **Blockchain Processing:** The blockchain component processes the request and evaluates its validity based on predefined rules and consensus mechanisms.
- **Blockchain Data Update:** If the request is valid and meets the required criteria, the blockchain is updated with the cryptographic hash representing the new data. This update is typically executed through a smart contract or a consensus process.
- **Timestamping:** To maintain a chronological history of the patient's EHR, the blockchain assigns a timestamp to the data update, recording when the modification occurred.
- **Audit Trail:** All actions related to the data update, as well as access to the EHR, are meticulously logged on the blockchain. This audit trail ensures transparency and provides a means for auditing and accountability.
- **Process Completion:** The data update process concludes successfully and the patient's EHR on the blockchain now includes the newly added or modified information.

This sequence diagram offers a simplified representation of the sequential interactions and steps involved in updating EHR data on a blockchain.

2.7 Case studies and current initiatives: Exploring blockchain-EHR integration

The integration of blockchain technology with EHR systems holds transformative potential in revolutionizing healthcare data management. In recent years, several projects, initiatives, and pilot implementations have emerged to explore this intersection, aiming to enhance data security, interoperability, and patient control. This section delves into notable case studies and ongoing initiatives that shed light on the successes achieved and lessons learned in the integration of blockchain with EHR systems [30].

2.7.1 MedRec: A pioneer in blockchain-EHR integration

One of the pioneering projects in this realm is MedRec, a decentralized EHR system developed by Ekblaw et al. [15]. MedRec leverages blockchain to provide patients with control over their medical records and enhances data accessibility for healthcare providers. Through encrypted patient records stored off-chain, MedRec tackles data scalability issues while utilizing blockchain's transparency and immutability to maintain data integrity. The project demonstrates that blockchain can offer a patient-centric approach to data sharing, fostering trust and enhancing data portability across healthcare providers.

2.7.2 Guardtime: Ensuring data integrity

Guardtime, in collaboration with Estonian eHealth Foundation, embarked on a journey to secure the integrity of healthcare records using blockchain. By implementing blockchain-based data timestamping and immutability, they aimed to prevent unauthorized tampering with medical records. The initiative aimed to establish an auditable trail of data modifications, ensuring the veracity of records while upholding compliance with data protection regulations.

2.8 Conclusion

The potential transformative impact of blockchain technology on EHR management is profound and far-reaching. This nascent synergy has the capacity to reshape healthcare data handling, catalyzing a shift where patients exercise unprecedented control over their records and providers access secure and accurate data. While challenges persist, including interdisciplinary collaboration, regulatory alignment, and user-centric design, the aspiration to create a more transparent, patient-centric, and secure healthcare ecosystem drives progress. The path towards blockchain-enabled EHR systems may be challenging, but it is paved with opportunities to redefine health care's future. The commitment to patient privacy, data security, and healthcare excellence will be the guiding light in shaping a landscape where blockchain's potential converges with EHRs' vital role, ultimately forging a path to improved patient care, streamlined processes, and a more resilient healthcare industry. As we stand at this crossroads, the collaborative efforts of researchers, practitioners, and stakeholders will steer the course towards a transformative future.

References

1. Azaria, A., Ekblaw, A., Vieira, T., & Lippman, A. (2016). MedRec: Using blockchain for medical data access and permission management. In International Conference on Open and Big Data (pp. 25–30).
2. Li, H., Zhu, X., Lyu, L., Guo, Z., & Wu, D. (2018). A secure privacy-preserving key management scheme for blockchain-based electronic health records system. IEEE Access, 6, 44849–44859.
3. Zohrevand, P., & Beznosov, K. (2018). Personal health records: Privacy and security considerations for mobile apps. International Journal of Medical Informatics, 112, 54–71.
4. Conoscenti, M., Vetrò, A., & De Martin, J. C. (2016). Blockchain for the internet of things: A systematic literature review. IEEE Access, 4, 2292–2303.
5. Shusterman, D., & Krawiec, R. J. (2017). Utilizing blockchain technology for personal health records. Journal of Health & Medical Informatics, 8(1), 261.
6. Roehrs, A., da Costa, C. A., & Righi, R. R. (2016). OmniPHR: A distributed architecture model to integrate personal health records. In 2016 IEEE 29th International Symposium on Computer-Based Medical Systems (CBMS) (pp. 459–464).
7. Iqbal, M. F., Asim, M., & Umair, M. (2019). A blockchain based framework for healthcare data sharing with patients consent. IEEE Access, 7, 114002–114011.
8. Alqarni, K. S., Almalki, F. A., Soufiene, B. O., Ali, O., & Albalwy, F., Authenticated wireless links between a drone and sensors using a blockchain: Case of smart farming. Wireless Communications and Mobile Computing, 2022, 4389729, 2022. https://doi.org/10.1155/2022/4389729
9. Gupta, S., Alharbi, F., Alshahrani, R., Kumar Arya, P., Vyas, S., Elkamchouchi, D. H., & Soufiene, B. O. Secure and lightweight authentication protocol for privacy preserving communications in smart city applications. Sustainability, 2023, 15, 5346. https://doi.org/10.3390/su15065346.
10. Samanthula, B. K., & Parikh, R. B. (2020). A blockchain based EHR sharing and access control scheme for COVID-19 pandemic. Journal of Medical Systems, 44(8), 1–11.
11. Du, J., Wang, S., & Fang, Y. (2019). A novel blockchain-based privacy-preserving EHR sharing scheme for healthcare 4.0. IEEE Access, 7, 13519–13527.
12. Haddad, P., & Aziz, A. (2019). A novel blockchain framework for data sharing in EHRs. Journal of Ambient Intelligence and Humanized Computing, 10(12), 4753–4763.
13. Othman, S. B., Almalki, F. A., & Sakli, H. (2022). Internet of Things in the Healthcare Applications: Overview of Security and Privacy Issues. In: Chakraborty, C., Khosravi, M.R. (eds) Intelligent Healthcare. Springer, Singapore. https://doi.org/10.1007/978-981-16-8150-9_9
14. Zhang, P., White, J., Schmidt, D. C., & Lenz, G. (2020). Blockchain technology use cases in healthcare: A systematic review. Journal of Medical Systems, 44(7), 1–14.
15. Ekblaw, A., Azaria, A., Halamka, J. D., & Lippman, A. (2016). A case study for blockchain in healthcare: "MedRec" prototype for electronic health records

and medical research data. In Proceedings of IEEE Open & Big Data Conference (OBD) (pp. 1–8).

16. Yin, S., Nong, G., Shao, L., & Zhang, W. (2019). An access control method of electronic medical records based on blockchain technology. Future Generation Computer Systems, 95, 511–517.

17. Roehrs, A., da Costa, C. A., da Rosa Righi, R., & da Silva, D. S. (2017). OmniPHR: A distributed architecture model to integrate personal health records. Journal of Biomedical Informatics, 71, 70–81.

18. Yin, J., Lamp, J., Cameron, K., Wurtz, R., & Chen, H. (2017). A blockchain framework for patient-centered health records and sharing behavior consent. In International Conference on Security and Privacy in Communication Systems (pp. 25–44).

19. Dagher, G. G., Marella, P. B., & Malluhi, Q. M. (2018). MedChain: Efficient blockchain-based healthcare system with decentralized access control. Journal of Medical Systems, 42(7), 130.

20. Xu, R., & Zhu, Y. (2018). Patient self-controlled medical record based on blockchain technology. Journal of Medical Systems, 42(8), 1–9.

21. Kang, J. M., Ryu, S. Y., & Kim, D. (2018). A survey of mobile blockchain: Architecture, consensus, and network. Journal of Communications and Networks, 20(4), 393–402.

22. Zohrevand, P., & Beznosov, K. (2017). A systematic literature review on blockchain technology for secure sharing of medical electronic records. In 2017 IEEE 19th International Conference on e-Health Networking, Applications and Services (Healthcom) (pp. 1–6).

23. Kuo, T. T., Kim, H. E., & Ohno-Machado, L. (2017). Blockchain distributed ledger technologies for biomedical and health care applications. Journal of the American Medical Informatics Association, 24(6), 1211–1220.

24. Mohsin, A., Jararweh, Y., Al-Ayyoub, M., Gupta, B. B., & Gupta, B. (2018). BCDS-health: Permissioned blockchain-based system for secure and efficient sharing of electronic health records. Future Generation Computer Systems, 86, 1106–1116.

25. Chen, M., Mao, S., & Liu, Y. (2014). Big data: A survey. Mobile Networks and Applications, 19(2), 171–209.

26. Pilkington, M. (2016). Blockchain Technology: Principles and Applications. Research Handbook on Digital Transformations, 1–33. Edward Elgar. https://ssrn.com/abstract=2662660

27. Shaikh, Z. A., Memon, A. A., Shaikh, A. M., Soomro, S., & Sayed, M. (2023). Blockchain in healthcare: Unlocking the potential of blockchain for secure and efficient applications for medical data management—A presentation of basic concepts. *Liaquat Medical Research Journal*, 5(2). https://doi.org/10.38106/LMRJ.2023.5.2-08

28. Ouaddah, A., Elkalam, A. A., & Ouahman, A. A. (2017). Towards a novel privacy-preserving access control model based on blockchain technology in IoT. In 2017 IEEE International Conference on Cloud Computing Technology and Science (CloudCom) (pp. 229–236).

29. Yin, J., Srinivasan, S., Wang, K., & Jiang, Z. (2018). A blockchain-based framework for data sharing with fine-grained access control in decentralized storage systems. Journal of Parallel and Distributed Computing, 118, 112–123.

30. Ekblaw, A., Azaria, A., Halamka, J. D., & Lippman, A. (2016). A case study for blockchain in healthcare: "MedRec" prototype for electronic health records and medical research data. In Proceedings of IEEE Open & Big Data Conference (pp. 1–8).

3

HEALTHCARE MONITORING SYSTEM WITH BLOCKCHAIN TECHNOLOGY TRACKING OPEN DONATIONS AND MINIMIZING THE SCOPE OF ORGAN TRAFFICKING

Puneeta Singh and Shrddha Sagar

3.1 Introduction

In the ever-evolving healthcare technology landscape, the Organ Management System stands out as a transformative initiative, harnessing the power of cutting-edge technologies such as blockchain, smart contracts, and Ethereum. Before delving into the specifics of our project, let's unravel the foundational technologies that underpin this innovative platform [1].

Blockchain is a decentralized and distributed ledger technology that ensures transparency, security, and immutability of data. In the context of the Organ Management System, blockchain serves as the bedrock of a tamper-resistant recordkeeping system [2]. By decentralizing data across a network of computers, the system guarantees the integrity of organ donation-related activities, providing an unparalleled level of trust and security. Blockchain, a revolutionary technology, operates on a decentralized network, fostering trust through consensus algorithms and ensuring transparent and secure transactions. Its immutable recordkeeping, powered by cryptographic hashes, prevents tampering and fraud. Smart contracts automate agreements, reducing the need for intermediaries, while transparency and traceability empower participants to view the entire transaction history. With various consensus mechanisms ensuring validity, blockchain facilitates secure, transparent, and tamper-proof transactions across distributed networks. These consensus mechanisms, such as Proof of Work (PoW), Proof of Stake (PoS), Delegated Proof of Stake (DPoS), and Practical Byzantine Fault Tolerance (PBFT), validate and agree on the state of the blockchain without a central authority [3].

At the heart of our project lies the implementation of smart contracts, self-executing contracts with the terms of the agreement directly written

DOI: 10.1201/9781003483113-3

into code. These contracts automate and enforce the execution of predefined rules, ensuring transparency and efficiency in transactions. In the Organ Management System, smart contracts play a pivotal role in governing and securing the organ donation process, adding an extra layer of trust to every interaction. Smart contracts, a hallmark of blockchain innovation, redefine the landscape of automated agreements. Pioneered by platforms like Ethereum, smart contracts are self-executing programs with coded terms, eliminating the need for intermediaries in contractual processes [4]. Operating on a decentralized network, these contracts execute actions automatically when predefined conditions are met, enhancing transparency, efficiency, and trust in various industries. Smart contracts have become integral to decentralized applications (DApps), powering functionalities ranging from finance to supply chain management [5]. Their versatility, combined with tamper-resistant execution on the blockchain, signifies a paradigm shift in how agreements are conceptualized and executed, offering a secure and automated foundation for the future of transactions and contractual relationships [6].

- **Public Blockchain:** It has great trust, no centralized authority, and allows for user writing and reading, but it also consumes a lot of energy [7].
- **Private Blockchain:** Access to or modification of the blockchain may be restricted to the particular entity that controls it. It is a decentralized blockchain with lower reliability. When the throughput is high, less energy is used [8].
- **Blockchain Consortium:** It can be owned by a group of companies, and each member of the group can read and write to it. Also referred to as a partially centralized blockchain, it consumes less energy and has a high throughput [8].
- **Hybrid Blockchain:** A hybrid blockchain may provide for read and write access for all participants, much like a public blockchain. It provides modest credibility and a little degree of centrality [9].

3.2 Review of related literature

According to Alqarni et al. [10], blockchain technology can potentially decrease the need for human labor by dividing the number of blocks it produces while also protecting Internet of Things (IoT) smart sensors from hackers and promoting transparency. There are numerous security vulnerabilities, such as delays in authentication and fabrication attacks.

To solve the security issue, Singh and Verma [11] propose utilizing blockchain technology in conjunction with the CIA (confidentiality, integrity, and availability) formulas. It could replace the current IoT system. They would have to cope with issues of integrity and secrecy.

Araujo-Inastrilla and Vitón-Castillo [12] suggest that Network Functions Virtualization (NFV), control and administrative functions, and integration with IoT devices can be used to deliver 5G technology. This article looks at a number of blockchain-related topics, including legislation and standardization. Artificial intelligence (AI) and blockchain technologies can assist in resolving these problems.

Lakhan et al. [13] state that the idea of a consensus process can be used to combine blockchain technology with IoT devices. The blockchain and its IoT sensors can generate hash-based authentication codes and establish block nodes using a random function utilizing a shared key. The winner of the election is the block node, also known as the offline quick election node. Before block nodes are updated for the blockchain process, AI techniques are also introduced to eliminate sensor outliers.

Ahmad et al. [14] have suggested that IoT sensors connect to one another and share information with each node. The author agrees that using decentralized techniques could potentially address a significant problem with centralized infrastructure.

Sun and associates [15] discuss the security, dependability, and transparency of the IoT as the three main problems. With the aid of blockchain technology's essential feature, decentralization, the most crucial aspect lies in the consensus process. This process ensures that all nodes in the network—which are interconnected and utilize smart contracts, data encryption, decryption, proof-of-work, and proof-of-stake mechanisms—operate cohesively and securely.

Tareen et al. [16] suggest that the IoT be used to record all patient data. When gathering data utilizing patient data, this study paid extra attention to security and patient privacy. It is challenging to maintain data integrity.

Singh [6] discusses the distributed nature of blockchain technology and its various uses, including consortium, public, and private blockchains. Additionally, a thorough explanation of blockchain, including privacy, secret data, and authentication, is given in this paper.

Pathak et al. [17] propose that intelligent logistics enables the quick and effective movement of goods. The IoT and new technologies have dramatically shortened lead times and made logistics management easier. It relies more on digital technology and uses fewer resources—people, transportation, paperwork, and other things. However, it could also result in issues with data theft and violation of privacy. Nevertheless, the integration of IoT and blockchain technologies will improve the security of the digital logistics system.

Elgamal et al. [18] propose despite the IoT security risks, the secure communication platform that blockchain technology provides can be used to remedy the issue. Blockchain technology will make use of smart contracts for security-related purposes.

TABLE 3.1 Research gap

Regional focus	Study deficit
QoS Result Achievement	• Without accounting for clustering, some published research have successfully transferred data directly to sink nodes, which negatively affects service quality by causing unnecessary delay [20]. • While many of the published articles conduct clustering, the quality of service is also adversely affected by the gateway's inadequate processing of the clustered data in terms of interval and delay [21]. • The routing protocols used in current research are limited, have poorer communication reliability, and suffer from transmission errors that also affect QoS [22].
Security Implementation	• Several ongoing initiatives prioritize data security over authentication, which affects patient privacy [23]. • Many state-of-the-art works employ sophisticated cryptographic techniques for data encryption and authentication, which raises energy consumption in WBAN-IoT networks [8]. • Due to some limitations in the current work, the WBAN-IoT environment is susceptible to serious attacks such as impersonation and false injection attacks, which only consider the bare minimum of security measures to ensure security [24].
Blockchain	• Conventional blockchain architectures are characterized by high energy consumption, latency, and scalability issues with block generation and validation time. Because of its resource constraints, WBAN-IoT is not suitable for these problems with typical blockchains [25].

Source: [Original (created by authors)].

David, explains how the healthcare sector operates and how it affects information technology [19] and the privacy and security of personal data. This technology improves their efficacy, resilience, and transparency.

Table 3.1 resume the related gap.

3.3 Problem statement

• The clustering procedure is ineffective because theClustering Feature (CF) computation can be time-consuming when many sensors are used, and it does not ensure that the best solution is always generated. This work reduces the amount of duplicate data, but it leaves anomalous (faulty) data unaccounted for. This implies considerable energy and bandwidth use for Cluster Heads (CHs).

• Interference arises when two sensors communicate simultaneously over the same channel. Multihop transmission via suboptimal nodes results in a decrease in delivery rate and an increase in energy usage.

3.4 Motivation

- **Organ Shortage Crisis:** The global shortage of organs for transplantation is a pressing issue. Millions of individuals require life-saving organ transplants, and the scarcity of available organs contributes to prolonged waiting times and increased mortality rates.
- **Inefficiencies in Traditional Systems:** Traditional organ donation systems often face inefficiencies, including delays in matching donors with recipients, lack of transparency in the allocation process, and challenges in maintaining secure and accessible medical records.
- **Geographical Barriers:** Geographical barriers can impede the timely identification and connection of potential organ donors with recipients. The Organ Management System aims to overcome these barriers by facilitating localized searches and connections.
- **Data Security and Trust Issues:** Concerns related to data security, privacy, and transparency in organ donation processes can create hesitancy among potential donors and recipients. The project addresses these issues by leveraging blockchain technology to ensure secure and transparent recordkeeping.
- **Complex Matching Process:** The current matching process for organ donation involves complex algorithms and manual assessments, leading to potential delays and inaccuracies. The Organ Management System seeks to streamline this process through the implementation of smart contracts, automating and optimizing donor-recipient matching based on predefined criteria.
- **Inefficient Communication Channels:** Communication gaps between potential donors, recipients, and healthcare providers can lead to missed opportunities and delayed organ matches. The proposed system integrates efficient communication channels, leveraging blockchain's transparency to enable seamless and secure information exchange among all stakeholders.
- **Inconsistent Organ Allocation Policies:** Varying organ allocation policies across regions and countries contribute to disparities in access to life-saving transplants. The Organ Management System promotes consistency and fairness by implementing standardized smart contracts that adhere to predefined allocation criteria, ensuring a more equitable distribution of organs.

3.5 Methodology/System model

3.5.1 Basic working of the system

The Organ Management System operates on a decentralized blockchain infrastructure to ensure transparency, security, and reliability in organ donation

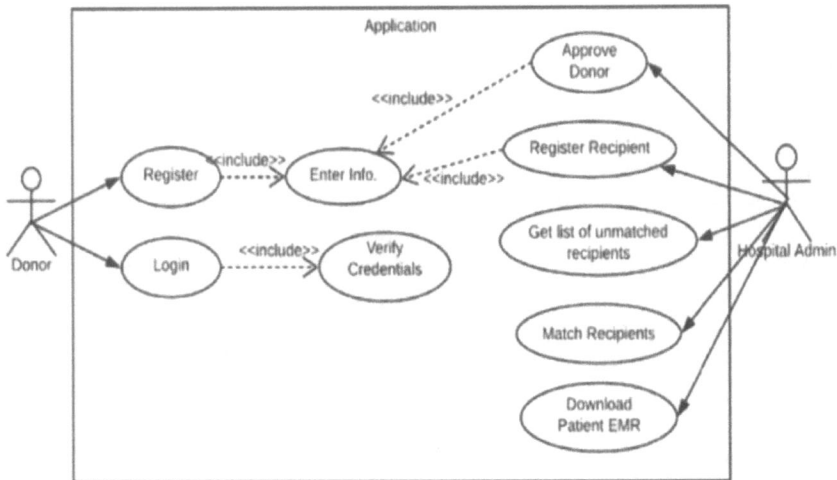

FIGURE 3.1 Blockchain network.

[Original (created by authors)]

transactions. The system involves three main actors: donors, recipients, and the blockchain network, see Figure 3.1.

- **Donors:** Donors register on the platform, creating a profile that includes medical history, blood type, and organ compatibility information. They express their willingness to be living donors and specify the organs they are willing to donate.
- **Recipients:** Recipients create profiles detailing their medical history, organ requirements, and urgency. They search for potential donors based on compatibility and geographical proximity.
- **Blockchain Network:** Serves as a decentralized ledger to record and validate organ donation transactions. Smart contracts manage the rules and conditions for organ donation, ensuring secure and transparent transactions.

3.5.2 Basic model of data flow

Figure 3.2 shows the model of data flow.

- **User Registration:** Donors and recipients register on the platform, providing necessary personal and medical information.
- **Profile Creation:** Users create detailed profiles, specifying their organ compatibility, medical history, and preferences.

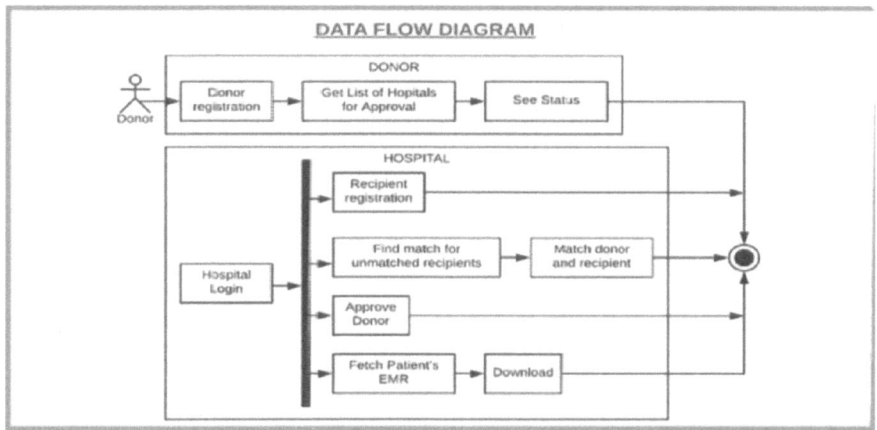

FIGURE 3.2 Data flow system.

[Original (created by authors)]

- **Search and Matching:** Recipients search for potential donors based on compatibility, location, and other relevant criteria. The system employs algorithms to match compatible donors with recipients.
- **Connection Establishment:** Once a match is found, users can initiate contact through the platform to discuss further details and arrangements.
- **Blockchain Transaction:** When both parties agree on the donation, a smart contract is executed on the blockchain, recording the transaction securely.
- **Medical Verification:** Before finalizing the transaction, medical professionals verify the compatibility and health of both parties.
- **Organ Donation Process:** The organ donation process is facilitated offline with medical professionals overseeing the transplant.

3.5.3 System architecture

The Organ Management System follows a microservices architecture to ensure scalability, maintainability, and flexibility. Figure 3.3 shows the communication flow between system architecture. The components include the following:

- **User Interface (ReactJS):** Provides a user-friendly frontend for donors and recipients to interact with the system.
- **Application Server (NodeJS):** Manages user requests, authentication, and communication with the blockchain network.
- **Blockchain Network:** Utilizes a decentralized network (e.g., Hyperledger Fabric) to store and validate organ donation transactions.

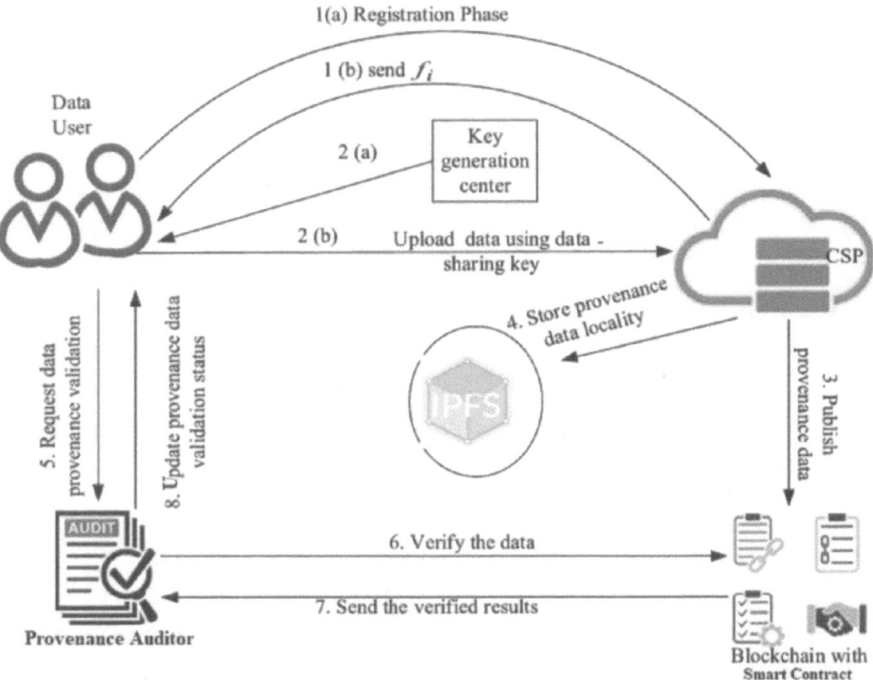

FIGURE 3.3 Communication flow.

[Original (created by authors)]

- **Database:** Stores nonsensitive user information and facilitates quick data retrieval.
- **Communication Flow:** Users interact with the front end, triggering requests to the application server. The application server communicates with the blockchain network to execute smart contracts and record transactions.

    User data is stored in a secure database for quick access and retrieval.

3.6 Results

The implementation of the Organ Management System has yielded significant positive outcomes in addressing the challenges inherent in traditional organ donation systems. The utilization of blockchain technology has successfully enhanced the efficiency, transparency, and security of the entire organ donation process.

- **Improved Matching Efficiency:** The introduction of smart contracts has notably streamlined the donor-recipient matching process, reducing delays and inaccuracies. The automated algorithms have enhanced the speed and accuracy of identifying compatible donors, thereby minimizing waiting times for recipients.

- **Enhanced Data Security and Transparency:** The integration of blockchain technology has successfully addressed concerns related to data security, privacy, and transparency. The decentralized and immutable nature of the blockchain ensures secure recordkeeping, instilling trust among donors, recipients, and medical professionals.
- **Overcoming Geographical Barriers:** The Organ Management System's localized search and connection features have effectively overcome geographical barriers, enabling swift identification and pairing of potential donors with recipients. This has significantly increased the accessibility of organ donation opportunities.
- **Promotion of Public Awareness:** Features designed to enhance public awareness have resulted in increased registrations of potential donors. The system's outreach initiatives have educated and engaged the community, contributing to a greater understanding of organ donation's impact on saving lives.
- **Precision in Matching Efficiency:** The introduction of smart contracts has not only expedited the matching process but has brought a level of precision previously unattainable. Automated algorithms analyze criteria with unparalleled accuracy, leading to swift and accurate donor-recipient pairings. This has translated into a substantial reduction in waiting times for recipients, offering a ray of hope in the face of the organ shortage crisis.
- **Fortified Data Security and Trust:** The integration of blockchain has acted as a robust shield against concerns related to data security and trust. The decentralized nature of the blockchain ensures that sensitive medical records remain secure, immutable, and accessible only to authorized personnel. This has significantly enhanced the confidence of donors, recipients, and healthcare professionals in the integrity of the organ donation process.
- **Overcoming Geographical Barriers with Precision:** The Organ Management System's capability to facilitate localized searches and connections has not merely overcome geographical barriers but has done so with precision. The system's ability to pinpoint potential matches within specific regions has revolutionized the accessibility of organ donation opportunities, offering a lifeline to those who were previously hindered by distance.
- **Catalyzing Public Awareness and Engagement:** The project's focus on public awareness initiatives has borne fruit, with a noticeable surge in donor registrations. Community engagement features have successfully educated the public on the critical impact of organ donation, resulting in

a surge of active participants. This not only contributes to the system's success but also indicates a positive shift in societal attitudes towards organ donation.

3.7 Conclusion

In summary, the Organ Management System stands at the forefront of transforming the global organ shortage crisis by ingeniously leveraging blockchain technology. This innovative project effectively addresses inherent inefficiencies in traditional systems, erases geographical barriers, and bolsters the overall transparency and security of organ donation processes. The implementation of a streamlined matching process, coupled with enhanced data security measures, not only expedites organ transfers but also fosters a heightened sense of trust among users. By successfully overcoming geographical limitations, the system significantly broadens the pool of potential donors, thereby making a profound impact on reducing waiting times for recipients. Moreover, the system's noteworthy contribution to public awareness and engagement underscores its potential to create a lasting impact on organ donation rates. The harmonious combination of technological innovation, security enhancements, and community involvement positions the Organ Management System as a pioneering force poised to revolutionize organ donation practices and ultimately save countless lives on a global scale.

References

1. Gupta, S., Alharbi, F., Alshahrani, R., Kumar Arya, P., Vyas, S., Elkamchouchi, D. H., & Soufiene, B. O. (2023). Secure and lightweight authentication protocol for privacy preserving communications in smart City applications. *Sustainability*, *15*, 5346. https://doi.org/10.3390/su15065346
2. Hajian, A., Prybutok, V. R., & Chang, H. C. (2023). An empirical study for blockchain-based information sharing systems in electronic health records: A mediation perspective. *Computers in Human Behavior*, *138*, 107471.
3. Hegde, P., & Maddikunta, P. K. R. (2023). Secure PBFT consensus-based lightweight blockchain for healthcare application. *Applied Sciences*, *13*(6), 3757.
4. Wenhua, Z., Qamar, F., Abdali, T. A. N., Hassan, R., Jafri, S. T. A., & Nguyen, Q. N. (2023). Blockchain technology: Security issues, healthcare applications, challenges and future trends. *Electronics*, *12*(3), 546. https://doi.org/10.3390/electronics12030546
5. Othman, S. B., Almalki, F. A., & Sakli, H. (2022). Internet of Things in the Healthcare Applications: Overview of Security and Privacy Issues. In: Chakraborty, C., Khosravi, M.R. (eds) Intelligent Healthcare. Singapore: Springer. https://doi.org/10.1007/978-981-16-8150-9_9
6. Singh, P., Sinha, P., & Raghav, A. (2023). A Blockchain IoT Hybrid Framework for Security and Privacy in a Healthcare Database Network. In: Arumugam Suresh Kumar, et al., (eds) *Dynamics of Swarm Intelligence Health Analysis for*

the *Next Generation*. (pp. 210–225). IGI Global. https://doi.org/10.4018/978-1-6684-6894-4.ch011

7. Sharma, P., Namasudra, S., Crespo, R. G., Parra-Fuente, J., & Trivedi, M. C. (2023). EHDHE: Enhancing security of healthcare documents in IoT-enabled digital healthcare ecosystems using blockchain. *Information Sciences*, 629, 703–718.

8. Ali, A., Al-Rimy, B. A. S., Alsubaei, F. S., Almazroi, A. A., & Almazroi, A. A. (2023). HealthLock: Blockchain-based privacy preservation using homomorphic encryption in internet of things healthcare applications. *Sensors*, 23(15), 6762.

9. Badri, S., Ullah Jan, S., Alghazzawi, D., Aldhaheri, S., & Pitropakis, N. (2023). BIoMT: A blockchain-enabled healthcare architecture for information security in the internet of medical things. *Computer Systems Science and Engineering*, 46(3), 3667–3684.

10. Alqarni, K. S., Almalki, F. A., Soufiene, B. O., Ali, O., & Albalwy, F. (2022). Authenticated wireless links between a drone and sensors using a blockchain: Case of smart farming. *Wireless Communications and Mobile Computing*, 2022, 4389729. https://doi.org/10.1155/2022/4389729

11. Singh, P., & Verma, S. (2019). Analysis on different strategies used in blockchain technology. *Journal of Computational and Theoretical Nanoscience*, 16(10), 4350–4355.

12. Araujo-Inastrilla, C. R., & Vitón-Castillo, A. A. (2023). Blockchain in health sciences: Research trends in Scopus. *Iberoamerican Journal of Science Measurement and Communication*, 3(2). https://doi.org/10.47909/ijsmc.56

13. Lakhan, A., Mohammed, M. A., Nedoma, J., Martinek, R., Tiwari, P., & Kumar, N. (2023). DRLBTS: Deep reinforcement learning-aware blockchain-based healthcare system. *Scientific Reports*, 13(1), 4124.

14. Ahmad, S., Arya, S. K., Gupta, S., Singh, P., & Dwivedi, S. K. (2023, May). Study of Cryptographic Techniques Adopted in Blockchain. In *2023 4th International Conference on Intelligent Engineering and Management (ICIEM)* (pp. 1–6). IEEE. 10.1109/ICIEM59379.2023.10166591.

15. Sun, M., Chai, Q., & Ng, C. T. (2023). Managing the quality-speed tradeoff in blockchain-supported healthcare diagnostic services. *Omega*, 120, 102911.

16. Tareen, F. N., Avi, A. N., Malik, A. A., Javed, M. A., Khan, M. B., Saudagar, A. K. J., ... Abul Hasanat, M. H. (2023). Efficient load balancing for blockchain-based healthcare system in smart cities. *Applied Sciences*, 13(4), 2411.

17. Pathak, R., Soni, B., & Muppalaneni, N. B. (2023, February). Role of Blockchain in Health Care: A Comprehensive Study. In *Proceedings of 3rd International Conference on Recent Trends in Machine Learning, IoT, Smart Cities and Applications: ICMISC 2022* (pp. 137–154). Singapore: Springer Nature Singapore.

18. Elgamal, E., Medhat, W., Abd Elfatah, M., & Abdelbaki, N. (2023, January). Blockchain in Healthcare for Achieving Patients' Privacy. In *2023 20th Learning and Technology Conference (L&T)* (pp. 59–64). IEEE. 10.1109/LT58159.2023.10092352.

19. David, S., Duraipandian, K., Chandrasekaran, D., Pandey, D., Sindhwani, N., & Pandey, B. K. (2023). Impact of Blockchain in Healthcare System. In: *Unleashing the Potentials of Blockchain Technology for Healthcare Industries*. (pp. 37–57). Academic Press. https://doi.org/10.1016/B978-0-323-99481-1.00004-3

20. Bennacer, S. A., Sabiri, K., Aaroud, A., Akodadi, K., & Cherradi, B. (2023). A comprehensive survey on blockchain-based healthcare industry: Applications and challenges. *Indonesian Journal of Electrical Engineering and Computer Science*, 30, 1558–1571.

21. Singh, P., Singh, A. P., & Gupta, A. (2021). Design Strategies for Mobile Ad-hoc Network to Prevent from Attack. *Proceedings of the 3rd International Conference*

on *Advanced Computing and Software Engineering* (pp. 194–201). SCITEPRESS - Science and Technology Publications, 194–201. 10.5220/0010566800003161.

22. Aloini, D., Benevento, E., Stefanini, A., & Zerbino, P. (2023). Transforming healthcare ecosystems through blockchain: Opportunities and capabilities for business process innovation. *Technovation, 119*, 102557.

23. Miriam, H., Doreen, D., Dahiya, D., & Rene Robin, C. R. (2023). Secured cyber security algorithm for healthcare system using blockchain technology. *Intelligent Automation & Soft Computing, 35*(2), 1–6.

24. Sinha, P., Singh, R., Roy, R., & Singh, P. (2022, March). Education and Analysis of Autistic Patients Using Machine Learning. In *2022 International Conference on Emerging Smart Computing and Informatics (ESCI)* (pp. 1–6). IEEE. 10.1109/ESCI53509.2022.9758322.

25. Kiania, K., Jameii, S. M., & Rahmani, A. M. (2023). Blockchain-based privacy and security preserving in electronic health: A systematic review. *Multimedia Tools and Applications, 82*, 28493–28519.

4

TRANSFORMING HEALTHCARE SERVICES IN SOUTH ASIA

Leveraging Blockchain Technology

*Mananage Shanika Hansini Rathnasiri,
Narayanage Jayantha Dewasiri, Rubee Singh,
Shahbaz Khan, and Ben Othman Soufiene*

4.1 Introduction

Technological progress in recent years has swiftly revolutionized multiple industries, and the healthcare sector is now on the verge of a digital transformation. Within the healthcare sector, the ongoing trend of digitalization has presented numerous prospects for enhancing the efficiency of diagnostic and therapeutic procedure [1]. In contrast, there are numerous obstacles such as data security risks, interoperability issues, and the fragmentation of patient information. However, there is a promising technology called blockchain that has the potential to bring about a significant change. Blockchain, a distributed and unchangeable system for recording information, which serves as the foundation for digital currencies such as Bitcoin, has expanded beyond its original financial uses and now holds significant promise in the healthcare field [2]. The healthcare business has been plagued by systemic inefficiencies for a long time. However, the decentralized, transparent, and cryptographically secure nature of blockchain technology offers a compelling answer to these problems [3].

The healthcare sector encounters a variety of enduring obstacles that hinder its effectiveness and efficiency [4]. Data security remains a critical concern, as regular data breaches continue to compromise highly sensitive patient information [5]. The sector is facing significant challenges with interoperability, which is impeding the smooth interchange of patient data among different healthcare systems. Furthermore, the presence of data silos hinders the provision of comprehensive patient care and impedes medical progress by causing information fragmentation across different healthcare professionals and systems. Traditional methods have been insufficient, leading to the

DOI: 10.1201/9781003483113-4

creation of isolated data sets, security breaches, and inefficiencies that undermine the quality of patient care and hinder advancements in medicine [6]. Nevertheless, in the face of these obstacles, blockchain technology arises as a promising solution for the healthcare business [7]. The intrinsic attributes of blockchain technology, namely decentralization, immutability, and cryptographic security, provide revolutionary solutions [8]. Through the utilization of blockchain technology, healthcare organizations have the potential to completely transform the way patient data is managed and shared. This can help overcome challenges related to interoperability and guarantee the integrity and security of data. The decentralized structure of blockchain facilitates the establishment of a safe and integrated system for electronic health records (EHRs), enabling smooth data exchange across healthcare providers while upholding patient privacy and autonomy [9].

The unchangeability of blockchain guarantees that once data is documented, it remains unaltered, hence ensuring the integrity and reliability of medical records [10]. Moreover, the openness of blockchain provides clear insight into data exchanges, promoting responsibility and reducing the chances of fraud or illegal entry [11].

This chapter aims to investigate the diverse uses of blockchain technology in the healthcare environment. The potential of blockchain is extensive and disruptive, since it can revolutionize various areas such as EHRs, supply chain management, clinical trials optimization, and billing and claims processing. However, like with any rising invention, the incorporation of blockchain in health care is not without hurdles. Obstacles like as regulatory constraints, scalability concerns, and the complexities of maintaining patient privacy require careful consideration. Hence, this chapter aims to offer a thorough comprehension of how blockchain technology has the potential to transform healthcare services by examining real-world case studies, practical implementations, and future prospects. Through elucidating its potential, analyzing present obstacles, and envisioning future prospects, our objective is to stimulate dialogues and encourage the integration of blockchain as a catalyst for beneficial transformation in the healthcare sector.

4.2 Methodology

In order to comprehend the utilization of blockchain technology in healthcare applications, we conducted a comprehensive analysis of existing literature utilizing a systematic literature review technique that adhered to a rigorous and well-structured approach. Employing a comparable methodology [12–14] and [15] examined a research conundrum that remains unresolved. The researchers conducted a comprehensive search by utilizing academic databases, search engines, and relevant banking periodicals such as Scopus and Google Scholar. We utilized alternate search terms, such as "blockchain technology and healthcare services," to examine the phenomenon. After identifying 98 publications in the first search, we applied rigorous inclusion and exclusion criteria to ensure that the selected papers were relevant to our study question and goals. The selection criteria were met by research that were published in conference proceedings, peer-reviewed journals, and publications specifically addressing the implementation of blockchain technology in the healthcare sector. We excluded studies that lacked sufficient information or were not relevant to our specific situation. The selection of studies was conducted by three unbiased reviewers. Initially, pertinent studies were identified through the process of evaluating abstracts and titles. The complete contents of these papers were subsequently assessed for eligibility based on the predefined criteria for inclusion and exclusion. Any conflicts among reviewers were resolved through discussion and, if necessary, consultation with a third reviewer.

We obtained relevant data from the selected research using a methodical and structured approach. The provided material encompasses key discoveries; blockchain technology; its applications in the healthcare services; and study characteristics such as authors, publication year, and research methodology. We utilized recognized quality assessment tools suitable for various types of studies to evaluate the rigor and quality of the selected studies. The studies were evaluated for their methodological rigor, representativeness of the sample, and clarity of the results. The systematic review included a final sample of 52 relevant studies for the analysis.

4.3   Applications of blockchain in healthcare services

The uses of blockchain technology in healthcare encompass multiple crucial disciplines, effectively tackling significant difficulties and transforming the industry [16]. Blockchain technology has the potential to revolutionize healthcare services by improving EHR management, protecting the integrity of the supply chain, maintaining data accuracy in research, and simplifying billing operations [17]. It offers benefits such as increased efficiency, enhanced security, and improved transparency.

4.3.1   Electronic health records

Blockchain technology presents a viable solution to the inherent difficulties of handling EHRs [18]. Blockchain demonstrates exceptional proficiency in the field of interoperability [19]. Healthcare systems frequently face challenges in exchanging data due to the presence of incompatible formats and isolated databases. The decentralized structure and cryptographic security of blockchain facilitate a unified and safe platform that promotes interoperability among diverse healthcare systems [20]. It guarantees the accessibility of patient data among different providers while upholding privacy and security.

Moreover, blockchain permits individuals to have authority over their health data [21]. By utilizing smart contracts and encryption techniques, individuals can securely disclose their health information to authorized parties, guaranteeing transparency and precision of data [22]. This patient-centric approach not only facilitates the exchange of information but also amplifies patient participation and inclusion in their healthcare choices.

The unchangeability of blockchain is essential for preserving the accuracy and consistency of data in EHRs [23]. Once data is stored on the blockchain, it becomes impervious to tampering and cannot be modified. This functionality guarantees the genuineness and dependability of medical records, diminishing the hazards linked to data manipulation or unlawful alterations, consequently fostering greater confidence in the healthcare system.

4.3.2 Logistics and operations management

The implementation of blockchain technology brings about a significant transformation in supply chain management in the healthcare sector, specifically in the monitoring and tracing of pharmaceuticals and medical devices [24]. Ensuring drug traceability is of utmost importance in the fight against counterfeit pharmaceuticals. The unchangeable nature of blockchain enables transparent monitoring of medications, tracing their journey from production to end-user delivery [25]. Each stage of the drug's transportation is meticulously documented, guaranteeing its genuineness and thwarting the entrance of fraudulent medications into the market.

Likewise, blockchain technology allows for the monitoring of medical devices, guaranteeing their genuineness and security. Blockchain technology establishes a continuous and secure record of the custody of medical devices, ensuring the verification of their source, production procedures, and distribution routes [26]. This process guarantees that medical devices adhere to regulatory standards and have not been compromised, hence improving patient safety and minimizing the likelihood of counterfeit or substandard devices.

4.3.3 Exploration of clinical trials and research

The utilization of blockchain technology has great potential in guaranteeing the reliability and openness of data in clinical trials and research initiatives [27]. Preserving the trustworthiness and dependability of research findings heavily relies on upholding data integrity. The unchangeable nature of blockchain guarantees that study data stays impervious to tampering, hence preventing any form of manipulation or fraudulent adjustments [28]. This feature is particularly essential for maintaining the integrity of clinical trial results and preventing any manipulation or prejudice in the data.

Moreover, blockchain enhances confidentiality for participants in clinical trials [29]. It enables the development of secure and transparent platforms in which people can provide data while maintaining their anonymity. By employing cryptographic methods and restricted access, blockchain technology facilitates the secure sharing of data among participants. This ensures the security of the information while also enabling transparent and verifiable records, thereby promoting confidence between researchers and participants.

4.3.4 Billing and claims handling

Blockchain technology optimizes the billing and claims processing procedures in the healthcare industry, resulting in decreased administrative expenses and enhanced operational efficiency [30]. Blockchain streamlines and expedites the billing and claims processes by utilizing smart contracts and decentralized ledgers [31]. Smart contracts automate payment arrangements between parties, guaranteeing precision, minimizing delays, and obviating intermediaries. This automation results in increased transaction efficiency, reduced billing errors, and improved transparency in financial activities within the healthcare system.

4.4 Implementation challenges and considerations

Although blockchain technology has the potential to bring about significant changes in health care, its adoption is hindered by challenges such as regulatory compliance, scalability, integration with current infrastructure, and safeguarding patient privacy [32]. To overcome these issues, it is imperative to foster collaboration among stakeholders, implement technological advancements, and establish regulatory frameworks that effectively balance innovation with adherence to healthcare standards and regulations [33].

4.4.1 Regulatory compliance

The integration of blockchain technology in the healthcare sector poses several regulatory hurdles and compliance concerns [34]. The healthcare sector functions within an intricate regulatory framework overseen by multiple legislations, including HIPAA (Health Insurance Portability and Accountability Act) and GDPR (General Data Protection Regulation). The primary objective of these pieces of legislation is to ensure the protection of patient data privacy, security, and the ethical utilization of healthcare information [35].

Navigating the integration of blockchain technology within the confines of these strict rules necessitates careful attention. The decentralized and immutable nature of blockchain technology raises concerns around data control and governance [36]. Ensuring adherence to rules becomes more complex when taking into account the necessity for data alteration or removal, particularly in situations involving patient demands or regulatory mandates. The task of reconciling the unchangeable record of blockchain with the need to comply with regulations on data modification or deletion presents a substantial difficulty. Moreover, there is a need for clear understanding of the legal and liability consequences that arise from data breaches or mistakes inside a system based on blockchain technology. The use of blockchain technology has a huge challenge in establishing frameworks that guarantee accountability, liability, and compliance with healthcare legislation [37].

4.4.2 Scalability and integration

The integration of blockchain into existing healthcare infrastructure raises significant concerns regarding scalability. Blockchain networks, particularly those that are public and permissionless, encounter constraints in terms of transaction velocity, capacity, and scalability [38]. Healthcare systems produce huge quantities of data and it is crucial to manage this volume effectively while ensuring efficiency [36].

The incorporation of blockchain technology into existing healthcare systems presents difficulties. Seamless integration between blockchain and established systems, such as EHR platforms, electronic prescribing systems, and other healthcare databases, necessitates careful strategizing and financial commitment. To achieve smooth data interchange between blockchain networks and existing systems, it is necessary to carefully analyze integration protocols and standards without causing any disruption to current operations [39].

Furthermore, it is necessary to address the scalability issues associated with the energy consumption and computational capacity needed for blockchain consensus methods [40]. It is crucial to provide scalable solutions that maximize resource utilization and guarantee the effectiveness and safety of blockchain networks in order to successfully adopt them in the healthcare sector.

4.4.3 Issues related to the protection of personal information and the right to privacy

Ensuring patient privacy and confidentiality is of utmost importance in the healthcare industry, and the incorporation of blockchain technology raises concerns around privacy [41]. Although blockchain provides improved security and openness, its intrinsic transparency poses a challenge in safeguarding sensitive patient data. The inherent unchangeability of blockchain, while beneficial for maintaining data integrity, presents difficulties in meeting patient demands for data alteration or deletion, especially when it comes to sensitive health information [42].

To tackle privacy concerns, it is necessary to incorporate privacy-enhancing technologies into blockchain networks. Methods such as zero-knowledge proofs, encryption, and selective data disclosure methods can facilitate safe and confidential transactions while maintaining the integrity of data [43]. Furthermore, it is essential to develop strong consent management systems that enable patients to regulate access to their data on the blockchain. Achieving adherence to privacy standards while using the advantages of blockchain technology necessitates a careful equilibrium between transparency, security, and the preservation of patient anonymity. Various real-life instances exemplify the effective integration of blockchain technology in the healthcare sector, highlighting its capacity for profound change [44]. An exemplification of this concept is Medicalchain, a platform that employs blockchain technology to transform the management of patient-centric healthcare data [45].

4.5 Use cases

The implementation of blockchain technology has had a profound effect on several healthcare situations, revolutionizing procedures and enhancing patient results. An important application is optimizing pharmaceutical supply networks. IBM's blockchain technology, developed in partnership with corporations such as Walmart and Merck, improves the capacity to track drugs from their creation to their distribution. Blockchain technology prevents the infiltration of counterfeit drugs into the market and guarantees patient safety and adherence to regulations by establishing an unchangeable record of the pharmaceuticals' entire journey.

Another significant application involves enhancing the efficiency and transparency of clinical trials. The Synaptic Health Alliance, which includes prominent healthcare corporations such as Aetna and Ascension, use blockchain technology to optimize the administrative procedures of clinical trials. The immutable ledger of blockchain guarantees visible and auditable records, so lowering administrative overhead, facilitating data sharing among stakeholders, and ultimately accelerating the development of new treatments and therapies.

Moreover, blockchain technology has been utilized to ensure the security of medical device data. Chronicled is a platform that utilizes blockchain technology to guarantee the genuineness and traceability of medical products. Chronicled facilitates healthcare practitioners in verifying the authenticity of medical devices, preventing the circulation of counterfeit items, and improving patient safety by assigning a distinct cryptographic identity to each device and documenting its history on the blockchain [46].

4.5.1 Case 1: Medicalchain

Medicalchain is an innovative platform that utilizes blockchain technology to revolutionize the administration of healthcare data [47]. This platform enables patients to have full ownership over their health records by utilizing blockchain technology for safe and decentralized storage. Medicalchain's architecture guarantees the integrity of patient data, making it resistant to tampering, while also facilitating convenient access and sharing among authorized healthcare practitioners. Patients have the ability to authorize particular healthcare personnel to securely access their records, which improves care coordination and treatment outcomes.

4.5.2 Case 2: Guardtime

Guardtime is a company that focuses on providing cybersecurity solutions for the healthcare industry by employing blockchain technology. Their keyless signature infrastructure (KSI) utilizes blockchain technology to guarantee the integrity and security of healthcare data. Guardtime's blockchain-based technology safeguards vital patient data against cyber threats and unlawful access by employing immutable records and cryptographic proofs. This solution greatly improves data security and authenticity, effectively addressing important compliance and privacy problems in the healthcare industry.

4.6 Future outlook for South Asia

The future prospects for South Asia in embracing blockchain technology in health care are highly encouraging, characterized by developing patterns that hold the potential to transform healthcare provision, diagnosis, and funding. Collaboration and collaborations among stakeholders are essential for fully harnessing the capabilities of blockchain technology. This collaboration will promote innovation; guarantee adherence to regulations; and eventually improve the quality, accessibility, and cost of healthcare services throughout the area.

4.6.1 Emerging trends

The potential of blockchain technology in health care across South Asia is highly promising, demonstrating a path towards substantial progress and breakthroughs. The healthcare scene in the region is set to undergo a revolutionary transformation due to emerging trends in the application of blockchain technology. Possible advancements involve the progression of interoperable blockchain networks, facilitating seamless data interchange among healthcare providers, augmenting care continuity, and enabling a full perspective of patients' health information across different regions and systems. Furthermore, the combination of artificial intelligence (AI) and Internet of Medical Things (IoMT) with blockchain technology is anticipated to enhance the effectiveness of healthcare services by facilitating predictive analytics, personalized medicine, and remote patient monitoring. This integration also guarantees the protection and accuracy of data.

Moreover, the investigation of decentralized financing (DeFi) methods in the healthcare sector is imminent. This entails utilizing blockchain technology for healthcare financing, insurance, and transparent income distribution models, which has the ability to democratize access to healthcare services and fund new healthcare projects. The rise of non-fungible tokens (NFTs) and their application in health care for distinct personal IDs, medical records, and intellectual property rights is a fascinating development that may gain popularity. These advancements indicate a significant change in the manner in which health care is obtained, provided, and funded in South Asia by incorporating blockchain technology.

4.6.2 *Collaborations and partnerships*

Collaborations and partnerships among stakeholders are crucial for the successful implementation and incorporation of blockchain technology in the healthcare sector of South Asia. The collaboration of several entities, such as government agencies, healthcare providers, technology corporations, research institutes, and regulatory authorities, is crucial to effectively address the complications involved in deploying blockchain technologies. Collaborative endeavors facilitate the creation of standardized procedures, compatibility guidelines, and regulatory structures customized to the healthcare requirements of the region [47].

Furthermore, cultivating collaborations promotes the interchange of knowledge, shares exemplary methods, and joint creation of inventive solutions tackle specific local difficulties. Collaborations among specialists in blockchain, healthcare professionals, and technology innovators enable the joint development of safe, scalable, and user-friendly blockchain solutions that specifically address the distinct requirements of South Asia's varied healthcare systems. These partnerships are essential for stimulating investment in research, infrastructure, and skill development required for the widespread implementation of blockchain technology, guaranteeing that the advantages of this technology are accessible and have a significant effect throughout the region [48].

4.7 Conclusion

The investigation into the possibilities of blockchain technology in the healthcare industry in South Asia has shown a landscape full of promising opportunities for transformation. Throughout this talk, significant elements demonstrating the influence of blockchain in health care have been emphasized. Blockchain has the potential to revolutionize healthcare services in the region. It may be applied in several areas, such as EHRs, supply chain management, clinical trials, and billing systems. Blockchain is considered an innovative technology that is expected to bring significant changes to the healthcare industry.

The future forecast encompasses various new trends, such as the integration of interoperable blockchain networks, the convergence of AI and IoT with blockchain, the investigation of decentralized finance models, and the application of NFTs in health care. These trends indicate a significant change in the way health care is provided, offering improved protection of data, seamless exchange of information, tailored treatment, and innovative financial structures that can make great health care accessible across South Asia. The revolutionary potential of blockchain technology in changing healthcare services across South Asia is unrivaled. The decentralized, secure, and transparent nature of this technology effectively tackles important issues like data security, interoperability, and patient privacy, while also promoting innovation and efficiency in healthcare systems.

The blockchain technology has the capacity to bring about significant changes in the healthcare sector, going beyond only technological breakthroughs. It represents a fundamental change in the way healthcare services are provided, focusing on the needs of the patients, improving efficiency, and ensuring transparency. By fostering collaborations, partnerships, and engaging stakeholders, the area can fully use the capabilities of blockchain technology to establish a future where health care is not only accessible but also customized to individual need, proactive, and focused on prevention.

In order for South Asia to effectively adopt blockchain technology in the healthcare sector, it is imperative to cultivate a cooperative environment that encourages creativity, allocates resources for research and infrastructure, and provides strong regulatory frameworks. This collaborative endeavor will guarantee the actualization of blockchain's revolutionary capacity, thereby establishing a healthcare environment that is both secure and efficient, with a primary emphasis on enhancing the welfare of individuals and communities throughout South Asia.

REFERENCES

1. Albanese, G., Calbimonte, J. P., Schumacher, M., & Calvaresi, D. (2020). Dynamic consent management for clinical trials via private blockchain technology. *Journal Of Ambient Intelligence and Humanized Computing*, 11(11), 4909–4926.
2. Al-Farsi, S., Rathore, M. M., & Bakiras, S. (2021). Security of blockchain-based supply chain management systems: Challenges and opportunities. *Applied Sciences*, 11(12), 5585.
3. Ali, O., Jaradat, A., Ally, M., & Rotabi, S. (2022). Blockchain Technology Enables Healthcare Data Management and Accessibility. In *Blockchain Technologies for Sustainability*. Singapore: Springer, pp. 91–118. https://doi.org/10.1007/978-981-16-6301-7_5

4. Aloini, D., Benevento, E., Stefanini, A., & Zerbino, P. (2023). Transforming healthcare ecosystems through blockchain: Opportunities and capabilities for business process innovation. *Technovation*, 119, 102557.
5. Alzahrani, S., Daim, T., & Choo, K. K. R. (2022). Assessment of the blockchain technology adoption for the management of the electronic health record systems. *IEEE Transactions on Engineering Management*, 70(8), 2846–863.
6. Attaran, M. (2022). Blockchain technology in healthcare: Challenges and opportunities. *International Journal of Healthcare Management*, 15(1), 70–83.
7. Attaran, M., & Gunasekaran, A. (2019). Blockchain-enabled technology: The emerging technology set to reshape and decentralise many industries. *International Journal of Applied Decision Sciences*, 12(4), 424–444.
8. Biancone, P., Secinaro, S., Brescia, V., & Calandra, D. (2019). Management of open innovation in healthcare for cost accounting using EHR. *Journal of Open Innovation: Technology, Market, and Complexity*. 5(4), 1–16.
9. Biancone, P., Secinaro, S., Marseglia, R., & Calandra, D. (2023). E-health for the future. Managerial perspectives using a multiple case study approach. *Technovation*, 120, 102406.
10. Boulos, M. N. K., Wilson, J. T., & Clauson, K. A. (2018). Geospatial blockchain: Promises, challenges, and scenarios in health and healthcare. *International Journal of Health Geographics*, 17(25), 1–10.
11. Chang, Y., Iakovou, E., & Shi, W. (2020). Blockchain in global supply chains and cross border trade: A critical synthesis of the state-of-the-art, challenges and opportunities. *International Journal of Production Research*, 58(7), 2082–2099.
12. Chattu, V. K. (2021). A review of artificial intelligence, big data, and blockchain technology applications in medicine and global health. *Big Data and Cognitive Computing*, 5(3), 41–50.
13. Dewasiri, N. J., Baker, H. K., Banda, Y. W., & Rathnasiri, M. S. H. (2022). The Dividend Decision Model: A Possible Solution for the Dividend Puzzle. In *Exploring the Latest Trends in Management Literature*. Bingley: Emerald Publishing Limited, pp. 249–267. https://doi.org/10.1108/973-1-80262-277-520231021
14. Dewasiri, N. J., Karunarathne, K. S. S. N., Menon, S., Jayarathne, P. G. S. A., & Rathnasiri, M. S. H. (2023). Fusion of Artificial Intelligence and Blockchain in the Banking Industry: Current Application, Adoption, and Future Challenges'. In Saini, A. and Garg, V. (Ed.) *Transformation for Sustainable Business and Management Practices: Exploring the Spectrum of Industry 5.0*. Emerald Publishing Limited, pp. 293–307. https://doi.org/10.1108/978-1-80262-277-520231021
15. Dewasiri, N. J., Karunarathna, K. S. S. N., Rathnasiri, M. S. H., Sood, K., & Saini, A. (2023). The Role of Health-Related Perceptions on Mobile Payment Adoption: Evidence from the Mobile Banking Industry in Sri Lanka. In Sood, K., Balusamy, B. and Grima, S. (Ed.) *Digital Transformation, Strategic Resilience, Cyber Security and Risk Management (Contemporary Studies in Economic and Financial Analysis, Vol. 111C)*. Leeds: Emerald Publishing Limited, pp. 67–86. https://doi.org/10.1108/S1569-37592023000111C004
16. Dewasiri, N. J., Pigera, A. K. M., Karunarathne, K. S. S. N., & Rathnasiri, M. S. H. (2023). Financial Services Employee Engagement and Attitude Toward Artificial Intelligence: Evidence from Sri Lanka. In Saini, A. and Garg, V. (Ed.) *Transformation for Sustainable Business and Management Practices: Exploring the Spectrum of Industry 5.0*. Bingley: Emerald Publishing Limited, pp. 231–245. https://doi.org/10.1108/978-1-80262-277-520231017
17. Dewasiri, N. J., Rana, S., & Kashif, M. (2021). Editorial – Theory building in marketing: Rationalizing South Asian perspective. *South Asian Journal of Marketing*, 2(1), 1–4. https://doi.org/10.1108/SAJM-03-2021-071

18. Esmaeilzadeh, P., & Mirzaei, T. (2019). The potential of blockchain technology for health information exchange: Experimental study from patients' perspectives. *Journal Of Medical Internet Research*, 21(6), e14184.

19. Farouk, A., Alahmadi, A., Ghose, S., & Mashatan, A. (2020). Blockchain platform for industrial healthcare: Vision and future opportunities. *Computer Communications*, 154, 223–235.

20. Grech, A., Sood, I., & Ariño, L. (2021). Blockchain, self-sovereign identity and digital credentials: Promise versus praxis in education. *Frontiers in Blockchain*, 4, 616779.

21. Jabbar, S., Lloyd, H., Hammoudeh, M., Adebisi, B., & Raza, U. (2021). Blockchain-enabled supply chain: Analysis, challenges, and future directions. *Multimedia Systems*, 27, 787–806.

22. Jaiman, V., & Urovi, V. (2020). A consent model for blockchain-based health data sharing platforms. *IEEE Access*, 8, 143734–143745.

23. Javed, I. T., Alharbi, F., Margaria, T., Crespi, N., & Qureshi, K. N. (2021). PETchain: A blockchain-based privacy enhancing technology. *IEEE Access*, 9, 41129–41143.

24. Khalid, M. I., Ahmed, M., & Kim, J. (2023). Enhancing data protection in dynamic consent management systems: Formalizing privacy and security definitions with differential privacy, decentralization, and Zero-Knowledge proofs. *Sensors*, 23(17), 7604.

25. Khan, D., Jung, L. T., & Hashmani, M. A. (2021). Systematic literature review of challenges in blockchain scalability. *Applied Sciences*, 11(20), 9372.

26. Khezr, S., Moniruzzaman, M., Yassine, A., & Benlamri, R. (2019). Blockchain technology in healthcare: A comprehensive review and directions for future research. *Applied Sciences*, 9(9), 1736.

27. Kuperberg, M. (2020, November). Towards enabling deletion in append-only blockchains to support data growth management and GDPR compliance. In 2020 IEEE international conference on blockchain (Blockchain) (pp. 393–400). IEEE.

28. Mackey, T., Bekki, H., Matsuzaki, T., & Mizushima, H. (2020). Examining the potential of blockchain technology to meet the needs of 21st-century Japanese health care: Viewpoint on use cases and policy. *Journal of Medical Internet Research*, 22(1), e13649.

29. Mackey, T. K., Kuo, T. T., Gummadi, B., Clauson, K. A., Church, G., Grishin, D., & Palombini, M. (2019). 'Fit-for-purpose?'–challenges and opportunities for applications of blockchain technology in the future of healthcare. *BMC Medicine*, 17(1), 1–17.

30. Nanda, S. K., Panda, S. K., & Dash, M. (2023). Medical supply chain integrated with blockchain and IoT to track the logistics of medical products. *Multimedia Tools and Applications*, 82, 32917–32939.

31. Omar, I. A., Jayaraman, R., Salah, K., Yaqoob, I., & Ellahham, S. (2021). Applications of blockchain technology in clinical trials: Review and open challenges. *Arabian Journal for Science and Engineering*, 46, 3001–3015.

32. Pandey, P., & Litoriya, R. (2020). Implementing healthcare services on a large scale: Challenges and remedies based on blockchain technology. *Health Policy and Technology*, 9(1), 69–78.

33. Politou, E., Casino, F., Alepis, E., & Patsakis, C. (2019). Blockchain mutability: Challenges and proposed solutions. *IEEE Transactions on Emerging Topics in Computing*, 9(4), 1972–1986.

34. Radanović, I., & Likić, R. (2018). Opportunities for use of blockchain technology in medicine. *Applied Health Economics and Health Policy*, 16, 583–590.

35. Rathnasiri, M. S. H. & De Silva, V. (2023). The role of shopping values, cognitive and affective evaluations on the relationship between store environment and store

patronage intention: A future research agenda. *Sri Lanka Journal of Management Studies*, 5(1), 100–120.

36. Reegu, F., Daud, S. M., & Alam, S. (2021). Interoperability challenges in healthcare blockchain system - A systematic review. *Annals of the Romanian Society for Cell Biology*, 25(4), 15487–15499.

37. Rejeb, A., Keogh, J. G., Simske, S. J., Stafford, T., & Treiblmaier, H. (2021). Potentials of blockchain technologies for supply chain collaboration: A conceptual framework. *The International Journal of Logistics Management*, 32(3), 973–994.

38. Rojnic, S. (2022). Blockchain application in healthcare: The example of Farma trust, medical chain and E-Hcert. *Amsterdam LF*, 14, 69.

39. Shelke, P., Sable, N. P., Dedgaonkar, S., & Mirajkar, R. (2023). Applications of Blockchain: A Healthcare Use Case. In *Nature-Inspired Methods for Smart Healthcare Systems and Medical Data*. Cham: Springer Nature Switzerland, pp. 67–88.

40. Sunny, J., Undralla, N., & Pillai, V. M. (2020). Supply chain transparency through blockchain-based traceability: An overview with demonstration. *Computers & Industrial Engineering*, 150, 106895.

41. Tanwar, S., Parekh, K., & Evans, R. (2020). Blockchain-based electronic healthcare record system for healthcare 4.0 applications. *Journal of Information Security and Applications*, 50, 102407.

42. Thapa, C., & Camtepe, S. (2021). Precision health data: Requirements, challenges and existing techniques for data security and privacy. *Computers in Biology and Medicine*, 129, 104130.

43. Villarreal, E. R. D., García-Alonso, J., Moguel, E., & Alegría, J. A. H. (2023). Blockchain for healthcare management systems: A survey on interoperability and security. *IEEE Access*, 11, 5629–5652.

44. Velmovitsky, P. E., Bublitz, F. M., Fadrique, L. X., & Morita, P. P. (2021). Blockchain applications in health care and public health: Increased transparency. *JMIR Medical Informatics*, 9(6), e20713.

45. Wang, Y., Singgih, M., Wang, J., & Rit, M. (2019). Making sense of blockchain technology: How will it transform supply chains? *International Journal of Production Economics*, 211, 221–236.

46. Yaqoob, I., Salah, K., Jayaraman, R., & Al-Hammadi, Y. (2021). Blockchain for healthcare data management: Opportunities, challenges, and future recommendations. *Neural Computing and Applications*, 34(14), 11475–11490.

47. Zachariadis, M., Hileman, G., & Scott, S. V. (2019). Governance and control in distributed ledgers: Understanding the challenges facing blockchain technology in financial services. *Information and Organization*, 29(2), 105–117.

48. Zarour, M., Ansari, M. T. J., Alenezi, M., Sarkar, A. K., Faizan, M., Agrawal, A., … Khan, R. A. (2020). Evaluating the impact of blockchain models for secure and trustworthy electronic healthcare records. *IEEE Access*, 8, 157959–157973.

5

CHALLENGES AND FUTURE DIRECTIONS OF BLOCKCHAIN TECHNOLOGY IN HEALTHCARE SETTINGS

Syed Immamul Ansarullah, Abdul Wahid Wali, Fayaz Ahmad Fayaz, and Muzaffar Ahmad Sofi

5.1 Overview of blockchain technology

Blockchain technology is a decentralized and distributed ledger system designed to facilitate secure, transparent, and tamper-resistant recordkeeping. At its core, a blockchain is a chain of blocks, where each block contains a list of transactions [1]. The technology operates on a peer-to-peer network, where multiple participants (nodes) maintain and validate the shared ledger. The key components of blockchain technology are as follows [2, 3]:

- **Blocks:** Each block in the chain contains a set of transactions. These transactions are bundled together and linked to the previous block through a cryptographic hash.
- **Cryptographic Hashing:** Hash functions are used to secure the integrity of data within each block. A change in any transaction would alter the hash, making tampering easily detectable.
- **Decentralization:** Unlike traditional centralized systems, blockchain operates on a decentralized network. Each participant has a copy of the entire blockchain, eliminating the need for a central authority.
- **Consensus Mechanisms:** These are protocols used to achieve agreement on the state of the blockchain. Popular mechanisms include proof-of-work (PoW) and proof-of-stake (PoS).

Blockchain technology revolutionizes various industries by introducing a secure, transparent, and decentralized approach to recordkeeping and value exchange. Blockchain serves as the underlying technology that empowers a range of applications [4]. The transformative potential of blockchain technology is

DOI: 10.1201/9781003483113-5

evident across industries. Whether revolutionizing financial transactions, automating contractual agreements, optimizing supply chain management, or safeguarding healthcare data, blockchain stands as a versatile and powerful tool with far-reaching implications for the future of various sectors.

5.2   Relevance of blockchain technology to healthcare settings

Blockchain technology holds significant promise in revolutionizing the healthcare industry by addressing critical challenges related to data management, security, and interoperability. The following are prominent applications of blockchain in healthcare settings:

- **Electronic Health Records (EHRs):** Traditional EHR systems often suffer from issues such as data fragmentation, security vulnerabilities, and a lack of interoperability between different healthcare providers due to their centralized nature. Blockchain addresses these challenges by ensuring secure and decentralized storage of EHRs. Patient records are distributed across the network, mitigating the risk of a single point of failure. This approach not only grants patients greater control over their data but also enables healthcare providers to access a comprehensive and tamper-resistant record. As a result, care coordination improves, leading to enhanced patient outcomes [5].
- **Data Security and Privacy:** Given the highly sensitive nature of healthcare data, it becomes a primary target for cyberattacks and unauthorized access, necessitating robust security measures. Traditional security protocols often fall short, prompting the adoption of blockchain, which employs advanced cryptographic techniques to fortify patient data. Each block in the blockchain is intricately linked to the preceding one through a cryptographic hash, introducing a formidable barrier against any attempts to alter information by unauthorized entities. This cryptographic foundation, coupled with the decentralized nature of blockchain, significantly enhances security by eliminating a central point of vulnerability, ensuring the integrity and confidentiality of healthcare data [5].
- **Interoperability:** The diversity in standards and formats for healthcare data across different systems poses a considerable obstacle to seamless data exchange among healthcare providers. Blockchain emerges as a solution by creating a standardized and decentralized ledger accessible to authorized participants. This innovation fosters interoperability by establishing a common platform for sharing and accessing healthcare data. As a result, healthcare providers gain access to a patient's complete medical history, enabling better-informed decisions and improving care continuity. The decentralized and standardized nature of blockchain thus acts as a catalyst in overcoming the challenges associated with interoperability, ultimately contributing to a more integrated and efficient healthcare ecosystem [6].

- **Supply Chain Management:** The pharmaceutical supply chain grapples with challenges such as counterfeit drugs, lack of transparency, and operational inefficiencies. Blockchain emerges as a transformative solution, offering end-to-end visibility throughout the supply chain. Every stage, from manufacturing to distribution, is meticulously recorded on the blockchain, ensuring unparalleled transparency. This transparency not only safeguards the authenticity and safety of medications but also serves as a formidable weapon against counterfeit drugs, ultimately streamlining the entire supply chain [6].
- **Clinical Trials and Research:** Clinical trials often encounter obstacles such as a lack of transparency, data inaccuracies, and the potential for fraud. Blockchain introduces a groundbreaking approach by employing smart contracts to automate and enforce the rules governing clinical trials. This innovation enhances transparency by providing a real-time, auditable record of trial data. Consequently, researchers and regulatory authorities gain increased confidence in the integrity and accuracy of clinical trial results, addressing long-standing challenges in the realm of medical research [6].
- **Patient Consent and Data Ownership:** The intricate task of managing and respecting patient consent preferences, often entangled with concerns about data ownership and ethical use, finds a robust solution in blockchain. This technology establishes a secure and transparent mechanism for handling patient consent, granting individuals control over who accesses their data and for what purposes. Beyond preserving patient autonomy, this approach fosters trust in the healthcare system, addressing the complexities associated with data ownership and consent management [7].
- **Billing and Insurance Claims:** Administrative processes related to billing and insurance claims are notorious for their cumbersome nature, susceptibility to errors, and time-consuming characteristics. Blockchain, through the implementation of smart contracts, revolutionizes these processes by automating and streamlining them. This not only reduces administrative overhead but also minimizes the risk of errors and fraud, leading to an accelerated reimbursement process for healthcare providers [8].
- **Public Health Surveillance:** The urgency of timely tracking and response to disease outbreaks for public health is indisputable, but traditional systems may lack real-time capabilities. Enter blockchain, which facilitates real-time tracking of disease outbreaks through a decentralized and secure platform. This innovative approach allows for the swift sharing of information among relevant parties, enabling quick and coordinated responses to emerging health threats and significantly enhancing public health surveillance capabilities [8].

5.3   Challenges in implementing blockchain in health care

Blockchain technology implementation poses several challenges that need to be addressed for successful integration. Addressing these challenges requires a collaborative effort from healthcare organizations, technology developers, regulators, and other stakeholders to create a supportive ecosystem for the successful integration of blockchain in health care.

- **Interoperability and Integration:** Healthcare systems often use diverse technologies and standards, leading to interoperability issues when integrating blockchain. To counter this, ongoing standardization efforts and the formulation of interoperability protocols are essential, ensuring a smooth fit into existing IT infrastructures [9].
- **Regulatory Compliance:** The healthcare industry is subject to strict regulations and compliance requirements, and integrating blockchain may raise legal and regulatory concerns. A collaborative approach between industry players and regulatory bodies becomes pivotal, creating clear guidelines and compliance frameworks [9].
- **Integration with Existing Systems:** Adapting legacy systems to work with blockchain technology can be complex and may require significant modifications. A phased integration strategy, modular approaches, and the incorporation of application programming interfaces (APIs) ease the coexistence of blockchain with established healthcare systems [9].
- **Data Standardization and Quality:** Ensuring consistent data standards and quality across a decentralized network is challenging, especially with diverse sources of information. The remedy lies in establishing industry-wide data standards, deploying data validation mechanisms, and leveraging smart contracts for meticulous data quality control [10].
- **Scalability:** As the number of transactions on the blockchain increases, scalability becomes a concern, potentially impacting transaction speed and network performance. Research and development efforts focused on scalable blockchain solutions, such as layer-two scaling is crucial to meet the escalating demands of healthcare applications [10].
- **Privacy and Confidentiality:** While blockchain ensures data security, there may be concerns regarding patient privacy and confidentiality, especially in a decentralized network. Implementing advanced privacy features, like zero-knowledge proofs, and robust consent mechanisms serve as solutions to address these privacy concerns effectively [10].
- **Costs and Resource Allocation:** Implementing blockchain solutions may require significant upfront investment, and ongoing maintenance costs can be substantial. Strategic measures such as cost-benefit analyses, collaborative funding models, and identifying cost-effective blockchain solutions are imperative to navigate these financial challenges [11].

- **Lack of Technical Expertise:** There is a shortage of skilled professionals with expertise in both blockchain technology and health care. Bridging this gap necessitates investments in workforce training, educational initiatives, and fostering collaboration between technology experts and healthcare professionals [11].
- **Resistance to Change:** Healthcare professionals and stakeholders may resist adopting new technologies, fearing disruptions to established workflows. Overcoming this resistance requires early engagement of stakeholders in the implementation process, comprehensive training, and a clear communication of the benefits that blockchain brings to health care [11].
- **Security Concerns:** While blockchain enhances security, there are still concerns about potential vulnerabilities, especially in the early stages of adoption. Mitigating these concerns involves regular security audits, collaboration with cybersecurity experts, and implementing consensus mechanisms prioritizing security [11].

5.4 Security and privacy

Ensuring robust security and safeguarding privacy are paramount considerations in blockchain technology. Addressing security and privacy concerns in implementing blockchain for health care involves a combination of advanced cryptographic techniques, careful design of smart contracts, proper identity management, and the strategic use of permission blockchains. Balancing transparency with privacy and regularly auditing the system for vulnerabilities are essential components of a secure and privacy-aware blockchain in health care [12].

5.4.1 Cryptographic techniques

- **Security Measure:** Cryptographic hashing is used to create a unique identifier (hash) for each block, securing data integrity.
- **Privacy Concern:** While hashes ensure data integrity, they are visible on the blockchain. Advanced cryptographic techniques, such as zero-knowledge proofs, enable parties to prove the authenticity of information without revealing specific details, enhancing privacy [12].

5.4.2 Patient consent and data ownership

- **Security Measure:** Blockchain facilitates transparent and secure management of patient consent preferences through smart contracts.
- **Privacy Concern:** Patient consent is crucial for privacy. Smart contracts can enforce and automate consent agreements, ensuring that patients have control over who accesses their data and for what purpose, thus protecting their privacy [13].

5.4.3 Decentralization

- **Security Measure:** Decentralization reduces the risk of a single point of failure, enhancing the overall security of the network.
- **Privacy Concern:** While decentralization is a security measure, the transparency of decentralized ledgers can pose privacy challenges. Implementing robust access controls and permissions is essential to protect sensitive patient information [13].

5.4.4 Identity management

- **Security Measure:** Blockchain enables secure and immutable identity management through cryptographic keys.
- **Privacy Concern:** Balancing identity verification with the need for anonymity or pseudonymity is crucial. Self-sovereign identity (SSI) frameworks, built on blockchain, allow individuals to control their digital identities, contributing to both security and privacy [13].

5.4.5 Smart contracts

- **Security Measure:** Smart contracts automate processes and enforce predefined rules transparently.
- **Privacy Concern:** The transparency of smart contract code can expose sensitive information. Properly encrypting sensitive data within smart contracts and carefully designing contract logic are essential for maintaining privacy [14].

5.4.6 Consensus mechanisms

- **Security Measure:** Consensus mechanisms ensure agreement on the state of the blockchain, preventing malicious activities.
- **Privacy Concern:** The choice of consensus mechanism can impact privacy. Proof-of-work, for example, exposes transaction details, while other mechanisms like zero-knowledge proofs in Zero-Knowledge Succinct Non-Interactive Argument of Knowledge (zk-SNARKs) enhance privacy. Selecting an appropriate mechanism depends on the desired balance between security and privacy [14].

5.4.7 Off-Chain storage for sensitive data

- **Security Measure:** Storing highly sensitive data off-chain, with references on-chain, enhances privacy.
- **Privacy Concern:** Striking a balance between transparency and the protection of sensitive data requires careful design. Encrypted databases or decentralized storage solutions can be used for off-chain storage while maintaining on-chain references for transparency [15].

5.4.8 Data minimization

- **Security Measure:** Implementing a principle of data minimization reduces the amount of sensitive information stored on the blockchain.
- **Privacy Concern:** Storing only essential information on the blockchain minimizes the exposure of sensitive data and reduces potential privacy risks. This practice aligns with privacy regulations and safeguards patient information [15].

5.4.9 Regular security audits

- **Security Measure:** Regular security audits help identify and address vulnerabilities in the blockchain system.
- **Privacy Concern:** Ensuring that security audits encompass both technical security and privacy considerations is crucial. The audits should evaluate the effectiveness of privacy features and compliance with privacy regulations [15].

5.5 Regulatory landscape

The regulatory landscape of blockchain in health care refers to the legal and regulatory framework governing the use, implementation, and operation of blockchain technology within the healthcare industry. This landscape encompasses laws, guidelines, and compliance requirements that dictate how blockchain solutions are developed, deployed, and utilized in the healthcare sector [16]. It addresses issues such as data privacy, security standards, interoperability, patient consent, and overall compliance with existing healthcare regulations.

5.5.1 Current regulations

- **GDPR (General Data Protection Regulation):** GDPR, applicable in the European Union, mandates strict data protection and privacy standards. Blockchain applications must comply with GDPR principles, ensuring transparent data processing, explicit user consent, and the right to be forgotten [16].
- **HIPAA (Health Insurance Portability and Accountability Act):** HIPAA in the United States regulates the privacy and security of protected health information (PHI). Healthcare blockchain solutions in the United States must align with HIPAA requirements, implementing measures to secure and protect PHI [17].
- **DSCSA (Drug Supply Chain Security Act):** DSCSA focuses on ensuring the traceability of pharmaceuticals throughout the supply chain. Blockchain

can assist in compliance by providing a transparent and traceable ledger, enhancing the security and authenticity of pharmaceutical supply chain data [17].

- **FDA (Food and Drug Administration) Oversight:** The FDA oversees medical devices, drugs, and other healthcare-related products. Blockchain applications related to medical devices and drug development may face scrutiny from the FDA to ensure safety, efficacy, and compliance with regulatory standards [17].

5.5.2 Proposals for future frameworks

- **Global Harmonization Efforts:** International collaborations are underway to harmonize regulations for cross-border blockchain applications in health care. The proposed framework involves continued efforts to establish a consistent global regulatory framework, promoting interoperability and ensuring regulatory compliance across diverse jurisdictions [18].
- **Tokenization Guidelines:** With the increasing prevalence of blockchain tokens, regulatory bodies may introduce guidelines to govern their legal and compliant use in health care. The proposed framework aims to clarify the regulatory status of blockchain tokens, addressing issues related to ownership, transferability, and compliance with securities laws to foster responsible and lawful token utilization [19].
- **Smart Contract Legal Recognition:** The legal recognition of smart contracts varies globally, presenting a need for regulatory clarity. Future frameworks are expected to address this by providing a clear stance on the legal validity of smart contracts. Standardized legal frameworks may be introduced to enhance the adoption of smart contracts in healthcare processes, ensuring legal certainty and reliability [19].
- **Privacy-Enhancing Technologies:** The transparent nature of blockchain has prompted regulatory responses to address privacy concerns. Proposed frameworks may offer guidance on the use of privacy-enhancing technologies within blockchain systems. Striking a balance between transparency and individual privacy, these frameworks aim to set standards for responsible data handling in healthcare blockchain applications [20].
- **Interconnected Health Data Marketplaces:** As health data marketplaces on blockchain gain traction, regulatory considerations become paramount. The proposed framework anticipates regulators introducing guidelines to ensure secure and ethical exchange of health data within interconnected marketplaces. Addressing issues of data ownership and compensation mechanisms, these frameworks seek to create a secure and transparent environment for health data exchange [20].

5.6 Future directions

As blockchain technology continues to evolve, its applications in health care are expected to advance significantly. Several future directions indicate the potential growth and impact of blockchain in the healthcare industry:

- **Scalability Solutions:** Scalability remains a current challenge for blockchain networks, particularly in healthcare applications where increasing transaction volumes impact overall performance. Ongoing research and development efforts are focused on scalable solutions such as sharding, sidechains, and layer-two protocols. These innovations hold significant promise for overcoming scalability issues and are anticipated to substantially enhance the performance of blockchain networks within healthcare settings [21].
- **Integration with Emerging Technologies:** The current status of blockchain in health care reflects a growing exploration of its synergies with other emerging technologies like artificial intelligence (AI) and the Internet of Things (IoT). Looking forward, the future direction envisions a seamless integration of blockchain with AI for advanced data analytics and IoT for real-time data collection. This convergence holds the promise of establishing comprehensive and secure healthcare ecosystems, fostering innovation and efficiency in data management and analysis within the healthcare domain [21].
- **Global Collaboration and Data Exchange:** Blockchain promotes transparency and trust, facilitating secure data exchange within localized networks. Expectations include the development of interoperable blockchain networks that enable global collaboration, data sharing, and research initiatives. Cross-border healthcare solutions leveraging blockchain may become more prevalent [22].
- **Enhanced Privacy Features:** Blockchain currently ensures security through cryptography, but efforts persist to elevate privacy features. Looking forward, the trajectory involves advancements in privacy-preserving technologies, specifically the integration of advanced zero-knowledge proofs and homomorphic encryption. These innovations are anticipated to play a pivotal role in fortifying privacy on the blockchain, especially when dealing with sensitive healthcare data. The future direction is geared towards establishing a more robust and confidential environment for healthcare information within the blockchain framework [22].
- **Tokenization of Healthcare Assets:** Some projects explore tokenizing healthcare assets, such as patient data or research findings, on the blockchain. The tokenization trend is expected to grow, creating new possibilities for secure and transparent management of healthcare assets. Tokenized systems can enhance data ownership and incentivize data sharing [23].

- **Regulatory Framework Development:** Regulatory uncertainty exists in various regions regarding the use of blockchain in health care. Anticipate the establishment of clearer regulatory frameworks specific to blockchain in health care. Collaborative efforts between regulatory bodies and industry stakeholders will contribute to the responsible and compliant adoption of blockchain technology [23].
- **Advanced Smart Contracts:** Smart contracts on blockchain automate predefined processes in a transparent manner. Evolution of smart contracts will involve more complex and customizable functionalities. This may include dynamic and self-executing contracts that adapt to changing conditions, enhancing automation and efficiency [24].
- **Distributed Autonomous Organizations (DAOs):** The concept of DAOs, organizations run by smart contracts on a blockchain, is gaining attention. Healthcare organizations may explore DAO structures for decentralized governance, decision-making, and resource allocation. DAOs could promote transparency and community involvement in healthcare systems [24].
- **Interconnected Health Data Marketplaces:** Blockchain facilitates secure data sharing but has not fully realized interconnected health data marketplaces. The development of secure, blockchain-based health data marketplaces will enable individuals to share their data securely for research or healthcare purposes, with transparent compensation mechanisms [25].
- **Environmental Sustainability:** PoW blockchain networks, like Bitcoin, raise concerns about energy consumption. Adoption of more energy-efficient consensus mechanisms, such as PoS or delegated PoS, will align blockchain technology with environmental sustainability goals in healthcare applications [25].

5.7 Conclusion

This research delves into the profound impact of blockchain technology on healthcare settings. As blockchain evolves, its applications in health care are poised for significant advancement. The study thoroughly examines the challenges in implementing blockchain in healthcare settings, detailing ongoing collaborative efforts to address these obstacles and develop comprehensive frameworks that unlock blockchain's transformative potential. This collective endeavor promises enhanced patient outcomes, streamlined operations, and the emergence of secure and interoperable healthcare systems. The research also provides a detailed exploration of the rules and guidelines governing how blockchain is used in health care, outlining the legal requirements that dictate the development, deployment, and utilization of blockchain solutions in the sector. Finally, it delves into the future of blockchain in health care, offering insights to healthcare professionals, technology experts, and regulatory bodies to foster continual improvement in the field.

References

1. Haleem, A., Javaid, M., Singh, R. P., Suman, R., & Rab, S. (2021). Blockchain technology applications in healthcare: An overview. *International Journal of Intelligent Networks*, 2, 130–139.
2. Agbo, C. C., Mahmoud, Q. H., & Eklund, J. M. (2019). Blockchain technology in healthcare: A systematic review. *Healthcare*, 7(2), 56.
3. Navadkar, V. H., Nighot, A., & Wantmure, R. (2018). Overview of blockchain technology in government/public sectors. *International Research Journal of Engineering and Technology*, 5(6), 2287–2292.
4. Othman, S. B., Almalki, F. A., & Sakli, H. (2022). Internet of Things in the Healthcare Applications: Overview of Security and Privacy Issues. In: Chakraborty, C., Khosravi, M.R. (eds) Intelligent Healthcare. Springer, Singapore. https://doi.org/10.1007/978-981-16-8150-9_9
5. Attaran, M. (2022). Blockchain technology in healthcare: Challenges and opportunities. *International Journal of Healthcare Management*, 15(1), 70–83.
6. Abu-Elezz, I., Hassan, A., Nazeemudeen, A., Househ, M., & Abd-Alrazaq, A. (2020). The benefits and threats of blockchain technology in healthcare: A scoping review. *International Journal of Medical Informatics*, 142, 104246.
7. Ben Fekih, R., & Lahami, M. (2020). Application of blockchain technology in healthcare: a comprehensive study. In *The Impact of Digital Technologies on Public Health in Developed and Developing Countries: 18th International Conference, ICOST 2020, Hammamet, Tunisia, June 24–26, 2020, Proceedings 18* (pp. 268–276). Springer International Publishing.
8. Hasselgren, A., Kralevska, K., Gligoroski, D., Pedersen, S. A., & Faxvaag, A. (2020). Blockchain in healthcare and health sciences—A scoping review. *International Journal of Medical Informatics*, 134, 104040.
9. Al-Asmari, A. M., Aloufi, R. I., & Alotaibi, Y. (2021). A review of concepts, advantages and pitfalls of healthcare applications in blockchain technology. *International Journal of Computer Science & Network Security*, 21(5), 199–210.
10. Hussien, H. M., Yasin, S. M., Udzir, N. I., Ninggal, M. I. H., & Salman, S. (2021). Blockchain technology in the healthcare industry: Trends and opportunities. *Journal of Industrial Information Integration*, 22, 100217.
11. Kaur, M., & Gupta, S. (2021). Blockchain Technology for Convergence: An Overview, Applications, and Challenges. In: *Blockchain and AI Technology in the Industrial Internet of Things* (pp. 1–17). IGI Global. https://doi.org/10.4018/978-1-7998-6694-7.ch001
12. Fatima, N., Agarwal, P., & Sohail, S. S. (2022). Security and Privacy Issues of Blockchain Technology in Health Care—A Review. In: *ICT Analysis and Applications* (Vol. 314, pp. 193–201). Springer, Singapore. https://doi.org/10.1007/978-981-16-5655-2_18.
13. Alqarni, K. S., Almalki, F. A., Soufiene, B. O., Ali, O., & Albalwy, F. (2022). Authenticated wireless links between a drone and sensors using a blockchain: Case of smart farming. *Wireless Communications and Mobile Computing*, 2022, 4389729, 13. https://doi.org/10.1155/2022/4389729
14. Shah, V., Thakkar, V., & Khang, A. (2023). Electronic Health Records Security and Privacy Enhancement Using Blockchain Technology. In: *Data-Centric AI Solutions and Emerging Technologies in the Healthcare Ecosystem* (pp. 1–13). Imprint: CRC Press. Pub. Location: Boca Raton, 12 October 2023.
15. Joshi, A. P., Han, M., & Wang, Y. (2018). A survey on security and privacy issues of blockchain technology. *Mathematical Foundations of Computing*, 1(2), 121–147. Doi 10.3934/mfc.2018007

16. Katuwal, G. J., Pandey, S., Hennessey, M., & Lamichhane, B. (2018). Applications of blockchain in healthcare: Current landscape & challenges. *arXiv preprint arXiv:1812.02776*.
17. Boulos, M. N. K., Wilson, J. T., & Clauson, K. A. (2018). Geospatial blockchain: Promises, challenges, and scenarios in health and healthcare. *International Journal of Health Geographics*, 17, 1–10.
18. Balasubramanian, S., Shukla, V., Sethi, J. S., Islam, N., & Saloum, R. (2021). A readiness assessment framework for blockchain adoption: A healthcare case study. *Technological Forecasting and Social Change*, 165, 120536.
19. Gupta, S., Alharbi, F., Alshahrani, R., Kumar Arya, P., Vyas, S., Elkamchouchi, D. H., & Soufiene, B. O. (2023). Secure and lightweight authentication protocol for privacy preserving communications in smart city applications. *Sustainability*, 15, 5346. https://doi.org/10.3390/su15065346
20. Soltanisehat, L., Alizadeh, R., Hao, H., & Choo, K. K. R. (2020). Technical, temporal, and spatial research challenges and opportunities in blockchain-based healthcare: A systematic literature review. *IEEE Transactions on Engineering Management*, 70(1), 353–368.
21. Saranya, R., & Murugan, A. (2023). A systematic review of enabling blockchain in healthcare system: Analysis, current status, challenges and future direction. *Materials Today: Proceedings*, 80, 3010–3015.
22. Andrew, J., Isravel, D. P., Sagayam, K. M., Bhushan, B., Sei, Y., & Eunice, J. (2023). Blockchain for healthcare systems: Architecture, security challenges, trends and future directions. *Journal of Network and Computer Applications*, 103633.
23. Khezr, S., Moniruzzaman, M., Yassine, A., & Benlamri, R. (2019). Blockchain technology in healthcare: A comprehensive review and directions for future research. *Applied Sciences*, 9(9), 1736.
24. Hussien, H. M., Yasin, S. M., Udzir, S. N. I., Zaidan, A. A., & Zaidan, B. B. (2019). A systematic review for enabling of develop a blockchain technology in healthcare application: Taxonomy, substantially analysis, motivations, challenges, recommendations and future direction. *Journal of Medical Systems*, 43, 1–35.
25. Kassab, M., DeFranco, J., Malas, T., Laplante, P., Destefanis, G., & Neto, V. V. G. (2019). Exploring research in blockchain for healthcare and a roadmap for the future. *IEEE Transactions on Emerging Topics in Computing*, 9(4), 1835–1852.

6

BLOCKCHAIN-ENABLED RADIOLOGY

Transformative Potentials and Implementation Hurdles

Kalyan Tadepalli and Amar Ratnakar Naik

6.1 Introduction to blockchain technology

Blockchain technology, originating from Bitcoin, represents a paradigm shift in digital infrastructure by enabling decentralized consensus through cryptographic ledgers. Its foundation, a distributed database, securely, transparently, and immutably records transactions without centralized intermediaries [1]. Chaining cryptographic blocks of transactions through decentralized nodes constantly validating the ledger achieves this. Initially devised for Bitcoin's permissionless value transfer, blockchain's architecture exhibits attributes conducive to enhancing trust and security across sectors. Disintermediation of transactions eliminates blind dependence on third parties, while distributed ledgers increase transparency, auditability, and data integrity. Cryptographic immutability fosters provenance tracking [2].

6.1.1 What is blockchain?

Blockchain technology functions as a sophisticated digital ledger, ensuring the secure and transparent recording of information. Unlike traditional databases, it bypasses the need for a central authority, fostering a more dependable and collaborative environment. This secure system offers a variety of applications beyond cryptocurrency. It can be used to track the movement of goods in a supply chain, guaranteeing authenticity and efficiency. Additionally, blockchain technology holds promise for revolutionizing voting systems by providing a verifiable and tamper-proof record of ballots. As the technology matures, we can expect even broader adoption across different industries, transforming the way we manage information and conduct transactions [3].

DOI: 10.1201/9781003483113-6

6.1.2 Key characteristics

Although still in its nascent stages, blockchain holds remarkable potential in advancing efficiency, security, patient control, and data analysis in health care if thoughtfully integrated. However, realizing these benefits requires addressing context-specific challenges around scaling complex blockchain systems, reconciling regulatory and compliance needs, and addressing data privacy concerns while maintaining utility. Blockchain's core characteristics, including decentralization, immutability, transparency, and cryptographic security, enable innovative applications across industries by distributing a tamper-evident ledger and establishing trust through mathematical consensus. These attributes have catalyzed solutions for supply chain tracking, identity management, voting systems, and beyond. As blockchain transitions from conceptual promise to practical large-scale implementations, holistic evidence-based analyses weighing quantitative metrics like efficiency and cost alongside qualitative dynamics spanning ethics, policy, and society are imperative to guide its prudent integration into critical systems like health care [4].

6.1.3 Detailed architecture

The backbone of blockchain architecture is cryptographically linked blocks that immutably record batches of transactions in a chronological chain. Each block contains a header with metadata including the hash of the previous block, timestamp, block version number, and nonce for cryptography. The hash links blocks sequentially, so tampering any block requires recomputing all subsequent hashes, rendering modifications practically infeasible. This chaining mechanism provides blockchain's characteristic security and immutability. When new transactions occur, network nodes validate and add them to a candidate block. Once consensus is reached per protocol rules, the block is permanently added to all nodes' ledgers. Each node thus maintains an identical record of all blocks in the chain from genesis block onward. This decentralized distribution eliminates centralized points of failure, enhancing integrity. The technology enabling the distributed blockchain ledger is called distributed ledger technology (DLT). It allows synchronized multiparty recordkeeping and validation across a decentralized network without central intermediaries. Unlike centralized databases, DLT has no single authority, improving transparency. Updates require consensus among nodes per predefined protocols. DLT thus facilitates trustless collaboration at scale, underpinning diverse blockchain applications from finance to supply chain tracking. Fundamentally, blockchain combines cryptographically immutable sequential chaining of transaction batches with decentralized consensus and recordkeeping to enable transparent, verifiable, tamper-proof transactions sans centralized trust.

6.1.3.1 Types of blockchains

There are two main classifications of blockchains based on access permissions: public and private blockchains. Additionally, there are hybrid blockchains that combine features of both.

- **Public (Permissionless) Blockchain:** Public, permissionless blockchains are open decentralized networks where anonymous participants can join freely and participate in consensus mechanisms and transaction validation. While permissionless architectures promote inclusivity, broad collaboration, and community innovation, their transparency can raise privacy concerns and public consensus mechanisms may encounter scalability constraints in high-volume environments.
- **Consortium (Public Permissioned) Blockchain:** Consortium blockchains represent a hybrid model governed by a group of organizations that control network participation and access. Allowing verified participants from member entities enhances security and efficiency for collaborative enterprise use cases while retaining some privacy and decentralization benefits.
- **Private (Permissioned) Blockchain:** In private, permissioned blockchains, one central entity determines participation and access control. Although sacrificing openness and inclusivity, permissioned architectures enable privacy, access restrictions, and higher transaction throughput valuable for regulated commercial applications.
- **Hybrid Blockchains:** Hybrid blockchains combine elements of both public and private blockchains, offering a flexible and customizable approach. These networks allow businesses to operate a private, permissioned network while also connecting to a public blockchain for specific tasks or transactions. This model provides the security and privacy of private blockchains with the transparency and integrity of public blockchains, making it an attractive option for various industries looking to leverage blockchain technology effectively.

Table 6.1 summarizes the prominent examples of each type of blockchain.

6.1.3.2 Consensus mechanisms

In a blockchain network, consensus mechanisms act as the foundation for trust and agreement. These protocols ensure that all participants (nodes) on the network come to a unified conclusion on the validity of transactions and the current state of the blockchain ledger. Here are some common types of consensus mechanisms:

- **Proof-of-Work (PoW):** PoW was the first consensus protocol implemented in Bitcoin. It involves miners competing to solve complex cryptographic

TABLE 6.1 Types of blockchain

Type	Main idea	Key characteristics	Examples
Public (Permissionless) Blockchain	Open, decentralized, anonymous	Inclusivity, scalability, privacy risk.	Bitcoin, Ethereum
Consortium (Public Permissioned) Blockchain	Semi-private, collaborative	Balance of efficiency, security.	R3 Corda Consortium, Enterprise Ethereum Alliance
Private (Permissioned) Blockchain	Centralized, private	Optimal for compliance, high throughput.	Hyperledger Fabric
Hybrid Blockchains	Flexible, customizable	Public/private blend, enhanced security.	DragonChain, Quorum

[Original (created by authors)]

puzzles, where the first miner to solve the puzzle is rewarded with the right to add the next block to the chain. This process of puzzle-solving requires significant computing power and electricity, making PoW energy-intensive. However, the computational work makes tampering with the blockchain expensive and resource-intensive, thereby providing security. A drawback is that PoW faces scalability limitations as the network grows due to the slow block creation rate. Variations like proof-of-capacity seek to improve sustainability.

- **Proof-of-Stake (PoS):** PoS offers a more energy-efficient alternative to PoW. Instead of mining, PoS involves validators being selected to propose new blocks based on the amount of cryptocurrency they have staked or locked up as collateral. This staking provides validators an economic incentive to maintain network integrity. Selection methods include randomized algorithms and taking turns. PoS enhances participation and security without high electricity demands, though concerns around centralization exist. Ethereum's planned transition to PoS highlights its increasing viability.
- **Delegated Proof-of-Stake (DPoS):** DPoS involves token holders voting to elect nodes as validators responsible for block creation, in contrast to PoS where any staker can validate. This introduces an element of democracy and decentralization in validator selection but means fewer nodes are involved in consensus. While less decentralized than PoW or PoS, DPoS enables much higher transaction throughput and efficiency needed for large-scale applications. DPoS is used by platforms like Ethereum on Steroids (EOS) and TRON.
- **Practical Byzantine Fault Tolerance (PBFT):** PBFT enables nodes on a network to reach consensus efficiently even when individual nodes fail or act maliciously. It does so through a voting mechanism among a set of trusted nodes. PBFT avoids the resource-intensive computational work of

PoW, allowing for faster transaction confirmation times. The trade-off is it is less decentralized. PBFT's efficiency suits high-throughput systems like financial transactions.

Various consensus protocols with different decentralization, security, efficiency, and scalability trade-offs exist. Selecting suitable mechanisms depends on the architecture, use case, and community needs. Ongoing blockchain research aims to optimize these factors, advancing in areas like energy efficiency, security, and scalability.

6.1.3.3 *Data storage in blockchain*

While blockchains themselves are not ideal for storing large amounts of data due to cost and immutability, data can still be integrated using two main approaches: hashing, where only a unique identifier of the data is stored on the chain, and off-chain storage, where the data resides elsewhere but a reference to it is placed on the blockchain for secure tracking and verification.

- **On-Chain Storage:** On-chain storage involves storing data directly within the blocks of a blockchain. By embedding data within the distributed ledger, on-chain storage ensures full decentralization and total transparency. All nodes maintain copies of the data, preventing central points of failure. Storing data on-chain also guarantees immutability, as the data cannot be altered without rewriting the entire blockchain. However, on-chain storage faces significant limitations in scalability and efficiency. Blockchains are designed for small transactional data, not large file storage. Storing extensive data sets on-chain leads to bloated block sizes, slowing down synchronization across nodes. This restricts the transaction throughput of the blockchain. On-chain data also incurs high gas costs for storage and access. Despite limitations, on-chain storage remains essential for critical records like financial transactions and smart contracts where immutability and transparency are paramount. Use cases include financial settlements, voting systems, verification of credentials, and any application where tamper-proof immutable data records are required. For all other large or sensitive data sets, off-chain storage is preferred.
- **Off-Chain Storage:** Off-chain storage involves storing bulk data off the main blockchain while using the blockchain itself for verification and coordination. Access references and hashes of the data are stored on-chain while the data itself is stored externally. This helps overcome scalability issues with on-chain storage. Storing data off-chain enables processing large data sets cost-effectively without bloating the blockchain or incurring high gas fees. It also enhances privacy as sensitive data need not be publicly visible on the chain. Only pointers to the data are stored on-chain along

with hashes or digital signatures for verification of the full data if needed. Off-chain storage dramatically improves scalability and reduces storage costs for applications like medical records, genomic data, or streaming media. However, it sacrifices the full transparency and decentralization of on-chain storage. Appropriate decentralization is still needed to avoid reintroducing central points of failure. The right balance depends on the specific application's priorities around transparency, privacy, decentralization, and costs. On-chain storage guarantees full transparency and decentralization but faces scalability issues, while off-chain storage provides efficiency at the cost of some decentralization. Trade-offs exist around immutability, privacy, and costs that inform when each approach is preferable. A combination of on-chain and off-chain storage is often optimal.

- **Decentralized File Storage:** Centralized models of data storage harbor critical risks to security, privacy, and reliability that decentralized approaches seek to overcome. InterPlanetary File System (IPFS) establishes a peer-to-peer method for securely storing and sharing files across a distributed network without a central point of control. By eliminating vulnerabilities from a centralized infrastructure, IPFS enhances resilience against data loss or censorship. The Filecoin blockchain protocol further strengthens this model by incentivizing participation and guaranteeing storage availability through an economic model. Alternatives like Storj and Sia exemplify blockchain-enabled cloud storage platforms that distribute data encryption and storage duties across multiple independent nodes. Users can lease excess storage capacities to the network in a transparent, verifiable process. Should individual nodes fail, data remnants across the network ensure integrity is preserved.

Compared to traditional cloud services consolidating power and data in single repositories, these decentralized architectures foster security through obfuscation. Files are split anonymously across unreliable peers, precluding total control or surveillance. Throughput demands are also more elasticity accommodated by market-driven node populations instead of constrained infrastructure. Decentralized solutions shelter sensitive patient data from exploitations of centralized weaknesses while facilitating universal access. Their economic models promise storage costs competitive with incumbent services as well.

Table 6.2 summarizes the most common storage methodologies followed in the Bitcoin ecosystem.

6.1.3.4 Data encryption and privacy in blockchain

Blockchains offer data security through encryption, but inherent transparency can expose information. While public blockchains might reveal some transaction details, hashing can be used to mask sensitive data. Additionally,

TABLE 6.2 Storage methodologies in blockchain

Storage mechanism	Advantages	Disadvantages	Applications
On-Chain Storage	Full decentralization, immutability, transparency	Scalability issues, high costs, slower sync	Financial records, voting systems, credential verification
Off-Chain Storage	Scalable, cost-effective, enhanced privacy	Partial decentralization, reduced transparency, possibility for emergence of central points	Medical records, streaming media
Decentralized File Storage	Resilient, no central control, participation is incentivised	Market-driven throughput, elastic demand response, competitive storage costs	Electronic health records

[Original (created by authors)]

privacy-focused blockchains with features like zero-knowledge proofs are emerging to provide stronger privacy guarantees.

- **End-to-End Encryption:** End-to-end encryption (E2EE) represents a robust cryptographic technique for fortifying data confidentiality in blockchain networks. By encrypting data on the sender's device and only allowing decryption by the intended recipient, E2EE eliminates third-party access to plaintext information during transit. This provides an additional confidentiality layer beyond the inherent cryptography of blockchain transactions. E2EE is pivotal for privacy-sensitive use cases like healthcare data sharing, financial transactions, and identity management platforms built on blockchain. It assures users that their data and communications cannot be intercepted by intermediary nodes on the network or external attackers. Specific E2EE implementations utilize elliptic curve cryptography and techniques like ephemeral key exchanges to ensure robust encryption with minimal overhead. Integrating E2EE into decentralized applications enhances trust and comfort with sharing sensitive personal information through blockchain ecosystems. As blockchain expands into domains requiring stringent data protection guarantees like health care, stringent privacy techniques like E2EE will be critical in complying with regulations and earning user trust.
- **Zero-Knowledge Proofs:** Zero-knowledge proofs (ZKPs) represent an advanced cryptographic technique that enables a prover to validate the veracity of a statement to a verifier without conveying any information

apart from the statement's validity itself. This seeming paradox provides a mechanism for transactions and computations on blockchains to be verified privately. ZKPs facilitate confidential cryptocurrency transactions where key metadata like sender, receiver, and amount remain hidden. This allows the creation of privacy-centric blockchains, critical for finance and healthcare applications. ZKPs can also execute private smart contracts where contract conditions and participant identities are concealed. Leading ZKP implementations include ZK-SNARKs and ZK-STARKs, which offer different optimizations around efficiency, security assumptions, and scalability. The rise of ZKPs underscores the growing recognition that public blockchain transparency alone does not guarantee sufficient privacy for many applications. As blockchain expands into highly sensitive domains, ZKPs present a way to meet stringent privacy requirements beyond relying only on encryption. Widespread ZKP adoption could expand blockchain applicability across sectors demanding both verifiability and confidentiality.

ZK-SNARKs (Zero-Knowledge Succinct Non-Interactive Argument of Knowledge): ZK-SNARKs enable one party to prove to another that a statement is true without revealing any information beyond the validity of the statement itself. This technology is foundational for privacy-centric cryptocurrencies like Zcash, allowing for the verification of transactions without disclosing any transaction details, thereby ensuring the anonymity and privacy of the transaction parties.

ZK-STARKs (Zero-Knowledge Scalable Transparent Argument of Knowledge): An advancement over ZK-SNARKs, ZK-STARKs provide similar ZKP capabilities without requiring a trusted setup. They are more scalable and quantum-resistant, offering enhanced security and privacy for blockchain transactions. ZK-STARKs are particularly useful in applications demanding high throughput and rigorous privacy requirements, including financial services and identity verification.

- **Homomorphic Encryption:** Homomorphic encryption represents a pioneering cryptographic technique with applications across industries grappling with privacy-sensitive data analysis. Within blockchain, homomorphic encryption holds the potential to rationalize the tension between leveraging data insights and preserving user confidentiality. Homomorphic encryption allows computations on ciphertexts, encrypted data, to generate outputs decrypting to the same results as if run on plaintext inputs. This mathematically ensures processing can transpire without access to the underlying information. Blockchain presents opportunities to extract value from networked data sets while guaranteeing user privacy. Homomorphic encryption facilitates this by creating secure computational environments. Voting systems exemplify how encrypted ballots can release tallies without divulging individual choices. Similarly, homomorphic encryption allows health data analysis yielding population-level insights absent, exposing personal medical profiles. Such capabilities address pressing needs across domains reliant on confidential analytics. Within blockchain, homomorphic encryption could revolutionize services from medical research collaboratives to financial auditing consortiums by concentrating networked computer power onto obfuscated contributions. Technical barriers persist, yet steady advances indicate homomorphic encryption's long-term viability when thoughtfully implemented. Continued cross-discipline cooperation will bolster privacy protections via encryption techniques while optimizing data-driven solutions' utility, benefiting all parties through distributed yet private progress.

- **Multi Party Computation:** Multi party computation (MPC) is a technique that allows multiple participants to collaboratively calculate a function using their inputs while keeping those inputs confidential. In the context of blockchain, MPC can improve privacy and security by enabling decentralized nodes to perform computations securely without exposing the underlying data. Integrating MPC into ecosystem features, like smart contracts and secure voting systems, can be supported. The key benefits include maintaining privacy-enhancing security and promoting decentralization. However, challenges such as overhead, protocol design, and interoperability issues need to be resolved for successful implementation.

- **Trusted Execution Environments:** Trusted execution environments (TEEs) create enclaves within processors where code and data are isolated from the operating system. TEEs play a role in protecting operations by establishing secure channels for processing sensitive data and enhancing the reliability of transaction validations. They offer isolation mechanisms and data security measures and contribute to building trust within networks. Despite facing obstacles like hardware dependency, potential vulnerabilities, and integration complexities in applications, TEEs have the potential to serve as a security component in blockchain infrastructure.

Table 6.3 summarizes some of the commonly used encryption protocols.

6.1.3.5 Smart contracts

The concept of smart contracts, initially proposed in the early 1990s, envisions a transformative approach to contractual agreements. These digital protocols autonomously execute contractual terms without relying on human intermediaries, offering significant potential for efficiency and reliability. Realizing this transformative application has necessitated advancements in enabling technologies and the identification of practical use case alignments.

TABLE 6.3 Encryption methodologies

Encryption method	Key idea	Advantage	Disadvantage	Typical scenarios
E2EE	Encrypts data	Ensures privacy	Complex implementation	Health care, finance
ZK-SNARKs	Proof with no info	Anonymity ensured	Trusted setup needed	Privacy-centric crypto
ZK-STARKs	Quantum-resistant, no trusted setup	Resource-intensive	High-throughput apps	High-throughput apps
Homomorphic Encryption	Enables encrypted data computations	Analysis without access	Computationally heavy	Voting, health data
Multi Party Computation	Private collaborative function calculation	Improved privacy and security	Overhead, protocol design	Smart contracts, secure voting
Trusted Execution Environment	Creates isolated enclaves in processors	Protects operations, enhances reliability	Hardware dependency, potential vulnerabilities	Security component in blockchain

[Original (created by authors)]

Open-source projects have played a pivotal role in evaluating alternative approaches to meet varying governance needs. Ethereum has emerged as a prominent model through its Ethereum Virtual Machine and Solidity smart contracting language. In contrast, Hyperledger Fabric focuses on permissioned distributed ledger systems, prioritizing enterprise interoperability through modularity and private network architectures ethereium review.

In the financial sector, smart contracts have facilitated activities such as lending, insurance, and securities trading through programmed rules that automate conditional payments. Supply chain applications have also benefited from smart contracts, enabling improved provenance traceability. Ongoing collaboration is standardizing environments to optimize platforms and languages for application-specific needs. Technical uncertainties remain regarding upgradability, cross-system compatibility, and jurisdictional arbitrage.

Table 6.4 summarizes some of the smart contracts.

6.1.4 Advanced concepts and technologies

- **Layer 2 Solutions (Lightning Network, State Channels, Plasma, Rollups [Optimistic Rollups, ZK-Rollups]):** One of the key challenges from the early days of blockchain has been scaling pressures arising from expanding user bases, which posed challenges to furthering adoption.

TABLE 6.4 Types of smart contracts

Comparative aspect	Ethereum	Hyperledger Fabric	Bitcoin	Ripple	Corda	EOS
Mechanism of Consensus	PoW/PoS Hybrid	Pluggable modules	PoW	XRP Ledger Consensus Protocol	Notary-based	DPoS
Native Currency	Ether	Nonexistent	Bitcoin (BTC)	XRP	Nonexistent	EOS Tokens
Transaction Visibility	Universally observable	Selectively disclosed	Universally observable	Selectively disclosed	Selectively disclosed	Configurable
Contractual Logic	Ethereum Virtual Machine (EVM)	Chaincode system	Scripting system	Ripple Consensus Ledger	Smart contracts (Flows)	WebAssembly (WASM)
System Governance	Decentralized autonomy	Permissioned membership	Decentralized	Permissioned	Permissioned	Decentralized autonomy
Programming Languages	Solidity, Vyper	Go, Java, JavaScript	C++, Script	RippleAPI (JavaScript)	Kotlin, Java	C++, WebAssembly
Network Architecture	Public and private	Consortium and private	Public	Permissioned	Private	Public

[Original (created by authors)]

On first-generation networks, all transactions occurred directly "on-chain," incurring latency and transaction costs that precluded high-frequency applications. Layer 2 technologies addressed this by developing dedicated "channels" that bundled numerous interactions, settling balances through periodic on-chain commitments.

The Lightning Network pioneered this approach for cryptocurrency micropayments through payment channels anchored to the parent blockchain. Channels allow near-instant off-chain settlements with throughput constrained solely by participating nodes. State channels generalized this concept to smart contract script executions. Yet channels remained point-to-point arrangements. Plasma expanded their scope through hierarchical "child chains" secured under the mainchain, partitioning validation workloads and improving efficiency. Rollups take a different approach, summarizing batched transactions into compressed blockchain "snapshots." By rerouting processing load and increasing transaction density, Layer 2 protocols overcome on-chain constraints impeding scalability. Optimizations like zero-knowledge rollups further realize privacy during validation. As frameworks evolve in synergy, Layer 2 thus enables blockchain growth through configurable offloading while safeguarding security properties.

- **Interoperability Solutions (Polkadot, Cosmos, Interledger Protocols, Cross-Chain Bridges):** Realizing blockchain's vision necessitated coordinated ledgers capable of inter-system cooperation. However, individual blockchains emerged in silos, using distinct protocols and featuring forks in data structures. Early on, proposals like Polkadot envisioned a domain-style hierarchy to route value and information between blockchains, akin to how DNS governs internet naming. Cosmos pioneered an alternative through independent yet intercommunicating "zones." The Interledger protocol provided a modular connection method for varied ledgers. Advancing in parallel, cross-chain bridges materialized for direct asset portability. Bridges serve as two-way conduits between blockchains by locking equivalent asset quantities on both ledgers. This allows migration without trusting counterparties with custody during transfer.

Currently, layering standardized inter-ledger communication over blockchain ecosystems advances toward unified semantic understandability sought since inception. Projects integrating advanced protocols promise networks cooperating as singular logical entities, fulfilling Satoshi Nakamoto's original vision of trusted global value transmission without centralized intermediation. Continued progress propels blockchain toward realizing its potential through interoperable plurality.

Table 6.5 highlights key similarities and differences between the various interoperability protocols.

- **Blockchain Scalability (Sharding, Sidechains, Off-Chain Computation):** Public blockchains like Bitcoin and Ethereum face inherent performance constraints due to their decentralized architecture, where each node replicates and validates the entire ledger. This places hard ceilings on transaction throughput and latency. However, myriad innovations are emerging to enhance blockchain scalability. Sharding involves partitioning the blockchain network into smaller segments called *shards*, each maintaining an independent subset of transactions and state while coordinating via a root chain. This parallel processing enables much higher transaction volume. Experiments like Ethereum's shard chains highlight the promise of this approach.

Sidechains are separate companion blockchains that link to and can transfer value to and from the main chain. By offloading transactions onto sidechains, the main chain is freed from congestion. Sidechains enable experimentation and customization for diverse use cases. Off-chain computation entails performing intensive computations off the main blockchain and simply submitting the final state root to the chain. This saves substantial computing resources and avoids blockchain bloat, significantly boosting performance.

- **Consensus Mechanism Innovations (Proof-of-Authority [PoA], Proof-of-Space and Time [PoST], Directed Acyclic Graphs [DAGs]):** The brilliance

TABLE 6.5 Interoperability protocols

Comparative aspect	Polkadot	Cosmos	Interledger protocol	Cross-chain bridges
Fundamental Concept	Heterogeneous multichain	Inter-blockchain communication (IBC)	Protocol for payments across payment networks	Connects two blockchains for asset transfer
Connector Entity	Relay chain	Hub and zones	Connectors	Bridge smart contracts
Communication Method	Shared security and messaging	IBC	ILP packet switching	Lock and Mint, Burn and Release
Governance	On-chain voting	On-chain governance by token holders	Depends on network participants	Varies by implementation
Consensus Mechanism	Nominated proof-of-stake (NPoS)	Byzantine fault tolerant (BFT) algorithms	Not applicable (agnostic to ledgers' mechanisms)	Dependent on the chains being connected
Native Token	DOT (Polkadot)	ATOM (Cosmos)	None (uses existing ledger assets)	Depends on the chains being connected
Use Cases	Interoperable smart contracts, pooled security	Scalable DApps, token transfers	Cross-ledger payments, micropayments	Asset transfers, cross-chain DApps

[Original (created by authors)]

of Bitcoin's PoW consensus catalyzed blockchain's inception. However, its computational intensity and associated energy demands have driven the exploration of alternative protocols.

Proof-of-authority (PoA) utilizes approved validators, conferring voting power based on reputation and domain expertise. This circumvents PoW's resource-intensity, enabling faster consensus finality. However, critics argue PoA reintroduces elements of centralization and trust. The applicability of PoA for public blockchains remains contested.

Proof-of-space (PoSpace) pivots mining towards a novel resource: unused hard disk space. By allowing "miners" to pre-allocate disk space that is randomly accessed during block proposals, PoSpace disrupts PoW's computational arms race for higher efficiency and environmental sustainability. However, some posit that economies of scale could lead to centralized mining pools under PoSpace as well.

Directed acyclic graphs (DAGs) completely reimagine blockchain's sequential data structure. By organizing transactions in a DAG, parallel execution

TABLE 6.6 Summary of consensus mechanisms

Consensus mechanism	Key idea	Challenge associated
Proof-of-Work (PoW)	Competitive cryptographic puzzle solving	Energy consumption, scalability issues
Proof-of-Stake (PoS)	Ownership stakes determine validation rights	Centralization through wealth accumulation
Delegated Proof-of-Stake (DPoS)	Elect validators via token-holder votes	Compromised decentralization, governance concerns
Practical Byzantine Fault Tolerance (PBFT)	Consensus through trusted node majority	Vulnerability to node collusion
Proof-of-Authority (PoA)	Authority based on identity and trust	Centralizes power, diminishes trustlessness
Proof-of-Space (PoSpace)	Disk space utilization instead of CPU	Centralization via economies of scale
Directed Acyclic Graphs (DAGs)	Transactions linked non-sequentially	Challenges in achieving consensus finality
Proof-of-History (PoH)	Sequence verification through historical records	Requires additional mechanisms for consensus finality

[Original (created by authors)]

unlocks vast scalability improvements. DAGs promise to resolve multiple limitations, including throughput constraints, latency, and cost. However, determinism and finality in DAG-based consensus remain active research challenges.

Proof-of-history (PoH) enables timestamps to be embedded directly into the blockchain. This minimizes the processing load since networks are informed about transactions' occurrences in a specific order and no confirmation is needed from other nodes.

In Table 6.6, we provide a succinct look at the central ideas and the challenges associated with each of the consensus mechanisms. While PoW's elegance is indisputable, its limitations instigated ingenious solutions that could profoundly shape blockchain's future. PoA, PoSpace, and DAGs highlight that consensus mechanisms have multifaceted trade-offs between decentralization, security, efficiency, and sustainability. Ongoing research and experimentation will undoubtedly uncover optimal solutions for different contexts and use cases.

- **Privacy Enhancements in Blockchain:** From inception, privacy and scalability posed challenges to blockchain networks. Mimblewimble offers a creative solution through revisions to standard transaction structure. It derives its name from the nonsensical Harry Potter charm, reflecting the protocol's whimsical reimagining of blockchain fundamentals. At its core, Mimblewimble achieves privacy and efficiency gains by merging numerous transactions before recording to the shared ledger. Individual amounts and addresses within consolidated transactions become obfuscated. By employing techniques like confidential transactions and CoinJoin, Mimblewimble obscures transaction details while retaining verifiability. These architectural augmentations enhance both privacy and performance. Privacy-enhancing technologies such as zk-SNARKs, Confidential Transactions, Ring Signatures, and Stealth Addresses provide mechanisms for ensuring that transaction outputs can be verified without exposing inputs, amounts, or other sensitive details. These technologies strike a balance between privacy and transparency, offering a more private and secure user experience in blockchain ecosystems.. Meanwhile, performance improvements arise from pairing multiple interactions into solitary "supertransactions," conserving storage and bandwidth resources. As an open-source project, Mimblewimble reflects the blockchain community's dedication to resolving inherent challenges through creative technical reassessment. By reenvisioning basic components, it illuminates potential for additional second-layer protocols to optimize core protocols, propelling continual progress. Wider consideration of such approaches could catalyze further optimization of scalability and privacy preservation across distributed systems.

• **Sustainable Blockchain Technologies:** The environmental impact of blockchain technology, particularly the energy-intensive nature of PoW consensus mechanisms, has prompted a search for more sustainable alternatives. The blockchain community is actively exploring energy-efficient consensus algorithms and models for carbon-neutral networks to address these concerns.

Alternatives to PoW, such as PoS, DPoS, and PoA, offer more energy-efficient mechanisms for achieving consensus on blockchain networks. These algorithms significantly reduce the computational power and energy required to maintain the network, aligning blockchain technology with sustainability goals.

Beyond improving energy efficiency, some blockchain projects are pursuing carbon neutrality through offsets and the use of renewable energy sources. Initiatives include the direct purchase of renewable energy credits, investment in sustainable energy projects, and the development of blockchain platforms specifically designed to facilitate carbon credit trading.

These efforts towards sustainable blockchain technologies reflect a growing recognition of the need to balance innovation with environmental responsibility. By adopting energy-efficient consensus algorithms and striving for carbon neutrality, the blockchain community can ensure that the benefits of this transformative technology are realized without compromising the health of our planet.

Table 6.7 presents an overview of the blockchain stack and the critical decisions that organizations must make when selecting and designing a blockchain solution.

From choosing the appropriate blockchain type that balances privacy with collaboration to selecting a consensus mechanism that ensures reliability and efficiency, each decision has a profound impact on the system's performance, security, and usability. The table outlines the key options within each category, including data storage solutions, smart contract platforms, and data

TABLE 6.7 Technology decisions while deciding on implementation

Decision	Options available	Key considerations
Blockchain Type	Private	Controls, ensures privacy
	Consortium	Promotes shared governance
	Hybrid	Leverages both, enhances access
Consensus Mechanism	PoA	Fast, energy efficient
	PBFT	Ensures network reliability
	DPoS	Balances efficiency, governance
Data Storage	On-chain	Secures critical data
	Off-chain	Solves scalability, performance
	Decentralized (IPFS, Filecoin)	Stores large files securely
Smart Contract Platform	Ethereum	Widely adopted, strong community
	Hyperledger Fabric	Privacy, permissioning features
	Corda	Privacy, regulatory compliance
Data Encryption and Privacy	End-to-end encryption	Secures data transmission
	ZKPs	Enhances privacy
	Homomorphic encryption	Encrypted data processing
Interoperability Framework	HL7 FHIR	Ensures effective communication
	Cross-blockchain protocols	Enables data exchange
	API gateways	Bridges technologies, systems
Identity and Access Management	Blockchain IDs	Secure digital identities
	RBAC on blockchain	Manages access control precisely
Compliance and Standards	DICOM	Standardizes imaging data
	Compliance smart contracts	Automates enforcement

[Original (created by authors)]

encryption methods, all of which contribute to the integrity and confidentiality of sensitive medical data.

In addition, interoperability frameworks and identity management are pivotal in ensuring seamless integration with existing healthcare systems and maintaining strict access controls. Finally, compliance with standards and regulations is non-negotiable in the healthcare domain, and Table 6.7 addresses how blockchain can be leveraged to meet these stringent requirements.

6.2 Blockchain's role in enhancing medical practice

6.2.1 Introduction to blockchain's role in medical practice

The healthcare industry is currently experiencing a revolution. The use of advanced digital systems to manage patient data and health records is replacing outdated paper-based methods. This shift aims to improve efficiency, accessibility, and the quality of care. However, there are challenges in integrating and managing sensitive medical data in this new digital landscape. Concerns about patient privacy, fragmented systems and flawed data management threaten to hinder the potential of health. Blockchain holds promise for addressing these obstacles. As it is founded on the triad of decentralization, immutability, and transparency, it seems uniquely suited to provide novel solutions to some of health care's traditional problems. From enhancing data security to enabling record interoperability, blockchain technology has the potential to transform healthcare operations. Successful implementation will require collaboration among technologists, medical professionals, and regulators as it moves from being a possibility to becoming a reality in health care [5, 6].

6.2.2 The pivotal role of blockchain in enhancing medical practice beyond basic data management

Blockchain technology's expansion within health care signals a significant shift, extending far beyond mere data management to revolutionize medical practices. Initially, blockchain served as a tool for secure data storage and access within health care, a response to the traditional systems' limitations in managing and safeguarding patient information efficiently [6]. However, its role has evolved, now playing a pivotal part in advancing medical practice.

The advent of blockchain in health care tackles the core issues of traditional systems—limited interoperability and the inefficiencies of isolated data management. By enabling seamless data exchange and integration among varied healthcare systems, blockchain facilitates improved continuity of care, a leap towards interconnected healthcare ecosystems [7]. Moreover, it addresses one of healthcare's most pressing concerns: patient privacy and data security [8].

Through its decentralized architecture and encryption mechanisms, blockchain ensures that patient information remains secure and private, mitigating risks of unauthorized access and breaches.

Beyond enhancing security and privacy, blockchain significantly streamlines healthcare operations. It reduces administrative burdens, expedites medical credential verification processes, and, by extension, contributes to cost savings and enhanced healthcare delivery [9]. This operational efficiency is pivotal in a sector where time and accuracy are of the essence. Furthermore, blockchain's impact extends to patient-centric care, empowering patients with control over their health data [7]. This empowerment fosters a patient-centric approach, allowing for personalized healthcare solutions and promoting patient engagement in their health management.

Blockchain's influence on health care transcends basic data management. It propels the sector towards more secure, efficient, and patient-centered practices. The future outlook for blockchain in health care is promising, marked by ongoing developments and the potential for innovative solutions [10]. As the field continues to evolve, the collaborative efforts of technologists, healthcare professionals, and policymakers will be crucial in realizing the full potential of blockchain to revolutionize medical practice and patient care.

6.2.3 Transitioning towards blockchain in health care

In an era marked by rapid technological evolution, the global healthcare sector faces a constellation of challenges that impede its efficiency and effectiveness. Among these, data breaches, systemic inefficiencies, and access barriers stand out as particularly pressing issues. Notably, the core difficulties of data security and interoperability within health care underscore the sector's vulnerability and highlight the urgency for innovative solutions. Blockchain technology emerges as a beacon of potential in this context, promising to revolutionize health care through its foundational principles of decentralization, immutability, and robust encryption. This transformative technology offers a pathway to not only bolstering data management but also to advancing healthcare practices beyond their current limitations. By enabling a secure, transparent, and seamless exchange of medical information, blockchain paves the way for a new era of health care characterized by enhanced operational efficiency and patient-centric care.

The anticipated impact of blockchain in the healthcare domain is profound, with the technology standing to redefine the paradigms of patient data management and healthcare delivery globally. As we look towards the future, the potential of blockchain to address the multifaceted challenges of the healthcare sector heralds a shift towards more integrated, secure, and patient-focused healthcare solutions.

This discussion sets the stage for a deeper exploration of blockchain's capabilities and its role in mitigating the challenges facing health care today, underscoring the technology's critical importance in the evolution of medical practices worldwide.

6.2.4 How blockchain technology is being integrated into healthcare systems

Integrating blockchain technology into healthcare systems heralds a paradigm shift, transitioning from conventional methods of data storage and exchange to a more secure, efficient, and patient-centered framework. This transition addresses the existing vulnerabilities of healthcare systems, such as fragmented data silos and security loopholes, by leveraging blockchain's decentralized, immutable, and transparent nature. Blockchain applications in health care extend from ensuring the secure exchange of patient data across different providers to enhancing drug traceability and managing medical records, showcasing practical benefits that include bolstered data security, improved interoperability, and enhanced patient control over personal health information. However, the path towards widespread adoption of blockchain in health care is fraught with challenges, including technical standards, regulatory hurdles, and the need for collaborative efforts among various stakeholders. These ongoing efforts and considerations underscore the potential of blockchain to revolutionize healthcare practices, promising a future where healthcare systems are more connected, secure, and centered around patient needs.

6.2.5 The theoretical foundation for blockchain's benefits in health care

Blockchain technology is being heralded as a revolutionary force in health care, offering solutions to long-standing issues like data security, patient privacy, and interoperability. Traditional healthcare systems are often siloed and fraught with security vulnerabilities, highlighting the urgent need for a system that can securely manage and share patient data. Blockchain's application in health care promises a decentralized, secure, and interoperable data management system, facilitating the seamless sharing of patient data across different providers. This technology has seen real-world applications ranging from secure patient data exchange to drug traceability and electronic medical records management, showcasing its practical benefits. Despite its potential, the widespread adoption of blockchain in health care faces challenges such as the need for technical standards, regulatory compliance, and collaboration among stakeholders. Addressing these challenges is crucial for harnessing blockchain's full potential to transform healthcare systems.

6.2.6   Setting the stage for blockchain in radiology

The advent of blockchain technology heralds a transformative era in health care, promising far-reaching implications beyond the conventional management of health data. Grounded in the pioneering insights of Gordon and Catalini, we observe a pivotal shift towards enhanced data security, patient privacy, and interoperability [7]. This evolution addresses the inherent challenges of healthcare systems marked by fragmented data silos and security vulnerabilities, paving the way for a decentralized, secure, and interoperable health data management framework. As elucidated by Hasselgren et al., blockchain's core attributes—distribution, decentralization, timestamping, data provenance, and nonrepudiation—emerge as vital solutions to the quandaries of healthcare informatics, driving the sector towards the ideals of Healthcare 4.0 [11].

In the realm of healthcare data management, blockchain technology fosters a patient-centric model, enabling secure and transparent verification of caregiver credentials and experience through immutable records on a blockchain. This model not only assures the integrity of healthcare treatments and evaluations but also upholds stringent privacy and security standards, aligning with regulatory frameworks such as GDPR and HIPAA.

As we navigate the complexities of technological integration and regulatory compliance, the forward-looking narrative of blockchain in health care is one of ongoing innovation and potential expansion, promising a more secure, efficient, and patient-centered healthcare ecosystem. The journey towards fully realizing the benefits of blockchain in health care is a collaborative endeavor, requiring the concerted efforts of technologists, healthcare professionals, and policymakers alike. Some of the current pressing problems we could potentially address using blockchain are highlighted in Table 6.8.

6.3   Introduction to radiology and its unique challenges

6.3.1   Introduction to radiology

Radiology is a branch of medicine that focuses on using and interpreting images to diagnose and treat diseases. It is at the forefront of integrating technology into health care. Over time, radiology has evolved from x-ray imaging to advanced techniques like MRI, CT scans, and PET imaging. This evolution signifies not an increase in complexity and capability but also highlights the crucial role radiology plays in modern diagnostics by enabling precise and early

TABLE 6.8 Adoption of blockchain technologies in the healthcare supply chain

Specialty	Key pain point	Traditional approach	Blockchain revolution
Electronic Health Records (EHRs)	Inefficiency in sharing, security	Centralized databases, lacks transparency, patient control	Secure, transparent sharing, patient data control [12]
Supply Chain Management	Lack of transparency, security	Centralized tracking systems, fraud prone	Improved traceability, security, efficiency [13]
Patient Data Privacy	Data breaches, lack of control	Centralized storage, limited patient access	Enhanced security, patient data control [14]
Pharmaceutical R&D	Drug development, trial efficiency	Isolated databases, manual stakeholder data sharing	Streamlined R&D, secure data collaboration [15–17]
Counterfeit Drugs	Combating counterfeit drugs	Manual tracking, physical security measures	Transparent, immutable drug origin, distribution records [18–20]
Healthcare Insurance	Fraud, claim processing inefficiency	Manual verification, error and fraud prone	Secured claims processing with smart contracts [21–23]
Medical Supply Chains	Inefficiencies, lack of real-time data	Centralized supply management, inaccuracies	Real-time tracking, efficiency with decentralized networks [19, 24]
Patient Identity Verification	Inefficient identification methods	Physical ID cards, documents, fraud prone	Secure, immutable identity verification systems [25, 26]
Data Interoperability	Lack of interoperable patient data	Siloed systems, proprietary formats	Seamless, secure data exchange across systems [7, 27]
Drug Traceability	Drug safety, combating counterfeits	Barcodes, RFID for track-and-trace, not foolproof	Secure, transparent drug traceability system [19]

[Original (created by authors)]

disease detection through visualization of internal body structures. Throughout its journey, radiology has embraced innovation expanding beyond reliance on x-rays to include various imaging techniques with specific applications and utilities. This evolution not only enhances diagnostic accuracy but also promotes less invasive and more patient-centered approaches in medicine.

Radiology faces common challenges shared by other medical specialties, such as concerns about data privacy, accuracy of diagnostic information, and the need for interdisciplinary collaboration. These challenges are amplified due to the nature of radiology being data intensive, generating volumes of high-definition images that require robust data management and security protocols. The storage, management, and analysis of imaging data in radiology pose challenges due to its voluminous and complex nature. To ensure accessibility and usefulness for high-resolution images require substantial digital storage and advanced data handling systems.

In the field of radiology, privacy and security concerns are particularly acute due to the nature of medical imaging. Striking a balance between accessibility and confidentiality is crucial for protecting patient data while enabling necessary image sharing among healthcare providers [28, 29]. However, this task becomes increasingly challenging in the face of growing cyber threats.

Radiology also faces a pressing challenge in achieving interoperability across diverse healthcare IT systems. The seamless exchange of medical imaging data across these systems is essential for patient care. Unfortunately, incompatible systems and formats often hinder the sharing and integration of imaging data into EHRs.

One unique aspect of radiology lies in its reliance on visualization techniques to drive diagnostics. This requires not only advanced imaging technologies but also sophisticated analytical tools that can accurately interpret these images. Furthermore, the field is characterized by the requirement for storage solutions that can handle large amounts of data and facilitate quick retrieval systems. This is crucial for managing archives of imaging data that are vital for long-term patient care.

Effective data management in radiology requires systems capable of handling the dual demands of archiving vast quantities of imaging data and facilitating rapid retrieval for diagnostic and treatment purposes. The goal is to ensure that historical and current images are readily available for comparison and analysis, a task that demands advanced digital infrastructure and meticulous data governance.

Radiology relies heavily on collaboration between radiologists, referring physicians, and other healthcare professionals. Communication and sharing mechanisms are essential in integrating radiological findings with other clinical data, enabling a comprehensive understanding of a patient's health status as well as planning effective treatment strategies.

The intersection of radiology with blockchain technology offers promising avenues to address these multifaceted challenges. By leveraging blockchain's capabilities for secure, decentralized data management, the field of radiology stands to gain significantly in terms of enhanced data security, improved interoperability, and more efficient collaboration across the healthcare continuum.

Table 6.9 presents an overview of the potential areas in the radiology workflow that could be addressed with blockchain.

TABLE 6.9 Potential areas in the radiology workflow that could be addressed with blockchain

Aspect of radiology workflow	Key pain point	Traditional solution (current practice)	Challenge with traditional solution
Privacy and Security of Imaging Data	Ensuring data confidentiality, integrity	Encryption, secure access protocols	Centralized systems vulnerable to breaches, unauthorized access
Interoperability and Data Sharing	Facilitating seamless data exchange across systems	HL7, DICOM standards for interoperability	Inconsistent standards implementation hampers data sharing
Patient Data Management and Consent	Managing patient consent for data sharing and use	Manual consent processes through patient portals	Time-consuming, limited patient control over data
Archiving and Retrieval of Imaging Data	Efficient data management amidst growing data volumes	Centralized digital archives with access control	Scalability, efficiency issues in retrieval, increased costs
Clinical Collaboration	Secure collaboration among healthcare professionals	Shared electronic health systems, team meetings	Synchronous meetings delay decision-making; limited access controls
Traceability and Data Integrity	Maintaining and verifying integrity of imaging data	Audit trails within Picture Archiving and Communication Systems (PACS) and EHR systems	Cumbersome audit trails, do not fully ensure data integrity
Access Control and Authorization	Restricting data access to authorized individuals	Role-based access controls in healthcare IT systems	Inflexible role-based systems, restrict or allow breaches
Real-Time Data Access	Providing immediate access to imaging data	Immediate data sharing protocols within networks	Delays due to encryption processes, system incompatibilities
Decentralized Data Storage	Reducing reliance on centralized data storage	Cloud-based storage solutions	Centralized storage risks data loss, service outages
Data Monetization and Intellectual Property	Managing and monetizing intellectual property	Licensing agreements, proprietary systems	Complex management, enforcement of intellectual property rights

[Original (created by authors)]

6.3.2 How blockchain can transform radiology

The potential impact of blockchain technology on the field of radiology is vast. It offers robust solutions to address the current challenges of data privacy, security, and interoperability. As we work towards integrating this technology into established clinical workflows, it becomes essential to conduct ongoing research and pilot programs to validate the practical benefits it brings to radiology. By leveraging blockchain, we can not only streamline radiological operations but also enhance the trust and effectiveness of services provided to patients. The unique characteristics of blockchain, such as decentralization, immutability, and transparency, provide specific advantages in the field of radiology. The use of immutable audit trails ensures legal compliance while facilitating data validation for research purposes without compromising patient privacy. Moreover, the transparent yet secure nature of blockchain networks fosters trust among stakeholders—a crucial element for collaborative radiological practices and multi-institutional research initiatives.

Securing data is of utmost importance to maintain patient trust and the integrity of the healthcare system. The architecture of blockchain provides resistance to tampering making it an ideal solution for safeguarding radiological data. Even if a cyberattack compromises a node, the remaining nodes in the network preserve untainted data, ensuring continuity and reliability across the radiology network [30].

To ensure treatment radiologists often need to collaborate with various healthcare providers requiring seamless interoperability of data. Blockchain can serve as a unified infrastructure that enables healthcare systems to securely access and share radiological data efficiently. This interoperability is achieved without compromising the integrity of the data since each transaction on the blockchain is authenticated and consistently maintained across systems [7, 27].

In radiology, timely collaboration plays a role in providing quick diagnoses and avoiding unnecessary delays. Blockchain facilitates this collaboration through contracts that automate various tasks, like releasing imaging studies to relevant parties based on predefined criteria. This capability has the potential to streamline findings and share them with referring physicians, thereby expediting patient management and potentially enhancing clinical outcomes [31].

Blockchain provides a solution to the growing complexities of data management in radiology. It enables the creation of a database where medical images and related metadata can be securely stored, easily accessed, and quickly shared when needed. Additionally, it ensures an unchangeable audit trail. This level of efficiency is particularly important for large-scale radiology practices dealing with large amounts of imaging data [31].

Smart contracts have the potential to revolutionize radiology by automating processes. These self-executing contracts, written directly into code can streamline consent procedures, image analysis requests and even financial transactions such as billing for radiological services. By reducing overheads and eliminating the chance of human error this automation allows healthcare professionals to focus more on providing quality patient care [32, 33].

Blockchain technology empowers patients to take charge of their radiological data. Through access mechanisms provided by blockchain, patients can manage who has access to their imaging data, set specific time frames for access permissions, and define conditions under which their data can be used. This empowerment aligns with the movement towards patient-centered care and reinforces the importance of involving patients in decision-making processes [32, 34].

6.4 Implementations of blockchain in radiology

The integration of blockchain in radiology and medical imaging is an emerging field with complex challenges and possibilities. Recent research illuminates blockchain's potential while also recognizing nuances and limitations. A predominant focus is using blockchain properties like decentralization, transparency, and cryptography for secure, accountable sharing of medical images and data [30, 35, 36]. But solutions must balance privacy, accessibility, scalability, and usability.

Multiple studies have proposed blockchain systems for permissions management, auditing, and provenance tracking to enable efficient yet controlled image sharing across providers [35, 37, 38]. Smart contracts automate notifications and access policies. Decentralized peer-to-peer networks facilitate availability without third-party intermediaries [34, 38]. However, blockchain cannot fully resolve regulatory constraints around protected health information. The design space remains large for optimized systems balancing security, functionality, and user experience.

A key application is using blockchain's tamper-proof, transparent nature for accountable, privacy-preserving collaborative modeling and distributed learning [39–41]. Locally trained deep-learning models can be aggregated to create more robust joint models while keeping raw data decentralized. But effective integration with healthcare IT systems is still needed. Studies also indicate blockchain's usefulness in crowdsourced labeling, model-sharing incentives, and persistent data set storage [42]. Yet adoption barriers remain regarding cost, scalability, and compatibility with clinical workflows.

Importantly, many studies are still conceptual or based on simulated experiments [39, 43]. Real-world evidence of clinical integration, scale, and tangible patient impact is largely lacking. Moreover, blockchain specifics like consensus mechanisms, platform architectures, encryption techniques, and smart contract logic can significantly impact properties like security, efficiency, interoperability, and privacy [38–40]. These nuances warrant investigation.

6.4.1   Data sharing and management

Ensuring data security and traceability is paramount in radiology given the sensitive nature of medical images. As healthcare data becomes increasingly digitized through EHRs, robust security frameworks are needed to prevent unauthorized access and data breaches involving protected health information. Blockchain technology presents a promising solution through its ability to securely record transactions in an immutable, distributed ledger without centralized authority.

Recent studies have explored applying blockchain to enhance data security and traceability in radiology. In seminal work, Aguiar et al. proposed a blockchain-based protocol for tracking user access to shared medical images [44]. Their approach addressed critical issues around data privacy and leakage in healthcare systems by embedding a unique token in Digital Imaging and Communications in Medicine (DICOM) file metadata. This token was then managed through the Hyperledger Fabric blockchain to control access to medical images by stakeholders like healthcare providers and patients. By recording access logs immutably on the blockchain, their protocol-enabled auditability of data leakage incidents to hold organizations accountable helps to comply with privacy regulations like the GDPR.

In related work, Patel developed a decentralized framework for securely sharing medical imaging data using blockchain [30]. By removing reliance on third parties as intermediaries, Patel's framework aimed to address inefficiencies and security vulnerabilities of traditional medical data sharing approaches. It established a blockchain-based ledger of radiological studies and patient-defined access permissions to provide a more secure and interoperable healthcare system. This demonstrated blockchain's potential for mitigating privacy concerns and streamlining the sharing of medical imaging across different healthcare providers to enhance efficiency and patient outcomes.

Taken together, these studies indicate blockchain technology's transformative potential for enhancing data security, traceability, and sharing capabilities in radiology. By leveraging blockchain attributes like decentralization, immutability, and transparency, proposed solutions provide secure, efficient, and patient-centered approaches to medical data management challenges. Future work in this area could help advance secure interoperability and optimize healthcare delivery through improved access to diagnostic imaging data.

6.4.2 Decentralized image management

One notable advantage of decentralized image management systems is that they empower patients to have control over who can access their medical images, unlike traditional centralized storage systems where healthcare institutions own the data. By distributing storage and utilizing the tamper-proof nature of blockchain technology, decentralized systems aim to ensure that only authorized parties across various healthcare providers can securely access medical images.

Jabarulla et al. proposed a framework based on technology for storing and sharing medical images in a way that prioritizes patient centricity while enhancing privacy and security [45]. Their system ensures the integrity of data by storing it in an append structure that cannot be tampered with. Mohsan et al. introduced an architecture that combines blockchain with IPFS for managing the storage of images and reports [34]. This architecture enables patients to maintain control over how their data is shared among authorized parties without relying on centralized servers.

The studies highlight the transformative potential of decentralized systems in addressing critical challenges in the management of medical images. By leveraging decentralized technologies, such as blockchain and distributed ledgers, these systems can tackle key vulnerabilities related to security, privacy, and the fragmentation of data silos in healthcare. The suggested methods utilize blockchain IPFS to guarantee that images are securely stored and shared while still allowing patients to maintain control and accessibility across various healthcare providers. Implementing these approaches on a larger scale could potentially improve the privacy, security, and interoperability of managing medical data. However additional research is required to assess how these methodologies can be integrated into healthcare workflows and determine the advantages compared to approaches.

6.4.3 Facilitating research through blockchain

Kuo has introduced a system based on contracts to share x-ray images on a blockchain network [37]. By incorporating access policies into these contracts, the approach allows controlled sharing of medical images among researchers with traceability. This not only safeguards data privacy but also facilitates decentralized sharing, offering a scalable solution to fragmented data access.

Similarly, Ortega et al. have developed a database for sharing electron tomography data using blockchain technology combined with peer-to-peer networks [36]. Their system provides a distributed solution for disseminating scientific imaging data sets exceeding 30 terabytes. Through an open-access model, their work encourages advancements by providing ample standardized data resources.

Both studies exemplify how blockchain can be utilized to manage rights, ensure transparency, and enable accessibility to medical research data. Such frameworks based on blockchain have the potential to enable secure collaboration as well as promote open science. However, for adoption, it is important to address scalability and integration with research workflow and sustainability. Future studies should focus on evaluating the real-world feasibility and quantitative impact of these technologies on imaging research. Nevertheless, these innovations underscore the power of blockchain in enhancing the credibility origin tracking and availability of medical imaging data.

6.4.4 *Privacy-preserving diagnostic tools*

The integration of blockchain and artificial intelligence (AI) offers promising avenues for developing privacy-preserving diagnostic tools, a critical need in radiology. Studies by Heidari et al. and Kumar et al. demonstrate the potential of combining these technologies for secure and accurate medical image analysis, particularly for COVID-19 detection [40, 46].

Heidari et al. proposed a blockchain-enabled AI method to diagnose COVID-19 from chest x-rays while preserving data confidentiality. Their approach utilizes AI for detection while blockchain provides security and privacy. This showcases the possibility of achieving high accuracy without compromising patient data, highlighting the value of integrating these technologies for ethical diagnostics.

Similarly, Kumar et al. developed a sophisticated framework integrating blockchain with homomorphic encryption for collaborative training on sensitive medical images. Their system allows different entities to jointly analyze images through encrypted gradient sharing, facilitating privacy-preserving federated learning. The validation demonstrates viability in maintaining strict data privacy while enabling collective training, offering a model for developing secure diagnostic tools.

Together, these studies demonstrate the transformative potential of blockchain and AI integration for radiology diagnostics. The capacity to enhance security and accuracy could pave the way for broader adoption in health care. Nonetheless, real-world implementation remains limited, warranting further research into translating these technologies into clinical practice. As blockchain and AI continue maturing, studies like these will likely accelerate the development of ethical and efficient diagnostic systems.

6.4.5 *Secure model training and image analysis*

The work by A. H. Mohsin et al. demonstrates an innovative application of blockchain technology and particle swarm optimization (PSO) for securing medical image data in radiology [47]. Their proposed model integrates blockchain and PSO-driven image steganography to conceal patient information within medical images while preserving diagnostic value. At its core, this approach leverages blockchain's decentralized and tamper-proof nature to create a secure environment for managing imaging data. By storing references to image hashes on the blockchain, data provenance can be reliably established. The use of PSO optimizes the embedding process to maximize capacity while minimizing image distortion. This dual mechanism aims to enhance security against unauthorized data access or modification. The authors suggest their model addresses pressing privacy concerns in digital radiology, including potential data breaches and lack of integrity controls. They argue that blockchain-steganography integration could foster collaborative research by securely transmitting images. However, clinical implementation and real-world validation remain open research areas.

While conceptual, this work highlights the promise of blending blockchain with data-hiding techniques like steganography for radiology applications. The proposed model offers one approach for reconciling the objectives of privacy, security, fidelity, and collaboration in medical imaging. Further research is needed to translate these principles into clinical systems and quantify the trade-offs involved. Nonetheless, Mohsin et al.'s study provides valuable insights into the translational potential of blockchain in redefining paradigms of security and trust in technology-enabled radiology.

6.4.6 Collaborative learning and model training

The integration of blockchain with AI in radiology is brought to the fore through the work of Yang Luo et al. [39]and Fadila Zerka et al. [41], demonstrating applications in collaborative deep learning while preserving privacy.

Luo et al. developed a framework leveraging blockchain technology to enable secure decentralized collaboration for medical image segmentation across institutions. Their approach facilitates collective model training without sharing sensitive medical data, overcoming key barriers to data sharing. Through integrating blockchain for a transparent collaborative mechanism, they address challenges in deploying AI under stringent privacy regulations. This exemplifies blockchain's potential as an infrastructure for privacy-preserving distributed learning systems to enhance diagnostic tools.

Similarly, Zerka et al. introduced a distributed learning approach combining sequential training with a blockchain platform for multicenter medical imaging. Their proposed system maintains data confidentiality by allowing health centers to participate in model training without centralizing information. It produces comparable results to centralized methods while improving security, privacy, and trust. This represents a significant step towards privacy-preserving AI adoption in radiology, securing model training processes through traceability.

Together, these studies demonstrate the feasibility and benefits of thoughtfully integrating blockchain with AI techniques in radiology. The capacity to resolve data sharing and privacy challenges while improving diagnostics and therapies highlights the transformative promise of these technologies. However, real-world implementation remains limited, warranting further research into translating these frameworks into clinical practice. As blockchain and AI mature, building on these foundations could propel radiology into an era of ethical and collaborative innovation.

6.4.7 Distributed learning for enhanced diagnostics

The work by Mohammadreza Noei et al. demonstrates the potential of integrating blockchain technology with deep learning for enhanced diagnostics in radiology while preserving data privacy [38]. Their proposed secure hybrid permissioned blockchain platform facilitates collaborative pneumonia classification from CT images among hospitals.

This platform allows hospitals to share trained neural network weights rather than actual patient data via the permissioned blockchain. By dividing a data set of 5,856 CT images evenly among five hospitals for localized training, each institution can leverage shared weights from others to improve their diagnostic models. This approach addresses traditional barriers to healthcare data sharing due to privacy concerns.

The study utilizes a 28-layer residual neural network architecture optimized for CT image analysis. This underscores the value of deep learning for pattern recognition in medical imaging. The permissioned blockchain ensures secure and verifiable exchange of model weights for collaborative learning while maintaining data privacy and integrity.

Results validate that the secure weight sharing improves diagnostic accuracy compared to isolated model training. Noei et al. demonstrate the potential to enhance radiology diagnostics through collaborative deep learning on decentralized blockchain platforms. While further real-world evidence is needed, this pioneering work illuminates pathways for transforming health care by synergizing blockchain security with AI capabilities for the common good.

6.4.8 System infrastructure and process optimization

The study by Jiyoun Randolph highlights the potential of blockchain technology to optimize workflow in teleradiology [43]. While acknowledging the benefits of teleradiology in facilitating remote diagnosis, Randolph notes significant technical and operational limitations arising from disparate systems.

The lack of integration between teleradiology platforms and on-site healthcare IT systems can lead to critical inefficiencies like delayed image availability and slow critical result communication. These factors extend radiology report turnaround times, negatively impacting timely diagnosis and treatment.

To address such limitations, Randolph proposes a permissioned blockchain system leveraging properties like decentralization, transparency, and immutability to enable secure, integrated platforms for teleradiology workflow. The proposed architecture aims to streamline image requests and critical result notifications through automation, minimizing reliance on manual processes. A prototype demonstrates the potential time savings and efficiency gains in radiology workflows from this approach.

Overall, Randolph's study provides valuable insights into optimizing teleradiology with blockchain-based automation. The prototype illustrates the feasibility of the proposed architecture to reduce steps and delays in image sharing and critical result communication. While an early conceptual model, this work establishes a foundation for further blockchain innovation to shape next-generation teleradiology platforms. Additional research incorporating user-centered design and evaluation of clinical integration at scale will be important to translate these architectural insights into patient care improvements.

6.4.9 Incentivizing collaboration in radiology

The work of Witowski et al. demonstrates the potential of blockchain technology to incentivize and optimize collaborative annotation of medical images [42]. Their proposed platform, MarkIt, aims to streamline the annotation process by integrating AI and blockchain functionalities. MarkIt expedites annotation for classification and object detection tasks, while transparently tracking user contributions to enable fair rewards calculation.

A key innovation is the permissioned blockchain back-end to securely share model weights, facilitating collaborative deep learning. MarkIt also ensures regulatory compliance and data privacy, critical considerations in medical imaging. The proof-of-concept with radiologists annotating 1,000 x-ray images showcases efficiency gains from the platform. Overall, this research highlights blockchain and AI's synergy in transforming data set annotation and model development workflows. Automated rewards dispensation based on traceable contributions could incentivize higher-quality annotations from medical experts. As MarkIt exemplifies, thoughtful blockchain integration can optimize data sharing, preserve privacy, and accelerate AI progress. However, real-world validation of clinical integration, legal compliance, and patient benefit is still necessary to translate these architectural insights into practice.

Table 6.10 presents an overview of the implementations of blockchain in radiology.

TABLE 6.10 Summary of the implementations of blockchain in radiology

Cluster	Solution	Radiology workflow addressed	Use in radiology
Data Sharing and Management	Blockchain protocol for medical image tracking [44]	Medical image sharing and access control	Secure and traceable image sharing
	Decentralized image management with blockchain [45]	Storage and sharing of medical images	Secure patient-centric image management
	Blockchain for x-ray image sharing [37]	Sharing of x-ray images for research	Efficient and secure image sharing
	Decentralized management of medical images/ reports [34]	Patient-centric data management	Secure storage and sharing
	Blockchain for electron tomography data sharing [36]	Scientific imaging data sharing	Decentralized data sharing for research
	Blockchain for decentralized image data sharing [30]	Cross-site image transfer	Secure and interoperable health system
Privacy-Preserving Diagnostic Tools	Blockchain and AI for COVID-19 detection [46]	COVID-19 detection in chest CT images	Privacy-preserving COVID-19 diagnosis
	Federated learning with blockchain for COVID-19 [48]	COVID-19 detection using CT imaging	Collaborative and privacy-preserving diagnosis
	Privacy-preserving model aggregation for images [40]	Medical image analysis and sharing	Secure collaborative model training
	Steganography-blockchain for COVID-19 data sharing [47]	Secure data sharing among hospitals	Enhanced data confidentiality and availability
Collaborative Learning and Model Training	Blockchain for collaborative model training [39]	Medical image segmentation	Privacy-preserving collaborative learning
	Blockchain for distributed machine learning [41]	Multi-institutional model development	Trustworthy and private model training
	Blockchain for CT image classification sharing [38]	Pneumonia classification from CT scans	Privacy-preserving distributed deep learning

(Continued)

TABLE 6.10 (Continued)

Cluster	Solution	Radiology workflow addressed	Use in radiology
System Infrastructure and Process Optimization	Blockchain for image sharing and notifications [43]	Teleradiology workflow optimization	Efficient image sharing and critical result notification
	Blockchain for collaborative AI annotation [42]	Medical image annotation	Efficient and incentivized crowdsourcing

[Original (created by authors)]

6.5 Current challenges in implementing blockchain in health care and radiology

6.5.1 Overview of blockchain challenges

Blockchain technology faces challenges when it comes to scalability and performance in the healthcare industry. These obstacles arise from the way blockchain systems are structured, which prioritizes both security and decentralization. As the number of transactions increases in decentralized systems (such as blockchain networks), several challenges can arise, including delays and increased costs. These issues stem from the limitations of the underlying consensus mechanisms, network capacity, and scalability.. These limitations can hinder the adoption of blockchain in health care for managing information, supply chains, and other data-intensive applications that require real-time access to information. To overcome these issues, various solutions, such as off-chain transactions and sharding, are being explored. The aim is to enhance scalability without compromising security.

Even though blockchain is renowned for its security, it still has vulnerabilities. The importance of security and privacy in the healthcare sector cannot be overstated, given the nature of patient information. Blockchain design philosophy makes it well suited to address these challenges. However, concerns arise regarding the potential for 51% attacks, which occur when a single entity gains control over the majority of network mining power [13, 49]. Moreover, privacy issues arise due to the nature of blockchain technology; while data is encrypted, the ledger remains accessible to the public. This dilemma emphasizes the need for measures that strike a delicate balance between transparency and privacy, ensuring both data security and confidentiality for patients.

6.5.2 Challenges in medical solutions using blockchain

Managing data in the healthcare industry, particularly when it comes to utilizing blockchain technology, presents challenges due to the need for consistency and compatibility across different medical systems. The healthcare sector generates a range of data, including patient records, clinical trial information, billing details, and other related data. By integrating technology into the healthcare sector, we aim to revolutionize this field by enhancing the sharing, management, and control of data for medical processes like prescribing medication and managing supply chains. Blockchain technology is renowned for its patient-centered approach as it ensures data integrity and protects information from unauthorized changes.

However, implementing technology successfully in the healthcare industry requires overcoming significant obstacles. One key hurdle lies in achieving presentation and transfer of health information across diverse organizations and systems. While blockchain has the potential to enhance interoperability, there needs to be a consensus on data formats, terminologies, and protocols. Additionally, access control methods must be sophisticated enough to safeguard confidentiality while allowing authorized individuals and entities to exchange necessary information [50, 51].

To effectively apply technology in the healthcare sector, it is crucial to carefully consider compliance with healthcare legislation such as HIPAA in the United States and GDPR in the European Union. These regulations ensure that patient health information remains confidential, secure, and accessible [51, 52]. Blockchain's decentralized ledger system offers a framework for protecting patient data and ensuring its authenticity. However, we must address concerns regarding privacy and the right to erasure due to the nature of blockchain ledgers and permanent data preservation.

To integrate blockchain into the healthcare industry's landscape, innovative approaches are required for data management and compliance. Proposed solutions include permissioned blockchains and combining on-chain references with off-chain data storage techniques. These strategies leverage the security and transparency benefits of technology while still upholding privacy and data protection regulations.

6.5.3 Blockchain implementation challenges in healthcare settings

Incorporating blockchain into the current healthcare IT infrastructure poses multiple barriers. An important issue to consider is the compatibility with existing systems, such as EHRs, which require smooth data interchange and immediate access. The specific requirements of healthcare data, such as the vast amount of confidential patient information, make it challenging to apply blockchain technology that was initially created to serve the requirements of other business verticals. Key challenges include system compatibility, data transfer, and the paramount concerns of maintaining the integrity and privacy of medical data [52]. Moreover, the healthcare industry's regulatory environment, including rigorous data protection legislation and standards, necessitates blockchain solutions to possess exceptional compliance and security measures. Furthermore, other stakeholders, such as medical services, doctor suppliers, and insurance payers, not having electronic medical records makes it difficult to transition to the blockchain architecture [13, 53].

Implementing blockchain in healthcare settings has substantial challenges in terms of user engagement and change management. Healthcare personnel may have concerns about adopting new technology, as they prioritize usability, data security, and the integrity of established procedures. Effective methods to promote adoption encompass the implementation of extensive training initiatives; transparent dissemination of the advantages of blockchain technology, such as heightened data protection and operational effectiveness; and active engagement of end users in the development phase to guarantee alignment with their requirements and preferences [13, 53, 54]. To properly manage this transformation, it is crucial to adopt a methodical approach that specifically tackles these concerns and showcases the benefits of blockchain technology in enhancing healthcare outcomes.

6.5.4 Specific challenges in implementing blockchain in radiological settings

Given that imaging files are inherently vast and complicated, managing and storing massive radiological data sets on blockchain networks presents certain challenges. Conventional blockchain systems, which are intended for handling smaller transactional data, have difficulties in terms of scalability and throughput when confronted with the large amount of data generated in radiology [51, 53, 55]. Addressing these problems requires improving blockchain designs to achieve higher scalability, integrating data compression techniques, and investigating hybrid models that utilize blockchain for metadata management while storing the actual image data off-chain. This technique preserves the security and integrity advantages of blockchain while addressing speed limitations. For prompt evaluation and treatment, it is essential to be able to view and analyze radiological data in real time. The decentralized nature of the blockchain provides a structure that allows authorized individuals from numerous locations to securely and promptly access imaging data. Nevertheless, practical implementation of this goal necessitates solving the latency challenges linked to blockchain transactions and guaranteeing the blockchain infrastructure's ability to effectively deal with scenarios with high demand. Improving blockchain protocols to achieve quicker consensus mechanisms and seamlessly integrating with current radiology information systems (RIS) and picture archiving and communication systems (PACS) are possible solutions to allow real-time operations [53, 55]. The integration of blockchain with radiology-specific technology entails harmonizing blockchain's functionalities with the sophisticated demands of radiological processes, including compatibility with various imaging modalities and adherence to medical imaging standards. The challenges encompass guaranteeing smooth integration without causing disruptions to current workflows, offering user-friendly interfaces for radiologists, and adhering to health data directives. The solutions aim to create blockchain-based apps that can seamlessly integrate with conventional radiology software and hardware. These applications should be capable of accommodating the unique data formats and protocols often employed in radiology.

Radiology depends significantly on reliable and consistent data. Any changes in medical images and accompanying metadata stay over a blockchain network could result in compromised patient care. Besides, integrating blockchain with PACS and RIS is challenging and achieving smooth data interchange between blockchain and traditional systems is a work in progress. Finally, blockchain networks must handle a large number of image-sharing transactions. Quick access to photos for accurate diagnoses is the need of the hour for a radiologist. Traditionally, blockchain transactions may create latency, owing to consensus procedures. Balancing security with speed is a delicate trade-off. Scalability alternatives, such as sharding or off-chain channels, require more reliable testing to meet radiology workflow [55].

Radiological pictures are huge files; thus, efficient storage and retrieval are required. Blockchain's decentralized nature can aid in the distribution of picture data across nodes; however, optimizing storage and retrieval techniques is difficult [54]. The integration of blockchain technology in the field of radiology requires careful consideration of regulatory and ethical aspects, especially when it comes to protecting patient privacy and ensuring data security. Blockchain's inherent immutability offers a reliable framework for secure and transparent data management. However, concerns arise regarding patient consent and the ability to modify or delete data in compliance with regulations such as HIPAA and GDPR [49, 54]. To address these challenges, it is crucial to develop innovative approaches for designing blockchain systems that adhere to regulations while leveraging the technology's strengths in terms of security and decentralization.

Table 6.11 presents a summary of the possible solutions offered by blockchain technology in radiology.

TABLE 6.11 Summary of the possible solutions offered by blockchain technology in radiology

Part of the radiology workflow concerned	Challenge	Possible solutions
Data Management and Storage [50, 51]	Managing large volumes of sensitive health data while ensuring privacy and compliance with regulations	Utilize blockchain for secure, decentralized storage solutions; implement advanced encryption and privacy-preserving techniques
Interoperability and System Integration [13, 52]	Difficulty integrating blockchain with existing healthcare IT infrastructures and ensuring seamless data exchange	Develop universal standards for interoperability; adopt middleware solutions to bridge blockchain networks with healthcare systems
Security and Privacy [49, 54]	Ensuring data confidentiality in the storage and exchange of patient data	Incorporate blockchain's immutable and transparent nature for data protection; utilize anonymous signatures and encryption for privacy
Regulatory Compliance [51, 52]	Navigating the complex landscape of healthcare regulations such as HIPAA and GDPR	Develop blockchain systems with built-in compliance mechanisms; engage with regulatory bodies to establish clear guidelines
Scalability and Performance [56, 57]	Blockchain's scalability issues in handling the vast amounts of data generated in health care and radiology	Explore storage optimization and blockchain redesign; adopt sharding, layer-two protocols, and new consensus mechanisms
User Adoption and Training [13, 53]	Resistance to new technology among healthcare professionals and the need for specialized knowledge	Implement comprehensive training programs; foster a culture of innovation and openness to change within healthcare settings
Supply Chain and Treatment Customization [13]	Customization required for individual patient care introduces complexity in supply chain management	Leverage smart contracts for automating agreements and processes; ensure supply chain–wide collaboration among stakeholders
Digital Transformation and Technology Resistance [13, 53]	Resistance to transitioning from traditional systems to blockchain-based solutions	Develop strategies to demonstrate the benefits of blockchain; focus on incremental implementation to ease the transition

[Original (created by authors)]

6.6   Conclusion and path forward

The integration of technology into the healthcare and radiology sectors presents obstacles. These challenges encompass scalability and performance concerns as issues regarding security, privacy, data management, standardization, regulatory compliance, integration with existing healthcare IT systems, and user adoption. In radiology, specifically, there are difficulties to tackle such as the handling and storage of sets of radiological data. It is essential to ensure real-time access and analysis while integrating with radiology technologies. Regulatory and ethical considerations also need attention in this context. Successfully addressing these challenges is pivotal for harnessing the benefits that blockchain technology offers in health care and radiology.

In summary, a collaborative approach that cuts across disciplines is crucial for realizing the power of blockchain technology in health care and radiology. Key areas that require focus include exploring architectures and consensus mechanisms, developing protocols for interoperability of health data, improving data management practices while promoting standardization, and ensuring compliance with regulations. Conducting pilot projects along with proof-of-concept studies will be instrumental in driving user acceptance through training programs and user-centered design methods. In relation to radiology, specifically, it is important to prioritize management of data sets, real-time processing capabilities, and address ethical concerns. Continual research and development efforts in these domains will guarantee that solutions in health care offer scalability, security compliance, and a user-friendly experience.

References

1. S. Aggarwal and N. Kumar, "History of Blockchain-Blockchain 1.0: Currency," in *Advances in Computers*, vol. 121, Elsevier, 2021, pp. 147–169. Accessed: Feb. 21, 2024. [Online]. Available: https://www.sciencedirect.com/science/article/pii/S0065245820300632
2. J. "Joey" Ryan and S. S. Smith, "History of Blockchain," in *The Emerald Handbook of Blockchain for Business*, Emerald Publishing Limited, 2021, pp. 15–29. Accessed: Feb. 21, 2024. [Online]. Available: https://www.emerald.com/insight/content/doi/10.1108/978-1-83982-198-120211004/full/html
3. S. S. Sarmah, "Understanding Blockchain Technology," *Comput. Sci. Eng.*, vol. 8, no. 2, pp. 23–29, 2018.
4. S. K. Panda, A. A. Elngar, V. E. Balas, and M. Kayed, *Bitcoin and Blockchain: History and Current Applications*, CRC Press, 2020. Accessed: Feb. 21, 2024. [Online]. Available: https://books.google.com/books?hl=en&lr=lang_en&id=iYr1Dw AAQBAJ&oi=fnd&pg=PT14&dq=history+of+blockchain&ots=Jq9Hxu-7mt &sig=LhMgW7S9KbWC5TbrjSs5RoqPt3Y
5. H. S. Andrew Fang, "Commercially Successful Blockchain Healthcare Projects: A Scoping Review," *Blockchain Healthc. Today*, vol. 4, 2021, doi: 10.30953/bhty. v4.166.

6. H. S. A. Fang, T. H. Tan, Y. F. C. Tan, and C. J. M. Tan, "Blockchain Personal Health Records: Systematic Review," *J. Med. Internet Res.*, vol. 23, no. 4, p. e25094, Apr. 2021, doi: 10.2196/25094.

7. W. J. Gordon and C. Catalini, "Blockchain Technology for Healthcare: Facilitating the Transition to Patient-Driven Interoperability," *Comput. Struct. Biotechnol. J.*, vol. 16, pp. 224–230, 2018, doi: 10.1016/j.csbj.2018.06.003.

8. A. AbuHalimeh and O. Ali, "Comprehensive Review for Healthcare Data Quality Challenges in Blockchain Technology," *Front. Big Data*, vol. 6, p. 1173620, 2023, doi: 10.3389/fdata.2023.1173620.

9. H. Fatoum, S. Hanna, J. D. Halamka, D. C. Sicker, P. Spangenberg, and S. K. Hashmi, "Blockchain Integration With Digital Technology and the Future of Health Care Ecosystems: Systematic Review," *J. Med. Internet Res.*, vol. 23, no. 11, p. e19846, Nov. 2021, doi: 10.2196/19846.

10. S. E. Chang and Y. Chen, "Blockchain in Health Care Innovation: Literature Review and Case Study From a Business Ecosystem Perspective," *J. Med. Internet Res.*, vol. 22, no. 8, p. e19480, Aug. 2020, doi: 10.2196/19480.

11. A. Hasselgren, K. Kralevska, D. Gligoroski, S. A. Pedersen, and A. Faxvaag, "Blockchain in Healthcare and Health Sciences - A Scoping Review," *Int. J. Med. Inf.*, vol. 134, p. 104040, Feb. 2020, doi: 10.1016/j.ijmedinf.2019.104040.

12. R. Malviya and S. Sundram, *Blockchain for Healthcare 4.0: Technology, Challenges, and Applications*, 1st ed., Boca Raton, CRC Press, 2023. doi: 10.1201/9781003408246.

13. O. Bak, A. Braganza, and W. Chen, "Exploring Blockchain Implementation Challenges in the Context of Healthcare Supply Chain (HCSC)," *Int. J. Prod. Res.*, pp. 1–16, Dec. 2023, doi: 10.1080/00207543.2023.2286491.

14. S. M. Idrees, P. Agarwal, and M. A. Alam, *Blockchain for Healthcare Systems: Challenges, Privacy, and Securing of Data*, 1st ed., Boca Raton, CRC Press, 2021. doi: 10.1201/9781003141471.

15. P. Tagde *et al.*, "Blockchain and Artificial Intelligence Technology in e-Health," *Environ. Sci. Pollut. Res.*, vol. 28, no. 38, pp. 52810–52831, Oct. 2021, doi: 10.1007/s11356-021-16223-0.

16. M. M. Schöner, D. Kourouklis, P. Sandner, E. Gonzalez, and J. Förster, "Blockchain technology in the pharmaceutical industry," *Frankf. Sch. Blockchain Cent. Frankf. Ger.*, 2017, Accessed: Feb. 21, 2024. [Online]. Available: http://explore-ip.com/2017_Blockchain-Technology-in-the-Pharmaceutical-Industry.pdf

17. C. Olsson and M. Toorani, "A permissioned blockchain-based system for collaborative drug discovery," in *ICISSP*, 2021, pp. 121–132. Accessed: Feb. 21, 2024. [Online]. Available: https://pdfs.semanticscholar.org/d35c/5be67a4786486ef9a6b998c4ad65bec8eeca.pdf

18. I. Haq and O. M. Esuka, "Blockchain Technology in Pharmaceutical Industry to Prevent Counterfeit Drugs," *Int. J. Comput. Appl.*, vol. 180, no. 25, pp. 8–12, 2018.

19. R. Kumar and R. Tripathi, "Traceability of counterfeit medicine supply chain through blockchain," in *2019 11th International Conference on Communication Systems & Networks (COMSNETS)*, IEEE, 2019, pp. 568–570. Accessed: Feb. 21, 2024. [Online]. Available: https://ieeexplore.ieee.org/abstract/document/8711418/

20. A. Kumar, D. Choudhary, M. S. Raju, D. K. Chaudhary, and R. K. Sagar, "Combating counterfeit drugs: A quantitative analysis on cracking down the fake drug industry by using blockchain technology," in *2019 9th International Conference on Cloud Computing, Data Science & Engineering (Confluence)*, IEEE, 2019, pp. 174–178. Accessed: Feb. 21, 2024. [Online]. Available: https://ieeexplore.ieee.org/abstract/document/8776891/

21. G. Saldamli, V. Reddy, K. S. Bojja, M. K. Gururaja, Y. Doddaveerappa, and L. Tawalbeh, "Health care insurance fraud detection using blockchain," in *2020 Seventh International Conference on Software Defined Systems (SDS)*, IEEE, 2020, pp. 145–152. Accessed: Feb. 21, 2024. [Online]. Available: https://ieeexplore.ieee.org/abstract/document/9143900/

22. D. Park and D. Ryu, "Blockchain in Health Insurance: Sharing Medical Information and Preventing Insurance Fraud," *Korean J. Financ. Stud.*, vol. 48, no. 4, pp. 417–447, 2019.

23. P. Pandey and R. Litoriya, "Implementing Healthcare Services on a Large Scale: Challenges and Remedies Based on Blockchain Technology," *Health Policy Technol.*, vol. 9, no. 1, pp. 69–78, 2020.

24. Y. Yue and X. Fu, "Research on medical equipment supply chain management method based on blockchain technology," in *2020 International Conference on Service Science (ICSS)*, IEEE, 2020, pp. 143–148. Accessed: Feb. 21, 2024. [Online]. Available: https://ieeexplore.ieee.org/abstract/document/9283738/

25. B. Houtan, A. S. Hafid, and D. Makrakis, "A Survey on Blockchain-Based Self-Sovereign Patient Identity in Healthcare," *IEEE Access*, vol. 8, pp. 90478–90494, 2020.

26. M. Shuaib, S. Alam, M. S. Alam, and M. S. Nasir, "Self-Sovereign Identity for Healthcare Using Blockchain," *Mater. Today Proc.*, vol. 81, pp. 203–207, 2023.

27. S. Schmeelk, M. Kanabar, K. Peterson, and J. Pathak, "Electronic Health Records and Blockchain Interoperability Requirements: A Scoping Review," *JAMIA Open*, vol. 5, no. 3, p. ooac068, Oct. 2022, doi: 10.1093/jamiaopen/ooac068.

28. M. Bak, V. I. Madai, M.-C. Fritzsche, M. T. Mayrhofer, and S. McLennan, "You Can't Have AI Both Ways: Balancing Health Data Privacy and Access Fairly," *Front. Genet.*, vol. 13, p. 929453, 2022, doi: 10.3389/fgene.2022.929453.

29. D. Chen, "Open Data: Implications on Privacy in Healthcare Research," *Blockchain Healthc. Today*, vol. 3, 2020, doi: 10.30953/bhty.v3.144.

30. V. Patel, "A Framework for Secure and Decentralized Sharing of Medical Imaging Data via Blockchain Consensus," *Health Informatics J.*, vol. 25, no. 4, pp. 1398–1411, Dec. 2019, doi: 10.1177/1460458218769699.

31. A. S. Tagliafico *et al.*, "Blockchain in Radiology Research and Clinical Practice: Current Trends and Future Directions," *Radiol. Med. (Torino)*, vol. 127, no. 4, pp. 391–397, Apr. 2022, doi: 10.1007/s11547-022-01460-1.

32. N. S. Ghorashi, M. Rahimi, R. Sirous, and R. Javan, "The Intersection of Radiology With Blockchain and Smart Contracts: A Perspective," *Cureus*, vol. 15, no. 10, p. e46941, Oct. 2023, doi: 10.7759/cureus.46941.

33. European Society of Radiology (ESR), "ESR White Paper: Blockchain and Medical Imaging," *Insights Imaging*, vol. 12, no. 1, p. 82, Jun. 2021, doi: 10.1186/s13244-021-01029-y.

34. S. A. H. Mohsan, A. Razzaq, S. A. K. Ghayyur, H. K. Alkahtani, N. Al-Kahtani, and S. M. Mostafa, "Decentralized Patient-Centric Report and Medical Image Management System Based on Blockchain Technology and the Inter-Planetary File System," *Int. J. Environ. Res. Public. Health*, vol. 19, no. 22, p. 14641, 2022.

35. X. Liao, J. Zhou, and J. Shu, "A blockchain enabled federal domain generalization based architecture for dependable medical image segmentation," in *2022 IEEE 6th Advanced Information Technology, Electronic and Automation Control Conference (IAEAC)*, IEEE, 2022, pp. 1655–1658. Accessed: Feb. 08, 2024. [Online]. Available: https://ieeexplore.ieee.org/abstract/document/9929625/

36. D. R. Ortega, C. M. Oikonomou, H. J. Ding, P. Rees-Lee, Alexandria, and G. J. Jensen, "ETDB-Caltech: A Blockchain-Based Distributed Public Database for Electron Tomography," *PLoS One*, vol. 14, no. 4, p. e0215531, 2019, doi: 10.1371/journal.pone.0215531.

37. M. M. Li and T.-T. Kuo, "Previewable Contract-Based On-Chain X-Ray Image Sharing Framework for Clinical Research," *Int. J. Med. Inf.*, vol. 156, p. 104599, Dec. 2021, doi: 10.1016/j.ijmedinf.2021.104599.
38. M. Noei, M. Parvizimosaed, A. S. Bigdeli, and M. Yalpanian, "A secure hybrid permissioned blockchain and deep learning platform for CT image classification," in *2022 International Conference on Machine Vision and Image Processing (MVIP)*, IEEE, 2022, pp. 1–5. Accessed: Feb. 08, 2024. [Online]. Available: https://ieeexplore.ieee.org/abstract/document/9738736/
39. J. P. Yang Luo, H. Su, T. Wu, and X. Wu, "Collaborative Modeling of Medical Image Segmentation Based on Blockchain Network," 2023, Accessed: Feb. 08, 2024. [Online]. Available: https://itiis.org/journals/tiis/digital-library/manuscript/file/38514/TIIS%20Vol%2017,%20No%203-15.pdf
40. R. Kumar *et al.*, "Blockchain and Homomorphic Encryption Based Privacy-Preserving Model Aggregation for Medical Images," *Comput. Med. Imaging Graph. Off. J. Comput. Med. Imaging Soc.*, vol. 102, p. 102139, Dec. 2022, doi: 10.1016/j.compmedimag.2022.102139.
41. F. Zerka *et al.*, "Blockchain for Privacy Preserving and Trustworthy Distributed Machine Learning in Multicentric Medical Imaging (C-DistriM)," *IEEE Access*, vol. 8, pp. 183939–183951, 2020.
42. J. Witowski *et al.*, "MarkIt: A Collaborative Artificial Intelligence Annotation Platform Leveraging Blockchain For Medical Imaging Research," *Blockchain Healthc. Today*, vol. 4, 2021, doi: 10.30953/bhty.v4.176.
43. J. Randolph, "Blockchain-Based Medical Image Sharing and Critical-result Notification," 2022, Accessed: Feb. 08, 2024. [Online]. Available: https://digitalcommons.kennesaw.edu/msit_etd/11/
44. E. J. De Aguiar, A. J. Dos Santos, R. I. Meneguette, E. Robson, and J. Ueyama, "A Blockchain-Based Protocol for Tracking user Access to Shared Medical Imaging," *Future Gener. Comput. Syst.*, vol. 134, pp. 348–360, 2022.
45. M. Y. Jabarulla and H.-N. Lee, "Blockchain-Based Distributed Patient-Centric Image Management System," *Appl. Sci.*, vol. 11, no. 1, p. 196, 2020.
46. A. Heidari, S. Toumaj, N. J. Navimipour, and M. Unal, "A Privacy-Aware Method for COVID-19 Detection in Chest CT Images using Lightweight Deep Conventional Neural Network and Blockchain," *Comput. Biol. Med.*, vol. 145, p. 105461, Jun. 2022, doi: 10.1016/j.compbiomed.2022.105461.
47. A. H. Mohsin *et al.*, "PSO–Blockchain-Based Image Steganography: Towards a New Method to Secure Updating and Sharing COVID-19 data in Decentralised Hospitals Intelligence Architecture," *Multimed. Tools Appl.*, vol. 80, no. 9, pp. 14137–14161, Apr. 2021, doi: 10.1007/s11042-020-10284-y.
48. R. Kumar *et al.*, "Blockchain-Federated-Learning and Deep Learning Models for COVID-19 Detection Using CT Imaging," *IEEE Sens. J.*, vol. 21, no. 14, pp. 16301–16314, Jul. 2021, doi: 10.1109/JSEN.2021.3076767.
49. Z. Wenhua, F. Qamar, T.-A. N. Abdali, R. Hassan, S. T. A. Jafri, and Q. N. Nguyen, "Blockchain Technology: Security Issues, Healthcare Applications, Challenges and Future Trends," *Electronics*, vol. 12, no. 3, p. 546, Jan. 2023, doi: 10.3390/electronics12030546.
50. S. Khatri, F. A. Alzahrani, M. T. J. Ansari, A. Agrawal, R. Kumar, and R. A. Khan, "A Systematic Analysis on Blockchain Integration With Healthcare Domain: Scope and Challenges," *IEEE Access*, vol. 9, pp. 84666–84687, 2021, doi: 10.1109/ACCESS.2021.3087608.
51. M. Attaran, "Blockchain Technology in Healthcare: Challenges and Opportunities," *Int. J. Healthc. Manag.*, vol. 15, no. 1, pp. 70–83, Jan. 2022, doi: 10.1080/20479700.2020.1843887.

52. E. Gökalp, M. O. Gökalp, S. Çoban, and P. E. Eren, "Analysing Opportunities and Challenges of Integrated Blockchain Technologies in Healthcare," in *Information Systems: Research, Development, Applications, Education*, S. Wrycza and J. Maślankowski, Eds., Lecture Notes in Business Information Processing, vol. 333., Cham, Springer International Publishing, 2018, pp. 174–183. doi: 10.1007/978-3-030-00060-8_13.

53. A. K. Tyagi, S. Dananjayan, D. Agarwal, and H. F. Thariq Ahmed, "Blockchain—Internet of Things Applications: Opportunities and Challenges for Industry 4.0 and Society 5.0," *Sensors*, vol. 23, no. 2, p. 947, Jan. 2023, doi: 10.3390/s23020947.

54. H. Taherdoost, "Blockchain and Healthcare: A Critical Analysis of Progress and Challenges in the Last Five Years," *Blockchains*, vol. 1, no. 2, pp. 73–89, Nov. 2023, doi: 10.3390/blockchains1020006.

55. M. A. Al-Shareeda, M. A. Saare, and S. Manickam, "The blockchain internet of things: review, opportunities, challenges, and recommendations," *Indones. J. Electr. Eng. Comput. Sci.*, vol. 31, no. 3, p. 1673, Sep. 2023, doi: 10.11591/ijeecs.v31.i3.pp1673-1683.

56. S. B. Othman, F. A. Almalki, H. Sakli, "Internet of Things in the Healthcare Applications: Overview of Security and Privacy Issues," in *Intelligent Healthcare*, C. Chakraborty and, M. R. Khosravi, Eds., Singapore, Springer, 2022, doi: 10.1007/978-981-16-8150-9_9

57 K. S. Alqarni, F. A. Almalki, B. O. Soufiene, O. Ali, and F. Albalwy, "Authenticated Wireless Links between a Drone and Sensors Using a Blockchain: Case of Smart Farming," *Wireless Communications and Mobile Computing*, vol. 2022, Article ID 4389729, p. 13, 2022, doi: 10.1155/2022/4389729

7

INTRODUCTION TO BLOCKCHAIN AND ARTIFICIAL INTELLIGENCE IN HEALTH CARE

Prabhjot Kaur, Sonia Dhiman, and Anand Muni Mishra

7.1 Introduction

Blockchain and artificial intelligence (AI) technology are novel developments in the healthcare sector. Data from Google polls that are carried out by multiple regulatory bodies is used to create healthcare indices. "Wellness indices are generated using data from numerous federal regulators' Google polls" [1]. Blockchain technology makes it easier to store the encrypted data that AI needs. Blockchain allows medical professionals to access patient health records, and AI will employ a variety of proposed algorithms, judgmental skills, and vast volumes of data. As a result, by implementing the latest developments, the healthcare process can be less expensive, well structured, and more democratic. Furthermore, cutting-edge technology has enhanced their capacity to manage huge data sets instantaneously, allowing for quicker illness recognition and discovery with automatic comparisons and treatment substitutes. The blockchain technique makes it possible to create and maintain "ledgers," or collections of content, as well as to analyze data securely and automatically [2]. Blockchain facilitates the prediction and analysis of health data. Numerous applications of technology have been demonstrated by research, including the evaluation of medical supply files, digital study with pharmaceutical awareness, the ability to reassemble, and the efficient application of health and therapeutic zones. Payers, healthcare providers, and medical specialists receive instant updates from the collected medical data [3]. This is further improved by blockchain and AI working together. Machines can identify patterns and trends in health thanks to AI. Furthermore, the industry for self-driving cars has proven that

DOI: 10.1201/9781003483113-7

it can use AI to create cars that can drive themselves. On the other hand, some companies are using machine learning to create techniques for identifying fraud and financial risks.

The medical treatment system is composed of three main components: (i) primary providers of medical treatment services, such as doctors, nurses, technicians, and hospital managers; (ii) emergency services; and (iii) consumers of health and health-related services, including individual patients [4]. In this work, we define health maintenance as the set of technology-enabled remote-control services expanded by participating service providers with the goal of advancing, maintaining, or improving the health of beneficiaries. Every year, the medical sector experiences an increase in security and privacy breaches. From 2010 to 2020, up to 37 million records may have been compromised; in 2021, over 300 breaches were disclosed. The increasing digitization of health care has facilitated the recognition of concerns around patient records access, ownership, safe storage, and medical data from related sources [5]. It is advised that blockchain be used to address important problems facing the healthcare industry, such as data protection laws compliance and safe record sharing. Blocks of immutable data that may be strongly traded without the involvement of third parties are stored in a particular type of database called a blockchain, which may be managed by a network of verified users, or nodes. Data is registered and stored using cryptographic signatures and consensus techniques, which are used as essential facilitators in their use [6, 7]. One of the main goals of utilizing blockchain technology (BCT) is data preservation, especially in the healthcare industry where a large volume of data is shared and disseminated.

The advancement of blockchain technology and its implementation in diverse settings have reached various phases of realization. The usage of smart contracts in sectors such as finance and real estate occupied the second phase of blockchain development, whereas cryptocurrencies occupied the first [8, 9]. The third stage of development concentrated on applying blockchain to non-financial industries like government, health care, and culture. Additionally, blockchain technology is in its fourth generation of evolution, thanks to the development of AI and cutting-edge technical capabilities like data immutability. The capacity of blockchain to create decentralized and trust-less transaction environments explains the aforementioned diversity in its application spectrum. Blockchain is a great fit for the healthcare industry because it can address important problems like automated claim authentication and public health management. Patients may now own their data and choose who can access it, thanks to technology that solves problems with data ownership and sharing [10]. Simultaneously, it facilitates the secure integration, modification, sharing, and timely retrieval of recorded data by appropriate authorities through consensus protocols. This is a big advantage of using this technology in the healthcare system because the way things are now done requires data to be stored by third parties. Lastly, due to the possibility of human mistakes, blockchain may enhance data management procedures' accountability; hence, lowering the possibility of improperly managing or abusing recorded data [11]. In light of the promising implications of blockchain technology for social and commercial transformation—a departure from preconceived notions—it seems that this is a debate over its inherent and secondary benefits.

According to a recent study, regardless of the widespread perception that blockchain technology's benefits might have been overstated, corporations will likely take a cautiously pragmatic approach and invest a significant amount of money in the future. It may be asserted that the hype surrounding this technology has not yet materialized. This may be because blockchains are being adopted widely, especially due to regulatory obstacles and other difficulties [12]. The lack of knowledge among the general public and some users, such as doctors or patients, about blockchain technology, its benefits for data processing, and its workings is another major barrier to the widespread adoption of blockchain. Organizational, societal, and implementation challenges—like security or governance issues—may prevent this technology from developing to the full extent expected during the planned stages of business transformation [13]. Widespread misconceptions over the application of blockchain systems to government regulations and law enforcement might worsen this. Current research endeavors are to facilitate the operational growth of blockchain technology and expedite its adoption by eliminating these challenges.

Launched in 2009, blockchain is a technology and architecture platform. Blockchain technology stores data in record ledgers that are dispersed throughout all of the computer systems that make up the blockchain infrastructure in a decentralized fashion. Peer-to-peer architecture is made up of network users, who engage in transactions, and blockchain miners, who assist in moving transactions forward in a distributed record [14]. The record is maintained in a distributed system of units that are constructed by the computation of cryptographic operations by each network participant. As seen in Figure 7.1, blockchain maintains anonymity and stores all data in a general, distributed way while providing a wealth of sophisticated features consisting of nonrepudiation, security, integrity, and traceability.

Blockchain applications can be found in the government, real estate, banking, and finance industries. While the fields of banking and finance have attracted more investigation, blockchain-enabled applications in health care have only lately begun to get greater interest. Numerous scholars have emphasized how blockchain technology may be used to solve current problems in healthcare applications [15]. Blockchain eliminates the requirement for a third party to mediate transactions between entities. It depends on validators—typically miners—who take the place of the middlemen and perform

FIGURE 7.1   Blockchain and healthcare relation.

[Original (created by authors)]

decentralized transaction validation. This is accomplished using a distributed consensus, which is the capacity of several untrusting persons to agree on anything. Within the realm of cryptocurrency, this computational issue is associated with the double-spending problem, which is how to verify that a given quantity of a virtual currency has not been used up without permission from a trustworthy third party (often a bank), which keeps records of every transaction and user balances.

The rest of the chapter is described as follows: Section 2 explains the healthcare applications, Section 3 discusses the applications related to blockchain, the need for blockchain in health care is explained in Section 4, some security issues of blockchain are discussed in Section 5, and block-chain technologies in health care are discussed in Section 6. The use of blockchain in health care is discussed in Section 7 along with benefits in Section 8 and some applications in Section 9. Section 10 concludes the chapter.

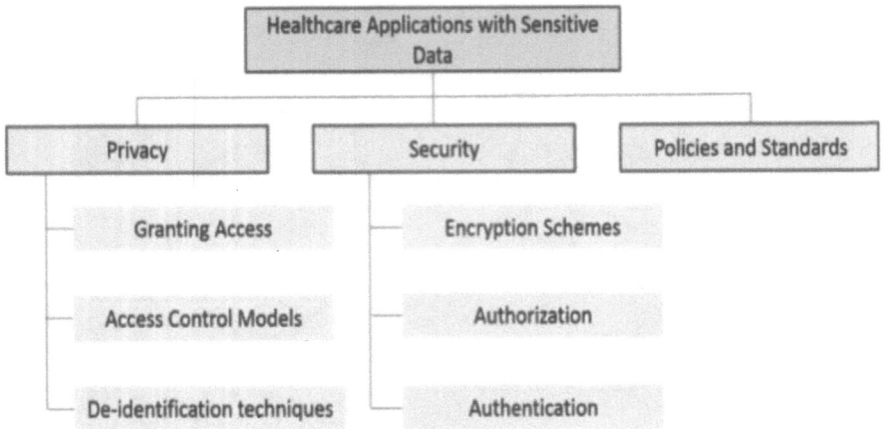

FIGURE 7.2 Healthcare applications requirements.

[Original (created by authors)]

7.2 Healthcare applications

The security and privacy of patient medical information is a special concern for the healthcare industry because of additional regulatory obligations. Recordkeeping and data sharing have become increasingly widespread in the internet age due to the use of mobile medical equipment and cloud-based storage, but there is also a higher chance of malicious attacks and the possibility that shared personal data could be exposed. Patients are visiting several doctors and have easier access to health information through smart devices, which raises concerns about data sharing and privacy [15, 16]. The healthcare sector is confronted with distinct demands, including those related to identification, interoperability, data sharing, medical record transfer, and mobile health issues, shown in Figure 7.2 and discussed below.

7.2.1 Data sharing

With civilian health records, there are intrinsic security issues as well as data-sharing and access concerns. Sharing medical records can be challenging at times since a person's complete medical data may be kept in multiple places. Healthcare practitioners also lack access to the most recent patient data if the records are situated elsewhere; thus, patients do not get a unified view of these dispersed records [17]. Healthcare records are spread across multiple hospitals, making record linkage—the idea of merging databases based on components that may or may not have a common identity, such as a Social Security number—challenging.

7.2.2 Data security

Major security needs for healthcare and medical data include access controls, authentication, and nonrepudiation of records. The availability, confidentiality, and integrity of medical data are all supported by these standards. To develop medical information, medical records, such as patient files, can be merged with medical data from body sensors and other apps [14, 18]. The transition of medical records from paper to digital format necessitates the implementation of role-based privileges and extra security measures to safeguard patient data. Furthermore, there may be problems with the protection of personal health information and healthcare data, including digital health records, or EHRs and EMRs, or PHRs, if different encryption standards are used in different systems. Disseminating a patient's medical records can have practical repercussions, and current measures to secure and protect documents have shown to be ineffective [19].

7.2.3 Interoperability

Interoperability is just another prerequisite that the healthcare industry must meet. Interoperability is the capacity to share and transfer data between several sources. Interoperability is primarily hampered by the use of centralized data storage in medical facilities. All data are kept in a single central database, or databank, which presents issues for healthcare practitioners using centralized data storage [20]. Patient agency, fragmented health information, poor availability of health information, lack of system compatibility, and data quantity and quality for medical studies are some of the specific problems that result from centralised storage of data. Many hospital data are created and maintained in one single area on a daily basis. If records are scattered throughout multiple institutions and disappear, patients will not be able to access the information [21]. A large number of records become dispersed as a result of the consolidated health recordkeeping system. Centralized data authority are required to supply a trustworthy database on an unreliable network.

7.2.4 Data access/mobility

Mobility is becoming a more crucial demand in the medical field since patients want their information to be portable as they are becoming increasingly mobile. The capability to transfer data becomes more crucial as the number of sensors, smart devices, and various internet-enabled gadgets increases. The difficulty of guaranteeing that data are safe and safeguarded by legal requirements is further exacerbated by the requirement for instantaneous data exchange and accessibility on any device from any location [22]. A rapidly expanding area of healthcare applications is mobile health, which makes use of gadgets like ubiquitous smartphones, body-area wireless networks with low power, and miniature sensors. Numerous problems with the widely used consolidated server architecture in health care also affect mHealth. Particular issues include user trust, access control, authentication, consent management, and data sharing. It requires significant resources to achieve security and protection in Internet of Things (IoT) or wireless sensor network (WSN), yet improper handling and compromised medical data may hurt the patient as well as future hopes for mobile health solutions.

Another kind of technology with possible security problems is wearable technology, which has uses in health care. Wearable technology raises unique privacy issues related to the sensitivity of health information and legal protection [23]. Privacy risks with sensors, gadgets, and smart technology include information disclosure, withholding services or information, non-audibility, altering information, repudiation, and loss of validity or authenticity. A wireless body area network (WBAN) deployment might include wearable body sensors. Among the security issues connected to WBAN deployments include data integrity, freshness, network availability, dependability, authentication, secure localization, secure management, flexibility, and accountability. Because WBAN devices are probably resource-constrained, it will be necessary to implement lightweight security solutions. Wearable health technology also carries additional risks, such as distorted data, malfunctioning or breaking devices, and data manipulation by users for their gain. Serious or even deadly health concerns could arise from an effective breach of essential equipment, including embedded healthcare devices that deliver insulin, which is a life-saving drug [2, 20].

IoT technology is spreading throughout the healthcare sector as more and more customers are eager to take an active role while making health-related decisions. In addition, patients have become more eager to participate actively in personalizing their treatment. One approach to individualizing health care and therapy is through smart sensors and smart devices that gather and send crucial medical information to the patient's physician, enabling them to monitor and assess chronic conditions remotely [24]. There are two types of assaults against wireless IoT systems: active and passive. When an attacker may change the destination of data packets or interfere with the routing protocols while they are being routed through the system, this is known as a passive attack. Active assaults occur when a hacker actively seeks for, steals, modifies, or obtains user data by taking advantage of a device or network vulnerability. A malevolent actor may employ many techniques to procure medical data from IoT devices, including data alteration, impersonation, eavesdropping, and playback, all aimed at obtaining confidential information from the target. Administrator security, physical security, information security, and general system security are some of the specific security flaws that hackers can take advantage of [10].

Particular privacy concerns that IoT applications for health care face include query privacy, location privacy, footprint privacy, owner privacy, and identity privacy. Privacy concerns are also present for third-party cloud providers when it comes to health record exchange between various healthcare facilities. Access control of patient data and medical information utilized and maintained by outside service providers is the subject of these privacy concerns. IoT technologies provide privacy risks due to inference attacks in addition to access control privacy implications. Malicious actors carry out inference attacks by combining data mining and wireless eavesdropping techniques to determine the significance of a given signal or message [25]. Wireless networks and IoT applications give rise to further privacy concerns. Among these worries is the possibility that, in an emergency, "healthcare data, such as a heart rate monitor, can be gained from the individual without the consent of the person." Concerning the distribution of critical information and its storage requirements, this topic poses privacy-related considerations. Until such concerns about privacy are resolved and patients can rest easy knowing that their records are safe in cloud-based infrastructures, such solutions are probably going to be widely used.

7.3 Blockchain applications

Blockchain has a wide range of applications across numerous industries that can take advantage of its inherent characteristics and technology. Applications are distinct from features in that the former are procedures that may be used with blockchain technology to meet new needs, while the latter are aspects of the system itself [7, 13]. Fraud detection, identity verification, and smart contracts are some of the applications that will be covered. These three applications shown in Figure 7.3 were investigated for the paper's objectives because of their potential to address the healthcare-related problems covered in the preceding section.

7.3.1 Smart contracts

One important use of blockchain technology is smart contracts, which allow a user or agent to utilize the blockchain to produce a legal document. Smart contracts, which are autonomous agents stored in blockchain technology, encapsulate transactions and convert them into contracts or other legal documents in order to perform legal services [26]. These scripts, known as smart contracts, are stored on the blockchain and have unique addresses that allow for their location and validation. In a decentralized way, smart contracts

Fraud Detection

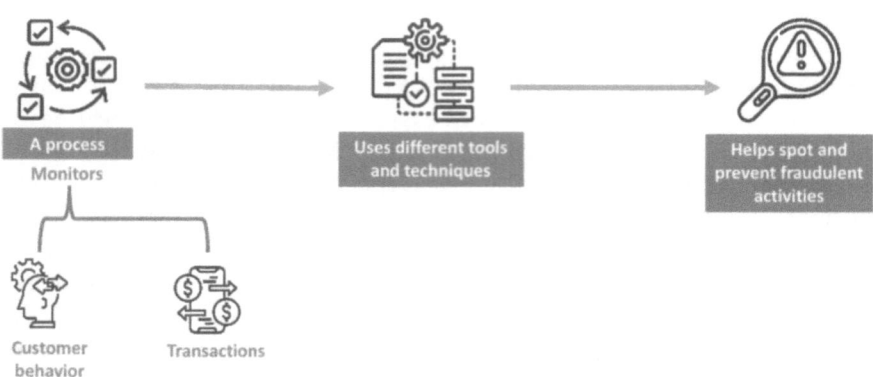

FIGURE 7.3 Applications of blockchain.
[Original (created by authors)]

offer a way to minimize contact between parties and guarantee fair exchange. The capacity to create documents alone, without the assistance of a notary or legal advisor, eliminates considerable time and expense obstacles and facilitates more efficient resource transfer.

7.3.2 Fraud detection

The identification of fraud is yet another use for blockchain. Validating a record or additional information source to find any instances of data tampering or other malicious activities is known as fraud detection. Examples of this include stopping the introduction of false reviews into online review platforms through vote stuffing and bad-mouthing, as well as fact-based fraud in the financial sector through loan applications [27]. A further field of research in fraud detection focuses on the relatively new idea of crowdsourcing. In order to acquire capital for a business, crowdfunding is a tactic used to convince a significant number of people to invest money or buy shares from the organization. Blockchain technology could be applied to crowdfunding by streamlining purchases and transferring equity more quickly, securely, and affordably. It can also be utilized as a low-cost platform.

7.3.3 Identity verification

Outside of the healthcare sector, other internet companies have discovered a variety of techniques for identity verification. Nowadays, a lot of companies and the governments utilize fingerprints and passports to identify people.

Although the government prepares and verifies all documentation, blockchain technology offers an alternative to government-sponsored identity verification [23]. Blockchain technology can confirm a user's identification with parties other than the government. Using blockchain technology to notarize contracts for businesses, marriages, and birth certificates is one example of this application. By utilizing the distributed ledger feature of the blockchain, an individual can demonstrate their existence at a specific location and time, and this can be independently verified by several users.

7.4   The need for blockchain in health care

Health care is one industry wherein blockchain is considered to hold a lot of value. Transforming health care requires giving data management, which benefits from connecting disparate systems and increasing EHR accuracy, top priority. Prescription medication management, supply chain management, pregnancy, and any related concerns can all be handled with blockchain technology. It can also be used to handle data exchange, access control, and the maintenance of an audit trail of medical procedures. Clinical trials, medical billing, contracting, medical record sharing, provider credentialing, and anti-counterfeiting medications are further healthcare domains that stand to gain from blockchain technology [11, 28]. A patient-centric approach is made possible by the transformation of healthcare services. Healthcare solutions built on blockchain technology have the potential to improve patient data security and dependability by giving people authority over their medical information.

The storing of patient medical data is essential in the healthcare sector. Due to their high level of sensitivity, cyberattacks frequently target sensitive data. It is essential to guarantee the security of any sensitive data. Another element is control over data, which is something the patient should ideally handle. Therefore, sharing and gaining access to control over patient healthcare data is another use case that can benefit from state-of-the-art modern technologies. Blockchain technology offers many access control mechanisms and is incredibly resilient to failures and attacks. Blockchain thus offers a solid foundation for medical data.

7.5   Security issues of blockchain technology

Blockchain has many uses in the healthcare sector that help researchers crack the genetic code by managing the drug supply chain, permitting the safe transmission of patient medical data, and enabling the secure transfer of patient medical records. The descriptions emphasize decentralization, immutability, and cryptography, all of which look secure because of the confidence that data is rarely altered without the knowledge of other participants

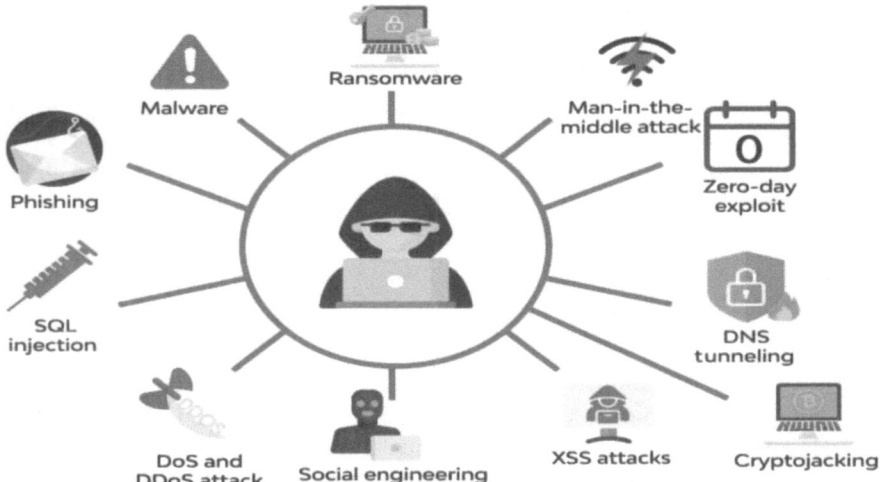

FIGURE 7.4 Types of attacks.

[Original (created by authors)]

and cryptographic security. The implementation of the data security system requires crypto graphical methods [29]. This does not imply that securities fraud and cyberattacks cannot occur on the blockchain. Due to its multi-disciplinary composite nature, extensive study, and numerous security incidents, blockchain technology is gradually exposing its security weaknesses at all levels.

Blockchain-based healthcare systems are small-scale centralized and EHRs are now kept digitally. Since blockchain technology will greatly benefit end users, numerous fund providers, medical researchers, and health ministries will need to work together to continue making blockchain technology a success. This will alter the healthcare industry.

There are numerous significant blockchain security issues and solutions shown in Figure 7.4.

- **51% Attacks:** The main duty of miners is to verify the transaction request and package data so they can investigate the next block in further detail. Since it has the potential to change the entire blockchain, a 51% attack is perhaps the riskiest in the blockchain sector. These attacks are more likely to happen early in the chain when there are not enough miners. To prevent 51% assaults, raise the hash rate, enhance mining pool supervision, and stay away from proof-of-work (PoW) consensus processes.
- **Sybil Attacks:** In a Sybil attack, cybercriminals fabricate fictitious network nodes and overwhelm the target network with phony identities, causing a system meltdown and obstructing chain transactions. Use the proper

consensus techniques, keep an eye on other nodes' activities, and look for nodes that are only forwarding blocks from a single user to prevent Sybil attacks [30].

- **Phishing Attacks:** Phishing assaults are becoming increasingly frequent on blockchain systems and are generating real problems. A phishing assault aims to obtain the user's credentials for the hacker. They are able to send phony emails that seem real to the wallet key owner. Obtain the qualifications and other information while the user submits their log-in credentials through a joined bogus hyperlink. By installing trustworthy anti-malware software or malicious link detection software and maintaining system and software updates, you may strengthen the security of your browser and device [15, 31]. To prevent phishing attempts, avoid turning on Wi-Fi when using an electronic wallet or other sensitive information, and do not click on unexpected URLs.
- **Routing Attacks:** Routing assaults are the next major safety and confidentiality concern in the field of blockchain. The anonymity of an account can be used by hackers to intercept data that is transferred to internet service providers (ISPs). The risk is that, frequently, these attacks will reveal assets or private information without the victim's knowledge. Users need to use strong passwords, protect their personal information, and change passwords often; employ secure routing mechanisms (with certificates); and self-educate about the hazards associated with information security to reduce routing assaults.
- **Role in Health Care:** A centralized institution is tasked with overseeing, directing, and monitoring the whole network under an organized architecture, like the one found in most EHR systems. AI is capable of carrying out intricate computational tasks and quickly analyzing vast volumes of patient data.

Though AI has demonstrated that it can execute many dynamic and cognitive tasks more quickly than a person, some doctors are still hesitant to use AI to affect a patient's well-being. Additionally, a survey conducted as part of a recent study found that the utilization of health services is inversely correlated with distance [32]. These days, blockchain and AI are the two technologies that have each shown promise for expansion in the healthcare sector.

The scientific community has expressed interest in the field of applying these techniques to the data processing of EHRs. On the other hand, the medical industry has seen a rise in the use of blockchain. To prevent the malicious alteration of patient records, it addresses the interoperability problems with the current EHR frameworks. Real-time AI solutions for clinical decision support systems and population health management are currently being used by a number of EHR-based programs, including Epic [33], to predict readmissions to hospitals, deaths, and patient deterioration.

Likewise, patients now have access to a blockchain-based platform known as MedRec. Researchers have used a variety of strategies based on blockchain and AI techniques to explore the aforementioned results. Several features allow the health sector to evaluate data at a high standard, but they also seriously compromise data security and limit the ability of experts to access their data for a limited period [31]. This report's main goal is to highlight the expert's contributions to give readers a better understanding of the function and effectiveness of AI blockchain in EHR systems. With a focus on AI and IoT that has not been combined before, this study assesses the impacts, suggests a study topic, and looks at the use of blockchain in agriculture, food, and health. Additionally, new technologies can now handle vast amounts of data better.

7.6 Blockchain technologies in health care

Applications for blockchain technology could be found in many different domains, such as finance, electricity, real estate, health care, social media, mathematics, transportation, entertainment, rights protection, government, nonprofit, technology, human resources, retail, education, and agriculture. We will talk about the three main uses of blockchain here, as well as how crucial it is to increasing life's value. Blockchain offers the medical industry a lot of benefits. For each patient, the technology has created a decentralized environment. Although this technology has not yet gained considerable traction in the industry, it will soon be widely used [34]. Patients' data is never discussed, nor where it goes after the hospital receives it nor how much is given to them for future use. Furthermore, carrying all of the reports at all times is not feasible. To steer clear of this predicament, technology has given rise to certain novel aspects of patient data reservation.

- **EHR (Digitalization):** Keeping track of each patient's information on paper is an extremely difficult and disorganized task. It is not anticipated for anyone to recall the specifics of every test, medical problem, allergy, and other conditions that the same person has, and any inaccuracy in the data could have disastrous consequences. In an emergency, testing the patient's body can waste a lot of time, and it might take longer to heal them until the report is received [34]. An EHR, which includes a patient's medical history, diagnosis, prescriptions, treatment plans, dates of immunizations, allergies, radiographic pictures, and laboratory and test results, is one technological solution to this issue. It enables the patient to have easier and more comfortable therapy by giving them access to the treating physician.
- **Laboratory Information System:** Allows medical professionals to examine all the data related to the patient's lab findings. The provider can examine

and study the test results to continue further treatment, regardless of the location of the test.

- **Diagnostic Imaging Repositors:** Allow the doctors to examine the diagnostic findings wherever the testing clinic is located and allow the providers to see and read the reports.
- **Drug Information System:** Protects the patient's past medication history [5].
- **Telehealth:** The method of providing health care when a patient and the clinic are in different places.
- **Privacy:** Confidentiality of the patient's information.

Utilizing EHRs is safe and secure. It is decentralized, nearly hard to temper, and extremely safe across nodes because it is based on blockchain technology. Every network node stores the hash function of the previous block in the chain, preventing outsiders from attempting to temper or block data through the snowball effect [16]. So, it will not take long to identify the tempered data. Since each node has a copy of the data and can download and store a copy of the file on its own, no data will be lost. A person's medical record is entirely safe and secure, even when it is stored on the blockchain. The patient may disclose the data by their wishes, without requiring the health institution's consent. The patient data will be their property. If you provide people with little incentives, you can inspire an increasing number of others to join this chain. A person may be eligible for rewards for managing their health well and taking good care of it. Additionally, you receive rewards for supplying your data for research projects [35]. Drug supply via blockchain technology can benefit pharmacies. Some scammers operate in the middle, stealing drugs from suppliers and sellers, and then reselling them illegally or at higher costs. A safe transaction between the buyer and seller can be made possible using blockchain. The miners would handle conducting all background checks and finalizing the purchase. Peer-to-Peer (P2P) connectivity will guarantee the medication's tracking until delivery.

7.7 The use of blockchain in health care

The healthcare sector has consistently been one of the most popular study fields over the past few decades, with new and more dependable solutions to support the sector as well as the community being found. Practitioners, medical experts, hospitals, therapists, patients, payers, and other stakeholders must all manage, access, and share health records in a safe, interoperable manner without modifying them. To confirm the authenticity of records, data provenance is also required. Blockchain technology can address some of the main issues the healthcare sector is currently facing and is being applied in a variety of scenarios [36]. However, more focused research is needed to put this technology to use in real-time applications. These are only a few of the health sector's uses for this technology.

Healthcare stakeholders may exchange data, preserve records, and authorize devices decentralized with the help of the MedRec platform. It is possible for patients to save their data and grant or deny access to their information. Because the logs, permissions, and records are exclusively saved on this blockchain and are pointers to data storage sites, this system offers complete confidentiality [6]. The Ethereum blockchain is being used by Gem to introduce the Gem Health Network in association with Philips Blockchain Lab. The purpose of this framework is to handle operating expenses. Better patient care is facilitated by interoperability among different providers who may access the same information, thanks to this shared infrastructure [8]. The guard time healthcare platform in Estonia facilitates direct communication between the healthcare provider and the patient. Guard Time Blockchain ensures safe, reliable, and auditable records by enabling transparent information sharing between the patient, doctor, and payer [9]. Research groups require the health data of their patients. In this regard, Health Bank has been offering patients a way to store and exchange their health information with research groups, which can be utilized for both pharmaceutical and scholarly purposes. Additionally, patients are receiving financial rewards from this platform for their contributions [18] developed an access control system for blockchain-based data sharing (BBDS) that is permission based. Data owners use a shared data pool to access their EMRs. This scalable and secure system offers an edge over HDG (Healthcare Data Gateways) by using digital signatures and cryptographic keys for user identification, authentication, and authorization.

7.8   Blockchain benefits

Since the launch of Bitcoin 10 years ago, other iterations of blockchain have been made available. Financial transactions are how blockchain technology was applied to digital assets. Among the industries with the greatest promise and focus is health care [19, 20]. Blockchain technology is altering governance and data management methods in healthcare applications. This is mainly because of its flexibility and unique way of securing, segmenting, and sharing medical data and services. Numerous current advancements in the healthcare industry are being driven by blockchain technology [21]. Current systems are not compatible with external systems and mainly transfer medical data inside the healthcare and medical areas. On the other hand, the evidence indicates that incorporating these systems into better standard, networked health care has several advantages, such as networking with different organizations and health informatics scholars [1]. Among the biggest issues faced by the health sector is securely handling the enormous volumes of medical information produced by regular business workings and transactions, as well as service delivery. Most of the healthcare data is useless; difficult to handle, understand, and exchange; and not standardized across systems [13].

Data security is a major concern for the healthcare sector. The antiquated IT architecture of the majority of healthcare organizations leaves them vulnerable to malware and other assaults. Sensitive health data is stored centrally. Blockchain technology can assist the healthcare industry in going digital by making it easier to share, process, manage, and minimize security risks related to data [23]. Furthermore, the development of computer programs, strategic planning, and infrastructure necessary for the healthcare industry to securely, reliably, and safely combine the many data sets at its disposal is still in its early stages.

The basic ideas of blockchain technology are illustrated in this section to help readers better grasp the remaining portions of the article. According to [7], a blockchain takes into account several kinds of digital ledgers, which, in order to safely store the data, are concurrently copied to multiple positions on a related system. A much-specified definition of distributed ledger technology (DLT) is blockchain's, which are databases that are simultaneously maintained across numerous sites. According to [8], each data block in the blockchain has a pointer to the previous data block in addition to its content. The blockchain is a network of linked data blocks that are connected via pointers in a shared record, each of which is represented by a hash address.

Patients and healthcare professionals can now communicate more easily and benefit from various benefits thanks to blockchain technology in the health sector. To increase the effectiveness and efficiency of healthcare systems, the healthcare industry is focusing its efforts on utilizing contemporary technologies [37]. We illustrate the significant blockchain benefits in the healthcare industry in this section, as shown in Figure 7.5.

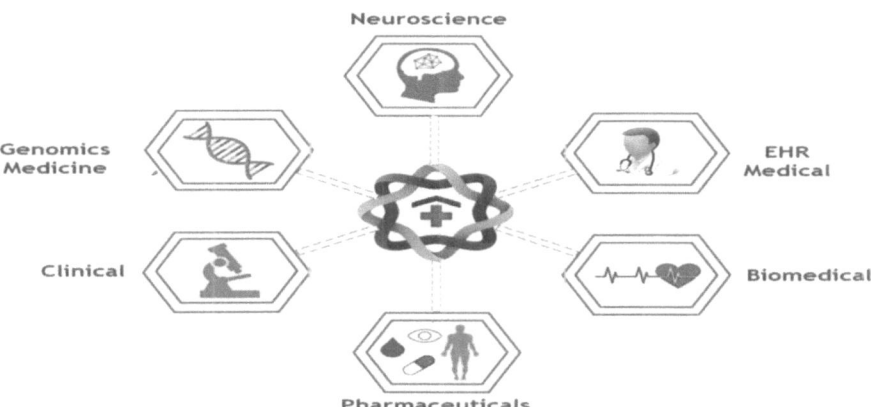

FIGURE 7.5 Blockchain benefits in the field of health care.

[Original (created by authors)]

7.8.1 Decentralization

In contrast to conventional databases, which are overseen by a single individual, a blockchain is a decentralized network similar to a timestamped record sheet and is encrypted to prevent deception and manipulation. When we talk about decentralization in relation to blockchain, we mean the movement of decision-making power from a central organization over a decentralized network. What makes this technology so important is its decentralized storage architecture, which improves data authentication and system security [38].

Each block also contains the transaction data, a timestamp, and the cryptographic hash of the previous block. It also contains the history of all previous blocks and transactions, which may be used to build a network or chain. Any change to any block's data sets off a series of events that could eventually cause the blockchain as a whole to freeze. Every machine connected to the network will lock simultaneously once the blockchain has processed the data, creating an irreversible record of the data. Every blockchain system specifies who can add blocks to the network as an alter authority and how this is done [28]. Once the information is placed in a certain block in the database, it is not feasible to edit or modify the data.

7.8.2 Trust and transparency

All participants will have access to the updated blockchain after the new block has been correctly added to the system. A data block is not added to the blockchain; instead, it is destroyed if it is faulty. Participants use consensus techniques as validation mechanisms to confirm that a data block is legitimate. By using consensus techniques, participants can quickly agree on the validity of the data block [39]. On the blockchain, data that has been captured and stored is visible to potential users and is rapidly updated. The transparency of the blockchain may make it more difficult for data to be lost or altered.

7.8.3 Security and privacy

A technique that shields data and transaction information in a block against external, internal, malevolent, or accidental threats is referred to as blockchain. It is common practice to identify and mitigate risks and provide relevant solutions to threats by utilizing IT and security policies, tools, and services. The capacity of an investor or organization to distinguish itself from other data and hence be able to communicate in a recognizable way is referred to as blockchain privacy. It is the ability to do transactions while divulging private information. By exercising cautious self-divulgation, users can also maintain compliance [40].

7.8.4   Availability and robustness

The blockchain structure is secure. As a result of its lack of centralized ownership and uniform block storage of medical data throughout the network, it lacks a single point of failure [41]. Without a central authority, many-to-one traffic flows are eliminated and all participating nodes' resources are used to ensure flexibility and resilience. This approach solves the issue of a single-phase failure and does away with delays as well.

7.8.5   Verifiability

The blockchain ensures the accuracy and integrity of the data, which can be verified even in the absence of the plaintext of the corresponding records. This feature is useful in the healthcare industry when processing insurance claims and managing the pharmaceutical supply chain require the verification of records [42]. Digital ledger software makes all healthcare data readily verifiable and available to all network users by enabling multiple sharing repetitions among all nodes on the blockchain. Blockchain automatically updates itself after a predefined amount of time to ensure the integrity of data and file synchronization.

7.9   Application in health care

7.9.1   Blockchain layer approach

The blockchain, apps, consensus, smart contracts, and transactions form the technological foundation of the blockchain's layers. These components are divided into several groups that correspond to the blockchain ecosystem.

7.9.2   Data management

A system to facilitate the safe and dependable management, distribution, and aggregation of EHR data has been established to embrace a patient-focused strategy to storing medical records, in addition to ensuring patient privacy and security with relation to the medical record handling demands, such as the patient-specified authorization policy [43]. They suggest a blockchain technology that permits authorized EHR data integration and sharing. In order to address issues with permission management, digital rights management, data management, data integrity, and data sharing, the MedRec system for medical data access and permission administration was proposed. The three different types of smart contracts that the authors used to manage the preferably massive count of record representations were patient-provider relationship (PPR) contracts, registrar contracts (RCs), and summary contracts (SCs) [44].

In a distinct study that was published, [45] presented a blockchain-based medical information exchange network. They also created a novel two-layer consortium blockchain and a procedure for anonymous information exchange. The security and dependability of users' exchange of medical records are enhanced by this technique. To prevent any manipulation or misuse, the data and transaction logs are thus kept in a dispersed manner. Demonstration of a smart contract–based remote healthcare system proposes a processing system for efficiently and sparingly storing medical device data in accordance with patients' health conditions [46]. To be more precise, they filter the sensor data before deciding whether or not to enter it onto the blockchain.

[47] has developed a mechanism for storing healthcare information and accelerating critical clinical working in addition to creating an access system based on smart contracts that permits communication between patients and providers. Additionally, Ethereum-based healthcare administration technologies are used in this study. By incorporating digital contracts into internet of medical things (IoMT) applications in e-healthcare, [7] proposed an efficient way to reduce the middlemen throughout the sharing of patient or medical records. They examine an IoMT-related service scenario as well.

7.9.3 Data security and privacy

Some authors established a secure and private healthcare system by implementing a blockchain-based Secure Healthcare System (SHS) architecture. This study confirms that the deployment of blockchain technology in SHSs may effectively address the problems and obstacles encountered by traditional SHSs. Additionally, the architecture of this system is proposed. [48] propose and develop an access control model for IoT-enabled smart healthcare devices and the medical system using blockchain-based smart contracts. Additionally, they build a plan on a private Ethereum blockchain.

The approach of research takes into account the entire medical system. To illustrate the selected dispersed and patient-focused intelligent contract–based authorization system, an example use case is given [6]. The authors also suggest a proactive smart contract–based distributed access control system.

A blockchain-based remote health monitoring (RHM) system was described by [26]. In order to safely communicate patient data with doctors without the data passing via other services, this study makes use of Tor disguised data off-chain delivery services. Based on several threat instances, the essay provides an evaluation of the security of the solution. The suggested new decentralized access control system described in [49] is based on the Tangle and gives users control over who can access their assets. The program verifies the work and it is checked using Automated Validation of Internet Security Protocols and Applications (AVISPA) tools, which validate security even while an attacker is present.

7.10   Conclusion

In conclusion, there may be uses for blockchain technology to assist in tackling a few of the current problems the healthcare industry is facing. The most thoroughly researched applications of blockchain technology in the healthcare sector include security, integrity, decentralization, availability, and authentication principles because of the general ledger and block-related infrastructure. These applications hold the greatest promise. The healthcare sector is having trouble keeping up with the rapidly advancing technology infrastructure that is centered on smart, internet-enabled IoT and sensing gadgets. Although these technologies make it easier for the healthcare industry to serve patients in a world where connections are growing daily, attackers can also take benefit from the flaws in such innovations, as well as in the actions of users and processes, to gain access and copy information, thereby making it more challenging for hospitals to exchange records. This could result in outdated data, which could lead to problems with health or inaccurate diagnosis, and even problems verifying a patient's identity. The chapter claims that this study has presented a number of use examples for the application of blockchain technology in the healthcare sector and will also cover techniques with potential applications in the field in the future. However, insufficient research and prototype implementations exist to assess the efficiency of these usage scenarios. The analysis also highlights the current state of the art for creating blockchain-based medical applications, along with any gaps in the field and prospective directions for future research.

References

1. Vyas S, Shabaz M, Pandit P, Parvathy LR, Ofori I. Integration of artificial intelligence and blockchain technology in healthcare and agriculture. Journal of Food Quality. 2022 May 28; 2022: 11. https://doi.org/10.1155/2022/4228448
2. Gorkhali A, Li L, Shrestha A. Blockchain: A literature review. Journal of Management Analytics. 2020 Jul 2;7(3):321–43.
3. Conoscenti M, Vetro A, De Martin JC. Blockchain for the Internet of Things: A systematic literature review. In 2016 IEEE/ACS 13th International Conference of Computer Systems and Applications (AICCSA) 2016 Nov 29 (pp. 1–6). IEEE.
4. Lin WC, Chen JS, Chiang MF, Hribar MR. Applications of artificial intelligence to electronic health record data in ophthalmology. Translational Vision Science & Technology. 2020 Jan 28;9(2):13.
5. Tutty MA, Carlasare LE, Lloyd S, Sinsky CA. The complex case of EHRs: Examining the factors impacting the EHR user experience. Journal of the American Medical Informatics Association. 2019 Jul;26(7):673–7.
6. Wenhua Z, Qamar F, Abdali TA, Hassan R, Jafri ST, Nguyen QN. Blockchain technology: Security issues, healthcare applications, challenges and future trends. Electronics. 2023 Jan 20;12(3):546.
7. Zheng Z, Xie S, Dai HN, Chen X, Wang H. Blockchain challenges and opportunities: A survey. International Journal of Web and Grid Services. 2018; 14(4):352–75.

8. Wong J, Murray Horwitz M, Zhou L, Toh S. Using machine learning to identify health outcomes from electronic health record data. Current Epidemiology Reports. 2018 Dec;5:331–42.
9. Sun J, Yao X, Wang S, Wu Y. Blockchain-based secure storage and access scheme for electronic medical records in IPFS. IEEE Access. 2020 Mar 24;8:59389–401.
10. Hölbl M, Kompara M, Kamišalić A, NemecZlatolas L. A systematic review of the use of blockchain in healthcare. Symmetry. 2018 Oct 10;10(10):470.
11. Saluja K, Gupta S, Vajpayee A, Debnath SK, Bansal A, Sharma N. Blockchain technology: Applied to big data in collaborative edges. Measurement: Sensors. 2022 Dec 1;24:100521.
12. Alhadhrami Z, Alghfeli S, Alghfeli M, Abedlla JA, Shuaib K. Introducing blockchains for healthcare. In 2017 International Conference on Electrical and Computing Technologies and Applications (ICECTA) 2017 Nov 21 (pp. 1–4). IEEE.
13. Kuo TT, Zavaleta Rojas H, Ohno-Machado L. Comparison of blockchain platforms: A systematic review and healthcare examples. Journal of the American Medical Informatics Association. 2019 May;26(5):462–78.
14. Gong X, Liu X, Jing S, Xiong G, Zhou J. Parallel-education-blockchain driven smart education: Challenges and issues. In 2018 Chinese Automation Congress (CAC) 2018 Nov 30 (pp. 2390–2395). IEEE.
15. Dey T, Jaiswal S, Sunderkrishnan S, Katre N. HealthSense: A medical use case of internet of things and blockchain. In 2017 International Conference on Intelligent Sustainable Systems (ICISS) 2017 Dec 7 (pp. 486–491). IEEE.
16. Zhang J, Xue N, Huang X. A secure system for pervasive social network-based healthcare. IEEE Access. 2016 Dec 29;4:9239–50.
17. Liu W, Zhu SS, Mundie T, Krieger U. Advanced block-chain architecture for e-health systems. In 2017 IEEE 19th International Conference on e-Health Networking, Applications and Services (Healthcom) 2017 Oct 12 (pp. 1–6). IEEE.
18. Xia Q, Sifah EB, Smahi A, Amofa S, Zhang X. BBDS: Blockchain-based data sharing for electronic medical records in cloud environments. Information. 2017 Apr 17;8(2):44.
19. Wadhwa S, Rani S, Verma S, Shafi J, Wozniak M. Energy efficient consensus approach of blockchain for IoT networks with edge computing. Sensors. 2022 May 13;22(10):3733.
20. Magyar G. Blockchain: Solving the privacy and research availability tradeoff for EHR data: A new disruptive technology in health data management. In 2017 IEEE 30th Neumann Colloquium (NC) 2017 Nov 24 (pp. 000135–000140). IEEE.
21. Elangovan D, Long CS, Bakrin FS, Tan CS, Goh KW, Yeoh SF, Loy MJ, Hussain Z, Lee KS, Idris AC, Ming LC. The use of blockchain technology in the health care sector: Systematic review. JMIR Medical Informatics. 2022 Jan 20;10(1):e17278.
22. Abu-Elezz I, Hassan A, Nazeemudeen A, Househ M, Abd-Alrazaq A. The benefits and threats of blockchain technology in healthcare: A scoping review. International Journal of Medical Informatics. 2020 Oct 1;142:104246.
23. Mazlan AA, Daud SM, Sam SM, Abas H, Rasid SZ, Yusof MF. Scalability challenges in healthcare blockchain system—A systematic review. IEEE Access. 2020 Jan 24;8:23663–73.
24. Durneva P, Cousins K, Chen M. The current state of research, challenges, and future research directions of blockchain technology in patient care: Systematic review. Journal of Medical Internet Research. 2020 Jul 20;22(7):e18619.
25. Tandon A, Dhir A, Islam AN, Mäntymäki M. Blockchain in healthcare: A systematic literature review, synthesizing framework and future research agenda. Computers in Industry. 2020 Nov 1;122:103290.

26. Merlo V, Pio G, Giusto F, Bilancia M. On the exploitation of the blockchain technology in the healthcare sector: A systematic review. Expert Systems with Applications. 2023 Mar 1;213 118897.
27. Gupta S, Alharbi F, Alshahrani R, Kumar Arya P, Vyas S, Elkamchouchi DH, Soufiene BO. Secure and lightweight authentication protocol for privacy preserving communications in smart city applications. Sustainability. 2023;15:5346. https://doi.org/10.3390/su15065346
28. O'Donoghue O, Vazirani AA, Brindley D, Meinert E. Design choices and trade-offs in health care blockchain implementations: Systematic review. Journal of medical Internet Research. 2019 May 10;21(5):e12426.
29. Hasselgren A, Kralevska K, Gligoroski D, Pedersen SA, Faxvaag A. Blockchain in healthcare and health sciences—A scoping review. International Journal of Medical Informatics. 2020 Feb 1;134:104040.
30. McGhin T, Choo KK, Liu CZ, He D. Blockchain in healthcare applications: Research challenges and opportunities. Journal of network and computer applications. 2019 Jun 1;135:62–75.
31. Alqarni KS, Almalki FA, Soufiene BO, Ali O, Albalwy F. Authenticated wireless links between a drone and sensors using a blockchain: Case of smart farming. Wireless Communications and Mobile Computing. 2022;2022, Article ID 4389729:13. https://doi.org/10.1155/2022/4389729
32. Anjum A, Sporny M, Sill A. Blockchain standards for compliance and trust. IEEE Cloud Computing. 2017 Oct 12;4(4):84–90.
33. Charles W, Marler N, Long L, Manion S. Blockchain compliance by design: Regulatory considerations for blockchain in clinical research. Frontiers in Blockchain. 2019 Nov 8;2:18.
34. Wang B, Lin Z, Wang M, Wang F, Xiangli P, Li Z. Applying blockchain technology to ensure compliance with sustainability standards in the PPE multitier supply chain. International Journal of Production Research. 2023 Jul 18;61(14):4934–50.
35. Meyers G, Keymolen E. Realizing a blockchain solution without blockchain? Blockchain, solutionism, and trust. Regulation & Governance. 2023 Sep 15;14:53–68.
36. Zidan F, Nugroho D, Putra BA. Securing enterprises: Harnessing blockchain technology against cybercrime threats. International Journal of Cyber and IT Service Management. 2023 Oct 31;3(2):167–72.
37. Patel S, Patel R, Akbari A, Makkala SR. An extensive study and review of privacy preservation models for the multi-institutional data. Journal of Information Security. 2023 Aug 8;14(4):343–65.
38. Liu J, Fan Y, Sun R, Liu L, Wu C, Mumtaz S. Blockchain-aided privacy-preserving medical data sharing scheme for E-healthcare system. IEEE Internet of Things Journal. 2023 Jun 20;10(24):21377–88.
39. Samaniego M, Deters R. Digital Twins and Blockchain for IoT Management. In Proceedings of the 5th ACM International Symposium on Blockchain and Secure Critical Infrastructure 2023 Jul 10 (pp. 64–74).
40. Akella GK, Wibowo S, Granzhi S, Mubarak S. A systematic review of blockchain technology adoption barriers and enablers for smart and sustainable agriculture. Big Data and Cognitive Computing. 2023 May 4;7(2):86.
41. Miličević K, Omrčen L, Kohler M, Lukić I. Trust model concept for IoT blockchain applications as part of the digital transformation of metrology. Sensors. 2022 Jun 22;22(13):4708.
42. Tan CL, Yeo SF, Tan KH, Kumar KM. Blockchain technology model towards smart agriculture: A proposed model. International Journal of Business and Technology Management. 2023 Mar 31;5(1):249–60.

43. Saranya R, Murugan A. A systematic review of enabling blockchain in healthcare system: Analysis, current status, challenges and future direction. Materials Today: Proceedings. 2023 Jan 1;80:3010–5.

44. Myrzashova R, Alsamhi SH, Shvetsov AV, Hawbani A, Wei X. Blockchain meets federated learning in healthcare: A systematic review with challenges and opportunities. IEEE Internet of Things Journal. 2023 Mar 31;10(16):14418–37.

45. Baysal MV, Özcan-Top Ö, Betin-Can A. Blockchain technology applications in the health domain: A multivocal literature review. The Journal of supercomputing. 2023 Feb;79(3):3112–56.

46. Othman, S.B., Almalki, F.A., Sakli, H. (2022). Internet of Things in the Healthcare Applications: Overview of Security and Privacy Issues. In: Chakraborty, C., Khosravi, M.R. (eds) Intelligent Healthcare. Springer, Singapore. https://doi.org/10.1007/978-981-16-8150-9_9

47. Yap KY, Chin HH, Klemeš JJ. Blockchain technology for distributed generation: A review of current development, challenges and future prospect. Renewable and Sustainable Energy Reviews. 2023 Apr 1;175:113170.

48. Ghosh PK, Chakraborty A, Hasan M, Rashid K, Siddique AH. Blockchain application in healthcare systems: A review. Systems. 2023 Jan 8;11(1):38.

49. Bali S, Bali V, Mohanty RP, Gaur D. Analysis of critical success factors for blockchain technology implementation in healthcare sector. Benchmarking: An International Journal. 2023 Apr 14;30(4):1367–99.

8

PATIENT EMPOWERMENT THROUGH SECURE DATA MANAGEMENT

Anuradha Reddy, G S Pradeep Ghantasala,
Mamatha Kurra, and R Mohan Krishna Ayyappa

8.1   Introduction

The healthcare background [1] is swiftly progressing, compelled by scientific progressions, varying enduring opportunities, and an accumulative emphasis on personalized care. In this dynamic environment, the concept of patient empowerment has arisen as a crucial strength reformatting the interactions between healthcare providers and those they serve. At the heart of this transformation lies the critical role of data management, which not only facilitates the seamless exchange of information but also ensures the safety and confidentiality of sensitive health information [2].

8.1.1   Overview of the healthcare landscape

The traditional healthcare model was characterized by a paternalistic approach, where healthcare decisions were predominantly made by professionals [3], leaving patients in a passive role. However, the contemporary healthcare landscape is marked by a shift towards patient-centered care. Patients are no longer mere beneficiaries of curative guidance; they are lively contributors in their healthcare journey. This shift is fueled by a growing awareness among individuals, facilitated by increased access to information through the internet and other digital channels.

The rise of protracted syndromes [4], aging populations, and the growing complexity of health care have further accentuated the need for a more collaborative and patient-centric approach. Patients today seek to be partners in their care, making knowledgeable conclusions that align with their ideals, preferences, and lifestyle.

DOI: 10.1201/9781003483113-8

8.1.2 Importance of patient empowerment

Enduring authorization is a complex model that encompasses the involvement of individuals in their healthcare decision-making processes, understanding their health conditions, and having the essential tackles to actively accomplish their well-being [5]. Authorized patients are further likely to follow the action procedures, participate in precautionary processes, and effectively communicate with healthcare benefactors, leading to improved fitness results.

Empowering patients is not only helpful on a distinct level but also pays to the overall efficiency and effectiveness of the healthcare system. It fosters nous of responsibility [6] and accountability, reducing unnecessary healthcare utilization and costs. Moreover, empowered patients often engage in healthier behaviors and lifestyles, promoting a proactive approach to health.

8.1.3 Role of information organization in health care

The digital transformation of health care has led to an unprecedented proliferation of health data. EHRs [7], wearable devices, and other health-related technologies generate vast amounts of information that, when managed effectively, can significantly contribute to patient empowerment. Data management includes the gathering, stowage, analysis, and secure distribution of this information, forming the backbone of modern healthcare systems.

Data management [8] in health care serves several crucial purposes. Firstly, it guarantees the accessibility of complete and precise patient info, assisting knowledgeable decision-making by healthcare providers. This is predominantly relevant in substitute situations where quick admittance to medicinal history can be lifesaving. Secondly, robust data management systems support care coordination among various healthcare professionals, promoting a holistic and collaborative approach to patient care.

Safety and confidentiality are the utmost in healthcare data management. Patients must trust that their sensitive information is controlled with the utmost overhaul. Monitoring agendas, such as the Health Insurance Portability and Accountability Act (HIPAA) [9] in the United States, establish standards for the safe handling of health data, fostering a secure environment for both patients and healthcare providers.

In conclusion, the healthcare landscape is undergoing a transformative shift towards patient empowerment, and data management plays a pivotal role in facilitating this evolution. As we investigate deeper into the niceties of patient empowerment through secure data management, it becomes evident that the connection of knowledge, patient engagement [10], and data security is shaping a new era of health care—one where persons are not just beneficiaries of care but active contributors in their fitness and well-being.

8.2 The evolution of patient empowerment: A journey through time

8.2.1 Historical perspective on patient–doctor relationships

The historical [11] narrative of patient–doctor relationships unveils a fascinating evolution, marked by a shift from a paternalistic model to one that places the patient at the center. In ancient times, healers held an esteemed but authoritarian role, making decisions on behalf of the patient with minimal input. The patient's role was passive, often limited to following prescribed treatments without much understanding.

As we progress through the centuries, a gradual transformation occurs. The Renaissance period saw the emergence of a more scientific approach to medicine [12], fostering the exchange of ideas and knowledge. However, the patient remained relatively marginalized in the decision-making process. It was during the 20th century that a paradigm shift began, catalyzed by societal changes, ethical considerations, and the acknowledgment of patients' rights.

8.2.2 Shifting towards patient-centered care

The latter half of the 20th century witnessed a pronounced move towards patient-centered care. The patient, once relegated to a passive role, began to be recognized as an active participant in their healthcare journey. This transformation [13] was driven by a confluence of factors, including the civil rights movement, bioethics, and the rise of informed consent. Patients demanded not only medical expertise but also respect, transparency, and the accuracy to be actively entangled in choices about their health.

The perception of communal decision-making gained prominence, emphasizing association between healthcare benefactors and patients. This tactic acknowledged the unique perspectives and values that patients bring to the table. It marked a departure from the traditional top-down communication style, fostering a more egalitarian and patient-centric model.

In recent decades, healthcare systems worldwide have adopted replicas such as patient-centered medical homes (PCMHs) [14] and accountable care organizations (ACCs), reinforcing the importance of patient engagement, communication, and individualized care plans. The shift towards patient-centered care recognizes the diverse needs of patients and seeks to tailor health care delivery accordingly.

8.2.3 Influence of technology on patient empowerment

Enter the 21st century—a technological renaissance that has further accelerated the empowerment of patients. The advent of ordinal fitness skills [15] has fundamentally altered the dynamics of patient–doctor associations.

Patients now have unprecedented access to health info through the internet, empowering them to be more informed partners in their care.

8.3 The significance of secure data management: Safeguarding the foundation of health care

8.3.1 Importance of health data security

In the contemporary healthcare background, where information flows as the essence of patient care, the prominence of health data security cannot be overstated. Health data encompasses a trove of sensitive information, including medical histories, treatment plans, and individual identifiers [16]. Safeguarding the safety of this information is paramount, not only to defend the privacy of individuals but also to maintain the integrity and trustworthiness of healthcare systems.

Health files safety goes beyond safeguarding information from unauthorized access; it is about preserving the privacy, veracity, and accessibility of information. Unauthorized access not only jeopardizes individual privacy but can also lead to distinctiveness robbery, insurance fraud, and other malicious activities. Moreover, the confidentiality of health data is intertwined with the trust patients place in the healthcare system [17]. A breach can erode this trust, hindering patients from fully engaging in their care and sharing critical information with their healthcare providers.

In an era where data is a cornerstone of medical research and innovation, health data security becomes integral to protecting the collective well-being of communities. Research institutions, pharmaceutical companies, and healthcare providers rely on robust security measures to protect the insights gleaned from health data, ensuring that advancements in medical knowledge are achieved without compromising individual privacy [18].

8.3.2 Risks associated with insecure data management

The risks associated with insecure data management in health care are multifaceted and extend far beyond the immediate implications for individual patients. One of the most pressing concerns is the potential for data breaches, which can result in the exposure of sensitive information on a massive scale. This not only puts patients at risk but also exposes healthcare providers to legal and financial repercussions.

Insecure data management also poses a threat to the continuity of patient care. If health records are compromised or altered, the accuracy and reliability of medical information come into question, leading to potential misdiagnoses, inappropriate treatments, and compromised patient safety. In the interconnected web of health care, a breach in one part of the system can have cascading effects, impacting the entire continuum of care.

The rise of ransomware attacks in the healthcare sector further underscores the urgency of securing health data. Cybercriminals target healthcare organizations, encrypting critical data and demanding payment for its release. Such attacks not only disrupt healthcare services but also highlight the vulnerabilities inherent in the interconnected digital infrastructure of modern health care.

8.3.3   Regulatory landscape (HIPAA, GDPR, etc.)

Recognizing the critical need to safeguard health data, various regulatory frameworks have been established globally to govern its management and protection. In the United States, HIPAA stands as a cornerstone of health data security. HIPAA mandates stringent safeguards to ensure the confidentiality, integrity, and availability of electronic protected health information (ePHI). Healthcare organizations must comply with HIPAA standards, implementing measures such as encryption, access controls, and regular audits to maintain compliance.

On the international stage, the General Data Protection Regulation (GDPR) governs data protection and privacy for individuals within the European Union (EU). GDPR applies to health data, emphasizing the importance of obtaining explicit consent for data processing, ensuring the right to be forgotten, and imposing strict notification requirements in the event of a data breach.

These regulatory frameworks serve as powerful tools to incentivize healthcare organizations to prioritize secure data management. They not only outline the expectations for data protection but also establish penalties for noncompliance, reinforcing the gravity of maintaining the highest standards of security in healthcare data management.

In conclusion, the significance of secure data management in health care cannot be overstated. It is a linchpin that upholds the trust of patients, the integrity of medical care, and the advancement of medical knowledge. As technology continues to evolve, so must our commitment to robust security measures, guided by a comprehensive understanding of the risks and a steadfast adherence to regulatory frameworks designed to protect the sanctity of health data.

8.4   Technologies shaping secure data management

In the ever-evolving landscape of health care, technological advancements play a pivotal role in shaping secure data management practices. This section explores key technologies, namely EHRs, health information exchange (HIE) [19], blockchain in health care, and cloud-based solutions, emphasizing their contributions to enhancing security and empowering patients.

8.4.1 Electronic health records

EHRs have reformed how patient data is documented, opened, and collective within healthcare systems. EHRs update data management by joining patient records into digital formats, allowing for efficient reclamation and bring up-to-date medical information. The transition from paper-based histories to EHRs not only expands healthcare transfer but also supports data security through access controls and audit trails. **Security Measures in EHRs:** Converse the security structures implanted in EHR systems, such as encryption, user authentication, and role-based access control. Discover how EHRs contribute to data integrity and condense the risks associated with manual recordkeeping.

8.4.2 Health information exchange

HIE simplifies the whole allotment of patient data between different healthcare units, helping care direction and falling replication of tests and procedures. This section discovers in what way HIE donates to secure data management by providing a uniform and secure framework for the conversation of health information across administrations. **Interoperability and Security:** Discourse the tasks and explanations associated to interoperability in HIE. Best part security proprieties and values that govern data exchange, guaranteeing that patient data remains confidential and secure throughout transmission.

8.4.3 Blockchain in health care

Blockchain technology has grown adhesion in health care for its probability to improve data security, transparency, and interoperability. Discover in what manner blockchain's decentralized and tamper-resistant nature can be leveraged to secure health data, update processes, and authorize patients with greater control over their data. **Securing Health Data with Blockchain:** Discourse obvious use cases of blockchain in health care, such as securing medical records, enabling secure data distribution, and supportive the integrity of clinical trials [20]. Address challenges and considerations associated to the acceptance of block chain in healthcare settings.

8.4.4 Cloud-based solutions

Cloud-based solutions have changed data storage, processing, and accessibility in health care. This section discovers how cloud technology contributes to protected data management by providing scalable and cost-effective explanations for storing and managing huge quantities of healthcare data. **Security Considerations in Cloud-Based Healthcare Systems:** Examine the security trials implemented by cloud service providers, as well as encryption, data backup, and submission with monitoring ideals. Discourse the benefits of cloud-based results in enhancing data accessibility for healthcare providers while maintaining robust security protocols.

In conclusion, the integration of technologies like EHRs, HIE, blockchain, and cloud-based solutions marks a significant leap forward in completing secure data management in health care. These technologies not only improve the competence of healthcare processes but also contribute to patient empowerment by ensuring the confidentiality and integrity of their health information. As we continue to embrace technological inventions, striking a balance between innovation and data security remains paramount in shaping the future of health care.

8.5   Interoperability and integration

Healthcare data interoperability and seamless integration are pivotal for realizing the full potential of patient empowerment through secure data management. In this section, we will navigate the challenges, explore solutions, and underscore the critical role of standards, such as HL7 (Health Level Seven) and FHIR (Fast Healthcare Interoperability Resources).

8.5.1   Challenges in healthcare data interoperability

The healthcare landscape is characterized by a multitude of disparate systems, each collecting and loading data in single formats. The lack of standardized protocols and formats poses a significant obstacle to interoperability. Healthcare providers often use different EHR systems that struggle to communicate with each other. Furthermore, diverse data sources, ranging from medical devices to wearable technologies, contribute to the complexity of achieving seamless interoperability. These challenges result in fragmented patient histories, hindering comprehensive and synchronized care.

8.5.2   Solutions for seamless data integration

To overcome interoperability tasks, healthcare organizations are increasingly implementing integration explanations that bridge disparate systems and facilitate smooth data conversation. Application programming interfaces (APIs) play a crucial role by enabling different software applications to communicate with each other. Middleware solutions act as intermediaries, translating data between incompatible formats. Data normalization techniques are employed to standardize diverse data sets, ensuring consistency and coherence.

Interoperability initiatives, such as Common Well Health Alliance and Care quality, purpose to establish a nationwide framework for healthcare data exchange. These collaborative efforts bring together healthcare stakeholders to define and implement interoperability standards, fostering a more connected and patient-centric healthcare ecosystem.

8.5.3 The role of standards (HL7, FHIR, etc.)

Healthcare standards play a central role in achieving interoperability and seamless data integration. HL7 [21], a widely adopted international standard, provides a framework for the exchange, integration, sharing, and recovery of electronic health information. It describes messaging formats and protocols for the exchange of clinical and administrative data.

Fast Healthcare Interoperability Resources (FHIR), developed by HL7, is gaining importance for its modern approach to healthcare interoperability. FHIR leverages web-based technologies and represents a more lightweight and flexible standard compared to its predecessors. Its modular structure allows for easier implementation and adaptability, making it well suited for the evolving healthcare landscape.

Standardized terminologies, such as SNOMED CT (Systematized Nomenclature of Medicine – Clinical Terms) and LOINC (Logical Observation Identifiers Names and Codes), contribute to semantic interoperability by ensuring consistent coding and terminology usage across healthcare systems.

In conclusion, addressing healthcare data interoperability requires a multifaceted approach that incorporates technological solutions, collaborative initiatives, and adherence to recognized standards. The adoption of interoperability standards like HL7 and FHIR [22], coupled with innovative integration strategies, lay the foundation for a seamlessly connected healthcare ecosystem. This interconnectedness, in turn, enhances the quality of patient care, supports informed decision-making, and ultimately contributes to the empowerment of patients through secure and comprehensive data management.

8.6 Patient access to health information

The empowerment of patients through access to their health information is a transformative aspect of modern health care. In this section, we will discover the significance of compromising patients' control over their health data, the benefits associated with this empowerment, and the challenges healthcare systems encounter in implementing robust patient data access policies.

8.6.1 Empowering patients with access to their data

Patient access to health information marks a standard shift in healthcare dynamics. Traditionally, medical information was often protected by healthcare providers, limiting patients' understanding of their own health. The advent of EHRs and patient portals has ushered in a new era, allowing individuals to access their health data conveniently. This empowerment encourages active patient participation in care results, fostering a collaborative relationship between patients and healthcare providers.

8.6.2 Benefits of patients having control over their health information

Granting patients control over their health information yields a multitude of benefits. First and foremost, it enhances patient engagement by providing a comprehensive view of their medical history, diagnoses, medications, and test results. This transparency fosters informed decision-making and encourages patients to take a proactive role in managing their health. Furthermore, authorized patients are better furnished to contribute in their care plans, adhere to prescribed treatments, and engage in preventive measures. The accessibility of health information also facilitates communication between patients and healthcare providers, enabling more meaningful and productive discussions during medical appointments.

8.6.3 Challenges in implementing patient data access

Despite the evident advantages, implementing common patient data access faces several challenges. Privacy and security concerns are dominant, as healthcare providers must ensure that sensitive information remains protected. Striking a balance between data approachability and maintaining confidentiality requires robust cybersecurity measures and adherence to regulatory standards such as HIPAA and GDPR. Technological barriers, including interoperability issues among different EHR systems [23], can hinder seamless patient data access. Ensuring a standardized and user-friendly interface across diverse healthcare platforms is essential for enhancing accessibility and usability.

Healthcare disparities also pose challenges, as not all patients may have equal access to digital tools or the ability to direct electronic health platforms. Bridging the digital divide is crucial to prevent exacerbating existing inequalities in healthcare access. Resistance to change within healthcare organizations and among healthcare providers can impede the implementation of patient data access initiatives. Training programs and change management strategies are vital to overcome resistance and cultivate a culture that embraces patient empowerment through data access.

In conclusion, patient access to health data is a cornerstone of patient empowerment in the digital age. There are several benefits of informed and engaged patients, contributing to improved health outcomes and a more patient-centric healthcare landscape. However, addressing the challenges associated with privacy, technology, disparities, and organizational resistance is imperative to ensure the successful implementation of patient data access initiatives. By navigating these challenges effectively, healthcare systems can create a more collaborative and empowering environment that places patients at the center of their care.

8.7 Data privacy and consent

In the era of digital health care, the connection of data privacy and informed consent is pivotal for establishing trust, respecting autonomy, and safeguarding individual rights. This section explores the critical importance of informed consent, the role of privacy-enhancing technologies, and the delicate balance required when navigating data distribution and privacy concerns.

8.7.1 Importance of informed consent

Informed consent is the cornerstone of principled and legal principles governing the use of personal health data. It represents an individual's voluntary and well-informed agreement to participate in any healthcare activity or research, understanding the potential risks and benefits. In the context of data privacy, obtaining informed consent is not merely a legal requirement but a fundamental ethical obligation to respect individuals' autonomy and privacy rights.

8.7.2 Privacy-enhancing technologies

Privacy-enhancing technologies (PETs) [24] are instrumental in mitigating privacy risks related with the collecting and processing of health data. Techniques such as anonymization, encryption, and differential privacy ensure that individuals' identities remain protected while still allowing for meaningful analysis. Anonymization, for instance, removes personally recognizable information, enabling the use of data for research without compromising individual privacy. Encryption adds an additional layer of security by encoding data, making it accessible only to authorized parties.

Differential privacy, a more advanced technique, presents controlled noise into data sets to protect individual individualities while still providing valuable insights. The integration of PETs not only aligns with privacy principles but also instills confidence in individuals that their sensitive health information is handled responsibly.

8.7.3 Balancing data sharing and privacy concerns

Achieving the delicate balance between data sharing and privacy concerns is a complex challenge. On one hand, sharing health data is critical for medical research, public health initiatives, and the development of innovative treatments. On the other hand, safeguarding individual privacy is non-negotiable. Striking this balance requires a nuanced approach that involves robust governance frameworks, transparent communication, and the incorporation of privacy-by-design principles into data distribution initiatives.

Healthcare organizations must approve comprehensive data governance guidelines that clearly outline how data will be used, who will have access, and the measures in place to protect individual privacy. Transparent communication with individuals about the purpose of data sharing, the potential benefits to public health or research, and the security measures in place is important for building trust.

Moreover, the concept of data minimization inspires limiting the gathering and retention of personal health data to what is strictly necessary for the intended purpose. Implementing strict access controls and regular audits further ensures that only authorized personnel have access to sensitive data.

In conclusion, navigating the landscape of data privacy and consent requires a holistic and ethical approach. Informed consent acts as a safeguard for specific autonomy, privacy-enhancing technologies deliver the technical foundation for responsible data handling, and a balanced approach to data sharing acknowledges both the societal benefits and the imperative to protect individual privacy. By upholding these principles, healthcare systems can foster a culture of trust, respecting the rights and privacy of individuals while harnessing the power of health data for collective well-being.

8.8 Telemedicine and remote patient monitoring

Telemedicine and remote patient monitoring (RPM) [25] represent transformative facets of modern health care, leveraging technology to bridge geographical gaps, enhance patient authorization, and optimize healthcare delivery. In this section, we will discover the effect of telemedicine on patient empowerment, the role of remote monitoring in data gathering, and the imperative of ensuring the security of remote healthcare data.

8.8.1 Impact of telemedicine on patient empowerment

Telemedicine, characterized by the provision of healthcare services through digital communication, has emerged as a powerful tool for empowering patients. One of its primary impacts is the democratization of access to health care. Patients, regardless of their geographical location, can connect with healthcare professionals, access medical advice, and participate in virtual consultations.

This increased accessibility fosters a sense of empowerment, especially for individuals in remote or underserved areas. Patients can take a more active role in managing their health by engaging in telehealth appointments, obtaining timely medical advice, and accessing educational resources. Additionally, telemedicine promotes continuity of care, enabling patients to maintain regular contact with healthcare providers without the constraints of physical distance.

8.8.2 Remote patient monitoring and data collection

RPM complements telemedicine by facilitating continuous data collection and analysis outside of traditional healthcare settings. Wearable devices, sensors, and smart technologies enable real-time tracking of vital signs, medication adherence, and other relevant health metrics. This constant stream of data provides healthcare professionals with a more comprehensive and dynamic understanding of a patient's health status.

The impact of RPM on patient empowerment is profound. Patients become active participants in their care, as they can monitor their health metrics in real time and gain insights into how lifestyle choices impact their well-being. For individuals with chronic conditions, RPM offers a proactive approach to management, allowing for early intervention and personalized adjustments to treatment plans.

8.8.3 Ensuring the security of remote healthcare data

The integration of telemedicine and RPM presents new attentions for ensuring the security of healthcare data, particularly when communicated and stored remotely. Patient privacy and data confidentiality must be paramount to maintain trust in these technologies.

8.8.4 Encryption and secure communication

Implementing robust encryption protocols is essential to safeguard patient data during transmission. Secure communication channels protect sensitive information from unauthorized access and interception. Whether it is video consultations, messaging platforms, or data transfer from wearable devices, encryption ensures that healthcare interactions remain confidential.

8.8.5 Authentication and access controls

Establishing strong authentication measures and access controls is critical to verify the identities of both patients and healthcare providers participating in telemedicine encounters. Multi-factor authentication adds an extra layer of security, reducing the risk of illegal access to patient records or telehealth platforms.

8.8.6 Compliance with regulatory standards

Adherence to regulatory standards, such as the HIPAA in the United States or equivalent data safety laws in other sections, is non-negotiable. Telemedicine platforms and remote monitoring systems must comply with these regulations to ensure the legal and ethical handling of patient data.

8.8.7 Device security and data integrity

Securing the devices used for telemedicine consultations and remote monitoring is crucial. Regular updates, endpoint protection, and data integrity measures moderate the risk of malware or unauthorized altering. Ensuring the security of the entire ecosystem, including wearable devices and monitoring equipment, contributes to a holistic approach to data protection.

As telemedicine and remote patient monitoring continue to evolve, addressing cybersecurity challenges and staying ahead of potential threats will be an ongoing endeavor. Technological advancements, including the integration of artificial intelligence (AI) for predictive analytics and continuous refinement of security protocols, will play a vital role in ensuring the sustained trust and adoption of these technologies.

In conclusion, the synergy between telemedicine, remote patient monitoring, and patient empowerment is redefining the healthcare landscape. By embracing these technologies, patients gain increased access to care, actively participate in health management, and contribute valuable data for personalized interventions. However, the successful integration of telehealth and RPM hinges on prioritizing the security of remote healthcare data. Through encryption, robust authentication, controlling compliance, and ongoing technological advancements, healthcare providers can harness the full potential of these innovations while maintaining the privacy and security of patient information.

8.9 Empowering vulnerable populations

Empowering vulnerable populations in health care involves addressing disparities in access, adopting personalized methods for various patient groups, and overcoming challenges related to digital health literacy. This section explores the complexities surrounding healthcare disparities, the importance of tailored approaches, and strategies to enhance digital health literacy.

8.9.1 Addressing disparities in healthcare access

Vulnerable populations, which may include individuals with lower socioeconomic status, ethnic minorities, the elderly, and those living in underserved areas, often face significant differences in healthcare access. Limited access to quality healthcare services can exacerbate existing health inequalities, leading to adverse outcomes. To address these disparities, healthcare systems must implement targeted interventions. This may involve increasing the availability of healthcare facilities in underserved areas, providing transportation provision, and leveraging telemedicine to bridge geographical gaps. Culturally competent care and outreach programs can help build trust within vulnerable communities, encouraging regular healthcare engagement.

8.9.2 Customized approaches for diverse patient groups

One size does not fit all in health care, particularly when dealing with vulnerable populations. Modified methods are important to address the unique needs and challenges faced by diverse patient groups. Tailoring healthcare interventions based on cultural, linguistic, and socioeconomic factors is critical to achieving positive health outcomes. Healthcare providers should engage in community partnerships and cooperate with community leaders to understand the exact needs of vulnerable populations. Culturally competent care involves identifying and respecting cultural differences, which can positively impact patient trust and participation in healthcare initiatives. Additionally, incorporating patient navigators or advocates can help guide individuals through the complexities of the healthcare system, fostering a more patient-centered approach.

8.9.3 Overcoming digital health literacy challenges

Digital health literacy is an integral module of authorizing vulnerable populations in an increasingly technology-driven healthcare landscape. However, many individuals within these populations face challenges related to understanding and utilizing digital health tools effectively.

- **Educational Initiatives:** Healthcare providers and public health organizations can implement educational initiatives to enhance digital health literacy. This may involve community workshops, informational pamphlets, and online resources designed to educate individuals on how to navigate digital health platforms, access telemedicine facilities, and interpret health data available online.
- **User-Friendly Technology:** Developing user-friendly digital health tools is crucial for overcoming barriers related to technology acceptance.

The design of applications and platforms should consider the diverse needs of users, including those with varying levels of digital literacy. Incorporating features such as simple interfaces, multilingual support, and accessibility options can make digital health tools more inclusive.

- **Partnerships with Community Organizations:** Collaborating with community organizations and grassroots initiatives can facilitate outreach efforts designed at improving digital health literacy. Local organizations often have a deeper understanding of the needs and challenges faced by their communities, making them valuable partners in designing and delivering targeted interventions.
- **Telehealth Support Services:** Providing dedicated support services for telehealth acceptance can authorize vulnerable populations to leverage digital health tools effectively. This may involve establishing helplines, virtual assistance, or community-based telehealth support centers where individuals can receive guidance on using telemedicine platforms.

8.10   Case studies and success stories

In the realm of health care, establishments that successfully implement secure data management not only enhance patient empowerment but also set precedents for industry-wide best practices. Examining real-world examples sheds light on the instructions learned, challenges overcome, and the transformative impact on patient care.

8.10.1   Success story: Mayo Clinic

Mayo Clinic, a renowned healthcare institution, exemplifies the integration of secure data management to empower patients. By implementing a comprehensive EHR system, Mayo Clinic ensures that patient data is accessible to authorized healthcare providers across its network. This seamless data exchange facilitates collaborative and patient-centered care, allowing different specialists to have a unified view of the patient's medical history.

Lessons Learned:

- **Interoperability Is Key:** Mayo Clinic's success underscores the importance of interoperability in healthcare data management. Integrating disparate systems and ensuring they "speak" to each other enhances the continuousness and quality of care.
- **Patient Access Empowers:** Providing patients with easy access to their medical records through the patient portal has empowered individuals to actively engage in their healthcare conclusions. Patients can review test results, understand treatment plans, and communicate efficiently with their healthcare team.

8.10.2 Success story: Kaiser Permanente

Kaiser Permanente, a leading healthcare provider, employs an integrated care model reinforced by strong data management practices. With a centralized EHR system, Kaiser Permanente ensures that patient data is constantly updated and accessible across its network of hospitals and clinics. This integration enhances care coordination, leading to more informed and collaborative decision-making.

Lessons Learned:

- **Data Governance Matters:** Kaiser Permanente's achievement highlights the significance of strong data governance policies. Standardized data management practices ensure data accuracy, integrity, and security, laying the foundation for effective patient care.
- **Proactive Care through Analytics:** By leveraging data analytics, Kaiser Permanente identifies trends and patterns in patient health. This proactive approach allows healthcare providers to intervene early, preventing complications and improving patient outcomes.

8.10.3 Success story: Cleveland Clinic

Cleveland Clinic exemplifies the successful implementation of secure data management through its use of advanced technologies, including blockchain. By adopting blockchain for health data exchange, Cleveland Clinic enhances the security and integrity of patient chronicles. This technology ensures that patient consent is recorded immutably, addressing privacy concerns and empowering patients with control over their data.

Lessons Learned:

- **Blockchain Enhances Trust:** Cleveland Clinic's use of blockchain highlights the role of this technology in development trust. Immutable records and transparent data sharing contribute to patient confidence in the security and privacy of their health data.
- **Privacy and Security Go Hand in Hand:** The success of blockchain implementation reinforces the importance of prioritizing both privacy and security. Striking a balance ensures that patients feel secure in sharing their data while maintaining control over who accesses it.

8.10.4 Lessons learned from real-world examples

- **Emphasizing Patient Education:** Across these case studies, a common thread is the importance on patient education. Successful organizations recognize the importance of educating patients about the benefits of secure

data management. Mayo Clinic, Kaiser Permanente, and Cleveland Clinic all provide educational resources and tools, empowering patients to actively participate in their healthcare journey.
- **Adapting to Technological Advances:** The success stories also highlight the necessity for organizations to adapt to technological advances continually. Whether integrating EHR systems, leveraging data analytics, or implementing blockchain, staying at the forefront of technology allows healthcare providers to enhance patient care and maintain the security of health data.

The lessons learned from these case studies underscore the evolving nature of secure data organization in health care. As technology continues to advance, organizations must remain agile, prioritize patient education, and leverage innovative solutions to empower individuals in their healthcare decisions.

In conclusion, the case studies and achievement stories presented here offer valuable insights into how secure data management can authorize patients and convert healthcare delivery. By learning from these examples, healthcare organizations can continue to refine their practices, prioritize patient-centered care, and stay at the forefront of the evolving landscape of healthcare data management.

8.11   Future trends: Emerging technologies in health care and data management

As we stand on the precipice of a new era in health care, the connection of emerging technologies and data management is shaping the future landscape. In this section, we explore the cutting-edge technologies poised to revolutionize health care and predict the trajectory of patient empowerment through secure data management.

8.11.1   Artificial intelligence and machine learning

AI and machine learning are becoming integral to health care by analyzing vast data sets to classify patterns, predict disease trajectories, and personalize treatment plans. Future Predictions:

- **Precision Medicine:** AI algorithms will enhance the understanding of individual patient features, enabling the development of highly personalized treatment plans tailored to genetic, lifestyle, and environmental factors.
- **Diagnostic Advancements:** Machine-learning models will evolve to deliver more accurate and timely diagnostics, improving early disease detection and intervention.

- **Predictive Analytics for Population Health:** AI will play a pivotal role in predicting and preventing public health issues by analyzing population-level data, allowing for proactive interventions and resource allocation.

8.11.2 Internet of Things and wearable technologies

The proliferation of Internet of Things (IoT) devices and wearables allows continuous monitoring of patient health metrics, creating a wealth of real-time data. Future Predictions:

- **Remote Patient Monitoring Evolution:** IoT devices and wearables will change to monitor an expanding array of health parameters, providing richer data sets for healthcare providers.
- **Integration with EHRs:** Seamless integration of wearable-generated data into EHRs will become standard practice, providing a comprehensive view of patients' health status.
- **Behavioral Health Monitoring:** Wearables will increasingly incorporate features for monitoring mental health, offering insights into stress levels, sleep patterns, and overall well-being.

8.11.3 Blockchain technology

Blockchain ensures secure, transparent, and immutable health data sharing, addressing concerns related to data integrity and privacy. Future Predictions:

- **Patient-Centric Data Ownership:** Blockchain will enable patients to have greater control over their health data, granting permission for specific data access and maintaining ownership.
- **Enhanced Interoperability:** Blockchain will contribute to improved interoperability between disparate healthcare systems, supporting seamless data exchange.
- **Clinical Trials and Research:** Blockchain will streamline and secure the management of clinical trial data, accelerating the pace of medical research and drug development.

8.11.4 5G technology

The rollout of 5G networks is transforming health care by providing high-speed, low-latency communication, facilitating real-time data exchange. Future Predictions:

- **Telehealth Transformation:** 5G will enable a seamless and immersive telehealth experience, with high-quality video consultations and real-time monitoring.

- **IoT Connectivity:** The increased bandwidth and low latency of 5G will support a more extensive network of interconnected medical devices and wearables.
- **Emergency Response:** 5G's low latency will enhance emergency response systems, enabling quick and reliable communication between healthcare professionals and emergency facilities.

In conclusion, the future of patient empowerment through secure data management is poised for a revolutionary transformation. Emerging technologies, from AI and IoT to blockchain and 5G, will usher in an era of personalized, accessible, and patient-centric health care. The predictions outlined here offer a glimpse into a future where individuals are not just recipients of healthcare services but active applicants in their health journey, empowered by secure and innovative data management practices.

8.12 Conclusion

In the preceding sections, we embarked on a journey through the dynamic landscape of health care, exploring the evolution of patient empowerment, the significance of secure data management, and the transformative impact of key technologies. As we conclude, let's recap the key points and underscore the ongoing importance of patient empowerment and secure data management in health care:

- **Historical Evolution of Patient Empowerment:** From a paternalistic model to patient-centered care, the historical development of patient–doctor relationships highlights the shift toward recognizing and respecting the autonomy of individuals in managing their health.
- **Influence of Technology on Patient Empowerment:** The advent of technology has played a pivotal part in empowering patients. Access to data, digital health tools, and the rise of patient-centered technologies have given individuals unprecedented control over their healthcare decisions.
- **Importance of Health Data Security:** The confidentiality, integrity, and availability of health data are paramount. Health data security is not only a legal and moral imperative but also crucial for maintaining trust in healthcare systems and ensuring the well-being of patients.
- **Risks Associated with Insecure Data Management:** Insecure data management poses significant risks, including unauthorized access, data manipulation, and potential breaches. These risks can lead to severe consequences, compromising patient privacy, and eroding the credibility of healthcare organizations.
- **Regulatory Landscape:** Regulations such as HIPAA and GDPR provide a framework for secure data management. Compliance with these

regulations is not only a legal requirement but also a commitment to defensive patient rights and development of a culture of responsible data handling.

- **Technologies Shaping Secure Data Management:** EHRs streamline data management, enhance accessibility, and contribute to the overall competence of healthcare processes. HIE facilitates seamless data exchange, fostering care coordination and reducing redundancies in healthcare services. Blockchain offers a decentralized and tamper-resistant result for securing health data, promoting transparency, and empowering patients. Cloud technology revolutionizes data storage and accessibility, providing scalable and secure solutions for managing vast healthcare data sets.

The Ongoing Importance of Patient Empowerment and Secure Data Management:

- **Patient-Centric Care:** The ongoing shift towards patient-centered care emphasizes the active involvement of patients in their healthcare journey. This not only enhances patient satisfaction but also contributes to better health outcomes.
- **Informed Decision-Making:** Empowered patients are equipped to make informed decisions about their health. Access to accurate and timely data fosters a cooperative approach between healthcare providers and patients.
- **Privacy and Trust:** Secure data management is foundational to preserving patient privacy and development trust. Patients must feel confident that their sensitive health information is handled with the utmost care and integrity.
- **Leveraging Technology for Empowerment:** The continuous integration of cutting-edge technologies in health care ensures that patients have access to innovative tools and platforms that facilitate self-management and proactive engagement in their health.
- **Interconnectedness and Interoperability:** The interconnected nature of healthcare systems necessitates a focus on interoperability. Seamless data exchange between different entities ensures continuity of care and a comprehensive view of patient health.
- **Regulatory Compliance:** Adherence to regulatory standards remains a non-negotiable aspect of healthcare operations. Compliance not only mitigates legal dangers but also demonstrates a commitment to ethical and responsible data management.
- **Continuous Innovation:** The landscape of health care and knowledge is in constant evolution. Staying ahead of emerging trends and accepting innovative solutions is essential for enhancing patient permission and ensuring data security in the face of new challenges.

In conclusion, the journey towards patient empowerment through secure data management is an ongoing and dynamic process. As we navigate the complexities of healthcare delivery, the principles of regarding patient autonomy, ensuring data safety, and leveraging technology for positive outcomes must remain at the forefront. The cooperative efforts of healthcare authorities, technology innovators, policymakers, and patients themselves will shape a future where individuals not only receive high-quality care but actively participate in their path to well-being. Balancing innovation with ethical considerations is the key to a healthcare ecosystem that truly authorizes individuals and prioritizes the sanctity of their health data.

References

1. Eysenbach, G., Powell, J., Kuss, O., & Sa, E. R. (2002). Empirical studies assessing the quality of health information for consumers on the world wide web: A systematic review. JAMA, 287(20), 2691–700. https://doi.org/10.1001/jama.287.20.2691. PMID: 12020305.
2. Othman, S. B., A.malki, F. A., & Sakli, H. (2022). Internet of Things in the Healthcare Applications: Overview of Security and Privacy Issues. In: Chakraborty, C., Khosravi, M.R. (eds) Intelligent Healthcare. Springer, Singapore. https://doi.org/10.1007/978-981-16-8150-9_9
3. Borycki, E. (2012). M-health: Can chronic obstructive pulmonary disease patients use mobile phones and associated software to self-manage their disease? Studies in Health Technology and Informatics, 172, 79–84. PMID: 22910504.
4. Anderson, R. M., & Funnell, M. M. (2011). Patient empowerment: Myths and misconceptions. Patient Education and Counseling, 79(3), 277–282.
5. Ant Ozok, A., Wu, H., Garrido, M., Pronovost, P. J., & Gurses, A. P. (2014). Usability and perceived usefulness of personal health records for preventive health care: A case study focusing on patients' and primary care providers' perspectives. 45(3), 613–628. doi: 10.1116/j.apergo.2013.09.005.
6. Archer, N., Fevrier-Thomas, U., Lokker, C., McKibbon, K. A., & Straus, S. E. (2011). Personal health records: A scoping review. Journal of the American Medical Informatics Association, 18(4), 515–522.
7. Barello, S., Graffigna, G., & Vegni, E. (2012). Patient engagement as an emerging challenge for healthcare services: Mapping the literature. Nursing Research and Practice, 2012, 1–7.
8. Bartlett, C., Simpson, K., & Turner, A. N. (2012). Patient access to complex chronic disease records on the internet. BMC Medical Informatics and Decision Making, 12(1), 87.
9. Alqarni, K. S., Almalki, F. A., Soufiene, B. O., Ali, O., & Albalwy, F. (2022). Authenticated wireless links between a drone and sensors using a blockchain: Case of smart farming. Wireless Communications and Mobile Computing, 2022, Article ID 4389729, 13. https://doi.org/10.1155/2022/4389729
10. Sezer, B. B., Turkmen, H., & Nuriyev, U. (2023). PPFchain: A novel framework privacy-preserving blockchain-based federated learning method for sensor networks. Internet of Things, 22, 100781. https://doi.org/10.1016/j.iot.2023.100781
11. Abaoud, M., Almuqrin, A., & Khan, M. F. (2023). Advancing federated learning through novel mechanism for privacy preservation in healthcare applications. IEEE Access, 11, 83562–83579. https://doi.org/10.1109/ACCESS.2023.3301162

12. Baucas, M. J., Spachos, P., & Plataniotis, K. N. (2023). Federated learning and blockchain-enabled fog-IoT platform for wearables in predictive healthcare. IEEE Transactions on Computational Social Systems, 10(4), 1732–1741. https://doi.org/10.1109/TCSS.2023.3235950

13. Moulahi, W., Jdey, I., Moulahi, T., Alawida, M., & Alabdulatif, A. (2023). A blockchain-based federated learning mechanism for privacy preservation of healthcare IoT data, Computers in Biology and Medicine, 167, 107630. https://doi.org/10.1016/j.compbiomed.2023.107630

14. Guduri, M., Chakraborty, C., Maheswari, U., & Margala, M. (2023). Blockchain-based federated learning technique for privacy preservation and security of smart electronic health records. IEEE Transactions on Consumer Electronics, 70(1), 2608–2617. https://doi.org/10.1109/TCE.2023.3315415

15. Gupta, S., Alharbi, F., Alshahrani, R., Kumar Arya, P., Vyas, S., Elkamchouchi, D. H., & Soufiene, B. O. (2023). Secure and lightweight authentication protocol for privacy preserving communications in smart city applications. Sustainability, 15, 5346. https://doi.org/10.3390/su15065346

16. Prokop, K., Połap, D., Srivastava, G. et al. (2023). Blockchain-based federated learning with checksums to increase security in internet of things solutions. Journal of Ambient Intelligence and Humanized Computing, 14, 4685–4694. https://doi.org/10.1007/s12652-022-04372-0

17. Vatambeti, R., Krishna, E. S. P., Karthik, M. G. et al. (2023). Securing the medical data using enhanced privacy preserving based blockchain technology in internet of things. Cluster Computing. https://doi.org/10.1007/s10586-023-04056-0

18. Jabarulla, M. Y., & Lee, H.-N. (2021). Blockchain-based distributed patient-centric image management system. Applied Sciences, 11, 196. https://doi.org/10.3390/app11010196

19. Chang, Y., Fang, C., & Sun, W. (2021). A blockchain-based federated learning method for smart healthcare. Computational Intelligence and Neuroscience, 2021, Article ID 4376418, 12. https://doi.org/10.1155/2021/4376418

20. Liu, W., He, Y., Wang, X., Duan, Z., Liang, W., & Liu, Y. (2023). BFG: Privacy protection framework for internet of medical things based on blockchain and federated learning. Connection Science, 35(1). https://doi.org/10.1080/09540091.2023.2199951

21. Qayyum, A., Ahmad, K., Ahsan, M. A., Al-Fuqaha, A., & Qadir, J. (2022). Collaborative federated learning for healthcare: Multi-modal COVID-19 diagnosis at the edge. IEEE Open Journal of the Computer Society, 3, 172–184. https://doi.org/10.1109/OJCS.2022.3206407

22. Nchinda, N., Cameron, A., Retzepi, K., & Lippman, A. (2019). MedRec: A Network for Personal Information Distribution. 2019 International Conference on Computing, Networking and Communications (ICNC), Honolulu, HI, USA, pp. 637–641. https://doi.org/10.1109/ICCNC.2019.8685631

23. Kuo, T. T., & Ohno-Machado, L. (2018). Modelchain: Decentralized privacy-preserving healthcare predictive modeling framework on private blockchain networks. arXiv preprint arXiv:1802.01746.

24. Wang, M., Guo, Y., Zhang, C., Wang, C., Huang, H., & Jia, X. (2023). MedShare: A privacy-preserving medical data sharing system by using blockchain. IEEE Transactions on Services Computing, 16(1), 438–451. https://doi.org/10.1109/TSC.2021.3114719

25. Kurniabudi, Stiawan, D., Darmawijoyo, Bin Idris, M. Y., Bamhdi, A. M., & Budiarto, R. (2020). CICIDS-2017 dataset feature analysis with information gain for anomaly detection. IEEE Access, 8, 132911–132921. https://doi.org/10.1109/ACCESS.2020.3009843

9

ENSURING DATA PRIVACY AND SECURITY WITH BLOCKCHAIN IN HEALTH CARE

Maitri Mohanty, Ambarish G. Mohapatra, Premansu Sekhara Rath, and Anita Mohanty

9.1 Introduction

The 21st century has witnessed an unprecedented proliferation of digital data, especially in the healthcare domain. Patient data, including medical records, treatment plans, and personal health information, has transitioned from traditional paper-based systems to EHRs and digital databases [1]. With this digital transformation comes a critical imperative: ensuring the security and integrity of patient data. Data security within the healthcare sector is paramount, not only to preserve patients' privacy but also to maintain trust and confidence in the healthcare ecosystem [2]. This introductory section sheds light on the significance of data security in health care and illuminates the prevalent challenges healthcare organizations face in managing patient data securely.

The table encapsulates the key aspects of incorporating blockchain technology into the healthcare domain. In terms of data security, blockchain offers immutable and tamper-proof data storage, ensuring the integrity of patient records [2]. However, challenges pertaining to scalability and significant energy consumption need to be addressed for wider adoption. Interoperability is significantly enhanced, allowing for seamless data exchange and a unified view of patient information across various healthcare systems [3]. Yet, integrating blockchain with existing systems poses integration complexities and necessitates standardization efforts. When it comes to data privacy, blockchain empowers patients to control data sharing and consent management [4].

Nevertheless, striking the right balance between data transparency and privacy, especially on public blockchains, remains a concern. Technology

DOI: 10.1201/9781003483113-9

TABLE 9.1 Blockchain in health care: Advantages, limitations, and future directions overview

Aspect	Advantages	Limitations	Future directions
Data Security	– Immutable, tamper-proof data storage	– Scalability concerns	– Implementing efficient consensus mechanisms
	– Robust encryption and access control	– Energy and computational resources required	– Research on quantum-resistant cryptographic tech
Interoperability	– Facilitates seamless data exchange	– Standardization challenges	– Interoperable blockchain solutions
	– Enables a unified view of patient data	– Integration complexities with existing systems	– Development of healthcare-specific standards
Data Privacy	– Patient-controlled data sharing	– Regulatory compliance (e.g., GDPR, HIPAA)	– Enhancing privacy-centric consensus mechanisms
	– Enhanced consent management	– Potential risk of data leakage through public blockchain	– Zero-knowledge proof and advanced encryption
Transparency	– Increased trust and accountability	– Privacy concerns related to complete data transparency	– Fine-grained access control mechanisms
	– Auditable, traceable data	– Balancing transparency with data confidentiality	– Hybrid blockchain solutions
Cost-Efficiency	– Reduces intermediaries and associated costs	– Initial setup costs and technology adoption barriers	– Research on cost-effective consensus algorithms

[Original (created by authors)]

promotes transparency, fostering increased trust and accountability through auditable and traceable data [5]. However, privacy concerns tied to complete transparency require solutions such as fine-grained access controls and hybrid blockchain models. Finally, blockchain enables cost-efficiency by reducing intermediaries and associated costs. Nonetheless, initial setup costs and the need to overcome technology adoption barriers call for continued research into cost-effective consensus algorithms and deployment strategies. To harness the full potential of blockchain in health care, ongoing research and development should focus on addressing these advantages, limitations, and future directions in Table 9.1.

9.1.1 Importance of data security in health care

In the realm of health care, the stakes associated with data security are exceptionally high. Patient data constitutes a treasure trove of sensitive and confidential information. Safeguarding this data is pivotal for protecting individuals' privacy and sustaining the integrity of healthcare services [6]. The advent of digital technologies, EHRs, telemedicine, and interconnected healthcare systems has exponentially increased the vulnerability of healthcare data to cyber threats and unauthorized access. Consequently, robust measures are indispensable to fortify data security, ensuring that patient information remains inaccessible to unauthorized entities and shielded against potential breaches. Figure 9.1 displays a taxonomy outlining various advantages of a blockchain-based healthcare system.

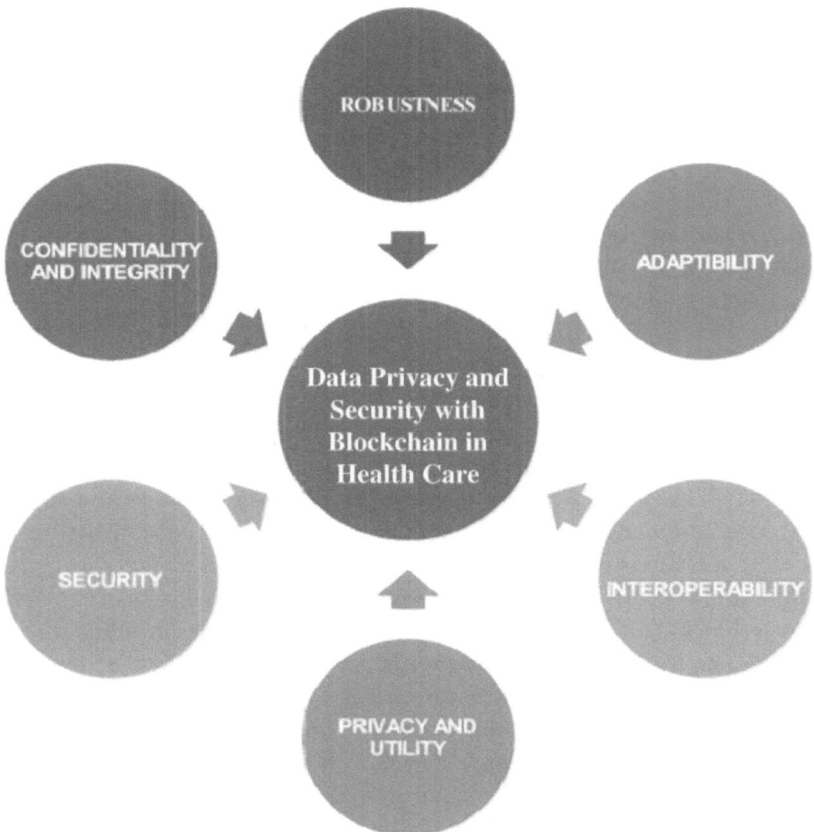

FIGURE 9.1 Enhancing security and preserving privacy through the utilization of blockchain in the healthcare sector.

Original (created by authors)

9.1.2 Current challenges in patient data management

Despite the advances in healthcare technology, managing patient data effectively remains a complex and multifaceted challenge. The conventional centralized approach to data storage, while widely used, exposes healthcare systems to a myriad of vulnerabilities [7]. Unauthorized access, data tampering, system failures, and ransomware attacks pose serious threats to the security and integrity of patient data [8]. Additionally, achieving interoperability among diverse healthcare systems remains a pressing issue due to the lack of standardized protocols and formats [8]. Compliance with regulatory requirements, such as the Health Insurance Portability and Accountability Act (HIPAA) in the United States, further compounds the challenges in managing patient data securely [9]. Addressing these challenges is pivotal to establishing a robust and secure framework for patient data management [10].

9.2 Understanding blockchain technology

A decentralized and distributed ledger system termed *blockchain technology* makes it possible to record transactions securely and openly across a network of computers. It was first created as the fundamental technology for the virtual currency known as Bitcoin, but it has subsequently found use in several sectors outside of banking. The following are essential aspects of comprehending blockchain technology [11]:

- **Decentralization:** Unlike centralized systems, Blockchain functions as a decentralized network, distributing data control among all nodes and providing resilience against a single point of failure.
- **Blocks and Chains:** Blocks are generated from grouping transactions, and each block has a timestamp, a reference to the block before it, and an identification number known as a cryptographic hash. Because of the blocks' linking, a chain is created; hence, the name blockchain.
- **Immutability:** It is very difficult to modify a block once it has been added to the blockchain. Blockchain technology creates immutability through consensus processes and cryptographic hashing, thereby rendering the record reliable and impervious to tampering.
- **Consensus Mechanisms:** Consensus strategies have been used to guarantee that all participants agree on the current state of the blockchain. Some popular ones include Practical Byzantine Fault Tolerance, Proof-of-Stake (PoS), Delegated Proof-of-Stake (DPoS), and Proof-of-Work (PoW; utilized by Bitcoin). Malicious acts and double spending are prevented by these processes.

- **Permission vs. Permissionless Blockchains:** Blockchains without permission, such as Ethereum and Bitcoin, allow anybody to sign in. On the contrary, permission blockchains are more suited for private or business applications since they limit access to individuals.

9.2.1 Core principles of blockchain

Decentralization is a fundamental tenet of blockchain technology, ensuring a peer-to-peer network devoid of a central authority [12]. Using cryptographic hashing, immutability guarantees the permanence and integrity of data [13]. Double spending is avoided by consensus procedures such as PoW or PoS, which establish consensus among nodes [14]. Using pairs of keys, cryptographic security safeguards transactions and authenticate participants. Replicated on every node, the distributed ledger improves transparency and thwarts central authority. By providing equal access to the same information, all parties involved can work towards transparency. This fosters a culture of distrust, making faith in a central authority unnecessary. Smart contracts increase effectiveness and dependability by using technology to automate and enforce agreements.

9.2.2 Key features for secure data management

Blockchain technology is essential to safe data management since it uses essential features to strengthen digital transactions. The cornerstone of cryptographic security is the use of secure key pairs and cutting-edge encryption to ensure the secrecy, integrity, and legitimacy of transactions. Since data is distributed among multiple nodes to thwart tampering and unauthorized access, its decentralized structure improves security by removing a single point of failure. Data integrity is guaranteed via immutability, which makes it extremely resistant to modifications made after recording [15]. Consensus techniques, such as PoW or PoS, establish participant agreement and safeguard the ledger. Strengthening security, the replicated distributed ledger across all nodes eliminates weaknesses seen in centralized databases. Due to its transparency, which allows everybody to see and authenticate the whole transaction history, blockchain promotes confidence. Permissioned networks offer an additional security layer through access limits. By streamlining and securing agreements and providing tamper-proof execution, smart contracts lessen the need for middlemen. When considered as a whole, these features form a strong and safe basis for blockchain data management, minimizing risks and maintaining transaction accuracy. Figure 9.2 depicts a biomedical security system integrating blockchain technology.

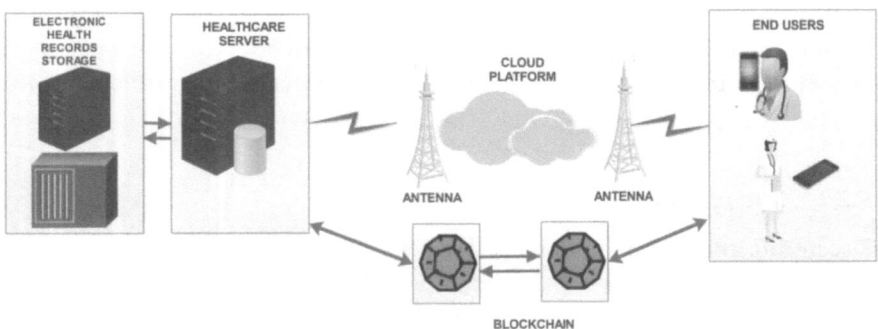

FIGURE 9.2 Blockchain-based biomedical security system.

[Original (created by authors)]

9.3 Leveraging blockchain for patient data security

By taking advantage of its decentralized and impenetrable structure, blockchain technology can be leveraged to enhance patient data security and address privacy concerns in the healthcare sector. Every patient transaction is safely documented in an unchangeable chain, improving record integrity and lowering the possibility of unwanted access. Public and private key pairs and other cryptographic security features of blockchain provide an additional degree of security, guaranteeing that patient data is only accessed by authorized healthcare providers. This satisfies legal mandates such as HIPAA. Transparency is promoted by giving patients ownership over their medical data through private key access, and sensitive data is dealt with securely using smart contracts, which automate consent management [16].

9.3.1 Cryptographic hash functions for data integrity

Cryptographic hash functions are essential for maintaining data integrity in several fields, such as blockchain technology and cybersecurity. These functions take any input data and output a fixed-length character string called the hash or digest. Characteristics such as collision resistance and the avalanche effect play a role in their significance. By rendering it computationally impossible for two different inputs to produce the same hash output, collision resistance guarantees uniqueness. The avalanche effect enhances sensitivity to changes by ensuring that even a slight change in the input data produces a noticeably different hash output. By comparing hash values before and after transmission, organizations using cryptographic hash functions can determine the integrity of the data and effectively identify any unauthorized modifications or corruption [17].

9.3.2 Decentralization and immutability for enhanced security

In the context of blockchain technology, decentralization and immutability are fundamental ideas that greatly improve security [18]. It describes how authority, processing, and control are dispersed throughout a network. In the context of blockchain, it indicates that a network of users rather than a single entity controls the system. A decentralized system is more resistant to attacks and single points of failure. The network is secure even in the event that one or more nodes are compromised. It is more difficult for a single organization to censor or regulate the flow of information or transactions when there is decentralization. This is especially important to preserving an open and free system. The lack of a central authority makes data tampering difficult.

Blockchain immutability ensures that data remains unaltered post-recording; once a block is added, it becomes unchangeable. This resistance to manipulation by participants eliminates the necessity for central authority. Immutability also simplifies auditability, enabling visual verification of the entire transaction history [16]. A strong security framework is produced when decentralization and immutability are combined. A decentralized and unchangeable blockchain provides a reliable and transparent platform for a variety of applications, including supply chain management, smart contracts, and financial transactions. It is impervious to a broad spectrum of security risks.

9.4 Patient data privacy and consent management

Blockchain technology revolutionizes healthcare consent and patient data privacy by ensuring safety through decentralized, immutable records. Patients remotely control data access via smart contracts, while transparent tools enable real-time monitoring for compliance. Blockchain's interoperability facilitates private data exchange among healthcare providers. Effective identity management and encrypted IDs reduce the risk of patient identity theft [19]. In summary, blockchain enhances security, empowers patients, and advances healthcare data platform privacy.

9.4.1 Empowering patients with data control

Blockchain technology empowers individuals by allowing direct oversight and decentralizing control over health data. Users can dictate and automate consent through smart contracts, specifying who can access data. Transparent tracking on blockchain encourages accountability, providing a clear audit trail for each data exchange. Interoperability enables the smooth and regulated sharing of health information among diverse healthcare providers. The inclusion of cryptographic identity management enhances verification and overall security. In conclusion, blockchain promotes a patient-centric paradigm, ensuring data autonomy and privacy in health care [20].

9.4.2 Smart contracts for automated consent management

The application of smart contracts in automated consent management makes consent-related processes more efficient and secure, streamlining the request, confirmation, and provision of consent across various transactions and interactions.

9.5 Encryption and access controls

Essential safeguards in blockchain technology include access restrictions and encryption. Encryption guarantees data confidentiality by transforming it into a secure code, while access controls manage permissions, determining who can access or modify blockchain data. Together, these elements enhance the security and integrity of blockchain-based systems.

9.5.1 Enhancing data security through encryption

Critical for bolstering data security in blockchain, encryption transforms data into a secure code, protecting it from unauthorized access and ensuring confidentiality within the blockchain ecosystem.

9.5.2 Implementing robust access control mechanisms

Ensuring the security and integrity of distributed ledgers in the ever-evolving domain of blockchain technology necessitates the implementation of robust access controls. Access control is pivotal in preventing unauthorized access and transactions, ensuring that only authorized users possess the necessary permissions to engage with the blockchain network. At the heart of this approach lies the formulation of authorization and permission procedures, delineating the specific tasks each user is allowed to execute. Identity management, facilitated by cryptographic methods and decentralized identity technologies, constitutes a crucial element in securely identifying users. The prevention of unauthorized transactions is facilitated by cryptographic keys and digital signatures, validating the legitimacy of each transaction before it is incorporated into the blockchain [21].

9.6 Ensuring interoperability and seamless data exchange

Facilitating information communication and ensuring interoperability within the context of blockchain is essential for establishing a cohesive and interconnected network. This entails seamlessly integrating various blockchain systems and platforms to facilitate the efficient transmission of data and transactions. Blockchain interoperability simplifies collaboration by enabling effective interaction among diverse blockchain networks and decentralized applications (DApps) [22]. Through the implementation of common standards and protocols, interoperability ensures easy sharing of data across different blockchain ecosystems, enhancing the overall effectiveness and efficiency of decentralized systems. The realization of the full potential of blockchain technology across a spectrum of applications, spanning from supply chain and finance to health care and beyond, hinges on the adoption of this interoperable approach.

9.6.1   *Standardizing data exchange with blockchain*

Leveraging blockchain technology to standardize data exchange is a fundamental approach to enhance reliability and effectiveness in information sharing. By establishing standardized protocols and formats, blockchain ensures consistent and uniform exchange of data among different parties in a network. This standardization contributes to a more transparent and collaborative environment across diverse sectors and industries, improving interoperability, streamlining communication, and facilitating seamless transactions.

9.6.2   *Facilitating secure interoperability among healthcare systems*

Securing and facilitating the sharing of patient data seamlessly incorporates blockchain technology, fostering secure interoperability among healthcare facilities. With its decentralized design and cryptographic security features, blockchain enhances the safety of medical records, ensuring secure sharing among diverse medical professionals. Through the establishment of standardized protocols, blockchain ensures uniform data formats and compatibility, facilitating effective communication among healthcare systems while maintaining robust security measures. Beyond promoting information sharing, this approach safeguards patient confidentiality and preserves data integrity throughout the healthcare system [21].

9.7   Case interoperability and seamless data exchange

In diverse applications, seamless interoperability, and effective data sharing within blockchain ecosystems are fundamental requirements. Whether in economic, supply chain, health care, or other sectors, the collaboration of various blockchain systems and platforms is crucial for streamlined and transparent operations. Ensuring the capability of different blockchain networks and applications to interchange data, transactions, and smart contract functionalities is vital for achieving comprehensive case interoperability. This fosters a more interconnected and collaborative environment, enabling blockchain technology to realize its maximum potential across a multitude of sectors.

Harnessing blockchain technology in healthcare applications has the potential to markedly enhance security, privacy, and data integrity, employing a range of mathematical models. Although machine learning (ML) and blockchain are typically viewed as distinct technologies, there are instances where their integration can be synergistic in healthcare applications [20, 22]. The ensuing concepts and mathematical models illustrate the convergence of ML and blockchain within the healthcare domain. These mathematical models are commonly utilized in the realm of blockchain technology for healthcare applications:

a **Federated Learning**
   Healthcare blockchain models may learn from decentralized patient data while preserving data confidentiality and privacy due to federated learning, a revolutionary concept in ML that enables model training across decentralized devices without centralized sharing of information. In federated learning, the iterative process involves adjusting model parameters θ based on the local data set Dt at each participant, as depicted in the equation:

$$\theta_{t+1} = \theta_t = \eta \nabla F(\theta_t, D_t)$$

   This formula represents the cooperative learning process among dispersed nodes, which enables the model to enhance its performance and accuracy without requiring the central exchange of private patient data.

b **Secure Multi-Party Computation**
   Secure multi-party computation (SMPC) ensures input privacy by enabling multiple parties to collaboratively compute a function over them. The process involves advanced cryptographic techniques, and the equations employed are contingent on the specific computation. SMPC equation

   Let $f(x1, x2\text{-------}xn)$ is the function to be computed jointly.
   Parties have private inputs x1, x2, ---------xn.

   It can provide cooperative ML tasks on healthcare blockchains without disclosing private patient information.

c **Homomorphic Encryption for Machine Learning**
   Machine learning tasks can be done with encrypted data sets by using homomorphic encryption, which enables calculations on encrypted data.

   $E(x)$ - specifies the encryption function that enables it possible to compute with encrypted data.
   $E(a).E(b) = E(a + b)$ Enabling addition operations on encrypted data due to its hType equation here.omomorphic characteristic.

This approach permits the study of confidential patient information in the healthcare sector without disclosing the original information.

d **Tokenization of Health Information**
Sensitive data must be tokenized in order to be represented by a token that protects its true contents.

Let D be the sensitive data.
Token (D) = Token where Token represents the tokenized form.

The process of tokenizing sensitive data and converting it into a tokenized format for usage in healthcare blockchains is represented by this equation.

Tokenization and ML models can be combined in healthcare blockchains to allow analysis without disclosing personally identifying information about patients.

e **Using Reinforcement Learning to Plan Treatments**
Let Q(s, a) show the predicted cumulative reward of performing action, or the action-value function "a" in state s.

Rt is the immediate reward one receives for acting at in state st.
α is the rate of learning.
γ is the discount factor.

$$Q(st, at) < -Q(st, at) + \alpha[Rt + y.\max a \, Q(st + 1, a) - Q(st, at)]$$

Reinforcement learning employs the Q-learning update rule, represented by this equation, enabling healthcare blockchains to optimize treatment plans and offer personalized recommendations while upholding patient data confidentiality.

f **Applying Predictive Analytics in Personalized Medicine**
Based on historical information, predictive analytics models predict illness risks or patient outcomes.

P (y|X) symbolizes the predictive analytics model and predicts the result y according to input features.
Θ represents the model parameters that have been obtained from previous information.
P (y|X,Θ) This equation describes the predictive analytics model, which uses input feature-based evaluation for predicting patient outcomes or disease risks.

To keep patient data confidential during the prediction process, this model must be implemented in a safe, privacy-preserving environment in a healthcare blockchain. Table 9.2 illustrates the utilization of predictive analytics for efficient sharing of relevant healthcare data.

TABLE 9.2 Use case: Predictive analytics and sharing relevant healthcare data

Aim	Facilitate the safe and confidential exchange of medical data for analytical purposes.
Steps towards Implementation:	
Blockchain for Data Sharing	Total Nodes (number of healthcare providers) 10 Daily Blockchain Transactions 1000 Level of Security for Blockchain 256-bit encryption
Tokenization in Relation to Privacy	Record Tokenization 50,000 Strength of the Tokenization Algorithm AES with 128-bit keys
Federated Learning for Predictive Analytics	Local Models Trained for Each Provider: 10 Iterations in Federated Learning: 20 Learning Rate (η) : 0.01
Employing Smart Contracts to Manage Consent	The quantity of smart contracts that have been created: 100 The consent terms defined for each contract: limitations on data usage and privacy settings
Results	Accuracy of Predictive Analytics Models: 90% Success Rate for Collaborative Disease Prediction: 85% Patient Being Satisfied with Data Security: 95%

Challenges and Considerations	(a) Regulatory Compliance:
	  Compliance Score: 98%.
	  Two privacy audits were carried out.
	
	(b) Interoperability:
	  Score for Interoperability: 75%
	  Healthcare System Integration Time: 6 months

[Original (created by authors)]

For purposes of demonstration only, these hypothetical numerical values are used. These values would be selected in a real-life scenario according to the needs, number, and features of the healthcare system that are being put into place.

9.8 Challenges and future directions

Future directions in blockchain encompass enhanced interoperability, sustainability, and privacy technologies, while challenges entail scalability, regulatory uncertainty, and the imperative for standardization [23].

9.8.1 Addressing challenges in blockchain implementation

Employing blockchain technology involves several problems that call for an intelligent and multidisciplinary approach.

- First and foremost, sharding and layer-2 protocols are two creative ways to address scalability issues frequently present in public blockchains.

- Clear compliance frameworks and proactive involvement with regulatory bodies play a pivotal role in resolving regulatory uncertainties. The challenges linked to standardization underscore the importance of collaborative efforts across the industry to formulate shared protocols, enhancing interoperability and fostering a more unified blockchain ecosystem.
- Addressing security concerns in blockchain involves implementing robust cryptographic measures and promoting user education, while transitioning from energy-intensive PoW to sustainable alternatives such as PoS is crucial to reduce environmental impacts.
- Ensuring confidentiality standards, especially in sensitive sectors like health care and finance, involves leveraging advanced technologies such as homomorphic encryption and zero-knowledge proofs. The establishment of cross-chain standards is imperative to tackle interoperability challenges, fostering seamless communication across diverse blockchain networks, ultimately necessitating collaboration in technology innovation, regulatory advocacy, and industry engagement for the full realization of blockchain's potential.

9.8.2   Future trends and potential innovations

- A popular trend has shifted towards blockchain-based decentralized health records, allowing consumers greater ownership over their information for enhanced safety and provider interoperability.
- The rising emphasis on interoperability in health care involves incorporating blockchain networks and standardized protocols to streamline data exchange and promote collaboration across systems.
- Blockchain technology is currently being employed to enhance pharmaceutical supply chain traceability, ensure transparency in novel ways, lessen the quantity of counterfeit medications, and improve the chain's overall effectiveness.
- The application of cutting-edge privacy-enhancing technology, such as zero-knowledge proofs, has become popular. This strategy effectively achieves an agreement between privacy and transparency, particularly when handling sensitive patient data.
- The current development involves integrating blockchain technology with artificial intelligence (AI) to promote advanced data analysis, dynamically improving predictive analytics, customized treatment plans, and medical research by employing AI synergies.
- The application of blockchain technology for delivering visible and unchangeable clinical trial data is currently widespread. This distinct approach to data integrity guarantee reduces fraud and boosts trust regarding the results of clinical trials.

9.9 Conclusion

Blockchain delivers a paradigm change in healthcare information management and has a profoundly revolutionary effect on patient data security. By providing restricted access and encrypting patient data, blockchain promises improved privacy. The integrity of patient data is guaranteed by a decentralized structure, which reduces the possibility of unwanted changes. By giving individuals more control over their health information, blockchain promotes confidence and transparency. The integrity of patient data is preserved by the auditable and tamper-resistant system that is ensured by the immutability of blockchain records. Essentially, blockchain offers itself as a game-changing technology that dramatically raises the bar for patient data protection throughout the healthcare industry.

References

1. Suhasini, M., & Singh, D. (2021). Blockchain based framework for secure data management in healthcare information systems. Annals of the Romanian Society for Cell Biology, 25, 16933–16946.
2. Gupta, R., Thakker, U., Tanwar, S., Obaidat, M., & Hsiao, K. F. (5–7 October 2020). BITS: A Blockchain-driven Intelligent Scheme for Telesurgery System. In Proceedings of the 2020 International Conference on Computer, Information and Telecommunication Systems (CITS), Hangzhou, China; pp. 1–5.
3. Chukwu, E., & Garg, L. (2020). A systematic review of blockchain in healthcare: Frameworks, prototypes, and implementations. IEEE Access, 8, 21196–21214.
4. Hathaliya, J. J., & Tanwar, S. (2020). An exhaustive survey on security and privacy issues in healthcare 4.0. Computer and Communications, 153, 311–335.
5. Guntur, L. N., Dornadula, G., & Nimbagal, R. N. (2022). Blockchain Technology: A Breakthrough in the Healthcare Sector. In: Idrees, S. M., Nowostawski, M. (eds) Transformations Through Blockchain Technology (pp. 137–160). Springer, Cham, Switzerland.
6. Saha, A., Amin, R., Kunal, S., Vollala, S., & Dwivedi, S. K. (2019). Review on "Blockchain technology based medical healthcare system with privacy issues". Security and Privacy, 2(5), e83.
7. Ali, A., Rahim, H. A., Pasha, M. F., Dowsley, R., Masud, M., Ali, J., & Baz, M. (2021). Security, privacy, and reliability in digital healthcare systems using blockchain. Electronics, 10(16), 2034.
8. Singh, S., Pankaj, B., Nagarajan, K., Singh, N. P., & Bala, V. (2022). Blockchain with cloud for handling healthcare data: A privacy-friendly platform. Materials Today: Proceedings, 62, 5021–5026.
9. Idrees, S. M., Agarwal, P., & Alam, M. A. (eds). (2021). Blockchain for Healthcare Systems: Challenges, Privacy, and Securing of Data. CRC Press.
10. Shah, V., Thakkar, V., & Khang, A. (2023). Electronic Health Records Security and Privacy Enhancement Using Blockchain Technology. In (Eds.) Alex Khang, Geeta Rana, R. K. Tailor and Vugar Abdullayev: Data-Centric AI Solutions and Emerging Technologies in the Healthcare Ecosystem (pp. 1–13). CRC Press.
11. Zaabar, B., Cheikhrouhou, O., Jamil, F., Ammi, M., & Abid, M. (2021). HealthBlock: A secure blockchain-based healthcare data management system. Computer Networks, 200, 108500.

12. Zhang, A., & Lin, X. (2018). Towards secure and privacy-preserving data sharing in e-health systems via consortium blockchain. Journal of Medical Systems, 42(8), 140.

13. Rani, P., Verma, S., Yadav, S. P., Rai, B. K., Naruka, M. S., & Kumar, D. (2022). Simulation of the lightweight blockchain technique based on privacy and security for healthcare data for the cloud system. International Journal of E-Health and Medical Communications (IJEHMC), 13(4), 1–15.

14. Othman, S. B., Almalki, F. A., & Sakli, H. (2022). Internet of Things in the Healthcare Applications: Overview of Security and Privacy Issues. In: Chakraborty, C., Khosravi, M.R. (eds) Intelligent Healthcare. Springer, Singapore. https://doi.org/10.1007/978-981-16-8150-9_9

15. Tanrıverdi, M. (2020). A systematic review of privacy-preserving healthcare data sharing on blockchain. Journal of Cybersecurity and Information Management, 5(2 SI 1), 31–37.

16. Patil, S. D., Kathole, A. B., Kumbhare, S., & Vhatkar, K. (2024). A blockchain-based approach to ensuring the security of electronic data. International Journal of Intelligent Systems and Applications in Engineering, 12(11s), 649–655.

17. Alqarni, K. S., Almalki, F. A., Soufiene, B. O., Ali, O., & Albalwy, F. (2022). Authenticated wireless links between a drone and sensors using a blockchain: Case of smart farming. Wireless Communications and Mobile Computing, 2022, Article ID 4389729, 13. https://doi.org/10.1155/2022/4389729

18. Gupta, S., Alharbi, F., Alshahrani, R., Kumar Arya, P., Vyas, S., Elkamchouchi, D. H., & Soufiene, B. O. (2023). Secure and lightweight authentication protocol for privacy preserving communications in smart city applications. Sustainability, 15, 5346. https://doi.org/10.3390/su15065346

19. Wang, B., & Li, Z. (2021). Healthchain: A privacy protection system for medical data based on blockchain. Future Internet, 13(10), 247.

20. Balasubramanium, S., Sivasankar, K., & Rajasekaran, M. P. (2021, March). A survey on data privacy and preservation using blockchain in healthcare organization. In 2021 International Conference on Advance Computing and Innovative Technologies in Engineering (ICACITE) (pp. 956–962). IEEE.

21. Wu, H., Dwivedi, A. D., & Srivastava, G. (2021). Security and privacy of patient information in medical systems based on blockchain technology. ACM Transactions on Multimedia Computing, Communications, and Applications (TOMM), 17(2s), 1–17.

22. Jennath, H. S., Anoop, V. S., & Asharaf, S. (2020). Blockchain for healthcare: Securing patient data and enabling trusted artificial intelligence. ACM Transactions on Multimedia Computing, Communications, and Applications (TOMM), Volume 17, Issue 2, Article No.: 60, Pages 1 - 17.

23. Steria, S. (2021). A blockchain-based healthcare platform for secure personalised data sharing. Public Health and Informatics - Proceedings of MIE, 281, 208.

10

AN ADVANCED SECURE MEDICAL FILE-SHARING SYSTEM BASED ON IPFS AND BLOCKCHAIN TECHNOLOGY

Mounira Tarhouni and Faten Chaabane

10.1 Introduction

Blockchain is a revolutionary decentralized and distributed ledger technology designed to provide a secure and transparent framework for recording transactions. Unlike traditional systems that rely on a central authority, blockchain operates as a peer-to-peer network, allowing multiple participants to interact without the need for intermediaries. Blockchain holds the promise of bringing about transformative changes across various industries, such as fintech, government, health, and supply chain [1].

The potential benefits of blockchain technology encompass a reduction in the costs and complexity of transactions between parties, heightened security measures, improved transparency, and enhanced regulatory capabilities.

The healthcare sector is often characterized as a traditionally rigid industry, resistant to change and slow to adopt innovative practices. Concerns related to health care, such as privacy, quality of care, and information security, have gained global attention in recent years. Blockchain technologies are emerging as a recognized solution to address challenges in information distribution within the healthcare domain. These technologies hold the potential to enhance immediate healthcare practices, including improvements in health service delivery and support for the quality of care. Several innovative information system solutions have been suggested to leverage blockchain-oriented applications in the healthcare sector. These evolving solutions are primarily crafted for healthcare professionals and patients, empowering them to make informed decisions related to treatments, care, and administrative arrangements for service support.

DOI: 10.1201/9781003483113-10

Jiang et al. [2] introduced BlocHIE, a blockchain-based platform for healthcare information exchange. This platform was designed to assess criteria for the exchange of healthcare data. Initially, authors scrutinize diverse prerequisites for sharing healthcare data originating from various sources. Drawing insights from this analysis, authors implement two loosely coupled blockchains to effectively manage distinct types of healthcare data. Subsequently, they integrate off-chain storage and on-chain verification methodologies to meet the dual demands of privacy and authenticability.

In [3], the authors proposed an architecture for sharing EHRs. This work is based on an encryption mechanism to encrypt the health data, access control to ensure the privacy, and confidentiality of health records. The proposed scheme has used a storage mechanism combining cloud and blockchain.

With a particular healthcare system, Ramani et al. [4] proposed a blockchain-based secure and effective data access method for the patient and the doctor to protect the confidentiality and privacy of the patients set by the elliptic curve cryptography (ECC) techniques. The proposed system is also capable of safeguarding patients' privacy. This scheme's security research reveals that it can withstand well-known attacks while retaining system integrity.

GuptaXia et al. [5] proposed MeDShare, a system that addresses the issue of medical data sharing among medical big data custodians in a trustless environment. The system employs smart contracts and an access control mechanism to effectively track the behavior of the data and revoke access to offending entities on detection of violation of permissions on data.

In [6], the authors have shown the various possibilities of creating reliable artificial intelligence (AI) models in e-health using blockchain, which is an open network for the sharing and authorization of information. Healthcare professionals will have access to the blockchain to display the medical records of the patient, and AI uses a variety of proposed algorithms and decision-making capability, as well as large quantities of data.

In [7], authors proposed an innovative IPFS-based storage model for blockchain. The miners deposit the transaction data into the IPFS network and pack the returned IPFS hash of transaction into the block. The proposed scheme is applied to the Bitcoin blockchain.

A blockchain-based framework integrated with InterPlanetary File System (IPFS) for EHR in healthcare management has been proposed by Jayabalan and Jeyanthi in [8]. This proposed framework empowers healthcare institutions to uphold fail-safe and tamper-proof healthcare ledgers in a decentralized fashion. Hospitals and doctors function as lightweight nodes, while patient nodes can operate as either full or lightweight nodes, enhancing the overall security and reliability of the system.

In this context, our chapter presents a cutting-edge mobile application that utilizes the IPFS and Ethereum technology to establish a secure and streamlined medical file-sharing platform. This innovative amalgamation capitalizes on the decentralized and immutable characteristics of blockchain, complemented by the efficiency and scalability of IPFS, offering a robust solution specifically designed for mobile environments.

10.2 Blockchain technology

A blockchain is an ever-expanding, decentralized ledger comprising records known as "blocks." These blocks are interconnected in a chain through a process called *mining*, where pending transactions are transformed into a cryptographic puzzle. Miners, individuals utilizing computer systems, solve this puzzle, generating a unique sequence of letters and numbers known as a hash for the block. Every block comprises crucial components, including a cryptographic hash of the preceding block, a timestamp, and transaction data. Additionally, it incorporates details from all antecedent blocks and transactions, intricately weaving a network or chain that ensures the integrity and coherence of the entire blockchain system [9, 10].

Any alteration to the data within a single block initiates a chain reaction that could potentially stall the entire blockchain. After processing the information, every computer in the network simultaneously secures the data, establishing a permanent, unchangeable digital record. The rules governing each blockchain system dictate the entities authorized to append new blocks to the chain and define how the procedure is done. At its core, a blockchain is a series of interconnected blocks, where each block contains a cryptographic hash of the previous block, creating an immutable chain of transaction history. This fundamental structure ensures the integrity and security of the recorded data.

Understanding how blocks are linked to form the blockchain is crucial for gaining insight into the functioning of this decentralized technology. As illustrated in Figure 10.1, the blockchain is essentially a chain of blocks, and each block contains a list of transactions. A block typically consists of a header and a body. The header contains metadata, including a timestamp, a reference to the previous block (hash), and other relevant information. The

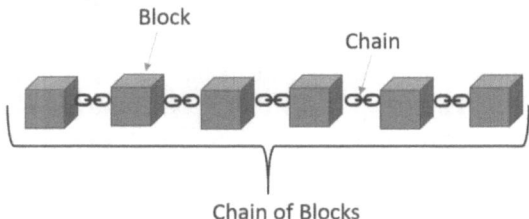

FIGURE 10.1 Blockchain architecture.

Original (created by authors)

concept of hashing plays a pivotal role. Each block is assigned a unique cryptographic hash based on its content, including the transactions and the previous block's hash.

This hash is a digital fingerprint that uniquely identifies the block. If any information in the block is altered, the hash changes, providing a tamper-evident mechanism.

The body of the block contains a set of transactions, each representing a transfer of value or data.

The distinctive advantages of blockchain lie in its capacity to facilitate the sharing of data and transactions across an unalterable peer-to-peer (P2P) network, thereby augmenting transparency and security.

Blockchain has the potential to address certain interoperability challenges within health care and can play a pivotal role in placing patients at the forefront of the ecosystem.

Blockchain can be applied to facilitate the access and sharing of patient medical records, mobile applications, remote monitoring, and medical data management systems. This application enables patients to retain ownership and control over their health records.

- **Header:** It serves the purpose of pinpointing a specific block within the entire blockchain. This component manages all blocks in the blockchain. Miners periodically hash the block header by altering the nonce value during routine mining operations. Additionally, the block header encompasses three sets of block metadata.
- **Previous Block Address/Hash:** It is employed to establish a connection between the (i+1)th block and the ith block through the use of hashing. In brief, it functions as a pointer to the hash of the preceding (parent) block in the chain.
- **Timestamp:** It is a system designed to validate the data within a block and allocate a specific time or date of creation for digital documents. The timestamp, represented as a unique string of characters, serves to distinctly identify the document or event and signifies its creation time.
- **Nonce:** A nonce is a numerical value utilized only once, integral to the proof-of-work (PoW) process within a block. This nonce is assessed by comparing it to the active target, and if it proves smaller or equal to the current target, it is deemed valid. Miners engage in the exhaustive testing of numerous nonces per second, persisting until they discover a valuable nonce that meets the validation criteria.
- **Merkle Root:** A data structure that forms the backbone of various data blocks, the Merkle Tree efficiently stores all transactions within a block by generating a digital fingerprint of the entire transaction set. This mechanism enables users to verify the eligibility of a transaction for inclusion in a block.

10.2.1 Mining techniques

Mining involves the creation of blocks that become permanently appended to the blockchain database. In certain blockchain applications, miners who successfully generate the initial valid block are rewarded, as seen in the case of Bitcoin. This reward, typically in the form of monetary compensation for financial applications [11], is provided by the system. Mining stands out as a pivotal concept in blockchain technology, enabling nodes to produce blocks subject to validation by others [12]. Nodes engaged in the creation of new blocks are termed "mining nodes," engaging in a competitive race to swiftly validate transactions and create a new block in order to secure the reward.

10.2.2 Consensus algorithms

Blockchain consensus algorithms are mechanisms that enable distributed nodes in a blockchain network to agree on the state of the system and validate transactions. Consensus is crucial for maintaining the integrity of the blockchain and ensuring that all participants have a consistent view of the ledger. Several consensus algorithms exist, each with its own set of characteristics and use cases [13].

The consensus algorithm of the blockchain is the logic that determines who can add new blocks to a blockchain and how nodes reach an agreement on the next transaction to be added to the chain. Consensus is a critical aspect of maintaining the integrity of the blockchain, ensuring that all participants share a consistent view of the ledger.

There are several major categories of blockchain algorithms:

- **Proof-of-Work (PoW)** is the most well-known consensus mechanism in the field of cryptocurrencies but is much less utilized due to its energy and hardware-intensive operation. It is the first consensus algorithm used by Satoshi Nakamoto in the creation of Bitcoin. The PoW consensus mechanism, therefore, requires a significant amount of energy and hardware to operate, and it is considered by many as the most secure solution for a network and for resisting censorship.
- **Proof-of-Stake (PoS)** is the second most prevalent consensus mechanism in the field of cryptocurrencies. Indeed, it is the most used due to its often-lower energy and hardware costs. PoS was introduced in 2011 to address the limitations of PoW networks, with Peercoin being the first cryptocurrency to implement the PoS mechanism. Unlike PoW, PoS operates with minimal computational power, relying instead on a certain number of tokens staked in a smart contract to secure the distributed network (blockchain). This process is known as "staking." Validators are randomly chosen to validate blocks and are rewarded in cryptocurrency.

- **Proof-of-Authority** (PoA) was proposed in 2017 by Gavin Wood, co-founder of Ethereum. He suggested a new practical and efficient solution to operate and secure the blockchain. Unlike PoW or PoS, PoA does not depend on computational power or the number of tokens a node possesses. Instead, it relies on the reputation of validators, referred to as "trusted entities." Block validation is carried out by validators who have been authoritatively selected.
- **Delegated Proof-of-Stake** (DPoS) Developed in 2014 by Daniel Larimer, the DPoS consensus algorithm is also an alternative to the PoW consensus algorithm. It is particularly well regarded in the community because this algorithm has been presented as a more efficient and democratic version of previous algorithms.

10.2.3 Smart contracts

Smart contracts are essentially software programs residing within a block-chain framework, designed to activate when specific predetermined conditions are satisfied. Their primary function is to facilitate the automatic execution of agreements, ensuring that all participants gain immediate certainty regarding the outcome, eliminating the need for intermediaries and minimizing time loss. Beyond agreement execution, these contracts also serve to automate entire workflows, seamlessly initiating subsequent actions as soon as the specified conditions are met.

10.3 Blockchain in e-health

Patients and healthcare practitioners are faced with the challenge of accessing, managing, integrating, and sharing health records securely. Patients should be able to manage their health records anywhere in the world, keep track of medical background, give access to data, and share those with any healthcare professional securely.

Blockchain technology is well suited for managing any type of digital data where authentication and consensus on data integrity are crucial. It proves particularly valuable in situations requiring shared write access for multiple parties. In the healthcare context, blockchain can be employed to ensure the safety and security of critical medical data.

The blockchain's limited storage capacity per block hinders its ability to store extensive data. Moreover, the requirement for duplicating block data across multiple network nodes leads to inefficient use of storage space. To address this, off-chain storage becomes essential for accommodating substantial data volumes while maintaining network efficiency and performance. Notably, solutions such as IPFS offer a means to reduce the cost implications for blockchain nodes by minimizing the data stored and processed by these nodes.

The integration of IPFS and blockchain empowers developers to architect decentralized and resilient systems, harnessing the advantages of distributed file storage and tamper-resistant transaction records. This synergy is particularly invaluable in applications where priorities include decentralization, safeguarding data integrity, and ensuring resistance to censorship.

In practical terms, this integration addresses several critical challenges. Firstly, the decentralized nature of IPFS facilitates efficient and scalable storage, ensuring that files are not reliant on a central server. The use of content addressing in IPFS ensures the integrity of stored data, as each file is uniquely identified by its cryptographic hash.

Ethereum was chosen for its advanced smart contract capabilities, which allow us to automate critical aspects of medical data management securely and transparently. Its widespread adoption and supportive ecosystem offer additional tools and libraries that accelerate development and ensure long-term viability.

10.4 Implementation

In assessing the system's performance, a comprehensive evaluation is conducted through the execution of a simulation on the Ethereum decentralized computing platform. This simulation involves the creation and execution of smart contracts, meticulously programmed in Solidity and deployed on the Ethereum platform. This approach thoroughly examines the system's performance on the Ethereum blockchain.

There are several programming languages that can be used to create this application, such as Python, JavaScript, etc. We have chosen to use Node. js for developing this application. In the context of our application, Node. js is much more than just a development choice; it is the diligent conductor orchestrating the symphony of our system's operations. Imagine Node.js as the backbone, seamlessly connecting the vibrant frontend with the complex, blockchain-powered backend, all while managing the flow of data like a skilled traffic controller. Whether it is handling user requests with the agility of a seasoned athlete, ensuring that each interaction with the Ethereum blockchain and IPFS network is as smooth as silk, or securing the gates of our digital world, Node.js does it all.

Firstly, we installed the necessary packages using import create from "ipfs-http-client." This imports the create function from the ipfs-http-client module. This line suggests the use of the IPFS HTTP client to interact with the IPFS network through HTTP calls, as shown in Figure 10.2.

Then, we created an IPFS client that connects to a local host and port, as shown in Figure 10.3.

To send medical files, we utilized the methods provided by the object using the "add" method, as shown in Figure 10.4.

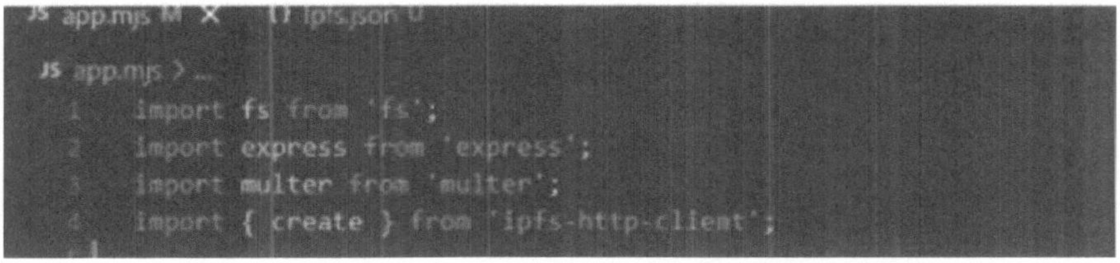

```
JS app.mjs M X    {} ipfs.json U

JS app.mjs > ...
  1    import fs from 'fs';
  2    import express from 'express';
  3    import multer from 'multer';
  4    import { create } from 'ipfs-http-client';
```

FIGURE 10.2 Client library for the IPFS HTTP Application Programming Interface (API)

[Original (created by authors)]

```
// Create an IPFS client that connects to your local IPFS Desktop node
const ipfs = create({ host: '127.0.0.1', port: 5001, protocol: 'http' });
```

FIGURE 10.3 Creation of IPFS client.

[Original (created by authors)]

```
// Retrieve additional parameters from the request body
const { userId, doctorId, description } = req.body;

// Upload the single file to IPFS using its path
const fileStream = fs.createReadStream(uploadedFile.path);
const ipfsFile = await ipfs.add(fileStream);
```

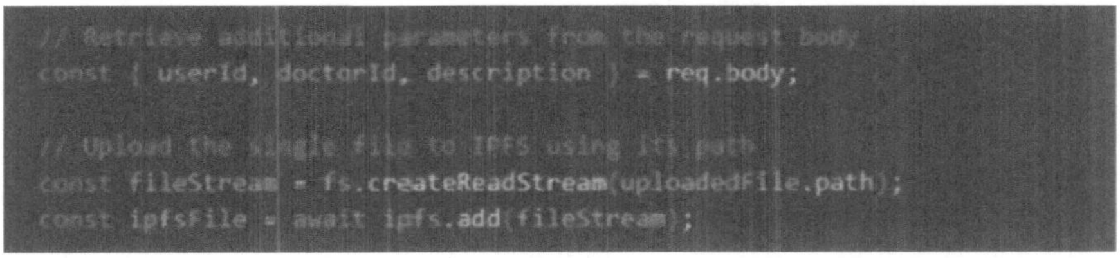

FIGURE 10.4 Storage of a document in IPFS.

[Original (created by authors)]

```
console.log(`File uploaded to IPFS with CID: ${ipfsHash}`);
```

FIGURE 10.5 Recovery of a document.

[Original (created by authors)]

To retrieve the data, we used the file hash that we stored in the IPFS system, "ipfsHash," as shown in Figure 10.5.

Finally, we obtained the content identifier (CID) of the data we added to IPFS, indicating that the addition operation was successfully completed, as shown in Figure 10.6.

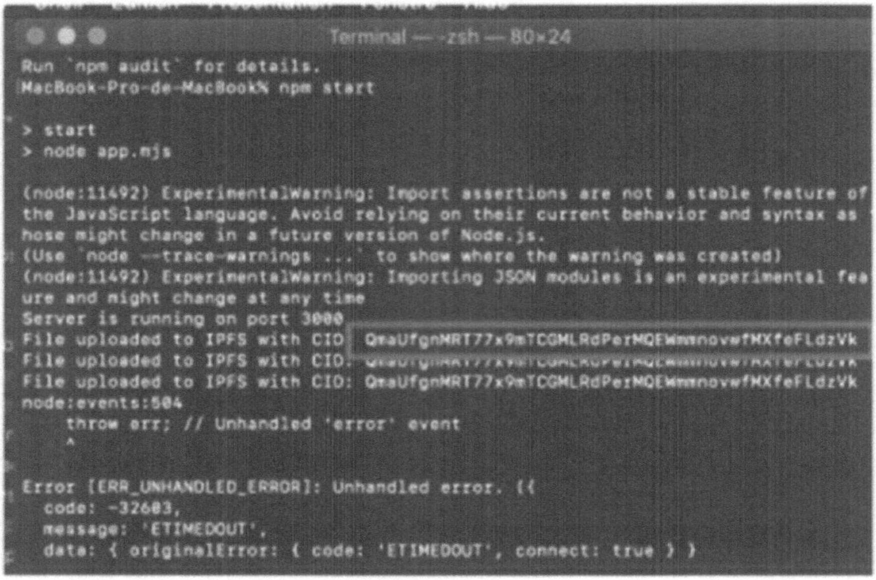

FIGURE 10.6 Content identifier (CID).

[Original (created by authors)]

10.4.1 *Integration of the blockchain with IPFS*

IPFS, functioning as a peer-to-peer content-addressed file-sharing system, leverages cryptographic hashes for data storage. This decentralized storage approach enhances efficiency. Combining blockchain with IPFS results in a robust file-sharing system. The integration of these technologies not only provides effective data storage but also contributes to reducing costs and maximizing decentralized storage capabilities.

Truffle served as our chosen framework for smart contract development, as it streamlines the creation, testing, and deployment process on the Ethereum blockchain. This framework not only simplifies but also streamlines the entire process, including the creation, compilation, deployment, and testing phases of smart contracts. Its comprehensive features contribute to an efficient and effective development workflow for Ethereum-based projects.

10.4.1.1 *Smart contract creation*

Within the "contracts" directory, a new Solidity file is crafted with the .sol extension, bearing the name "ipfs.sol," as depicted in Figure 10.7. Following this, the Solidity code is incorporated into the file, as exemplified in Figure 10.8.

To compile our smart contract, we execute the following command: truffle compile.\\.

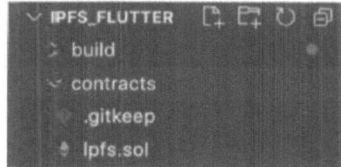

FIGURE 10.7   Creation of a smart contract.

[Original (created by authors)]

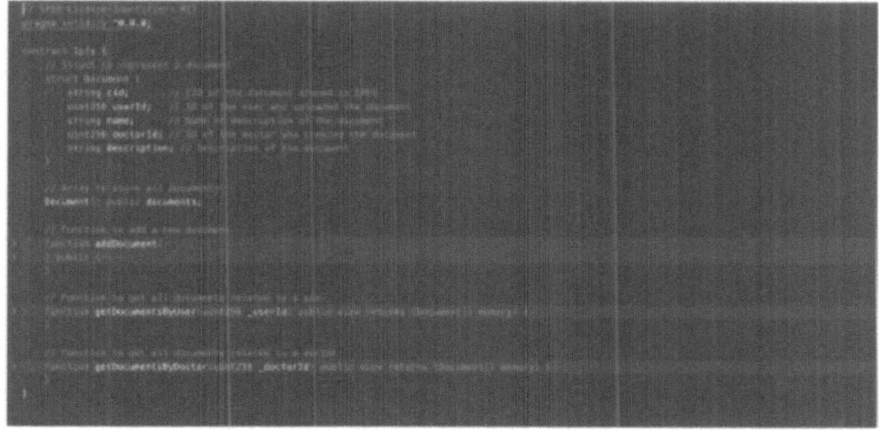

FIGURE 10.8   Code of the smart contract.

[Original (created by authors)]

This will generate the output files in the "build/contracts" directory of our project, which represent our API that we will use for further integration. Next, we create a migration file in the "migrations" directory to specify how to deploy our contract on a blockchain. We will use JavaScript to define the deployment steps, as illustrated in Figure 10.9.

Finally, we execute the migration with the following command: truffle migrate.

This will deploy our smart contract on the blockchain specified in our Truffle configuration. To use this contract in our previously developed application, we need the contract's address.

We have previously obtained the contract that we are going to deploy using Truffle. To use this contract in our existing node application, we need two elements: the contract's ABI, which is automatically generated during the compilation of our contract and is stored in the "build/contracts" directory, and the contract's address (Figure 10.10).

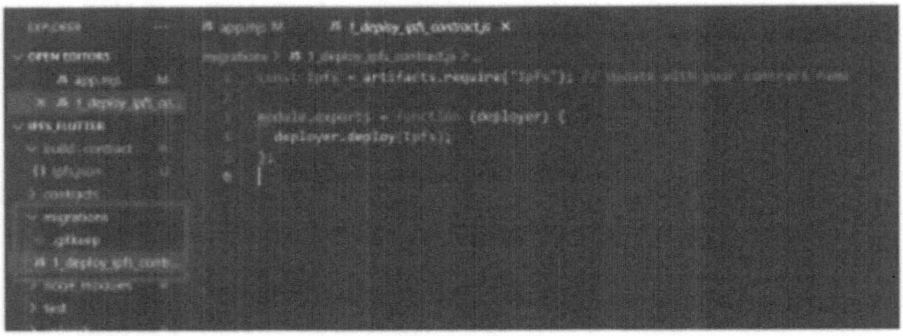
const Ipfs = artifacts.require("Ipfs");
module.exports = function (deployer) {
deployer.deploy(Ipfs);
};

FIGURE 10.9 Migration of smart contract.

[Original (created by authors)]

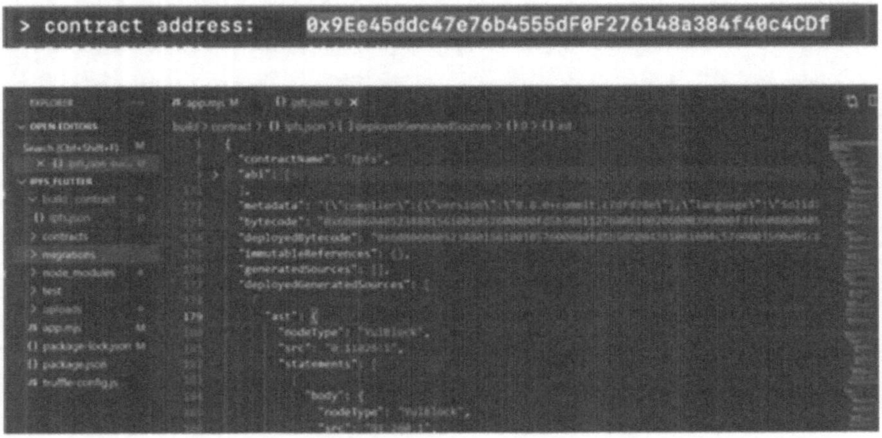
> contract address: 0x9Ee45ddc47e76b4555dF0F276148a384f40c4CDf

FIGURE 10.10 Contract's ABI and address.

[Original (created by authors)]

10.4.2 Mobile application

In this step, we will integrate the blockchain and IPFS. We need to import the "web3," "HDWalletProvider," and "json" packages, as shown in Figure 10.11.

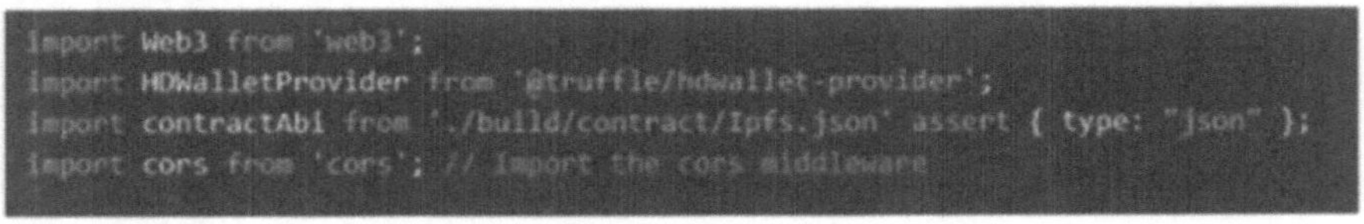
import Web3 from 'web3';
import HDWalletProvider from '@truffle/hdwallet-provider';
import contractAbi from './build/contract/Ipfs.json' assert { type: "json" };
import cors from 'cors'; // Import the cors middleware

FIGURE 10.11 Required package for integration of blockchain and IPFS.

[Original (created by authors)]

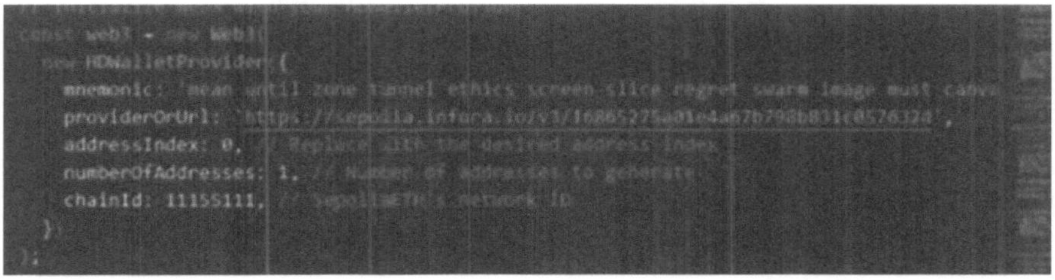

FIGURE 10.12   Infura API call.

[Original (created by authors)]

FIGURE 10.13   Contract address.

[Original (created by authors)]

Infura is a service that provides infrastructure nodes to interact with decentralized blockchains such as Ethereum. Therefore, calling the Infura API is typically necessary to access blockchain functionalities, as shown in Figure 10.12.

Usage of web3 and HDWalletProvider: Web3 is a JavaScript library that simplifies the interaction of decentralized applications with the Ethereum blockchain, as shown in Figure 10.13.

After retrieving the IPFS CID, as mentioned in the previous section, we can now send this value to the blockchain using the "set" function, as illustrated in Figure 10.14.

Finally, we can observe, using Etherscan as shown in Figure 10.15, the blocks and transactions on the blockchain.

10.4.2.1   Spring Boot + MySQL

Spring Boot, with its suite of security features, acts as the fortress wall, defending the application from potential threats and vulnerabilities. It simplifies the implementation of authentication and authorization mechanisms, ensuring that only legitimate users can access sensitive information. This framework automates many of the tedious security configurations, allowing us to focus on developing features without compromising on safety. MySQL, our chosen database, complements Spring Boot's security measures by providing a reliable foundation for data storage. It ensures the integrity and confidentiality of the data through robust access control and encryption capabilities. Together, Spring Boot and MySQL forge a backend system that is not

```
const rawTx = {
    nonce: nonce,
    gasPrice: web3.utils.toHex(gasPrice), // Convert gas price to hex format
    gasLimit: gasLimit,
    to: contractAddress,
    value: '0x00',
    data: data,
};

const signedTx = await web3.eth.accounts.signTransaction(rawTx, '3a09dc7fc5cbadefba6a

web3.eth
    .sendSignedTransaction(signedTx.rawTransaction)
    .once('transactionHash', (hash) => {
        console.log(`Transaction hash: ${hash}`);
    })
    .once('receipt', (receipt) => {
        console.log('Transaction receipt:');
        console.log(receipt);
        res.json({ ipfsHash });
    })
    .on('error', (error) => {
        console.error('Error sending transaction:', error);
        res.status(500).json({ error: 'Internal Server Error' });
    });
```

FIGURE 10.14 Contract address.

[Original (created by authors)]

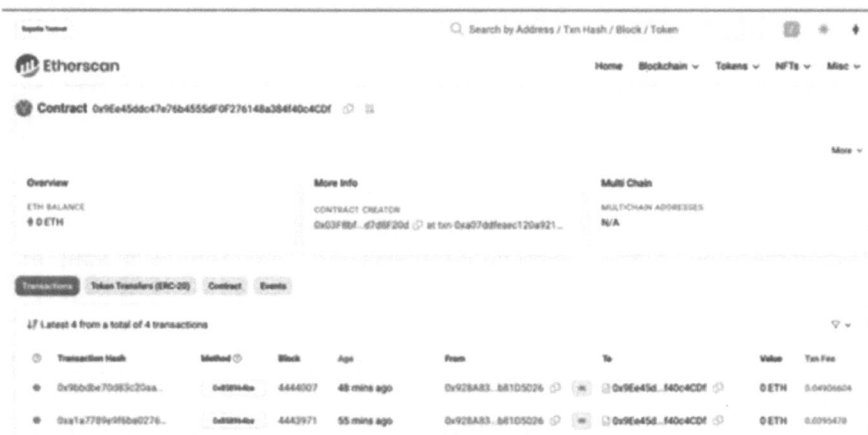

FIGURE 10.15 Etherscan interface.

[Original (created by authors)]

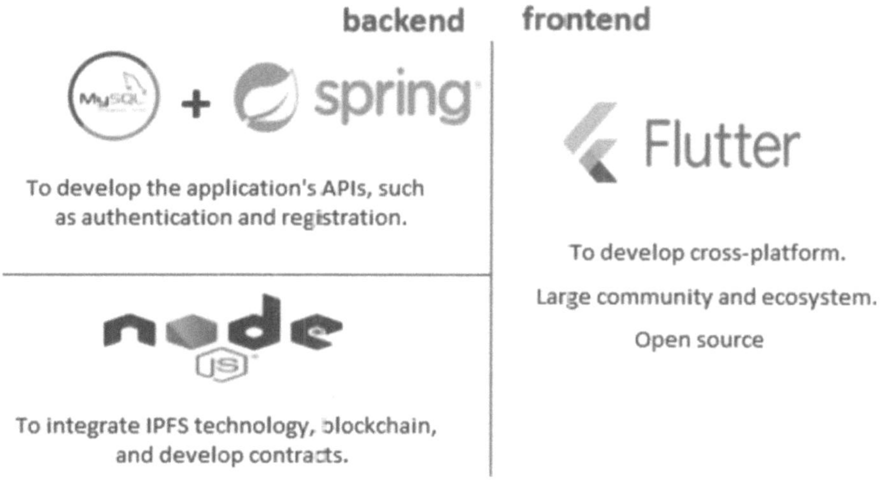

backend **frontend**

To develop the application's APIs, such
as authentication and registration.

To develop cross-platform.

Large community and ecosystem.

Open source

To integrate IPFS technology, blockchain,
and develop contracts.

FIGURE 10.16 Proposed system architecture.

[Original (created by authors)]

just resilient against attacks but also capable of swiftly recovering from any breaches, thus maintaining the application's stability and trustworthiness, as illustrated in Figure 10.16.

In essence, the combination of Spring Boot and MySQL does not just support our application; it elevates it. By integrating these technologies, we have constructed a backend that stands as a bastion of security and a beacon of reliability, ensuring that our users' data is protected, and the system's performance is unwavering, even as we scale and evolve in the dynamic landscape of digital health care.

- Node.js

    For managing medical records on the blockchain and decentralized file storage, we turn to Node.js in combination with blockchain and IPFS technologies. This combination ensures data security and enables efficient access.

    Node.js is a JavaScript runtime built on the V8 JavaScript engine. It allows developers to execute JavaScript code outside of a web browser, making it suitable for server-side development. Node.js is known for its non-blocking, event-driven architecture, making it efficient for handling concurrent operations. It has gained popularity for building scalable and high-performance applications, especially in scenarios where real-time capabilities are crucial. Node.js is commonly used to develop web servers, APIs, and various types of networked applications.

- **Flutter**
  For the user interface, we are using the Flutter framework, which provides a smooth and consistent user experience. Flutter transforms the development process to build, test, and deploy mobile, web, desktop, and embedded experiences from a single codebase.
      The use of Spring Boot, Node.js, Flutter, blockchain, and IPFS technologies in a medical application can create a comprehensive ecosystem that addresses the security, privacy, and accessibility needs of medical data. Each of these technologies brings specific advantages to the application.
- **Robust and Secure Backend:** Spring Boot facilitates the development of a robust backend with integrated security features such as user management, session handling, and endpoint security.
- **Easy Integration with Databases:** It allows connecting the application to a database to securely store medical information.
- **Node.js:** Node.js is a runtime environment that allows developers to execute JavaScript code outside of a web browser. It is built on Google Chrome's V8 JavaScript engine and is widely used for building scalable, high-performance applications, particularly on the server side.
- **Asynchronous Processing:** Node.js excels in asynchronous processing, which is valuable for managing numerous real-time medical queries simultaneously.
- **Scalability:** The event-driven nature of Node.js enables efficient scalability, crucial for constantly expanding medical applications.
- **Reactive User Interface:** Flutter provides a reactive and appealing user interface for mobile applications, essential for a modern user experience in the healthcare sector.
- **Cross-Platform Development:** It enables the development of a medical application that works on both Android and iOS with a common source code.
- **Data Security:** Blockchain ensures the integrity of medical data, preventing unauthorized alterations.
- **Traceability:** Blockchain technology allows tracking the origin and modifications made to data, providing complete traceability.
- **Decentralized Storage:** IPFS offers decentralized storage, enhancing the resilience and availability of medical data.
- **File Sharing:** Facilitates secure sharing of medical files among different stakeholders while ensuring confidentiality.

10.5 Conclusion

The implementation of a secure medical file-sharing system, based on IPFS and blockchain technology, aims to create a robust platform ensuring the security and integrity of medical data. Our solution relies on the decentralization provided by IPFS and the inherent security of the blockchain, thus ensuring maximum confidentiality. The system incorporates mechanisms for verifying the authenticity of data through the use of hashes on the blockchain, making any alterations detectable. The sharing process occurs in an encrypted and efficient manner, providing a reliable solution for the secure exchange of sensitive medical information.

References

1. Othman, S. B., Almalki, F. A., & Sakli, H. (2022). Internet of Things in the Healthcare Applications: Overview of Security and Privacy Issues. In: Chakraborty, C., Khosravi, M.R. (eds) Intelligent Healthcare. Springer, Singapore. https://doi.org/10.1007/978-981-16-5150-9_9
2. Jiang, S., Cao, J., Wu, H., Yang, Y., Ma, M., & He, J. (2018). Blochie: A blockchain based platform for healthcare information exchange. In 2018 IEEE International Conference on Smart Computing (SMARTCOMP) (pp. 49–56).
3. Alqarni, K. S., Almalki, F. A., Soufiene, B. O., Ali, O., & Albalwy, F. (2022). Authenticated wireless links between a drone and sensors using a blockchain: Case of smart farming. Wireless Communications and Mobile Computing, Article ID 4389729, 13. https://doi.org/10.1155/2022/4389729
4. Ramani, V., Bracken, A., Liyanage, M., Ylianttila, M., & Kumar, T. (2018). Secure and efficient data accessibility in blockchain based healthcare systems. In IEEE Global Communications Conference (GLOBECOM) (pp. 206–212).
5. Gupta, S., Alharbi, F., Alshahrani, R., Kumar Arya, P., Vyas, S., Elkamchouchi, D. H., & Soufiene, B. O. (2023). Secure and lightweight authentication protocol for privacy preserving communications in smart city applications. Sustainability, 15, 5346. https://doi.org/10.3390/su15065346
6. Tagde, P, Tagde, S, & Rahman, M. H. (2021). Blockchain and artificial intelligence technology in e-health. Environmental Science and Pollution Research International, 28(38), 14757–14767.
7. Zheng, Q., Li, Y., Chen, P., & Dong, X. (2018). An innovative IPFS-based storage model for blockchain. In 2018 IEEE/WIC/ACM International Conference on Web Intelligence (WI) (pp. 704–708).
8. Jayabalan, J., & Jeyanthi, N. (2022). Scalable blockchain model using off-chain IPFS storage for healthcare data security and privacy. Journal of Parallel and Distributed Computing, 164, 152–167, ISSN 0743-7315. https://doi.org/10.1016/j.jpdc.2022.03.009
9. Guo, H., & Yu, X. (2022). A survey on blockchain technology and its security. Blockchain: Research and Applications, 3(2), 100067. Retrieved from https://www.sciencedirect.com/science/article/pii/S2096720922000070
10. Bhutta, M. N. M., Khwaja, A. A., Nadeem, A., Ahmad, H. F., Khan, M. K., Hanif, M. A., & Cao, Y. (2021). A survey on blockchain technology: Evolution, architecture and security. IEEE Access, 9, 61048–61073.
11. Salman, T., Zolanvari, M., Erbad, A., Jain, R., & Samaka, M. (2019). Security services using blockchains: A state of the art survey. IEEE Communications Surveys Tutorials, 21(1), 858–880.
12. Kaushik, A., Choudhary, A., Ektare, C., Thomas, D., & Akram, S. (2017). Blockchain—Literature survey. In 2017 2nd IEEE International Conference on Recent Trends in Electronics. Information Communication Technology (RTEICT) (pp. 2145–2148). doi: 10.1109/RTEICT.2017.8256979
13. Sankar, L. S., Sinchu, M., & Sethumadhavan, M. (2017). Survey of consensus protocols on blockchain applications. In 2017 4th International Conference on Advanced Computing and Communication Systems (ICACCS) (pp. 1–5).

11

A SURVEY ON SECURITY ENHANCEMENTS OF ELECTRONIC HEALTH RECORDS THROUGH BLOCKCHAIN TECHNOLOGY

Shahd Rashed Abdulla Alhebsi, Alanoud Eisa Faraj Alfalahi, and Thangavel Murugan

11.1 Introduction

EHRs are a digital form of recording a patient's medical data and displaying it to the user through application or online, allowing easier and faster access process at any time they need it. EHRs can store data such as personal statistics such as name, age, Body Mass Index (BMI), medical history, laboratory test result, allergy, immunization status, and more. All this type of data is displayed for the patient through the account that they created and can access to check on with no limitation. Furthermore, this data will be displayed for the doctor for medication and diagnosis purposes [1].

EHRs can provide numerous types of advantages that may help in healthcare services. EHRs also provide easy access and efficient care for both professionals and the patient. Moreover, another benefit of EHRs can help in eliminating and reducing the risk of human error when inserting data into the database. Also, EHRs may help the patient to understand their data more and know what each term means, providing them with the ability to track their health and motivation to improve it. One more benefit related to the EHRs is their contribution to enhancing research and data analysis with the help of data mining. It is easier to use EHR data to identify trends and patterns that can help in discovering new meditation or medicines or new types of diseases [2].

On the other hand, EHRs may also involve some disadvantages that can affect the patients. EHR implementation may be expensive and need a lot of money or investors to start this technology, including the cost of developing the software, hardware, and the salary of the people who will join in building it. Moreover, EHRs may impose some difficulties for the patient and the health provider because it is a new technology, and the health provider may

DOI: 10.1201/9781003483113-11

not have the time to adapt to it. Some of the patients, especially the elderly, may have difficulty in using EHR technology. EHRs store sensitive data related to the patient medical data and may contain some private data so there is a potential for data breaches and some data security and privacy concerns [3].

EHR security will be the target that every researcher acquires to achieve as it is one of the challenges that needs to be solved as soon as possible. Solving or enhancing the security of EHRs may help the patient and boost the trust of the patient in the newest technology and utilize it more. Another reason that we need to increase the security of the EHR system is that there is a legal and ethical obligation to build protection of patient data and there is a law that this called the Health Insurance and Portability and Accountability Act (HIPAA). Ensuring the security of EHRs also means ensuring data integrity and protecting it from unauthorized modification and ensuring the patient data is protected from being stolen and sold to a third party that may use this data with bad intentions in mind. Furthermore, safeguarding patient medical data will prevent identity theft and any other fraudulent action [4].

Blockchain technology can provide data integrity and ensure that the data is being accessed by the authorized user and no modification has happened to the data. Blockchain also can safeguard the patient data that is stored somewhere in the network [5]. Data integrity can be garnered using different blockchain mechanisms and features and some of these features include cryptography, consensus mechanisms, smart contracts, permissioned and permissionless blockchains, and hash function (see Figure 11.1).

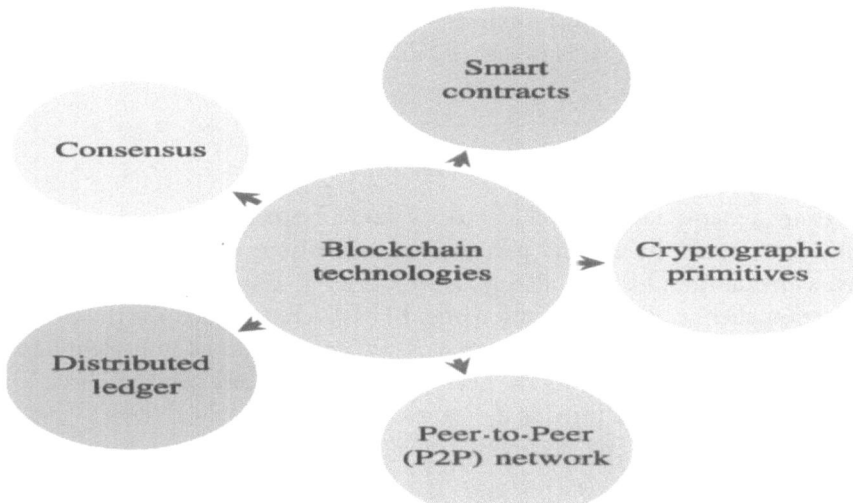

FIGURE 11.1 Different blockchain mechanisms and features.

Original (created by authors)

Blockchain technology uses cryptography, which is the science of writing secret code that cannot be understood by anyone other than the sender and receiver to ensure confidentiality of the data. Also, another use of blockchain is the smart contract, which can ensure and verify the data did not change during transmission. The hash function is also included in blockchain technology, where it always produces an output that is fixed in size, no matter what the size of the message, as an input to the function. The hash function can provide security to the data of the patient as well as data integrity [6].

Blockchain technology and some of its features can be integrated into health care and boost the security of EHRs through using those various features of blockchain. For example, blockchain can facilitate easy enhancement of data between hospitals while maintaining the security of the exchange data. Blockchain technology cryptographic features can provide data confidentiality of patient medical records and securely store them to ensure data security and privacy [7].

The purpose of the literature survey is to conduct analysis and perform a comprehensive study about other researcher solutions and what they use from features, functions, technologies, and methods, especially related to blockchain technology to enhance the security of EHRs, as it is some of the most important data to humans. Contribute to the enhancement of healthcare services by creating and developing the optimal solution to all the challenges that face the other authors and researchers using blockchain technology and enhance the security of electronic health records. After investigating the solution that is developed by the researcher in the field of a blockchain, we will understand each of these solutions and then establish the solution that will be used to safeguard the EHR using a blockchain and improve and boost security and privacy [8].

11.2   Overview of electronic health records

EHRs are a method in which the patient's data are stored in a digitalized way where it contains the medical part of the information related to the patient, such as meditation history, allergy, laboratory test results, and personal information such as BMI, age, and name. EHRs were founded for the benefit of sharing patient data across different healthcare locations in a secure and much easier process, allowing the health provider to access the data check for the patient's health and provide a diagnosis [9].

EHRs facilitate different benefits. Some of the key advantages include:

- Efficiency and productivity increase by comparing it with the traditional method of storing patient data.
- Reduces the time to insert the data by the manual method, which will decrease human errors and mistakes.

- Reduces redundancies and improves consistency in sharing the data between different hospitals.
- Reduces the cost of spending because shifting to EHRs may decrease the need to purchase paper and focuses the spending on other resources that may be necessary.
- The accuracy will be increased sufficiently due to the elimination of manual entering of records by humans.
- Engages the patient to easily access their data and monitor their health accordingly.
- Legal and regulation compliance for security including different laws created to maintain the security and the privacy of the health portion of patient data.

While adopting EHRs brings numerous benefits to healthcare services, some other challenges and problems need to be addressed in a more focused mind. EHRs keep track and store the patient's health data and because it stores the data it needs to be secure and comply with the law as these data are important to the patient and are sometimes considered private and the patient does not want it to be accessible by anyone other than the healthcare provider and themselves. Some challenges that might occur for the EHR if it is not secure enough are data breaches, where its unauthorized access to the health portion of patient data, modification of the data by unauthorized persons, integrity concerns, and other types of challenges. These challenges need to be solved immediately with solutions that will provide EHR safety and security.

11.3 Blockchain technology

Transactions across a network of computers need to be secure, tamper-resistant, and transparent. With the use of blockchain technology, all the transaction records and other types of data that need to be stored, such as EHRs, where the need to have data that are secure, accomplish data integrity and the records need to resist unauthorized modification of data. Blockchain is a technology that is distributed and decentralized by creating a chain of blocks and each block is connected to the previous block, allowing more secure and hard-to-break relationships [10].

The principles that are involved in the blockchain are as follows: decentralization and distribution, hash function, cryptography, smart contract, and permissioned and permissionless networks. All these principles can help the blockchain to achieve its design.

- **Decentralization and Distribution:** Removing the need to rely on a central authority, making the block more secure and trusted. Also reducing the risk of failure as the blocks are distributed.

- **Hash Function:** The hash function is used to evaluate the integrity of the blocks, making it more secure. The hash function will get an input message that can vary in size and produce a fixed hash or digest.
- **Cryptography:** It is the science of converting the plaintext to a ciphertext using a technique or a method. There are two types of techniques used in cryptography: symmetric key and asymmetric key.
- **Permissioned and Permissionless Networks:** Different types of networks, such as permissioned, restrict access to blocks while permissionless allows anyone to access the block.

Blockchain can be identified based on the three types of blockchain: public, private, and hybrid (see Figure 11.2). Each one of the types contains some feature and provides other functionality that the other two types need for special cases and purposes [11]. For example, a public allows anyone to access and participate, meaning the public can access the block and validate the transaction if it is used for those purposes. Also, a single cannot have complete control over all the blocks on the network while the participant can do so. The private blockchain type is the opposite of the public, where certain people can validate and access the block in the network, restricting access to the authorized user only and it may be centralized or partially decentralized, without relying on a central authority. Finally, the hybrid blockchain type is in between the first two types, in which it combines the functionality of the public and private blockchain.

Blockchain technology can be used in different sectors and have different impacts and purposes for different types of industries. Here are the potential sectors and industries where a blockchain can be applied:

- **Healthcare:** It can be used to secure the transmission of patient medical data, such as EHRs.
- **Government:** Secures voting for electing a new ministry for the country; reduction of fraud action.

4 Main Types of Blockchain

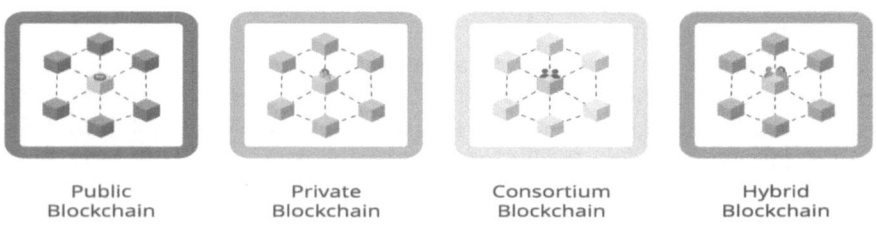

| Public Blockchain | Private Blockchain | Consortium Blockchain | Hybrid Blockchain |

FIGURE 11.2 Blockchain types.

[Original (created by authors)]

- **Finance and Banking:** Can be used in cryptocurrency and ensure the security of Bitcoin and transactions.
- **Intellectual Property:** Proof that the intellectual property owner is the one who owns the design or the invention.
- **Legal and Regularity:** Compliance with the law reduces the need to trust a third party.
- **Education:** Secure and evaluate the integrity of the academic credentials, such as employee information (e.g., Social Security number) or student information (e.g., grades).

11.4   Blockchain technology in health care

Blockchain technology can offer a lot of different advantages in the act of deploying it in the healthcare system. Facilitating healthcare services is one of the advantages that would occur if the system implemented blockchain technology; for example, it would help in providing data integrity and ensure that the data have not changed during transmission, making sure that the patient health data in EHRs maintains their privacy when sharing with other hospital healthcare systems. Blockchain can utilize real-time updates to the data stored in EHRs, making the process faster during an emergency, increasing the trust of the patient in the EHR technology when using blockchain technology.

The adoption of blockchain technology can initiate the bridge for the transition from a country to a leader in technology innovation. Blockchain technology was implemented in various sectors and industries to perform and facilitate different purposes. Blockchain technology in the healthcare sector was one of the main foci, as it can be crucial to implement it. Examples of implementation of blockchain in health care include the following:

- Blockchain can be used in EHRs for the main purpose of ensuring data integrity and enhancing the security of the record.
- Pharmaceutical management can also be an area to implement blockchain, ensuring the medication and drugs are safe, according to the country's law.
- The safe transition of patient health records across the country makes it easier for the person who is outside the country to get treatment in another country.
- Blockchain can also facilitate the process of telemedicine and remote patient monitoring with the help of Internet of Things (IoT) devices.

Despite the advantages and advancement of blockchain technology and any other technology, some limitations and challenges can be encountered when using blockchain technology. Here are some of the challenges and limitations that occur in health care. First, it might be difficult to make changes to the block in the blockchain because of an immutable record. If the user wants to make a change, the user needs to make a change in all the blocks that follow the target block. Second, scalability is a concern when talking about a blockchain, as there will be big data that need to be stored in a secure place. Third, the security and privacy of EHRs might cause an issue when implementing blockchain technology. Finally, the cost of implementing blockchain technology in health care might be an expensive and intensive resource.

11.5   Security enhancements of EHR through blockchain: Research works

The objective of the research is to investigate the ability of blockchain technology to establish a private by-design IoT system and ensure the CIA triad—Confidentiality, Integrity, and Availability is applied in the created system [5]. The work ensures that the data produced from the IoT applications using the blockchain and peer-to-peer approaches is not produced by the centralized companies, where the decision is produced from the top level to ensure the integrity of the decision. With the use of layer architecture, the research claims that the problem of untrusted data can be solved in which it stores only a limited portion of the data in the blockchain.

Because the IoT is a dynamic environment, the existing frameworks that depend on third-party auditors are not good enough to ensure the verification of the data integrity on the applications. So, [8] has conducted a framework using a blockchain to provide a more reliable framework for IoT systems without the use of third-party auditors. The objective of the research is to create a blockchain framework that will help verify the data integrity of the IoT application without the help of a third-party auditor to ensure the integrity of the data transmitted through the IoT system. Replacing the issues of the existing framework that uses the Integrity Management Service, which raises the integrity issues. So, the research has established a blockchain framework that replaces third-party auditors and increases the reliability of the services provided. The solution also includes the use of the protocol to verify the data integrity for both the data owner and the data client. The work also focuses on the improvement of the random environment of IoT applications and improves the smart contract to verify the data on a large scale.

Clinical and precision medicine needs to have strong powerful blockchain technology to provide data integrity and privacy for identifying clients. The authors in [9] have proposed a new architecture that will provide a solution for that problem and enhance the security of health information. The objective of the research is to establish a novel platform for clinical and medical data that demands precision and accuracy in its handling. The work aims to describe the requirements for building blockchain technology, and it also assists other researchers in making decisions when developing new architectural ideas. The research creates a new platform that will provide trust across the internet when transmitted. To accomplish the trust needed, the researchers use the concept of distributed and parallel computing mechanisms with a ledger. Smart contracts can also be used to provide assurance of the communication entity rather than the use of an institution to transmit the data. The system will give the right to patients to be able to access their data and to investigate the variety of data. The research work only explains the blockchain that they created to use in the health sector for data that need precision when handling. Therefore, there is no experimental result as in its conceptual paper. The researchers aim in the future to investigate and learn about big data analysis and the use of machine learning and its properties to boost their solution.

[10] aims to provide a solution for the challenges and limitations that are limited to the data privacy and security concerns in the healthcare system The research work aim is to provide a system that will work in mobile to maintain the data collection and sharing between the data owner and the health provider to discuss the patient case and research purposes. Moreover, the research work aims to address the challenges in the existing solution and to overcome these challenges using blockchain technology, specifically the use of Hyperledger Fabric. The proposed solution is a mobile healthcare system that is a secure and decentralized platform for health data. The system works as follows: (i) The health data related to the patient will be collected using wearable devices. (ii) The data will be stored in the cloud server on a trusted platform. The ownership of the data is the patient, and they have the right to deny or allow any action. (iii) The user can request medical treatment and can revoke the request when finished to ensure the doctor has no access to the data after the treatment. (iv) The system uses the Merkle tree method to ensure the quality of the data process. (v) Any type of update or modification of the data will be recorded in the blockchain network to improve data privacy. The system is tested and evaluated against a large number of records and found that the result is fast and shows at low latency, which means that the system can work for a large record in no time.

[12] mentions that there is a need to create a new system to ensure data integrity. The objective of the research is to provide a new system to protect communication in a cloud-based application. However, the researchers aim to establish a trustworthy and resilient architecture with high security. The researchers want the system to verify the data integrity in the IoT system. DroneChain is the system the author proposed and it is a blockchain-based drone system. The components of DroneChain are a drone, cloud server, control system, and blockchain network. It is a system of a collection of drones where the control system is used to give commands for drone distribution

and communication purposes. The blockchain is included to provide data integrity and to provide trust in the system. Also, the cloud server provides storage and the capacity needed for the collection of large amounts of data. Future work mentioned is to extend the system and make it used in different IoT applications.

The researchers seek to provide a system that will solve all the limitations that will combine blockchain technology with Peer-to-Peer (P2P) cloud storage. Such that the framework will establish a trust communication of the transferred data in the cloud server, [13] created a way to break the existing solution into two parts: provable data possession (PDP) and scalable and efficient provable data possession (SE-PDP). To establish a framework that will be able to encase the verification process and make it more open and auditable. Using a blockchain-based P2P cloud server, the researchers aim to provide solutions to challenges in the current framework. Using the P2P cloud storage features and combining the blockchain with a framework that will be used in identifying data integrity is the proposed solution. The researchers make use of the Merkle tree properties to be the storage for the hash values generated to identify the entity to provide the system with a trust level. The use of the verification process established by the researchers can ensure the data is not tempered with. The research has conducted a prototype and done a pervasive simulation to test if the framework is effective in verifying data integrity. The result shows that the system is flexible and improves the data integrity.

[6] aims to enhance and improve the security and data integrity verification of EHRs using the Merkle tree approach. To propose a solution using blockchain technology in a private network and to help identify the data integrity with the help of the Merkle tree–based approach, the researchers seek to simplify blockchain technology and propose a solution with that feature created while avoiding data mining. It makes use of cryptography to secure the content in the blockchain. The proposed approach went through different test types and shows that the approach is found to be robust and can protect against different modifications, whether accidental or intentional. Compared to the old approach, the new approach has low processing overhead. The approach was tested using a well-known database called MIMIC-III and the outcome of the test had high-quality results.

Cloud storage servers, where most of the sensitive data is stored, are vulnerable to modification and data breach vulnerabilities. Additionally, these systems lack openness and accountability. [4] aim to provide a solution that is tamper-proof and can verify data integrity accurately in the health sector. The solution that uses blockchain technology will modify the block to add the transaction; however, the approach that is proposed by the researchers will append a metadata file as a transaction to the blockchain. This solution will help in avoiding the unnecessary rewrite of the data in the block. It ensures the cloud storage system is not changed by monitoring the files in the server. The proposed solution is efficient for the data in the archives that is not modified frequently but accessed often. The result shows that the solution response time and cost are reasonable.

The data that is collected about people increases, which results in the challenges that occur when sharing data in health care between institutions due to the lack of data reliability and trust that the data will be transmitted as it was sent without modification. The objective of [3] is to provide a healthcare system that is standardized and able to be shared, called Sharechain. It will ensure that the data is transparent to the user and ensure its interoperability. It will provide a framework that will solve all the addressed problems, making it the solution that will combine all the features. SHAREChain is the proposed solution by the researchers and it is a healthcare framework that will provide data interoperability and ensure its reliability. The blockchain technology type of this solution uses consortium blockchain. It prevents the copying of stored data. The system that the researchers used is called XDS (Cross-Enterprise Document Sharing).

Transparency of transactions in e-health systems may lead to problems with data integrity and privacy for the data in health systems. The objective of [6] can be achieved by the blockchain-based solution called the eHealth Integrity model, based on a permissioned blockchain that the researchers designed and aims to ensure the data integrity of electronic health information. The system can be integrated to be used in assigning the help of verifying the EHR integrity. The blockchain-based model called BEIM (blockchain-enabled integrity management) is the proposed system and the desire to build a system that will ensure the data integrity and accuracy of healthcare data in a digital format. The researchers seek to add the feature of removing the information from the system and they can enable this functionality using permissioned blockchains with off-chain storage. The researchers suggest a system that will guarantee the integrity and accuracy of healthcare data using blockchain-based technology. The proposed system failed to provide any experimental results. Testing the system in the laboratory environment also implements an approval of the concept of the proposed solution so that it can be published in the future. The test process will be conducted such that it confirms how the number of nodes, network latency, and other threats affect verification speed.

To provide a Blockchain-Based Data Integrity Verification for Large-Scale IoT Data and ensure the data integrity when transmitted/stored and pressed. Reducing the computational and communication overhead using a dynamic blockchain-based approach to ensure the data integrity of IoT data stored in cloud storage is the objective [14]. The researchers will allow the update in real time of IoT data that is on the cloud server. The proposed solution was conducted with the idea of data integrity assurance in mind for IoT devices. The proposed system is blockchain-based data integrity verification for large-scale IoT data that uses a combination of properties of blockchain technology. It allows real-time data modification in data that is stored on a cloud server while ensuring the integrity of the data without relying on a third party. The researchers analyzed the performance of the proposed algorithm and found that the schema provided is feasible. Regarding the security of the proposed system, the researchers analyzed the scenario that can happen to the system and found that the system can combat malicious attacks.

The problem or the challenge of the limitation of the importance of ensuring data integrity on the cloud server also provides confidence in third-party auditors. [15] proposed a solution that is based on consortium blockchain, aiming to provide the ability to trust the data integrity and the third-party auditor using the properties in the blockchain technology. To protect anonymity and user privacy, the researchers make use of an identity mixer based on zero-knowledge proof. Also, the researchers did use the Hyperledger Fabric, which will generate a digital certification to prove the communication. The proposed schema based on consortium blockchain can achieve data integrity for IoT security at a reasonable time cost.

Nowadays, the data collection about personal information is increasing with the bloom of technology; thus, there is a need for a system that can store the data securely and efficiently. In all the states the data can be taken, there is a long list of threats and problems related to it, such as data modification, data breaches, and unauthorized disclosure. [16] proposes a system that will be able to solve all the current issues, including the security related to the storage where the data is stored. To ensure that the data is secure and cannot be modified, the proposed solution aims to use blockchain technology to store checksums. The researchers aim to provide a system that can be used in a scalable environment where fast responses are needed. RIVAChain is the proposed solution, which is a blockchain-based ledger system. It is a system in which it stores the data in a storage that can resist modification or any of the data corruption. Enabling the validation of the integrity of file transfers without needing the data source to compute file checksums for each transfer. The system uses a hash function to create a unique value that will be passed to the blockchain to avoid tampering with the data. The result shows the evaluation of the performance as well as the scalability of the Rivachain system. The result shows that the proposed system can show high results of throughput and calculate the checksum at a low time rate.

The scope of [17] is tactical data link (TDL) and blockchain and its application. TDL is a point-to-point data transmission method that lacks security as the data transmission occurs in plaintext and no encryption is performed to secure the data. Year by year, TDL faces such development, including the problem of plaintext its solved using encryption. The objective of the design goal of the TDL chain is to aim at transmission control fully automated. Automated transmission can be done by achieving the following: data consistency, access control, data auditing, and autonomy and intelligence. The proposed solution in TDL chain is an intelligent data transmission control system based on blockchain technology. It aims at solving the problem of inconsistency in sharing multiple chains in the TDL. It involves the use of blockchain technology and its properties, a cloud server, and a certificate authority. Ciphertext-Policy Attribute-Based Encryption (CP-ABE) will make it possible for the TDL chain to access the data on the cloud server and blockchain. The system went to several experiments to evaluate the performance and achieve some metrics. The experiment was focused on efficiency. The testing was focused on the following parameters: the efficiency of smart contracts to make a response, low latency response to an event quickly, throughput of the massive amount of data stored in the blockchain successfully, and the cost of communication. Optimization and development of the TDL chain system, including strengthening the blockchain network's scalability and performance, looking into more effective encryption techniques, and carrying out more thorough security study and testing.

The [18] researchers aim to provide the security and privacy of the trading data system for both the user and the data being traded. The proposed solution is a blockchain-based personal data trading system that consists of using DID (decentralized identifiers) and VC (verifiable credentials). Decentralization is the system infrastructure to manage personal data and allow the user to store and use their data more reliably. The system works as follows before the user trades their data user needs to authenticate the identity and claim that they are the owner of the data being traded. DID is used to help in the authentication process and VC to ensure ownership. The authors illustrate the system with users' data and use the features of the DID and VC to prove that trading user data can be achieved effectively and efficiently using the proposed system. There is a database that will record the history of all the previous transactions in a blockchain that will offer immutably, reliability, and security.

The problem statement is to verify the data integrity in a distributed system for big data analysis to avoid any conflict or loss of trust when data is modified or changed from when it was sent. The nature of this system makes it difficult to verify the data integrity. [19] will provide a solution that will verify the data integrity to fulfill the trust. A blockchain-based system that provides verifiable integrity over Hadoop Distributed File System (HDFS) called Clouseau. The system will be used to detect malicious action while ensuring the data integrity of the data provides trust. The aim is to provide a system that will not affect the read-write operation. The system will ensure data integrity in a distributed system in which the environment of this system makes it difficult to provide data integrity and trust of the data. To ensure data integrity, the system will use Merkle proofs and smart contracts, which will ease the process of data verification. The system will allow the user to choose the right configuration based on their needs, while providing security. Clouseau is a system that provides efficacy in spotting malicious activity and maintaining data integrity in distributed systems. The researchers tested the performance of the system to evaluate the throughput and latency of the read-write operation. Moreover, the system can detect malicious activity and modification of data integrity.

[20] proposed a multilayer blockchain-based EHR system. A multilayer blockchain-based EHR solution tackles problems with healthcare data management. The system's goals are to build a PDP-like data verification mechanism to safeguard data integrity and to offer a hierarchical structure that supports the operational hierarchy in health organizations. The system design is as follows: semi-node and full node of health organization reduce storage costs while keeping data security in the system the author will build. The researchers evaluated the performance of the system and found that the result is high throughput increases as the number of full nodes increases more than 30, but the throughput decreases when the number of nodes increases from 4 to 30.

[21] proposed a system using blockchain technology in the field of information security and offers an assurance of data integrity. The system creates a message authentication code that will be stored in a block with a hash value to provide data integrity. The hash values are created using the algorithm of the SHA-256 after the encrypted. Blockchain-based data integrity assurance method is better than the current system as it is more robust and evolving. The system was tested in blockchain-based integrity using penetration testing. The proposed system is implemented and deployed the system in a real-time environment to assure data integrity of the data used in the system; the system should be tested more to ensure that the system can be more robust and function in the required scope.

[22] propose a schema or a solution for the problem of verifying the data integrity of the IoT network. The solution is based on blockchain technology that will be used for IoT networks. The researcher aims to provide a solution that will enhance the data integrity of the IoT network and improve its security. The proposed system aims to verify the data integrity of this network that uses IoT devices. The system process is in three steps and the three stages are (i) Setup stage: the data will be sliced into small parts, and the key is generated in this step. (ii) Processing stage: then the data that is sliced will combine again in the blockchain and will be sent to a cloud server. (iii) Verification stage: verify the data integrity. The blockchain for IoT can be used efficiently for the IoT application. The researchers have tested the

performance of the system with three parameters: for example, memory utilization, accuracy rate, and end-to-end delay. Memory utilization is how much memory the IoT application uses during the verification process. Accuracy rate is how much of the data verification was predicted successful. End-to-end delay is the time calculated for the packet to be sent from the source to the destination in a network. The proposed scheme is better in terms of end-to-end delay.

The challenges that occur to the IoT application are because it is growing in popularity and there are not enough studies related to the issue of security and privacy. In the agriculture sector, IoT devices are used to transmit sensing data that is stored in a database so there is a problem of data integrity, which is what the authors will seek to solve. [11] aim to propose solutions to all the issues that exist in the current paper research, where they only focus on implementing IoT rather than focusing on security and data integrity. The researchers proposed a blockchain implementation that will use Ethereum to ensure smart irrigation security and integrity. The type of network used in a proposed blockchain solution is divided into three types: public, which means anyone can access; only authorized users can access the blockchain; and only people with permission can access this network. The system is built with the following components: (i) IoT sensor: its task is to transmit the data to the blockchain using a type of protocol called MQTT (Message Queuing Telemetry Transport). (ii) Ethereum ensures the security of the system. (iii) The data repository is used to contain the result and store it. (iv) Users. The result was found after testing the private blockchain network with different types of tests, such as software unit testing, smart contract testing, and data integrity testing.

The objective of [23] is to safeguard the data collection that is collected in a cloud server provider (CSP) and stored in cloud edge collaborative storage. This information can result in user privacy concerns. The researchers aim to provide a solution based on blockchain technology that will help in improving the security and privacy issues on the Internet of Vehicles (IoV). The proposed solution used bilinear mapping, which is a function that creates a transformation in a linear path; third-party audit (TPA), the cloud server provider is used for storage resources, the data generator collects data about the IoV, edge node stores the data that is collected from the data generator, the data user is the user of the data and blockchain technology used to verify the data integrity and effectiveness of the transaction. The system was evaluated and found that: (i) Data was encrypted to avoid data being stolen, so the system could achieve data privacy at a certain level. (ii) Third-party audit is not trusted. (iii) Cloud server providers and edge nodes produce time overhead to provide evidence of the data integrity. (iv) Reduces the time overhead of third-party auditors.

As the big data analysis is rising, there is an issue in trusting the data that is stored on a cloud server. [24] objective is to perform an evaluation of off-chain transaction queueing delay and to guarantee data integrity in a blockchain-based system. The researchers shed light on a protocol that is used off-chain and how it affects the performance of the queueing model. The proposed solution is a queueing methodology for creating a proof that considers how long off-chain transactions (OTXs) take to process. Particularly in the case of regularly updated data, such as IoT data, the model aids in estimating the mean OTX queueing time and determining if the implemented off-chain strategy is successful in guaranteeing data integrity. The study illustrates how variables like the OTX batch size and the OTX rate impact the OTX queueing delay and gives theoretical and simulated figures to support the validity of the conclusions. The researchers evaluate the OTX queueing delay to evaluate the result of the queuing model. Also, there is a comparison that the author constructed to compare the values of the result of the test. There is a numerical parameter that is used in the evaluation process, such as OTX batch size and the OTX rate, that affect the OTX queueing delay.

There are issues with safeguarding the data integrity of sensor data that is stored and used by low-power IoT devices on public blockchain networks. [25] also addresses the drawbacks of off-chain options and the high transaction costs connected with on-chain storage. These problems are addressed by the proposed data protection protocol, which also offers a reasonably priced and secure method of storing and validating sensor data on open blockchains. The objective of the research is to provide a protocol that seeks to address issues with extending battery life for IoT devices used with public blockchain networks, lowering transaction fees, and protecting the data integrity of recorded sensor data. Also, it provides a safe and affordable way to store and validate sensor data on open blockchains for low-power IoT devices. The proposed solution is a data security protocol that addresses the drawbacks of both on-chain and off-chain storage while combining their advantages. The proposed solution uses different combinations of smart contracts, decentralized web applications, and public blockchains aiming to protect data security, save transaction costs, and extend battery life. The following actions are part of the protocol: (i) Data gathering: Gathers information about sensors, such as sensor ID, start time, delta time, and data hash. (ii) Encryption of the data: A symmetric key encryption method to encrypt the collected data. (iii) Implementation of smart contracts: To store and authenticate the encrypted data, smart contracts are introduced onto the public blockchain. (iv) Data validation: A decentralized web application is created to validate the information that is collected on the public blockchain. An ESP32S2 device is used as a proof of concept to confirm the evaluation and effectiveness of the data storage mechanism. The study assesses and tests the solution's energy use, memory utilization, and security. The researchers found that low-power sensor nodes could mention the data integrity of the public blockchains if data is transmitted using Wi-Fi.

Table 11.1 discusses the related research findings.

TABLE 11.1 Summary of research findings

References	Problem addressed	Proposed solution	Result	Pros and cons
[1]	The development of a decentralized IoT application using blockchain technology	Layer architecture to store only a limited portion of untrusted data in blockchain and peer-to-peer approaches, ensuring data integrity and decision-making integrity.	Selected 35 papers based on a designed mechanism to create a system for IoT applications using blockchain technology.	The advantage of the paper is that it ensures the integrity of the blockchain technology and compares it with different solutions. Found various ways for how to use blockchain technology.
[2]	Blockchain-based framework for IoT systems, eliminating the need for third-party auditors, thereby ensuring data integrity and reliability in the dynamic environment of the IoT.	A blockchain framework to replace third-party auditors, improve service reliability, and use a protocol for data integrity verification for both data owners and clients.	The study implemented a prototype that will demonstrate the function that the authors work to implement. The IoT is insufficient to generate the smart contract.	The advantage of the proposed framework is that it is more reliable and data integrity is enhanced. However, the disadvantage on the other hand is that IoT linked to smart contracts is not efficient enough.
[3]	A new architecture for clinical and precision medicine that also strengthens health information security.	The study aims to create a trust-based platform using distributed computing, ledgers, and smart contracts, ensuring patient access to and investigation of their data.	The study explains a blockchain designed for precision data handling in the health sector but lacks experimental results as in its conceptual paper.	One aim of the study is to provide a way to hide the identity of the patient that was not done by any of the other papers.
[4]	Data privacy and security challenges in the healthcare system, focusing on secure cloud server sharing and user access control.	Mobile healthcare system uses wearable devices to collect and store patient health data, ensuring privacy and quality through the Merkle tree method and blockchain network.	The system, tested against numerous records, demonstrated fast performance and low latency, enabling quick record access, and underwent security analysis.	The advantage of this paper is that the authors have solved all the limitations of other designs that are provided and constructed a system with optimal solutions that address all the problems.

(Continued)

TABLE 11.1 (Continued)

References	Problem addressed	Proposed solution	Result	Pros and cons
[5]	To design a secure cloud-based IoT system for data integrity in drone transmission, utilizing blockchain technology to ensure high protection in the growing drone usage.	DroneChain is a blockchain-based drone system comprising a drone, cloud server, control system, and blockchain network, ensuring data integrity and trust, and providing storage capacity for large data collections.	The study does not provide any experimental or empirical results.	Providing a system with high reliability and responsibility while offering a level of security and ensuring the integrity of the drone system that will be used for a delivery purpose to shorten the time and location.
[6]	Combining blockchain technology with P2P cloud storage to address limitations in scalability, efficiency, security, and data verification processes.	Solution using P2P cloud storage, blockchain, and Merkle tree properties for data integrity and verification, ensuring trust and preventing tampering.	A prototype and pervasive simulation to evaluate the effectiveness of a framework in verifying data integrity, demonstrating its feasibility and improvement.	The paper has solved the problem of an untrusted verification mechanism by the use of an untrusted third party and utilizing blockchain technology for that purpose.
[7]	The issue is enhancing the security and privacy of medical records in the health sector, as they are crucial for patient data collection and doctor access.	A Merkle tree–based blockchain solution for identifying data integrity in private networks, simplifying the technology, and avoiding data mining through cryptography.	Tested using the MIMIC-III database, it is robust and low processing, ensuring protection against accidental or intentional modifications, resulting in high-quality results.	Provide a lightweight solution to overcome the error whether it is intentional or by mistake, which can be costly.

(Continued)

TABLE 11.1 (Continued)

References	Problem addressed	Proposed solution	Result	Pros and cons
[8]	Cloud storage servers storing sensitive data are vulnerable to modification and data breaches, lacking transparency and accountability, resulting in subpar data integrity.	A blockchain technology solution that adds a metadata file as a transaction, avoiding unnecessary data rewrites and ensuring a secure cloud storage system.	The proposed solution efficiently manages frequently accessed archives data, demonstrating reasonable response time and cost, and advancing data reservation in cloud storage through 11 nodes in a cluster.	The disadvantage is the framework takes a lot of time to make a response so it is suitable for data that is rarely modified or updated. The advantage of the usage of Endolith is best for a file in which the time to respond is not critical.
[9]	The growing collection of personal data poses challenges in healthcare data sharing due to the lack of reliability and trust in the transmission of data without modification.	SHAREChain is a healthcare framework utilizing consortium blockchain technology for data interoperability and reliability, with an XDS system consisting of five properties.	There are no results discussed in the paper for the proposed system.	The proposed system can solve all the limitations in the current data-sharing system, which provides interoperability and reliability.
[10]	The authors propose a blockchain-based solution to address data integrity and privacy issues in e-health systems, ensuring transparency in transactions.	A blockchain-based model called BEIM ensures data integrity and accuracy in health care, enabling information removal using permissioned blockchains and off-chain storage.	The proposed system failed to provide any experimental results.	Incorporating two different approaches to provide privacy for the system proposed. The study has provided a method to remove the content of the block without exposing the content and traceback to its origin.

(Continued)

TABLE 11.1 (Continued)

References	Problem addressed	Proposed solution	Result	Pros and cons
[23]	Blockchain-based data integrity verification for large-scale IoT data is being developed to ensure data integrity during transmission, storage, and pressing due to the exponential popularity of IoT applications.	The proposed blockchain-based data integrity verification system for IoT devices ensures data integrity by allowing real-time modification of cloud-stored data without relying on third parties.	The study evaluated the proposed algorithm's performance and security, confirming its feasibility and potential to combat malicious attacks in various scenarios.	A new integrity verification system can be used to provide the integrity of the blockchain. The system is still in the creation stage, where it cannot provide integrity for different types of data, such as graphs, images, etc.
[12]	A blockchain technology solution to address the challenge of ensuring data integrity in cloud servers, thereby enhancing confidence in third-party auditors.	Proposed consortium blockchain solution for IoT device data integrity, ensuring trust, anonymity, and privacy through zero-knowledge proof identity mixer and Hyperledger Fabric digital certification.	The study tested a proposed schema based on consortium blockchain for IoT security, demonstrating its potential to achieve data integrity at a reasonable time cost.	Through the use of Hyperledger Fabric, the author can solve the issue of the untrusted third-party auditor. The experiment proved that the system is feasible and can ensure integrity.
[13]	The increasing collection of personal information necessitates a secure and efficient data storage system to mitigate threats such as data modification, breaches, and unauthorized disclosure.	RIVAChain is a blockchain-based ledger system that securely stores data, ensuring the integrity of file transfers without requiring file checksums, and uses a unique hash function for data validation.	The Rivachain system demonstrated high performance and scalability, achieving high throughput and low latency in checksum calculations, even with large data sizes.	Using Rivachain. the transfer time to the blockchain can be reduced by 50%, minimizing the overhead.

(Continued)

TABLE 11.1 (Continued)

References	Problem addressed	Proposed solution	Result	Pros and cons
[22]	The system and security models of the TDL chain, a blockchain network relying on encryption and certificate authority for data storage and entity identification.	The proposed TDL chain solution utilizes blockchain technology, a cloud server, and a certificate authority to address inconsistencies in sharing multiple chains in the TDL.	The smart contract effectively manages data transfer, intelligently makes decisions for TDL containing data, and ensures efficient data transmission, allowing for further system throughput improvement.	The system can guarantee secure data; the disadvantage of the system is that the throughput is not as high as it is expected to be.
[11]	Integrating traditional blockchain with edge-cloud storage aims to improve credibility and address resource inadequacy.	A Merkle tree for data integrity verification employs various sampling strategies and utilize smart contracts to ensure process integrity.	The study experimented with three loss function variables to enhance the framework's security and efficiency.	The framework offers better performance, data storage security, and dependability, but has higher overhead.
[24]	Utilizing a third party, faces issues such as inefficient data security due to its centralized database, making it susceptible to breaches and hackers.	The proposed blockchain-based personal data trading system utilizes decentralized identifiers (DIDs) and verifiable credentials (VCs) for authentication and ownership, ensuring reliable data storage and usage.	The study demonstrates the efficient use of the proposed system, which utilizes DID and VC features, and a blockchain-based database for user data storage.	The advantage of this paper is that it avoided the use of a centralized system, meaning the users themselves can authenticate and provide their identity on their own.

(Continued)

TABLE 11.1 (Continued)

References	Problem addressed	Proposed solution	Result	Pros and cons
[18]	The problem statement involves verifying data integrity in a distributed system for big data analysis to prevent trust loss due to changes in data.	Clouseau, a blockchain-based system, to ensure data integrity in distributed systems using Merkle proofs and smart contracts, allowing user-defined configurations while ensuring security.	Clouseau is a system that effectively detects malicious activity and maintains data integrity in distributed systems, demonstrating high throughput and latency in read-write operations.	The study has provided a demonstration to help the users know and understand the system better.
[25]	MB-EHR is a blockchain-based EHR system for healthcare data management.	MB-EHR is a blockchain-based EHR system with efficient data storage and verification mechanisms.	The study evaluates the performance of MB-EHR, revealing that an increase in full nodes results in a decrease in system throughput.	MB-HER is a blockchain-based solution for hierarchical EHR systems.
[15]	Discusses research gaps in blockchain implementation in IoT ecosystems.	Proposes three solutions for implementing blockchain technology in IoT ecosystems.	Blockchain technology can meet IoT efficiency standards and ensure data integrity.	Blockchain technology ensures data integrity in IoT ecosystem databases.
[14]	To address the rising cyber threat, highlighting the challenges of verifying and managing data integrity in information security, thereby addressing new security and privacy issues.	A proposed blockchain system for information security, ensuring data integrity through message authentication codes and SHA-256 hash values, encrypted with asymmetric key cryptography and recipient public key.	Blockchain-based data integrity assurance method offers robust and evolving security, as tested through penetration testing using tools like Wireshark, OpenSSL, and Nmap in five rounds.	The study claims that the proposed blockchain integrity security management is more robust compared to the existing solution. One more advantage is that the block is immutable to change, making it more secure.

(Continued)

TABLE 11.1 (Continued)

References	Problem addressed	Proposed solution	Result	Pros and cons
[16]	The issue pertains to security and privacy concerns in IoT networks and applications, despite their growing popularity due to their ease of use.	The proposed system utilizes a blockchain technique for IoT networks, ensuring data integrity through three stages: setup, processing, and verification, making it efficient for IoT applications.	The study tested the system's performance using memory utilization, accuracy rate, and end-to-end delay parameters, finding the proposed scheme was better in terms of end-to-end delay.	The proposed system security is achieved and the integrity of the system. The disadvantage of the system is that as the number of blocks increases, the memory consumption increases, so it has a shortage in dealing with large amounts of data.
[17]	To address security and privacy issues in the growing IoT application in agriculture, focusing on data integrity in sensing data stored in databases.	The proposed blockchain implementation uses Ethereum for smart irrigation security, divided into public, authorized, and permission-only networks. Components include IoT sensors, Ethereum, data repositories, and users.	The private blockchain network underwent various tests including software unit, smart contract, and data integrity testing, all of which yielded successful results in various scenarios.	The system advantage is that it ensures the integrity of the data that is stored in the blockchain 100%.
[26]	Limitations of the cloud service provider, data damage recovery, and the problem of third-party unauthorized disclosure.	A new data storage system is proposed using Merkle tree properties and blockchain smart contracts.	It was analyzed and tested using some techniques and found to be efficient and powerful.	Repair and recover the data damage, authenticate the user, and provide a high level of security and privacy.
[19]	The nonstop availability of data in the server of the public cloud data.	The system uses a verifiable delay function VDF, zero-knowledge privacy, and a smart contract for verification.	The task involves authenticating data, ensuring no information leakage, and ensuring a sound protocol.	Saved space in their devices helps improve the security of the enterprise.

(Continued)

TABLE 11.1 (Continued)

References	Problem addressed	Proposed solution	Result	Pros and cons
[20]	The Internet of Vehicles (IoV) involves collecting user and vehicle data on cloud servers, posing security and privacy concerns due to low integrity and trust.	The proposed system utilizes bilinear mapping, TPA, cloud server, data generator, edge node, and blockchain technology to transform IoV data, verify transaction integrity, and enhance user experience.	The system's data encryption ensures privacy, but third-party audits are not trusted. Reducing time overhead for data integrity is suggested.	Ensuring the security and integrity of the IoV data. Also, another advantage reduces the minimum overhead of the system performance. It also increases the efficiency of the entire system.
[27]	Researchers are exploring blockchain technology to address trust issues in cloud server data, but the technology's short transaction time limits its application in large data sets.	The proposed solution uses a queueing methodology to estimate off-chain transaction queueing time, assess data integrity in IoT data, and consider factors like batch size and rate.	The study assesses the OTX queueing delay and compares results using numerical parameters like batch size and OTX rate, highlighting their impact on the queuing model.	The study's advantage is that it ensures the integrity of the block by the proposed system as well as the delay of the OTX. The disadvantage of the study it was hard to understand as it provided a lot of calculations and formulas.
[21]	The study proposes a data protection protocol for low power IoT devices on public blockchain networks, addressing issues with data integrity, transaction costs, and off-chain options.	The proposed solution combines on-chain and off-chain storage for data security, utilizing smart contracts, decentralized web applications, and public blockchains for data gathering, encryption, smart contract implementation, and data validation.	The ESP32S2 device is used to evaluate a data storage mechanism, proving its effectiveness, energy use, memory utilization, and security for low-power IoT devices.	The advantage that the authors achieved is that it focuses on low-power IoT devices and improves their efficiency and integrity. The use of smart contracts prove the security tool used is free from vulnerabilities.

[Original (created by authors)]

11.6   Research gaps and potential areas for future work

Numerous efforts have been made for the sake of securing EHRs in the modern health system. Some of the work was accomplished using blockchain technology, the Merkle tree–based approach, establishing an application, IoT, etc. There exist more technologies that can be utilized for EHRs and ensure their security and privacy. For example, there is a potential to use machine learning as well as data mining to check for abnormal patterns and trends to increase the efficiency of EHRs. The security of EHRs can be an issue if they do not meet certain levels. To avoid this problem, biometric authentication can be used to make it more secure and ensure the identity of the person trying to access the account. Intrusion detection systems (IDSs) and intrusion prevention systems (IPSs) must be implemented to create a level of defense that will be detected before the bad action happens. IPS will act to prevent the bad action and the level of threat can be decreased exponentially.

11.7   Discussion and conclusion

After investigating the literature survey and understanding the key feature, how the design works, the purpose, and the problem statement, the authors address and create a solution. A lot of researchers aim to use blockchain technology for data integrity purposes for EHRs. However, different literature surveys used different types of blockchain and different techniques and features. There are some authors who have implemented an application or a website to accomplish their objective. One of the most used techniques is called the Merkle tree approach, which is used to ensure the integrity of the record on the blockchain.

There are some areas where researchers cannot investigate EHRs. Machine learning can be used to predict abnormal events in EHRs. ML techniques can be used to predict disease and create treatment plans. Even though there are some researchers who have created a mobile application and use a blockchain for it, this area lacks investigation; for example, there could be a chance for researchers to create an app for mobile use and integrate the EHR and make sure that it is secure enough to be deployed for users.

This research domain can be viewed as important in the modern healthcare system because it deals with patient medical records and sometimes these records can be private and have information that is critical to the user and the patient does not want to disclose this information to anyone else other than their healthcare provider or maybe family. An EHR is a factor that leverages the health industry boost to the researcher to make their work and contribute to making it more secure and advance this technology more.

References

1. Conoscenti, M., Vetro, A., & De Martin, J. C. (2016, November). Blockchain for the internet of things: A systematic literature review. In 2016 IEEE/ACS 13th International Conference of Computer Systems and Applications (AICCSA) (pp. 1–6). IEEE.
2. Nagpal, D., Alsubaie, N., Soufiene, B. O., Alqahtani, M. S., Abbas, M., & Almohiy, H. M. (2023). Automatic detection of diabetic hypertensive retinopathy in fundus images using transfer learning. Applied Sciences, 13, 4695. https://doi.org/10.3390/app13084695
3. Liang, X., Zhao, J., Shetty, S., Liu, J., & Li, D. (2017, October). Integrating blockchain for data sharing and collaboration in mobile healthcare applications. In 2017 IEEE 28th Annual International Symposium on Personal, Indoor, and Mobile Radio Communications (PIMRC) (pp. 1–5). IEEE.
4. Liang, X., Zhao, J., Shetty, S., & Li, D. (2017, October). Towards data assurance and resilience in IoT using blockchain. In MILCOM 2017-2017 IEEE Military Communications Conference (MILCOM) (pp. 261–266). IEEE.
5. Yue, D., Li, R., Zhang, Y., Tian, W., & Peng, C. (2018, December). Blockchain-based data integrity verification in P2P cloud storage. In 2018 IEEE 24th International Conference on Parallel and Distributed Systems (ICPADS) (pp. 561–568). IEEE.
6. Othman, S. B., Almalki, F. A., & Sakli, H. (2022). Internet of Things in the Healthcare Applications: Overview of Security and Privacy Issues. In: Chakraborty, C., Khosravi, M.R. (eds) Intelligent Healthcare. Springer, Singapore. https://doi.org/10.1007/978-981-16-8150-9_9
7. Sharma, B., Sekharan, C. N., & Zuo, F. (2018, November). Merkle-tree-based approach for ensuring the integrity of electronic medical records. In 2018 9th IEEE Annual Ubiquitous Computing, Electronics & Mobile Communication Conference (UEMCON) (pp. 983–987). IEEE.
8. Renner, T., Müller, J., & Kao, O. (2018, March). Endolith: A blockchain-based framework to enhance data retention in cloud storage. In 2018 26th Euromicro International Conference on Parallel, Distributed and Network-Based Processing (PDP) (pp. 627–634). IEEE.
9. Lee, A. R., Kim, M. G., & Kim, I. K. (2019, November). SHAREChain: Healthcare data sharing framework using Blockchain-registry and FHIR. In 2019 IEEE International Conference on Bioinformatics and Biomedicine (BIBM) (pp. 1087–1090). IEEE.
10. Alqarni, K. S., Almalki, F. A., Soufiene, B. O., Ali, O., & Albalwy, F. (2022). Authenticated wireless links between a drone and sensors using a blockchain: Case of smart farming. Wireless Communications and Mobile Computing, 2022, Article ID 4389729, 13. https://doi.org/10.1155/2022/4389729
11. Yue, D., Li, R., Zhang, Y., Tian, W., & Huang, Y. (2020). A blockchain-based verification framework for data integrity in edge-cloud storage. Journal of Parallel and Distributed Computing, 146, 1–14.
12. Dong, G., & Wang, X. (2020, May). A secure IoT data integrity auditing scheme based on a consortium blockchain. In 2020 5th IEEE International Conference on Big Data Analytics (ICBDA) (pp. 246–250). IEEE.
13. Alhussen, A., & Arslan, E. (2020, December). RIVAChain: Blockchain-based integrity verification for file transfers. In 2020 IEEE International Conference on Big Data (Big Data) (pp. 3255–3261). IEEE.
14. Salagrama, S., Bibhu, V., & Rana, A. (2022). Blockchain-based data integrity security management. Procedia Computer Science, 215, 331–339.

15. Rodrigues, C. K. D. S., & Rocha, V. (2021). Towards blockchain for suitable efficiency and data integrity of IoT ecosystem transactions. IEEE Latin America Transactions, 19(7), 1199–1206.
16. Chanal, P. M., & Kakkasageri, M. S. (2022, August). Secured data integrity scheme for internet of things. In 2022 2nd Asian Conference on Innovation in Technology (ASIANCON) (pp. 1–5). IEEE.
17. Sumarudin, A., Putra, W. P., Puspaningrum, A., Suheryadi, A., Anam, I. S., Yani, M., & Hanif, I. (2022, December). Implementation of IoT sensor data integrity for irrigation in precision agriculture using blockchain Ethereum. In 2022 5th International Seminar on Research of Information Technology and Intelligent Systems (ISRITI) (pp. 29–33). IEEE.
18. Konsta, A., Mytilinis, I., Doka, K., Niarchos, S., & Koziris, N. (2021, April). Clouseau: Blockchain-based data integrity for HDFS clusters. In 2021 IEEE 37th International Conference on Data Engineering (ICDE) (pp. 2725–2728). IEEE.
19. Huang, Y., Yu, Y, Li, H., Li, Y., & Tian, A. (2022). Blockchain-based continuous data integrity checking protocol with zero-knowledge privacy protection. Digital Communications and Networks, 8(5), 604–613.
20. Qi, H., Li, H., Yu, W., & Wang, C. (2023, June). IoV edge data integrity audit method based on blockchain. In 2023 International Conference on Blockchain Technology and Information Security (ICBCTIS) (pp. 180–186). IEEE.
21. Khor, J. H., Sidorov, M., Ong, M. T., & Chua, S. Y. (2023). Public blockchain-based data integrity verification for low-power IoT devices. IEEE Internet of Things Journal, vol. 10, no 14, pp. 13056–13064, 15 July15, 2023, doi: 10.1109/JIOT.2023.3259975.
22. Yang, X., Li, Y., Chen, L., Feng, W., & Yan, Z. (2020, November). TDL-chain: An intelligent data transmission control system in tactical data link based on blockchain. In 2020 IEEE International Conference on Blockchain (Blockchain) (pp. 305–312). IEEE.
23. Wang, H., & Zhang, J. (2019). Blockchain-based data integrity verification for large-scale IoT data. IEEE Access, 7, 164996–165006.
24. Yoon, D., Moon, S., Park, K., & Noh, S. (2021, October). Blockchain-based personal data trading system using decentralized identifiers and verifiable credentials. In 2021 International Conference on Information and Communication Technology Convergence (ICTC) (pp. 150–154). IEEE.
25. Wu, H., Li, L., Paik, H. Y., & Kanhere, S. S. (2021, May). Mb-EHR: A multilayer blockchain-based EHR. In 2021 IEEE International Conference on Blockchain and Cryptocurrency (ICBC) (pp. 1–3). IEEE.
26. Haifeng, M., & Ji, Z. (2022, November). Block-chain-based cloud storage integrity verification scheme for recoverable data. In 2022 7th International Conference on Intelligent Informatics and Biomedical Science (ICIIBMS) (Vol. 7, pp. 280–285). IEEE.
27. Seike, H., Aoki, Y., & Koshizuka, N. (2023, April). Evaluating off-chain transaction queueing delay to ensure data integrity by blockchain. In 2023 8th International Conference on Cloud Computing and Big Data Analytics (ICCCBDA) (pp. 68–75). IEEE.

12

BLOCKCHAIN FOR HALAL INTEGRITY IN HEALTH CARE

Enhancing Compliance, Ensuring Benefits

Md Mahfujur Rahman

12.1 Introduction to Halal health care and blockchain technology

12.1.1 Defining Halal health care

Halal health care represents a significant evolution in the healthcare sector, integrating Islamic teachings into various aspects of medical care and product development [1]. This innovative approach extends beyond the compliance with Islamic dietary laws, encompassing a broader spectrum of ethical, moral, and spiritual values rooted in Islam. It is about providing a healthcare system that is not only physically beneficial but also spiritually uplifting for Muslim patients. This holistic care model is particularly significant given the growing global Muslim population, which is actively seeking healthcare solutions that resonate with their religious and cultural values. Halal health care, therefore, plays a crucial role in meeting these specific needs, ensuring that medical treatments, pharmaceuticals, and healthcare practices do not contravene Islamic principles. [2] emphasizes the importance of this approach in modern health care, acknowledging the need for systems and solutions that are both innovative and faith aligned.

12.1.2 Unlocking the potential: The importance of blockchain technology

12.1.2.1 Trust with immutability

Trust is the mutual reliance and expectation between partners that they can depend on one another to behave in a predictable and reasonable manner [2]. Trust is a fundamental attribute of blockchain technology [3]. Blockchain's

DOI: 10.1201/9781003483113-12

immutability fortifies the cornerstone of successful partnerships—trust. It ensures an unchangeable recording of transactions using cryptographic techniques and hash values, preventing the spread of false information and self-regulating agents' behavior without requiring central authorities [4]. Immutability guarantees that once data is stored, it cannot be modified or altered, thereby enhancing security and data integrity.

12.1.2.2 Transparency

Transparency is defined as the extent to which pertinent information on a transaction is easily accessible to all parties engaged in it, including external observers. Transparency is a crucial factor in evaluating the supply chain's effectiveness, considering the increasing level of security provided by blockchain technology. Blockchain ensures transparency by enabling every member to possess an identical copy of all data. The approval of the majority of nodes is required to add transaction blocks to the ledger, eliminating fraudulent activities and ensuring transparency across the entire supply chain. This transparency is an essential factor in evaluating the supply chain's performance and guarantees compliance, safety, and accuracy throughout various phases [4]. Blockchain technology has the capacity to enhance the transparency of systems, leading to a reduction in failures [5].

12.1.2.3 Decentralized technology with security

The decentralized character of blockchain, as described in [5] and [6], implies that there is no controlling authority or one individual in charge. A network is maintained by a set of nodes, which improves security and reduces interference. Blockchain eliminates the need for central authority, prohibiting individuals from manipulating the network's attributes to their benefit. Cryptographic hashing protects every piece of data on the blockchain.

12.1.2.4 Distributed ledgers, consensus, and speedier settlement

Utilizing distributed ledgers, blockchain ensures that every participating node has an identical copy, guaranteeing consistency. Consensus mechanisms ensure a single shared record among all nodes, enhancing truthfulness and honesty. Blockchain has the potential to expedite asset trade settlements, bypassing existing intermediaries and allowing for faster, more flexible transactions. Miners can be rewarded for maintaining accurate records, contributing to overall system efficiency [6].

12.1.3 The nexus of Halal health care and blockchain

The convergence of blockchain technology with Halal health care is a promising development in the medical field. Blockchain can significantly enhance the trustworthiness and compliance of healthcare services and products with Islamic standards, from their production to their distribution [5]. This technology ensures a transparent and verifiable trail of Halal certifications and transactions, building confidence among consumers and stakeholders in the Halal healthcare market.

Moreover, blockchain's role in patient data management is of paramount importance. It offers a secure and efficient platform for storing and sharing patient information, ensuring compliance with both privacy standards and Islamic ethical principles. The implementation of smart contracts on blockchain platforms can streamline healthcare processes, ensuring they adhere to Halal principles. These contracts automatically execute agreed-upon terms, reducing the need for intermediaries and minimizing the potential for errors and breaches in compliance [6].

The integration of blockchain in Halal health care extends beyond ensuring compliance with religious doctrines; it represents an opportunity to elevate the overall quality of healthcare delivery. By enhancing transparency and trust in Halal certification processes and supply chains, blockchain technology could become a crucial factor in improving healthcare services in the Islamic world. This synergy between advanced technology and faith-based principles leads to a more inclusive and ethically aligned healthcare system, addressing the specific needs of the Muslim population and fostering a comprehensive approach to health and well-being.

Thus, the fusion of Halal health care and blockchain technology represents a significant stride towards an integrated, ethically aligned, and technologically advanced healthcare system. This integration not only assures adherence to Islamic principles but also propels the healthcare sector towards greater efficiency, transparency, and trust. As we continue to navigate the complexities of modern health care, the role of innovative solutions such as blockchain in enhancing Halal compliance becomes increasingly pivotal, promising a future where health care is both technologically advanced and religiously conscientious.

12.2 The importance of Halal compliance in health care

12.2.1 Ethical and religious imperatives

Halal compliance in health care transcends dietary laws and extends into the broader ethical and religious imperatives of Islam [6]. The term "Halal," meaning "permissible" in Arabic, serves as a guiding principle influencing various aspects of a Muslim's life, including healthcare decisions. Ethical considerations in Halal health care are intertwined with Islamic teachings on the sanctity of life, beliefs about the afterlife, and the conviction that life and death are determined by God's will.

Life is considered a sacred gift in Islam, shaping the approach to health care. Practices like euthanasia and suicide are prohibited, reflecting the belief in divine sovereignty over life and death [7]. This perspective influences medical decisions, such as the implementation of Do Not Resuscitate (DNR) orders, where ending life-sustaining treatments in specific cases is viewed as permissible under Islamic law. The Islamic concept of death, perceived as the soul's journey to the afterlife, informs the Muslim approach to end-of-life care. Discontinuing life support in medically futile situations is acceptable in Islam, as long as it is clearly communicated and differentiated from practices like euthanasia, which are not permitted [8].

12.2.2 Halal health care: Consumer preferences and quality assurance

Halal products have gained increasing significance, aligning with Islamic teachings emphasizing the consumption of what is "Halal" (lawful) and "Tayyib" (good and clean), as outlined in the Qur'an and other Islamic teachings [9]. The integration of Islamic principles into health care, spanning pharmaceuticals and medical tourism, emerges as a substantial and growing global concern. Fueled by the expanding Muslim population's demand for healthcare services and products adhering to Islamic principles, this trend holds profound implications for the healthcare industry.

12.2.2.1 Consumer preferences and quality assurance in Halal pharmaceuticals

The escalating demand for Halal-certified pharmaceuticals mirrors a global apprehension, particularly among Muslim consumers, for products aligning with Islamic dietary laws and religious beliefs. With the Halal pharmaceutical market poised for significant expansion, Malaysia assumes a pivotal role in both domestic and international contexts. This study illuminates consumer preferences driving the demand for Halal pharmaceuticals, rooted in religious adherence and considerations of quality and safety. The inclination towards Shariah-compliant manufacturing and ingredients signifies a broader shift, where Halal certification denotes not just religious compliance but also product quality and safety. This shift towards Halal pharmaceuticals signifies a comprehensive approach to health, harmonizing physical well-being with spiritual adherence and resonating with both Muslim and non-Muslim consumers alike [10].

12.2.2.2 Halal medical tourism: A growing industry

Over the past two decades, the concept of Halal has gained significant prominence in the realm of international medical tourism. The remarkable expansion of the global Muslim population plays a pivotal role in propelling the development of Halal tourism. Anticipated to reach 2.2 billion by 2030, constituting 26.4% of the projected global population of 8.3 billion, the Muslim demographic's growth is reshaping healthcare trends. The term "Halal," rooted in the Qur'an and Sunnah, denotes actions or things deemed acceptable according to Shari'ah, the Islamic legal system. Halal-friendly healthcare services have evolved as a substantial component of the broader healthcare delivery system, garnering global recognition. The surge in demand for Halal-friendly healthcare services is evident, driven by the substantial and expanding market segment of Muslim visitors [11].

12.2.3 Impact of noncompliance in Halal health care

12.2.3.1 Ethical and religious misalignment

Noncompliance with Halal principles in healthcare settings can lead to a misalignment between provided healthcare services and the ethical and religious expectations of Muslim patients. The commitment to incorporate Islamic principles into the work ethic of healthcare establishments, as exemplified by the Islamic Hospital Consortium, is crucial. However, failure in this alignment can create a sense of discomfort and dissatisfaction among patients, impacting the doctor–patient relationship. The holistic approach, emphasizing not only technical aspects but also the alignment with Islamic ethics, underscores the importance of ensuring Shari'ah compliance in all facets of healthcare services [12].

12.2.3.2 Quality of care and patient experience

Noncompliance with Shari'ah principles in healthcare settings can compromise the quality of care provided to Muslim patients, potentially leading to suboptimal health outcomes. This noncompliance manifests in various challenges faced by Muslim patients in conventional hospitals, creating a distinctive context for the demand for Shari'ah-compliant healthcare services [13]. Muslim patients encountering noncompliance often experience privacy issues during treatment, cross-gender interactions, and concerns about the Halal status of pharmaceuticals. These challenges contribute significantly to the heightened demand for healthcare services that align with Shari'ah principles, as highlighted by authors in [14] and [15]. The intricacies of providing health care in accordance with Islamic values become particularly relevant in addressing the unique needs and preferences of Muslim patients.

The views of al-Imam al-Ghazali on medical treatment emphasize the permissibility of treatment in cases where potential side effects may exist. This perspective becomes essential in the context of Shari'ah-compliant health care, where navigating potential side effects while ensuring adherence to Islamic principles becomes a critical consideration. Additionally, the hadith of Prophet Muhammad, cited in [15], reinforces the encouragement for Muslim patients to seek treatment, assuring them that there is a cure for every ailment, known to some and unknown to others. This hadith serves as a guiding principle for Muslim patients facing health challenges, providing spiritual support and emphasizing the compatibility of seeking medical treatment with Islamic teachings. In essence, the impact of noncompliance in this context lies in potentially hindering individuals from following the guidance of Prophet Muhammad to seek medical treatment, find assurance in the availability of cures, and benefit from both known and unknown medical solutions. It emphasizes the importance of aligning healthcare practices with Islamic teachings to ensure that individuals receive the necessary support and encouragement for their well-being [16].

12.3   Halal health care: Certification and regulatory challenges

12.3.1   Operational challenges in Halal certification implementation

The enactment of the Halal Law and subsequent government regulations brings forth a myriad of practical challenges for the pharmaceutical industry. The complexities arise from the burdensome nature of Halal certification, which pharmaceutical businesses find challenging to implement. The Association of Pharmaceutical Companies advocates against applying Halal certification to medicines, arguing that the diverse composition of medicines, including potentially forbidden materials, makes compliance difficult [16].

Additionally, the Halal Products Certification Agency (BPJPH), tasked with guaranteeing Halal products, faces challenges in examining a vast number of products within a short time frame. With the pharmaceutical industry needing Halal certification, the capacity of the certification agency must be continually enhanced. Experts in specific production processes and drug development become essential in addressing the unique challenges posed by different segments of the pharmaceutical production chain [17].

Furthermore, compliance costs pose a significant concern, estimated to be as much as S\$4.4 billion. Pharmaceutical companies are burdened with costs related to reprinting labels, disposal of finished goods, and the regular renewal of Halal certificates. The potential rise in prices due to compliance costs may lead to a decline in sales, impacting companies' financial stability. The law's strict penalties for noncompliance, including two-year jail terms or fines, add further pressure on businesses [18].

The lack of understanding of the Halal concept among the community, associating it primarily with religious matters, presents an additional obstacle.

The intricate process of Halal certification for medicines, involving investigations into manufacturing processes and ingredients, adds complexity and higher costs. This regulatory layer not only increases production costs but also introduces uncertainties that may disrupt the pharmaceutical business and supply of medicines to the public. The greatest challenge lies in the potential disruption to the distribution system and supply chain, particularly considering the significant percentage of active ingredients in imported medicines lacking Halal certification [19].

12.3.2 Regulatory challenges

The Halal Law introduces fundamental flaws that pose significant regulatory challenges, particularly in its attempt to establish a legal framework for halal certification and labeling. Article 4, stating that "Products that entered, distributed, and traded in Indonesia must be certified as halal," creates a potential contradiction. The obligation implied in Article 4 suggests that non-Halal products may be restricted from entering or being traded in Indonesia, impacting the pharmaceutical industry. However, Article 26 provides a contradictory provision allowing the entry and distribution of non-Halal products, provided they bear appropriate labeling. This inconsistency may create confusion among drug producers and companies operating in Indonesia [19].

Moreover, there is a challenge related to the absence of implementing regulations, such as the Presidential Regulation (PR) and the Regulation of the Ministry of Religious Affairs (PMARMRA). Despite the finalized draft, the lack of published regulations creates legal uncertainty. Additionally, as a member of the World Trade Organization (WTO), Indonesia is bound by the Technical Barrier to Trade (TBT) Agreement, raising concerns about the creation of trade barriers that contradict the TBT Agreement. Balancing Halal requirements with international agreements becomes crucial to avoid unnecessary trade obstacles [20].

12.4 Blockchain: A technological solution for Halal healthcare compliance

12.4.1 Blockchain and its fundamentals application in Halal certification

Blockchain technology, with its decentralized and transparent nature, is increasingly gaining recognition as a transformative force in various industries. In the context of Halal certification, the application of blockchain offers a novel solution to address challenges related to authenticity, traceability, and global standardization.

12.4.1.1 Benefits of blockchain in Halal certification and real-time update

Blockchain technology's decentralization serves as an ideal fit for the intricate demands of Halal food traceability, which is an important factor for patients' food supply. By addressing global challenges such as the lack of a universally recognized Halal certification system, the dissemination of inaccurate data on Halal products, inadequate regulation of raw materials, and difficulties in managing centralized regulatory systems, blockchain provides a comprehensive solution. Blockchain enables real-time updates on the condition and status of Halal products, facilitating easy access for consumers seeking accurate information. The transparency afforded by blockchain ensures that end-consumers can make informed decisions about the products they consume, fostering a holistic understanding of Halal product information [16].

12.4.1.2 WhatsHalal app and consumer engagement

Consumers benefit from the integration of blockchain through applications like WhatsHalal. Leveraging blockchain, the app becomes a gateway for consumers to access tertiary services such as food delivery and restaurant reservations. Additionally, consumers contribute to the ecosystem by making product inquiries and providing feedback. This information loop, enabled by blockchain, allows producers to enhance their processes based on real-time consumer insights [17].

12.4.1.3 Smart contracts for expedited certification

The implementation of smart contracts within blockchain technology aims to streamline the Halal certification application process. Smart contracts bring transparency and traceability by publicly verifying information that is immutably recorded on the blockchain. Data such as Halal testing results, laboratory and venue inspections, evaluations of equipment and supplies, and analysis results of component ingredient lists are all securely stored on the blockchain. Certifying bodies can swiftly review this information, saving both time and resources in the certification process.

12.4.1.4 Digital Halal certification for authenticity

The development of digital Halal certification on the blockchain facilitates easy tracking of authenticity. This innovation not only validates Halal certification but also positions Indonesia as a champion of global Halal standards. By leading the harmonization of standards, Indonesia supports businesses in navigating straightforward and transparent procedures, contributing to the establishment of a global benchmark for Halal practices.

12.4.2 Enhancing supply chain transparency with blockchain

12.4.2.1 Blockchain revolutionizing Halal healthcare supply chain

The primary objective of the Halal healthcare supply chain is to ensure the availability of Halal medical supplies, including drugs, equipment, and services, to maintain public health. Efficient supply chain management involves establishing robust linkages between suppliers and customers while aiming for high customer satisfaction at a reasonable cost [17]. The structure of a blockchain-based Halal healthcare supply chain, as illustrated in Figure 12.1, underscores the transformative potential of blockchain technology in optimizing Halal healthcare logistics.

12.4.2.2 Traditional versus blockchain-powered Halal supply chains

In the conventional Halal healthcare supply chain, a manufacturer dispatches Halal medical products to a distribution hub or distributor, with raw materials

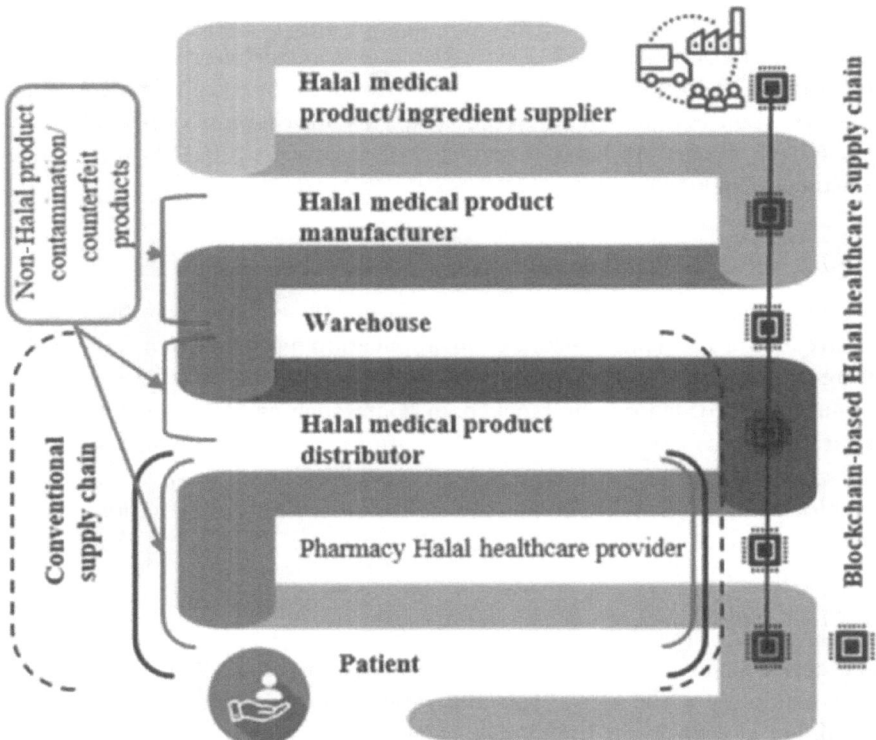

FIGURE 12.1 Halal healthcare supply chain using blockchain.

Original (created by authors)

sourced from various Halal vendors. Distributors play a pivotal role in securely delivering Halal medical products to healthcare providers, pharmacies, or directly to patients. The implementation of the InterPlanetary File System (IPFS) [18] as a decentralized protocol further enhances data security and accessibility for stakeholders, ensuring resilience against potential challenges.

The transformative potential of blockchain is evident in Figure 12.3, where traditional supply chains (depicted by red and blue lines) involve intermediaries like distributors. Blockchain empowers stakeholders, including pharmacies, healthcare professionals, and patients, to directly engage with manufacturers, placing the Halal patient at the forefront. Facing challenges related to counterfeiting, blockchain's transparency and immutability features provide a robust solution for tracking and tracing Halal pharmaceuticals throughout the supply chain, ensuring data integrity in a decentralized Halal healthcare supply network. Every transaction, securely recorded on the blockchain, establishes a foundation for comprehensive data management and analysis [19].

12.4.2.3 *Blockchain integration in the Halal healthcare supply chain*

The Halal healthcare supply chain focuses on ensuring the availability and accessibility of Halal-certified medical supplies, including pharmaceuticals, medical equipment, and healthcare services, while adhering to Islamic principles. Its primary goal is to maintain public health by providing products and services that align with ethical and religious requirements, ensuring trust and compliance among Muslim consumers [19]. The structure of a blockchain-based Halal healthcare supply chain, as illustrated in Figure 12.1, underscores the transformative potential of blockchain technology in optimizing the Halal healthcare supply chain.

The conventional Halal healthcare supply chain typically involves a Halal medical product manufacturer, which then dispatches Halal medicinal items to a distribution hub or a Halal product distributor. Raw materials for manufacturing are supplied by various Halal vendors. Distributors play a crucial role in securely delivering Halal medical products to Halal healthcare providers, Halal pharmacies, or directly to patients in emergency situations.

The implementation of the IPFS, as described in [19] and [20], offers a decentralized protocol for storing healthcare industry segment-wise details in a distributed file system. IPFS may utilize data addressing to uniquely identify each department globally, facilitating access by stakeholders such as Halal suppliers, manufacturers, warehouses, distributors, Halal pharmacies, Halal healthcare providers, and Halal patients. The decentralized nature of IPFS ensures resilience against malware attacks or server failures, enabling data access from alternative systems.

In the conventional supply chain, an interaction between stakeholders (Halal manufacturer, distributor, pharmacy, healthcare practitioners, and patients) might take two forms, as shown by the black dotted and black straight-line colors in Figure 12.1. The product is usually stored in the Halal manufacturer's warehouse once it has been manufactured. A distributor, or middleware, picks up pharmaceuticals or other products from a warehouse and distributes them to other parties. This scenario is shown by the black dotted color in Figure 12.1. In the other scenario, highlighted with a black straight line, stakeholders (pharmacies, healthcare professionals, and patients) can buy pharmaceuticals directly from the manufacturer, bypassing intermediaries like distributors. The patient is at the heart of the system, and we must serve them.

Healthcare supply networks are complicated, diverse, and constantly evolving. As shown in Figure 12.1, non-Halal contamination or counterfeiting of products is possible on multiple fronts. Some of these include: 1) when pharmaceuticals are shipped from the manufacturer to the warehouse; 2) when pharmaceuticals are stocked in the warehouse; and 3) when they are shipped from the warehouses to other stakeholders such as the distributor, pharmacy, healthcare professionals, and patients. To anybody at any level, identifying and tracking non-Halal contamination or counterfeit product determination is incredibly tough. Hence, powerful technology, such as blockchain technology, is needed for flawless monitoring and tracking. Blockchain is a transparent, traceable, and distributed ledger technology that has the potential to solve many of the challenges of traditional supply chains [20]. Because of the blockchain network's immutability feature, every single transaction from the supplier to the end user will be recorded, and no one can modify it. These blockchain network details are utilized for data management and data analysis systems. Blockchain-based Halal healthcare supply chain with a fully decentralized structure offers a transformative approach to managing medical products and services. This system connects all stakeholders—including clients, pharmaceutical companies, healthcare providers, and regulatory bodies—through a distributed ledger, ensuring transparency, security, and compliance with Halal standards.

12.4.3 Navigating Halal healthcare data management with blockchain

In the ever-evolving landscape of healthcare technology, the incorporation of blockchain technology establishes a symbiotic relationship with Islamic principles, revolutionizing the landscape of medical data management within the Halal healthcare domain. This transformative integration brings forth a myriad of dimensions, each contributing to the enhancement of healthcare services and adherence to Halal principles [21].

12.4.3.1 Uncertain and complex nature of medical data

The intricate characteristics of patient data, often vague and inconsistent, pose challenges. Blockchain, fortified by cryptographic techniques, provides a decentralized solution, ensuring the integrity and reliability of medical data. This aligns with Islamic principles emphasizing transparency and honesty in health care [21].

12.4.3.2 Decentralization of healthcare information

A paradigm shift is observed in decentralizing healthcare information, empowering individuals to manage their health journey. Blockchain's architecture facilitates patient control over health records, ensuring transparency and confirmed consent. This resonates with Islamic principles that prioritize individual autonomy and equitable access to information [21].

12.4.3.3 Reliable clinical trial management

The reliability of clinical trials is vital for advancing medical knowledge. Blockchain enhances efficiency by automating data processes and improving transparency in clinical trial management. From an Islamic ethical standpoint, this aligns with the emphasis on maintaining high standards in healthcare practices [22].

12.4.3.4 Outcome-based blockchain contracts for cost estimation

Blockchain's innovation in linking clinical outcomes to costs transforms the approach to cost estimation. This transparency aligns with Islamic principles of fairness and openness in financial transactions. Blockchain's feature of connecting clinical outcomes to costs resonates with these principles, providing a clear and accountable mechanism for cost estimation in health care [23].

12.4.3.5 Security and confidentiality of medical data

Ensuring the security and confidentiality of medical data is paramount. Blockchain's decentralized, secure, and counterfeit-resistant nature makes it well suited for protecting and sharing sensitive medical information. From an Islamic perspective, safeguarding privacy and upholding confidentiality are crucial. Blockchain aligns with these principles, providing a secure platform where individuals can trust that their medical information is protected. The cryptographic mechanisms employed add an extra layer of protection, ensuring the authenticity and integrity of medical data. This resonates with the broader Islamic value of trustworthiness [24].

12.4.3.6 Efficient exchange of electronic medical records

Efficiently exchanging electronic medical records remains a challenge in health care. Blockchain addresses this by providing a secure and transparent platform for data exchange. This efficiency aligns with Islamic values of trust and confidentiality in transactions. In Islam, maintaining confidentiality and trust in exchanges, especially those related to sensitive medical information, is crucial. The blockchain's contribution to efficient data exchange supports the broader Islamic value of trustworthy transactions [25].

12.4.3.7 Verification and authenticity of medical data

Blockchain's role in enabling users to store medical data with verifiable authenticity enhances trust in the information. From an Islamic perspective, trust is fundamental in all aspects of life. Blockchain's cryptographic algorithms ensure the confidentiality and integrity of medical data, aligning with Islamic principles of trustworthiness and data integrity. This fosters confidence in the accuracy of medical information, promoting a trustworthy healthcare ecosystem. The ability to verify authenticity aligns with the broader Islamic principle of ensuring truthfulness and integrity in dealings [26].

12.4.3.8 Implementation challenges and prototypes

The ongoing development of blockchain applications in health care reflects the dynamic nature of technological advancements. Current projects are often in prototype stages, open to ongoing improvements. This aligns with Islamic principles of continuous improvement and innovation in healthcare services while ensuring ethical considerations. In Islam, the pursuit of knowledge and advancements in technology is encouraged, provided they align with ethical considerations. The development of blockchain applications in health care aligns with the Islamic ethos of seeking progress while maintaining ethical standards. The challenges encountered during implementation underscore the importance of thorough testing and refinement, ensuring that the final solutions align with both technological excellence and ethical considerations. It reflects the Islamic principle of seeking excellence in endeavors while adhering to ethical standards and continuous improvement [27].

Table 12.1 outlines essential dimensions where blockchain technology plays a pivotal role, addressing challenges and reshaping the landscape of medical data handling within the realm of Halal health care. Each dimension highlights the specific role blockchain assumes, emphasizing its alignment with fundamental Halal healthcare principles. The intersection of technology and ethical considerations is carefully explored, offering insights into how blockchain fosters transparency, security, and reliability while adhering to Islamic values in healthcare practices. Explore the key dimensions, blockchain's role, and their profound alignment with Halal healthcare principles in this comprehensive table.

TABLE 12.1 Key dimensions, blockchain's role, and alignment with Halal healthcare principles

No.	Dimension	Blockchain's role	References	Halal healthcare principle
1	Uncertain and Complex Nature of Medical Data	Blockchain provides a decentralized, secure, and reliable solution for managing uncertain medical data. It ensures data integrity through cryptographic methods and hash functions	[29]	Ensures the integrity and reliability of medical data, aligning with the Islamic principles of honesty and transparency in health care
2	Decentralization of Healthcare Information	Blockchain decentralizes medical information, improving availability, efficiency, transparency, and credibility. It facilitates complete longitudinal health records, enhancing patient control and confirmed consent	[30]	Decentralization aligns with Islamic principles by providing more control to individuals over their health information while maintaining transparency and credibility
3	Reliable Clinical Trial Management	Blockchain tools, combined with electronic data collection, offer automatic aggregation, replication, and distribution of clinical data. This ensures greater revision, tracking, and control compared to traditional systems	[31]	Improves the reliability of clinical trials, essential for maintaining ethical standards in health care according to Islamic principles
4	Outcome-Based Blockchain Contracts	Blockchain enables outcome-based contracts, linking clinical outcomes to costs. This simplifies cost estimation in medical care, reducing complexity and enhancing recordkeeping	[32]	Aligns with the Islamic principle of fairness and transparency by linking costs directly to outcomes in medical care

(Continued)

TABLE 12.1 (Continued)

No.	Dimension	Blockchain's role	References	Halal healthcare principle
5	Security and Confidentiality of Medical Data	Blockchain's decentralized, secure, and counterfeit-resistant nature makes it suitable for protecting and sharing medical data. It ensures safe storage, prevents forgery, and allows users to verify the authenticity of their data	[33]	Enhances the security and confidentiality of medical data, addressing concerns about privacy and unauthorized access in line with Islamic principles
6	Efficient Exchange of Electronic Medical Records	Blockchain facilitates secure and efficient exchange of electronic medical records. It ensures privacy and security, addressing challenges related to data leakage and confidentiality breaches	[34]	Enables a more efficient and secure exchange of medical records, promoting confidentiality and trust in accordance with Islamic values
7	Verification and Authenticity of Medical Data	Blockchain allows users to store important medical data with verifiable authenticity. Cryptographic algorithms ensure data confidentiality, providing an extra layer of security	[35]	Provides verifiable authenticity and confidentiality of medical data, aligning with Islamic principles of trust and data integrity
8	Implementation Challenges and Prototypes	Current projects using blockchain in health care are mostly prototypes in development. They are open source, but effective methods for medical data management based on blockchain technologies are still evolving	[36]	The ongoing development aligns with Islamic principles of continuous improvement and innovation in healthcare services while ensuring ethical considerations

[Original (created by authors)]

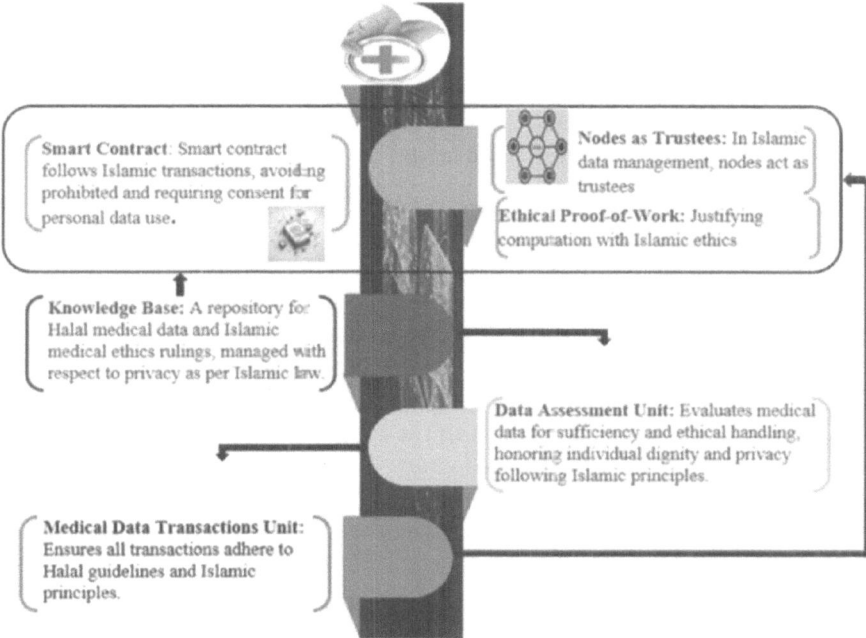

FIGURE 12.2   Structure of the Halal healthcare blockchain-based medical data management system with Islamic principles.

Original (created by authors)

Drawing insights from the analysis of established medical data management systems utilizing blockchain technologies, as detailed by [28], we have crafted a Halal healthcare blockchain-based medical data management system infused with Islamic principles. This innovative system, meticulously developed to align with the ethical foundations of Islamic health care, is visually represented in Figure 12.2.

12.5   Integrating blockchain into Halal healthcare systems

12.5.1   Concerns in the implementation of blockchain for enhanced benefit

Blockchain technology, though revolutionary, faces challenges, especially in the implementation of a Halal healthcare blockchain system. This section scrutinizes the issues associated with blockchain implementations, shedding light on crucial aspects that require consideration for the creation of a resilient and ethical Halal healthcare blockchain framework to ensure more benefit [36].

12.5.1.1 Throughput and latency challenges

Addressing the throughput challenge, as emphasized by Porru et al. [37], is pivotal. The current Bitcoin network processes a modest 3 to 20 transactions per second (tps), significantly lagging behind established networks like VISA (2000 tps) and Twitter (5000 tps). This limited throughput poses a significant obstacle to blockchain's widespread acceptance, especially in Halal health care, where timely transactions are crucial [38]. The time factor is critical in blockchain implementations, and the delay in transaction processing poses a hurdle for universal technology acceptance. In the case of Bitcoin, the time needed to complete one transaction is approximately 10 minutes, while VISA achieves transaction completion within seconds [39]. Such latency issues impact the efficiency of blockchain in time-sensitive applications like Halal health care.

12.5.1.2 Size, bandwidth, and scalability challenges

The sheer size of the blockchain in the Bitcoin network, exceeding 50,000 MB in February 2016, raises concerns about scalability and bandwidth utilization [40]. With the potential to grow 214 PB each year, scalability becomes a prominent issue for handling the increasing volume of transactions, a critical consideration for a robust Halal healthcare blockchain system. Scalability emerges as a significant challenge, necessitating a large number of full nodes to ensure decentralized security. The scalability limits are intricately linked to data size, transaction processing rate, and data transmission latency. Achieving scalability without compromising security is essential for the successful implementation of a Halal healthcare blockchain.

12.5.1.3 Cost implications and data malleability

Blockchain, while decentralized, is not free from costs, impacting its attractiveness as a decentralized solution. Users bear transaction and computational power costs, potentially steering them toward centralized alternatives where fees may be less overt. In the context of Halal health care, addressing cost-related challenges is imperative for widespread adoption. Data malleability poses a potential threat in blockchain implementations, where attackers can modify and rebroadcast transactions, complicating transaction confirmation [41]. Addressing data malleability is crucial for ensuring the integrity and authenticity of medical transactions within a Halal healthcare blockchain.

12.5.1.4 Authentication, privacy, and security considerations

Incidents like the Mt. Gox case underscore authentication challenges in blockchain transactions. The compromise of customer private keys raises concerns about the security of healthcare data in a Halal blockchain system. Robust authentication mechanisms are essential to safeguard against unauthorized access and data breaches. Privacy concerns arise from the problem of multiple addresses in blockchain systems, allowing users to create numerous addresses that researchers attempt to cluster [42]. Address clustering, while performed for legitimate purposes, raises privacy considerations. Balancing privacy and transparency are crucial for Halal healthcare blockchain implementations.

12.5.1.5 Double-spending attacks and security issues

Susceptibility to double-spending attacks, as observed in Bitcoin, is a noteworthy security concern. In health care, the integrity of transactions is paramount, and mitigating the risk of double-spending attacks is crucial for building trust in Halal healthcare blockchain systems. The speculative nature of publicly distributed ledgers raises security concerns, with the potential for a 51% attack on the Bitcoin blockchain [43]. Security breaches, such as Distributed Denial of Service (DDoS) attacks and account hacking, emphasize the need for robust security measures in Halal healthcare blockchain implementations.

12.5.1.6 Addressing wasted resources

The energy expenditure in Bitcoin mining, approximately $15 million per day, raises environmental and efficiency concerns [34]. Addressing the environmental impact of mining is essential for creating a sustainable and ethical Halal healthcare blockchain system.

12.5.2 Integrity and quality strategies for Halal healthcare blockchain compliance

Ensuring the trustworthiness of a blockchain system is paramount, demanding high data integrity, security, reliability, and node privacy [35]. In the context of Halal health care, addressing specific challenges becomes crucial to developing a robust and ethical blockchain framework.

12.5.2.1 Throughput enhancement and scalability solutions

To tackle throughput issues, one potential solution is increasing the size of each block. However, this approach introduces size-related problems. A more nuanced strategy involves tailoring blockchain size for specific applications, avoiding a one-size-fits-all approach. This adaptability ensures optimal performance across diverse applications. Calability is a significant concern, and one approach is deploying multiple blockchains for distinct purposes. Blockchains can interconnect, enhancing security across different applications. This strategy allows miners to focus on blockchains of suitable size, maintaining a satisfactory level of security [44].

12.5.2.2 Authentication and privacy measures

Innovations like the BlueWallet device set the standard for **next-generation authentication in cryptocurrency and beyond**. By combining robust security with ease of use, such devices can address broader authentication challenges in sectors like finance, healthcare, and IoT, ensuring secure digital interactions in an increasingly connected world. Additionally, proposed certification systems offer guarantees for transactions between certified users, adding a layer of trust to Bitcoin addresses. Two-factor authentication for Bitcoin wallets, incorporating smartphones, presents another layer of security. Addressing privacy concerns, permissioned blockchains offer a more controlled environment, allowing developers to grant specific permissions. The Chain-Anchor system proposes identity and privacy preservation for permissioned blockchains, introducing a layer above the blockchain for enhanced security. A Halal healthcare blockchain could adopt such models to balance privacy and transparency effectively [45].

12.5.2.3 Human resource information management

Proposed models for human resource information management, based on blockchain, enhance authenticity and decision support for organizations. Leveraging consensus mechanisms, smart contracts, and payment functions, this model provides a foundation for secure and reliable human resource information handling in a Halal healthcare setting [46].

12.5.2.4 Energy efficiency and data storage optimization

In pursuit of energy efficiency, modifying blockchain blocks by adding extra bytes to optimize timestamps presents an alternative to the energy-intensive proof-of-work (PoW) efficiency. Exploring proof-of-stake (PoS), where mining power depends on the amount of Bitcoin held, introduces a more sustainable consensus mechanism. The challenge of data storage capacity in current blockchain implementations demands a strategic design choice. Balancing cost efficiency, performance, and flexibility requires deciding what data and computation should be on-chain and what should be stored off-chain. Common practices involve storing raw data off-chain and critical metadata and hashes on-chain [46].

12.5.2.5 Quality assurance through testing

Ensuring the security and reliability of blockchain software is crucial. Continuous testing, as advocated by IBM, offers a robust approach. The testing process involves careful consideration of factors such as the platform's nature (public or private) and integration testing with other applications. Early involvement of the testing team is imperative for real-scenario testing to identify potential impacts on the broader system [47].

12.5.2.6 Enhanced software architecture and evaluation metrics for blockchain performance

Adopting specific design notations, patterns, and modeling languages enhances the quality of software implementing blockchain technology. Defining metrics for complexity, communication, resource consumption, and performance aids in evaluating and improving the software process. Evaluation of blockchain performance relies on qualitative and quantitative metrics. These include submission throughput, maximum/average validation throughput, average transaction validation latency, latency volatility, security, confidentiality, transaction fees, hardware requirements, scalability, complexity, and smart contract limitations. These metrics offer a comprehensive view of a blockchain system's efficiency and reliability [48].

12.5.2.7 Integration into established systems

In the context of Islamic and Halal principles, the integration of blockchain into established supply chain systems refers to incorporating blockchain technology into existing logistical and operational processes [49]. This integration aims to enhance transparency, traceability, and accountability within the supply chain, aligning with Islamic principles of fairness, honesty, and ethical business practices, including those related to Halal standards. Table 12.2 provides an overview of key considerations and strategies for implementing a Halal healthcare blockchain system while adhering to Islamic principles.

TABLE 12.2 Key considerations and strategies for Halal healthcare blockchain implementation

Topic	Description	Challenges/ Considerations	Solutions/ Strategies	References	Islamic/Halal principle
Throughput Enhancement	Tailoring blockchain size for specific applications to improve throughput without size-related issues.	Avoiding one-size-fits-all, size limitations	Application-specific blockchain sizing	[50]	Fairness, efficiency, resource optimization
Scalability Solutions	Interconnecting multiple blockchains enhances security and allows scalability with suitable sizes.	Security maintenance, scalable framework	Multiple interconnected blockchains	[51]	Security, efficiency
Authentication and Privacy	Solutions like BlueWallet and certification systems ensure secure transactions and user privacy.	Trust and privacy in controlled environments	Use of secure hardware tokens, permissioned blockchains	[52]	Trust, privacy, ethical conduct
Human Resource Management	Enhances decision support and authenticity in human resource information handling.	Secure handling and authenticity verification	Blockchain models for HR management	[53]	Authenticity, decision support
Energy and Data Storage Optimization	Energy-efficient modifications and PoS for sustainability; strategic data storage design.	Energy consumption, storage capacity management	PoS, on-chain/off-chain data strategies	[54]	Sustainability, efficiency, cost-effectiveness
Quality Assurance and Testing	Continuous software testing and early team involvement for security and reliability.	Platform nature, integration testing challenges	Early testing, continuous testing procedures	[55]	Reliability, robustness
Software Architecture	Improved software quality with specific design notations, patterns, and metrics for performance.	Complexity, resource consumption measurement	Design notations, performance metrics	[56]	Efficiency, quality

(Continued)

TABLE 12.2 (Continued)

Topic	Description	Challenges/ Considerations	Solutions/ Strategies	References	Islamic/Halal principle
Performance Evaluation	Comprehensive evaluation of blockchain's efficiency and reliability with various metrics.	Measurement of throughput, latency, and security	Implementation of qualitative and quantitative metrics	[57]	Efficiency, security
System Integration	Blockchain integration into existing systems for transparency and accountability.	Complexities of existing systems and integration efforts	Seamless interoperability and system adaptation	[58]	Transparency, accountability, ethical practices

[Original (created by authors)]

12.6 Benefits of blockchain-enabled Halal health care

12.6.1 For patients: Assurance and trust

12.6.1.1 Data ownership and privacy

In Islamic teachings, privacy and individual rights are paramount. Blockchain applications such as Fast Healthcare Interoperability Resources and Blockchain-Based Multi-level Privacy-Preserving Location Sharing Scheme empower patients with control over their health data. This mirrors the Islamic respect for privacy and personal rights and the empowerment through blockchain aligns with the Halal principle of safeguarding personal [59].

12.6.2 Ensuring quality care through integrity

The immutable and transparent nature of blockchain technology supports the safeguarding of patient records. This adherence to data integrity and confidentiality is in harmony with the Islamic values of trustworthiness and excellence, ensuring care delivery that meets the high standards required by Halal healthcare protocols. Such a system aligns with Islamic values of excellence (Ihsan) and trustworthiness (Amanah), guaranteeing that care delivery is of the highest quality and is consistent with Halal healthcare standards [60].

12.6.3 Efficiency and Islamic stewardship

Blockchain technology in health care optimizes business processes, improves patient outcomes, and lowers costs, thus enhancing operational efficiency and cost-effectiveness. Thus, utilizing blockchain allows healthcare providers to streamline operations, reflecting the Islamic principle of efficient resource management. This optimization not only improves the quality of care but also enhances cost-effectiveness, embodying the Islamic ethos of stewardship and environmental consciousness [61].

12.6.4 Shariah compliance and value enhancement

The ability of blockchain to standardize healthcare operations and ensure regulatory adherence is a valuable aspect for Halal healthcare providers. This capability facilitates compliance with Shariah law and bolsters the overall value offered to the Muslim community, aligning with Islamic principles of communal welfare and ethical conduct [62].

The integration of blockchain technology into Halal health care marks a significant evolution towards more ethical, transparent, and patient-centered medical services. This innovative approach empowers patients by ensuring secure control over their medical records in strict adherence to Islamic privacy principles. By leveraging blockchain's inherent security and transparency features, healthcare providers can offer cost-effective, Halal-compliant care that not only meets Islamic dietary laws and religious beliefs but also enhances patient satisfaction through improved service delivery.

Operational excellence is achieved by streamlining Shariah-compliant processes, minimizing errors and unnecessary costs, and thus embodying the Islamic commitment to excellence and fiscal prudence. This advancement ensures the delivery of healthcare services that are not just efficient but also ethically sound, fostering a trust-based relationship between patients and providers. Financial stewardship through blockchain enables the healthcare sector to enhance revenue generation with cost-effective methods while promoting Islamic economic responsibility. It improves healthcare networking by establishing trust and reducing informational disparities, which are crucial in Halal practices.

Innovation and ethical compliance are driven within the Islamic ethical framework, utilizing blockchain to spur growth and ensure ongoing compliance with Shariah laws. This fosters a culture of continuous improvement in healthcare processes, making them more efficient and compliant.

Collaborative partnerships constructed via distributed ledger technology ensure Halal compliance and data privacy, extending health care's reach and efficacy. This creates a more interconnected and interoperable healthcare ecosystem, facilitating seamless exchange and access to Halal-compliant healthcare services across borders.

Figure 12.3 shows the transformative impact of blockchain technology on Halal health care, highlighting its role in empowering patients with secure control over their medical records, streamlining Shariah-compliant healthcare delivery, and fostering innovative, ethical compliance. It encapsulates the essence of patient empowerment, operational excellence, financial stewardship, innovation, and collaborative partnerships, all underpinned by blockchain's capabilities in ensuring Halal compliance and extending healthcare reach.

Patient Empowerment:
- ✓ Ensures secure control over medical records.
- ✓ Provides cost-effective, Halal-compliant health care.
- ✓ Boosts patient satisfaction.

Operational Excellence:
- ✓ Streamlines Shariah-compliant healthcare delivery.
- ✓ Minimizes errors and unnecessary costs.
- ✓ Enhances transparency and trust.

Collaborative Partnerships:
- ✓ Construct distributed systems for Halal compliance.
- ✓ Fosters interoperability for extended healthcare reach.

Innovation and Compliance:
- ✓ Drives innovation within the Islamic ethical framework.
- ✓ Advances Shariah-compliant healthcare processes.

Financial Stewardship
- ✓ Boosts revenue with cost-effective methods.
- ✓ Improves healthcare networking for trust and efficacy.

FIGURE 12.3 Blockchain technology's incorporation into Halal health care signifies a transformative leap towards achieving a value-based, patient-empowered healthcare system.

Original (created by authors)

12.7 Blockchain-enabled Halal health care streamlines auditing and compliance

Blockchain technology offers a compelling solution to these challenges. It enables healthcare institutions to manage their data in a verifiable, tamper-proof, and permanent manner, thereby reinforcing the trustworthiness of the stored health data. This feature of blockchain allows auditors to efficiently verify transactions on blockchain platforms, streamlining the audit process and ensuring rigorous compliance with both legal and Islamic regulatory standards [63].

In Halal health care, the auditing process is integral to ensuring compliance with Shariah laws, alongside healthcare policies, procedures, rules, and regulations. Traditional healthcare data management systems are often hindered by their manual nature and lack of sophisticated coordination, making them susceptible to data breaches and unauthorized changes. These limitations can compromise the auditing process and its quality, challenging the Islamic principle of trustworthiness (Amanah).

Moreover, blockchain-based healthcare data auditing contributes to the improvement of patient services and ensures that healthcare institutions meet crucial legal requirements and regulations [64]. It also helps in eliminating unnecessary data redundancies, supporting the Islamic ethos of resource optimization (Iqtisad) and efficiency (Itqan), which are essential for the delivery and management of exceptional Halal healthcare services.

Table 12.3 offers a comprehensive analysis of how blockchain technology revolutionizes auditing and compliance in Halal health care. It delves into the

TABLE 12.3 Enhanced impact of blockchain on Halal healthcare auditing and compliance

Aspect	Benefit detail	Impact on auditing process	Alignment with Islamic principles	Regulatory impact
Data Management	Blockchain ensures that healthcare data is managed in a way that is verifiable, tamper-proof, and permanent, enhancing the trustworthiness of the data stored.	Facilitates a more efficient audit process by enabling auditors to verify the authenticity and integrity of healthcare data with ease.	Upholds the Islamic principle of Amanah (trustworthiness) by ensuring data integrity and security, fostering a reliable healthcare environment.	Significantly improves data integrity and reliability, which are critical for regulatory audits and compliance checks.
Compliance	Automates and standardizes compliance processes to adhere to Shariah laws alongside healthcare regulations, ensuring consistent application across institutions.	Reduces the complexity of compliance verification, allowing for real-time monitoring and reporting of compliance status.	Supports the Islamic ethos of adherence to legal and Shariah standards, ensuring that healthcare services are provided in an ethically compliant manner.	Streamlines regulatory adherence, making it easier for healthcare institutions to meet and exceed legal and ethical standards.
Operational Efficiency	Leverages smart contracts and blockchain's immutable ledger to streamline healthcare operations, reducing manual errors and inefficiencies.	Enhances the quality and speed of audits by automating the tracking of transactions and patient data, reducing the likelihood of errors.	Reflects Islamic values of Itqan (excellence) and Iqtisad (resource optimization) by promoting efficient and error-free healthcare service delivery.	Contributes to a reduction in audit time and complexity by automating processes, leading to more efficient regulatory oversight.

(Continued)

TABLE 12.3 (Continued)

Aspect	Benefit detail	Impact on auditing process	Alignment with Islamic principles	Regulatory impact
Data Redundancy	Utilizes blockchain's distributed ledger technology to eliminate duplicate records and ensure that all data entries are unique and accurate.	Simplifies the data management process, reducing the time and resources required for auditing redundant data.	Promotes the efficient use of resources and stewardship, aligning with Islamic values by avoiding waste and ensuring accuracy in healthcare data management.	Minimizes storage requirements and management costs by reducing redundant data entries, leading to operational and financial efficiencies.
Transparency and Trust	Blockchain technology enhances transparency in healthcare transactions and data management, building trust among patients, providers, and regulators.	Enables a transparent audit trail of all transactions and data changes, facilitating thorough and straightforward audits.	Aligns with Islamic principles of transparency and mutual trust (Muta'amin) among stakeholders in the healthcare system.	Bolsters patient and public trust in the healthcare system by providing clear, auditable records of transactions and data management practices.

[Original (created by authors)]

operational, compliance, ethical, and regulatory benefits of integrating blockchain, showcasing its pivotal role in enhancing healthcare data management, ensuring Shariah compliance, and fostering an environment of trust and efficiency.

By integrating blockchain technology into Halal healthcare systems, regulators and healthcare providers can significantly enhance the auditing process, ensuring adherence to both Shariah and healthcare regulations while promoting Islamic principles of trustworthiness, efficiency, and stewardship. This technology not only streamlines operations and reduces errors but also establishes a transparent and trustworthy healthcare environment. The comprehensive application of blockchain across various aspects of healthcare data management exemplifies a forward-thinking approach to addressing current challenges in healthcare auditing and compliance, setting a new benchmark for operational excellence and ethical compliance in the Halal healthcare sector.

12.8 Conclusion

In exploring the intersection of blockchain and Halal health care, several key findings have emerged. The complexities associated with Halal certification in health care pose challenges related to ethical alignment, quality of care, cultural sensitivity, legal and regulatory compliance, community trust, and patient satisfaction. Noncompliance not only jeopardizes the well-being of Muslim patients but also impacts the reputation and trustworthiness of healthcare institutions. The demand for Shariah-compliant healthcare alternatives is on the rise, signaling a need for robust solutions.

Looking ahead, the future of Halal health care with blockchain holds tremendous potential. Blockchain's decentralized nature, coupled with its ability to provide real-time updates and enhance transparency, positions it as a catalyst for a globally recognized Halal healthcare framework. The technology not only aligns with Islamic principles but also facilitates compliance, contributing to improved patient care and community relationships.

In concluding this chapter, it is evident that blockchain has the power to enhance Halal integrity in health care. However, successful implementation requires collaboration between healthcare institutions, regulatory bodies, and technology developers. To navigate the complexities of Halal certification, it is recommended that stakeholders actively engage in the development and adoption of blockchain solutions. Collaboration should extend to the formulation of global standards to ensure harmonization and facilitate international recognition of Halal healthcare practices.

Moreover, continuous research and development in blockchain applications for health care can further refine and optimize existing solutions. As the field evolves, stakeholders should remain adaptive and proactive in embracing innovations that align with the evolving needs of the Muslim community.

Thus, the fusion of blockchain and Halal health care marks a significant milestone in the pursuit of compliance, transparency, and patient-centric care. By embracing this technology, the healthcare industry can not only meet the unique requirements of Muslim patients but also set new standards for integrity and trust in healthcare practices.

Acknowledgment

We extend our gratitude to the Institute of Halal Management, Islamic Business School, Universiti Utara Malaysia, for their support in this work.

References

1. Abu-Elezz, I., Hassan, A., Nazeemudeen, A., Househ, M., & Abd-Alrazaq, A. (2020). The benefits and threats of blockchain technology in healthcare: A scoping review. *International Journal of Medical Informatics*, *142*, 104246.
2. Alexander, C., & Wang, L. (2019, 11–14 April) Cybersecurity, information assurance, and big data based on blockchain. In: *Paper Presented at the IEEE Southeast Conference*. Huntsville, USA.
3. Alzeer, J., Rieder, U., & Abou Hadeed, K. (2018). Rational and practical aspects of Halal and Tayyib in the context of food safety. *Trends in Food Science & Technology*, *71*, 264–267.
4. Atzori, M. (2015). Blockchain technology and decentralized governance: Is the state still necessary? *Available at SSRN 2709713*.
5. Aziz, Y. A. A. (2013). *The Fiqh of Medicine*. (S. Afsar, Ed.) (p. 86). IMAK Ofset Turkey.
6. Bamert, T., Decker, C., Wattenhofer, R., & Welten, S. (2014). Bluewallet: The secure bitcoin wallet. In *Security and Trust Management: 10th International Workshop, STM 2014, Wroclaw, Poland, September 10-11, 2014. Proceedings 10* (pp. 65–80). Springer International Publishing.
7. Cao, Y., Sun, Y., & Min, J. (2020). Hybrid blockchain-based privacy-preserving electronic medical records sharing scheme across medical information control system. *Measurement and Control*, *53*(7–8), 1286–1299. https://doi.org/10.1177/0020294020926636
8. Centobelli, P., Cerchione, R., Del Vecchio, P., Oropallo, E., & Secundo, G. (2022). Blockchain technology for bridging trust, traceability and transparency in circular supply chain. *Information & Management*, *59*(7), 103508.
9. Chen, F., Huang, J., Wang, C., Tang, Y., Huang, C., Xie, D., Wang, T., & Zhao, C. (2021). Data access control based on blockchain in medical cyber physical systems. *Security and Communication Networks*, *2021*, 3395537. https://doi.org/10.1155/2021/3395537
10. Chen, Y., Meng, L., Zhou, H., & Xue, G. (2021). A blockchain-based medical data sharing mechanism with attribute-based access control and privacy protection. *Wireless Communications and Mobile Computing*, *2021*, 6685762. https://doi.org/10.1155/2021/6685762
11. Decker, C., & Wattenhofer, R. (2014). Bitcoin transaction malleability and MtGox. In *Computer Security-ESORICS 2014: 19th European Symposium on Research in Computer Security, Wroclaw, Poland, September 7-11, 2014. Proceedings, Part II 19* (pp. 313–326). Springer International Publishing.
12. Dietrich, F., Ge, Y., Turgut, A., Louw, L., & Palm, D. (2021). Review and analysis of blockchain projects in supply chain management. *Procedia Computer Science*, *180*, 724–733. https://doi.org/10.1016/j.procs.2021.01.295
13. Dutta, P., Choi, T. M., Somani, S., & Butala, R. (2020). Blockchain technology in supply chain operations: Applications, challenges and research opportunities. *Transportation Research Part E: Logistics and Transportation Review*, *142*, 102067.
14. Efendi. (2018, May 2). Halal industry can help Indonesia in international trade - Lifestyle - The Jakarta Post. Retrieved January 31, 2024.
15. Herrera-Joancomartí, J., & Pérez-Solà, C. (2016). Privacy in bitcoin transactions: new challenges from blockchain scalability solutions. In *Modeling Decisions for Artificial Intelligence: 13th International Conference, MDAI 2016, Sant Julià de Lòria, Andorra, September 19–21, 2016. Proceedings 13* (pp. 26–44). Springer International Publishing.

16. Hovorushchenko, T., Hnatchuk, Y., Herts, A., Moskalenko, A., & Osyadlyi, V. (2021) Theoretical and applied principles of information technology for supporting medical decision-making taking into account the legal basis. *In: CEUR-WS*, vol 3038, pp 172–181.

17. Hovorushchenko, T., Moskalenko, A., & Osyadlyi, V. (2023). Methods of medical data management based on blockchain technologies. *Journal of Reliable Intelligent Environments*, 9(1), 5–16.

18. Majah, I. (1953). *Sunan Ibn Majah*. (Q. I. Yazid, Ed.) (pp. 1137–1138). Cairo: Dar Ihya" al-Kutub.

19. Jadhav, J. S., & Deshmukh, J. (2022). A review study of the blockchain-based healthcare supply chain. *Social Sciences & Humanities Open*, 6(1), 100328.

20. Kakavand, H., Kost De Sevres, N., & Chilton, B. (2017). The blockchain revolution: An analysis of regulation and technology related to distributed ledger technologies. *Available at SSRN 2849251*.

21. Kashmanian, R. M. (2017). Building greater transparency in supply chains to advance sustainability. *Environmental Quality Management*, 26(3), 73–104.

22. Khezr, S., Moniruzzaman, M., Yassine, A., & Benlamri, R. (2019). Blockchain technology in healthcare: A comprehensive review and directions for future research. *Applied Sciences*, 9(9), 1736.

23. Kim, S., & Huh, J. (2020). Artificial neural network blockchain techniques for healthcare system: Focusing on the personal health records. *Electronics*, 9(5), 763. https://doi.org/10.3390/electronics9050763

24. Kim, T., Lee, S., Chang, D., Koo, J., Kim, T., Yoon, K., & Choi, I. (2021). DynamiChain: Development of medical blockchain ecosystem based on dynamic consent system. *Applied Sciences-Basel*, 11(4), 1612. https://doi.org/10.3390/app11041612

25. Koteska, B., Karafiloski, E., & Mishev, A. (2017, September). Blockchain implementation quality challenges: A literature. In *SQAMIA 2017: 6th workshop of software quality, analysis, monitoring, improvement, and applications* (Vol. 1938, p. 8).

26. Levashenko, V., Zaitseva, E., Kvassay, M., & Deserno, T. (2016, 23–25 September). Reliability estimation of healthcare systems using fuzzy decision trees. In: *Paper Presented at the Federated Conference on Computer Science and Information Systems* (pp 331–340). Lviv, Ukraine. https://doi.org/10.15439/2016F150

27. Li, X., Jiang, P., Chen, T., Luo, X., & Wen, Q. (2017). A survey on the security of blockchain systems. *Future Generation Computer Systems*, 107, 841–853. https://doi.org/10.1016/j.future.2017.08.020

28. Mann, C., & Loebenberger, D. (2017). Two-factor authentication for the bitcoin protocol. *International Journal of Information Security*, 16, 213–226.

29. Mayer, R. C., Davis, J. H., & Schoorman, F. D. (1995). An integrative model of organizational trust. *Academy of Management Review*, 20(3), 709–734.

30. Mougayar, W. (2016). *The Business Blockchain: Promise, Practice, and Application of the Next Internet Technology*. John Wiley & Sons.

31. Muflih, B. K. (1999). The importance of halal consumption in forming a civilized Muslim. *Muslim World*, 89(3–4), 208.

32. Naimat, N., Mustafa, M. S. A., Nasrijal, N. M. H., & Mahat, I. R. (2023). Challenges and opportunities in the halal pharmaceutical industry in Malaysia. *Information Management and Business Review*, 15(4), 73–78.

33. Nakamoto, S. (2008). Bitcoin: A peer-to-peer electronic cash system. *Decentralized Business Review*. Retrieved from https://bitcoin.org/bitcoin.pdf

34. Naserirad, M., Tavakol, M., Abbasi, M., Jannat, B., Sadeghi, N., & Bahemmat, Z. (2023). Predictors of international Muslim medical tourists' expectations on

halal-friendly healthcare services: A hospital-based study. *Health Services Management Research*, 36(4), 230–239.

35. Norazmi, M. N., & Lim, L. S. (2015). Halal pharmaceutical industry: Opportunities and challenges. *Trends in Pharmacological Sciences*, 36(8), 496–497.

36. Notheisen, B., Cholewa, J. B., & Shanmugam, A. P. (2017). Trading real-world assets on blockchain: An application of trust-free transaction systems. in the Market for Lemons. *Business & Information Systems Engineering*, 59, 425–440.

37. Porru, S., Pinna, A., Marchesi, M., & Tonelli, R. (2017, May). Blockchain-oriented software engineering: Challenges and new directions. In *2017 IEEE/ACM 39th International Conference on Software Engineering Companion (ICSE-C)* (pp. 169–171). IEEE.

38. Rahmah, M., & Barizah, N. (2020). Halal certification of patented medicines in Indonesia in the digital age: A panacea pain? *International Journal Systematic Reviews in Pharmacy*, 11(12), 210–217.

39. Rahman, M. K., Zainol, N. R., Nawi, N. C., Patwary, A. K., Zulkifli, W. F. W., & Haque, M. M. (2023). Halal healthcare services: Patients' satisfaction and word of mouth lesson from Islamic-Friendly hospitals. *Sustainability*, 15(2), 1493.

40. Rahman, M. M. (2024). Ensuring Halal Compliance in AI-Driven Healthcare Solutions: Balancing Innovation and Faith. In *Federated Learning and AI for Healthcare 5.0* (pp. 298–320). IGI Global. https://doi.org/10.4018/979-8-3693-1082-3.ch015

41. Salama. (2017, October 12). Indonesia in Top 10 World Halal Consumers - HalalFocus.net - Daily Halal Market News. Retrieved January 31, 2024, from https://halalfocus.net/indonesia-in-top-10-world-halal-consumers/

42. Shariff, S. M., & Rahman, A. R. A. (2016). Shariah compliant hospital; From concept to reality: A Malaysian experience. *Bangladesh Journal of Medical Science*, 15(1), 1.

43. Shrier, D., Wu, W., & Pentland, A. (2016). Blockchain & infrastructure (identity, data security). *Massachusetts Institute of Technology-Connection Science*, 1(3), 1–19.

44. Swan, M. (2015). *Blockchain: Blueprint for a New Economy*. O'Reilly Media. Inc, Sebastopol, CA.

45. Syed, T., Alzahrani, A., Jan, S., Siddiqui, M., Nadeem, A., & Alghamdi, T. (2019) A comparative analysis of blockchain architecture and its applications: Problems and recommendations. *IEEE Access*, 7, 176838–176869. https://doi.org/10.1109/ACCESS.2019.2957660

46. Taheri. (2020, August 14). Overview of Health Care in Islamic History and Experience. Retrieved January 18, 2024, from https://ethnomed.org/resource/overview-of-health-care-in-islamic-history-and-experience/

47. Tieman, M., Darun, M. R., Fernando, Y., & Ngah, A. B. (2019). Utilizing blockchain technology to enhance halal integrity: The perspectives of halal certification bodies. In *Services–SERVICES 2019: 15th World Congress, Held as Part of the Services Conference Federation, SCF 2019, San Diego, CA, USA, June 25–30, 2019, Proceedings 15* (pp. 119–128). Springer International Publishing.

48. Tith, D., Lee, J. S., Suzuki, H., Wijesundara, W. M. A. B., Taira, N., Obi, T., & Ohyama, N. (2020). Application of blockchain to maintaining patient records in electronic health record for enhanced privacy, scalability, and availability. *Healthcare Informatics Research*, 26(1), 3–12.

49. Wang, S. M. (2015). Identifying niche markets for Taiwan's inbound tourism. *International Journal of Organizational Innovation*, 7(3), 96–114.

50. Westphal, E., & Seitz, H. (2021) Digital and decentralized management of patient data in healthcare using blockchain implementations. *Front Blockchain*, 4, 732112. https://doi.org/10.3389/fbloc.2021.732112

51. Xiao, Y., Xu, B., Jiang, W., & Wu, Y. (2021). The HealthChain blockchain for electronic health records: Development study. *Journal of Medical Internet Research*, 23(1), Article e13556. https://doi.org/10.2196/13556
52. Yaga, D. J., Mell, P., Roby, N., & Scarfone, K. (2018). Blockchain technology overview *US National Institute of Standards and Technology*, 10.6028/nist.ir. 8202
53. Yaqoob, I., Salah, K., Jayaraman, R., & Al-Hammadi, Y. (2021). Blockchain for healthcare data management: Opportunities, challenges, and future recommendations. *Neural Computing and Applications*, 34, 11475–11490.
54. Yaqoob, S., Khan, M. M., Talib, R., Butt, A. D., Saleem, S., Arif, F., & Nadeem, A. (2019). Use of blockchain in healthcare: A systematic literature review. *International Journal of Advanced Computer Science and Applications*, 10(5), 644–653.
55. Yli-Huumo, J., Ko, D., Choi, S., Park, S., & Smolander, K. (2016). Where is current research on blockchain technology?—A systematic review. *PLoS One*, 11(10), e0163477.
56. Zaitseva, E., & Levashenko, V. (2016). Construction of a reliability structure function based on uncertain data. *IEEE Transactions on Reliability*, 65(4), 1710–1723. https://doi.org/10.1109/TR.2016.2578948
57. Zaitseva, E., Levashenko, V., Rabcan, J., & Krsak, E. (2020). Application of the structure function in the evaluation of the human factor in healthcare. *Symmetry*, 12(1), 93. https://doi.org/10.3390/sym12010093
58. Zawawi, M., & Othman, K. (2018). An overview of Shari'ah compliant healthcare services in Malaysia. *Malaysian Journal of Consumer and Family Economics*, 3(1), 91–100.
59. Zelbst, P. J., Green, K. W., Sower, V. E., & Bond, P. L. (2020). The impact of RFID, IIoT, and blockchain technologies on supply chain transparency. *Journal of Manufacturing Technology Management*, 31(3), 441–457.
60. Zhang, L., Peng, M., Wang, W., Su, Y., Cui, S., & Kim, S. (2021). Secure and efficient data storage and sharing scheme based on double blockchain. *CMC-Computers, Materials & Continua*, 66(1), 499–515. https://doi.org/10.32604/cmc.2020.012205
61. Zhang, P., White, J., Schmidt, D. C., Lenz, G., & Rosenbloom, S. T. (2018). FHIRChain: Applying blockchain to securely and scalably share clinical data. *Computational and Structural Biotechnology Journal*, 16, 267–278. https://doi.org/10.1016/j.csbj.2018.07.004
62. Zhang, R., George, A., Kim, J., Johnson, V., & Ramesh, B. (2019). Benefits of blockchain initiatives for value-based care: Proposed framework. *Journal of Medical Internet Research*, 21(9), e13595.
63. Zheng, Z., Xie, S., Dai, H., Chen, X., & Wang, H. (2017, 25–30 June) An overview of blockchain technology: Architecture, consensus, and future trends. In: *Paper Presented at the IEEE International Congress on Big Data* (pp 557–564). Honolulu, Hawaii. https://doi.org/10.1109/BigDataCongress.2017.85
64. Zou, R., Lv, X., & Zhao, J. (2021). SPChain: Blockchain-based medical data sharing and privacy-preserving eHealth system. *Information Process Management*, 58(4), 102604. https://doi.org/10.1016/j.ipm.2021.102604

13

NONPROBABILISTIC APPROACH TO SOLVE MULTIOBJECTIVE OPTIMIZATION MODEL WITH APPLICATIONS IN BLOCKCHAIN TECHNOLOGY

Paresh Kumar Panigrahi and Sukanta Nayak

13.1 Introduction

In recent times, data has played a crucial role both in people's social lives and in scientific research. This is due to the continued growth of big data and internet technologies, and the spreading and sharing of research documents is becoming gradually important to drive both societal and scientific progress. In this regard, the importance of data in blockchain technology cannot be overstated. It forms the foundation for the trust, security, and functionality of the entire system. The immutability, transparency, and decentralization provided by blockchain are only possible because of the reliable and secure handling of data. In various sectors, the use of big data has significantly benefited society and the economy. For example, industries dealing with medical, financial, energy, and meteorological data have seen notable advancements. However, the development of big data technologies, while improving convenience and efficiency in many areas, has also introduced numerous data security challenges. These security issues have made it more difficult to ensure the privacy and protection of sensitive information. In this context, people are scared to share and store date on the server, which has number of drawbacks in our daily use. In this context, blockchain technology offers a promising approach for data sharing, thanks to its key properties. Once data is added to a blockchain, it cannot be altered, deleted, or tampered with, ensuring the integrity and immutability of the information. This makes blockchain an ideal solution for securely sharing sensitive data across various sectors, such as healthcare, finance, and supply chain management. Cryptographic security is another feature of blockchain technology that guards against manipulation. Before adding new data to the

DOI: 10.1201/9781003483113-13

blockchain, each network communication is encrypted, and hashes guarantee the accuracy of transaction information. features. On the other hand, the prerequisites for secure and effective data exchange are not met by simply combining blockchain with data sharing.

Blockchain is designed to provide data availability and resistance to tampering in a decentralized setting. It is immutable and specifically suited to improve the security, availability, and integrity of Internet of Things (IoT) data while improving IoT applications [1]. It is a distributed ledger technology with encryption that may be used in a variety of industries to create tamper-proof real-time data [2, 3]. Additionally, this platform offers an IoT device ecosystem that is dependable.

Moreover, the IoT network is used for a suitable task; some of the IoT will perform better than others. The crucial issues are examined and figuring out which nodes are most appropriate. Getting the proper nodes at the right time and choosing them carefully helps reduce typical IoT-related uncertainties about things like resource allocation, network longevity, and data collection confidence [4]. Choosing the node instead of optimizing node numbers and locations might address the energy and routing problems [5]. In this scenario, the nodes can be arranged in order, and only a subcategory of nodes is stimulated at any given time for a given mission. Node selection contributes to energy efficiency by choosing the right subset of nodes depending on the job criteria [6]. Moreover, there is a choice between individual-based selection, where each node is assessed independently, and group-based selection, where potential clusters are evaluated as a consistent unit and the optimal set is chosen. So, evaluations are focused on the task specifications and constraints [7]. Due to a number of shortcomings, the most recent selection techniques in particular are not appropriate for localization tasks. As a result, this study utilizes blockchain technology to enhance the privacy and security of the system. Additionally, incorporating an edge platform has the potential to enhance system efficiency, minimize latency, and optimize overall performance. In this regard, an optimization model is designed for selecting a suitable node for a specific task, depending on the input parameters. The primary goal of the researcher is to minimize execution time, power consumption, response time, and delay, minimizing the processing cost associated with offloading workloads.

Here, the focus of this research is on resource allocation and scheduling methodology grounded in a linear optimization model. The Linear Programming (LPP) involves a single objective function that needs to be maximized or minimized subject to linear constraints. But, in real practice, LPP possesses ambiguous solutions for imprecise objective functions and constraints. The nature of this impreciseness may occur due to randomness and/or fuzziness of the coefficients, constants, and decision variables. As such, these make the system difficult to handle. Here we have considered fuzzy uncertainties in our investigation. To deal with fuzziness, we can apply a fuzzy programming technique. Accordingly, fuzzy programming is adopted with LPP.

Numerous researchers have focused on the fuzzy linear programming problem. Meanwhile, in 1970, [8] proposed the concept of fuzzy linear programming in decision-making problems. Then, the general idea of an optimization problem handled with fuzzy uncertainty was proposed by [9], whereas [10] formulated the linear programming problem in the presence of fuzzy parameters. In general, we get two types of LPPs if fuzzy uncertainties are incorporated. These are fuzzy LPP (either objective function is fuzzy or constraints are fuzzy) and fully fuzzy LPP (both the objective function and constraints are fuzzy).

In this regard, many researchers presented different approaches to solve a fuzzy linear programming problem. A few of the relevant research works are discussed here. The authors [11–14] contributed in the area of fuzzy linear programming problem (FLPP) and developed many methods to find the optimal solution. In this regard, [14] introduced a fully fuzzy linear programming problem (FFLPP). Further, the authors [15–19] proposed several approaches to solve FFLPP with different types of fuzzy numbers. In light of this, researchers presented different methods to solve FFLPP. A few of the related research studies are discussed here. In [15], the authors used the lexicography method to solve the FFLPPs. In [18], the authors proposed a method to solve FFLPPs with trapezoidal fuzzy numbers, and [20] used a modified technique to solve FFLPP with the triangular fuzzy number to obtain the optimal solution. Furthermore, [21] proposed a method to solve a nonlinear model for a FFLPP with the unrestricted fuzzy variable using the ranking function. In addition, various types of fuzzy numbers are taken into account for investigation. But it has also been noted that the same system with a different scenario needs to optimize two or more objective functions. As such, there is an essence to investigate a multiobjective linear programming problem (MOLPP) with uncertainties.

Many complex problems occur in the field of economics, social science, engineering, and medical can be formulated in terms of MOLPP with uncertainties. Initially, the MOLPP with fuzzy parameters was proposed by [22]. Then, [23, 24] proposed a method to solve the MOLPP to find the optimal solution with fuzzy uncertainty. In [25], the authors targeted the MOLPP with a fuzzy coefficient that can be transformed into the interval from by using the parametric representation. Besides, [26] has included a flexible constraint based on $\alpha-$ cut for solving a fuzzy multiobjective quadratic programming problem. Furthermore, from recent research, it has been found that the uncertainties arise due to the error estimation while handling the same with intervals. There are different approaches to deal with the MOLPP to solve the coefficient of objective function taken as an interval and with interval parameters [27, 28]. In this context, a new type of interval typed triangular fuzzy number with the MOLPP was presented by [29].

From the above literature review, it is seen that there are many methods to handle Fuzzy Multi-Objective Linear Programming Problems (FMOLPP), but there is a scope to explore for finding an effective solution of the same based on the width analysis. As such, the major focus of this study is to develop an alternate approach to handle FMOLPP effectively. In this context, we have hybridized the concept of fuzzy set theory with well-known weighted sum method to develop a fuzzy weighted sum method. Then various theorems are proposed to establish the efficacy of the proposed method. An example problem is considered to illustrate the proposed method. The obtained results are compared with the existing method of width analysis and found a good agreement with tight width.

The structure of this paper is as follows. Section 13.2 includes the preliminaries of fuzzy numbers and fuzzy arithmetic operations. Section 13.3 describes the standard MOLPP formulation. Section 13.4 presents a fuzzy MOLPP formulation. In Section 13.5, we have analyzed the fuzzy weighted sum method and its three types of computation. Finally, in Section 13.6, an example problem is demonstrated through the fuzzy weighted sum method and the solutions are reported.

13.2 Preliminaries

In this segment, we will see the basics of fuzzy set and triangular fuzzy number (TFN) with its arithmetic operations.

Definition 2.1 [30]: A fuzzy number $\tilde{A} = [x_L, x_N, x_R]$ is said to be a TFN if the membership values are defined as

$$\mu_A(x) = \begin{cases} f_L, & x_L \leq x \leq x_N \\ f_R, & x_N \leq x \leq x_R \\ 0, & \text{otherwise} \end{cases} \tag{13.1}$$

where, f_L is the left monotonically nondecreasing function and f_R is the right monotonically nonincreasing function. These functions can be represented as $f_L = \dfrac{x - x_L}{x_N - x_L}$ and $f_R = \dfrac{x_R - x}{x_R - x_N}$.

Definition 2.2 [31]: A TFN, $\tilde{A} = [x_L, x_N, x_R]$, is said to be a nonnegative TFN if and only if $x_L \geq 0$ and $x_L \leq x_N \leq x_R$.

Definition 2.3 [32]: An arbitrary TFN, $\tilde{A} = [a_L, a_C, a_R]$, can be expressed in the following interval form by using the α-cut

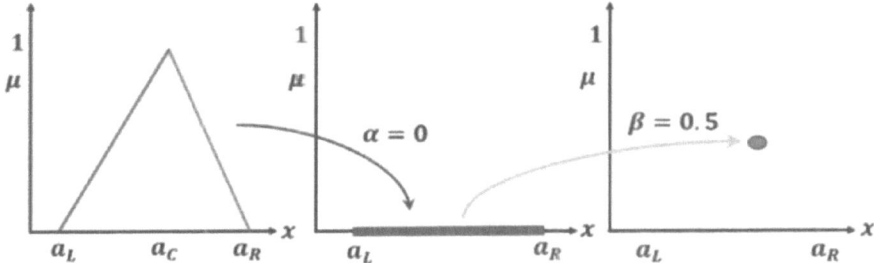

FIGURE 13.1   Sketch diagram of fuzzy parametric.

[Original (created by authors)]

Definition 2.4 [33]: The midpoint of a TFN, $\tilde{A} = [a_L, a_C, a_R]$, is defined as $A(\alpha)_M = \dfrac{\xi_L + \xi_R}{2}$, where $\alpha \in [0,1]$.

Definition 2.5 [34]: The width of a TFN, $\tilde{A} = [a_L, a_C, a_R]$, is written as $A(\alpha)_w = \xi_R - \xi_L$, where $\alpha \in [0,1]$.

Consider a TFN, $\tilde{A} = [a_L, a_C, a_R]$, where a_L, a_C, and a_R are the left, center, and right values of the TFN. To computational propose the TFNs can be converted into interval by using $\alpha -$ cut of the parametric. Then, the interval can be converted into crisp [33], which is represented in the Figure 13.1. The same crisp form can be used for a computational purpose by using the traditional arithmetic operations given in [34].

Definition 2.7 [35]: If $\tilde{A}(\alpha) = [\xi_L, \xi_R] = \left[A(\alpha)_M, A(\alpha)_w \right]$ and $\tilde{B}(\alpha) = [\zeta_L, \zeta_R] = \left[B(\alpha)_M, B(\alpha)_w \right]$ are two TFNs, then the order relation $\leq_{RM}$ is defined as $\tilde{A}(\alpha) \leq_{RM} \tilde{B}(\alpha)$ if $A(\alpha)_R \leq B(\alpha)_R$ and $A(\alpha)_M \leq B(\alpha)_M$.

Definition 2.8 [36]: If $\tilde{A}(\alpha) = [\xi_L, \xi_R] = \left[A(\alpha)_M, A(\alpha)_w \right]$ and $\tilde{B}(\alpha) = [\zeta_L, \zeta_R] = \left[B(\alpha)_M, \bar{E}(\alpha)_w \right]$ are two TFNs, then the order relation $\geq_{LM}$ is defined as $\tilde{A}(\alpha) \geq_{LM} \tilde{B}(\alpha)$ if $A(\alpha)_L \geq B(\alpha)_L$ and $A(\alpha)_M \geq B(\alpha)_M$.

13.3 MOLP formulation

Consider the following MOLP problem statement.

$$\text{Max(Min)} \; F_i = \sum_{j=1}^{k} c_{ij} x_j$$

Subject to the constraints

$$\sum_{j=1}^{k} a_{tj} x_j \leq b_j, \, t = 1, 2 \ldots, m$$

$$x_j \geq 0, \tag{13.2}$$

$$j = 1, 2, \ldots, k, \, i = 1, 2, \ldots, n$$

All the objective function, coefficient matrix, and right-hand side vector are represented through a TFN [i.e., (c_{ij}, a_{tj}, b_j)]. Take two vectors: $a = (a_1, \ldots, a_n)^t$ and $b = (b_1, \ldots, b_n)^t$ in R^n. Then, $a \leq b$ if $a_t \leq b_t$ for $t = 1, \ldots, n$ and there is at least one $1 \leq m \leq n$ with $a_m \leq b_n$. Also, $a < b$ if $a_t < b_t$ for $t = 1, \ldots, n$.

Definition 3.1 [28]: A feasible solution to the initial value $x^0 = \left(x_1^0, \ldots, x_k^0\right)^t$ of a MOLP problem is efficient if there is no another feasible solution $x = (x_1, \ldots, x_k)^t$ such that $\left(F_1(x), \ldots, F_n(x)\right)^t < \left(F_1(x^0), \ldots, F_n(x^0)\right)^t$.

Definition 3.2: A feasible solution $x^0 = \left(x_1^0, \ldots, x_k^0\right)^t$ of a MOLP problem is weakly efficient if there is no another feasible solution: $x = (x_1, \ldots, x_k)^t$ such that $\left(F_1(x), \ldots, F_n(x)\right)^t \leq \left(F_1(x^0), \ldots, F_n(x^0)\right)^t$.

Definition 3.3: Consider a vector $(w_1, \ldots, w_n)$, such that $w_i \geq 0$, $i = 1, \ldots, n$. The weighted sum linear programming problem corresponding with the MOLP problem is as follows.

$$\text{Min} \sum_{i=1}^{n} \sum_{j=1}^{k} w_i c_{ij} x_j$$

Subject to the constraints

$$\sum_{j=1}^{k} a_{tj} x_j \leq b_j, \; t = 1, \ldots, m$$

$$x_j \geq 0, \, j = 1, \ldots, k \tag{13.3}$$

Theorem 1 [28]: A feasible solution, $x^0 = \left(x_1^0, \ldots, x_n^0\right)^t$, is a weakly efficient solution to the MOLP problem if there exists a weight $w = (w_1, \ldots, w_p)$ with $w_i \geq 0$, $i = 1, \ldots, p$, such that x^0 is an optimal solution to the problem.

Theorem 2: A feasible solution $x^0 = \left(x_1^0,\dots,x_n^0\right)^t$ is an efficient solution to the MOLP problem if there exists $w = (w_1,\dots,w_p)$ with $w_i > 0$, $i = 1,\dots,p$, such that x^0 is an optimal solution to the MOLP problem.

The next section includes a FMOLPP.

13.4 Fuzzy MOLP formulation

In this section, we investigate a FMOLPP. A FMOLPP can be formulated as follows:

$$\text{Max(Min) } F_1 = \sum_{j=1}^{k}\left[c_{1j}^L,c_{1j}^N,c_{1j}^R\right]x_j = \left(f_1^L(x),f_1^N(x),f_1^R(x)\right)$$

$$\text{Max(Min) } F_2 = \sum_{j=1}^{k}\left[c_{2j}^L,c_{2j}^N,c_{2j}^R\right]x_j = \left(f_2^L(x),f_2^N(x),f_2^R(x)\right)$$

$$\vdots$$

$$\text{Max(Min) } F_n = \sum_{j=1}^{k}\left[c_{nj}^L,c_{nj}^N,c_{nj}^R\right]x_j = \left(f_n^L(x),f_n^N(x),f_n^R(x)\right)$$

Subjected to the constraints

$$\sum_{j=1}^{k}[a_{tj}^L,a_{tj}^N,a_{tj}^R]x_j \le [b_j^L,b_j^N,b_j^R]$$

$$x_j^L \le x_j^N, x_j^N \le x_j^R, x_j^L \ge 0,$$

$$t = 1,2,\dots,m,\ j = 1,2,\dots,k$$

(13.4)

To solve the FMOLPP by using the fuzzy weighted sum method, one needs three types of computations (i.e., left, center, and right computations). The computations are discussed in Section 5.

Definition 4.1: A feasible solution $x^0 = \left(x_1^0,\dots,x_k^0\right)^t$ of a FMOLPP is left midpoint (LM) efficient if there is no feasible solution: $x = (x_1,\dots,x_k)^t$ such that $\left(F_1(x),\dots,F_n(x)\right)^t < \left(F_1(x^0),\dots,F_n(x^0)\right)^t$, i.e., $F_n(x^0) >_{LM} F_n(x)$.

Definition 4.2: A feasible solution $x^0 = \left(x_1^0,\dots,x_k^0\right)^t$ of a FMOLPP is LM weakly efficient if there is no feasible solution: $x = (x_1,\dots,x_k)^t$ such that $\left(F_1(x),\dots,F_n(x)\right)^t \le \left(F_1(x^0),\dots,F_n(x^0)\right)^t$, i.e., $F_n(x^0) \ge_{LM} F_n(x)$.

Definition 4.3: A feasible solution $x^0 = \left(x_1^0, \ldots, x_k^0\right)^t$ of a FMOLPP is the center (N) efficient if there is no feasible solution: $x = \left(x_1, \ldots, x_k\right)^t$ such that $\left(F_1(x), \ldots, F_n(x)\right)^t < \left(F_1(x^0), \ldots, F_n(x^0)\right)^t$, i.e., $F_n(x) <_N F_n(x^0)$.

Definition 4.4: A feasible solution $x^0 = \left(x_1^0, \ldots, x_k^0\right)^t$ of a FMOLPP is the N weakly efficient if there is no feasible solution: $x = \left(x_1, \ldots, x_k\right)^t$ such that $\left(F_1(x), \ldots, F_n(x)\right)^t \leq \left(F_1(x^0), \ldots, F_n(x^0)\right)^t$, i.e., $F_n(x) \leq_N F_n(x^0)$.

Definition 4.5: A feasible solution $x^0 = \left(x_1^0, \ldots, x_k^0\right)^t$ of a FMOLPP is the right midpoint (RM) efficient if there is no feasible solution: $x = \left(x_1, \ldots, x_k\right)^t$ such that $\left(F_1(x), \ldots, F_n(x)\right)^t < \left(F_1(x^0), \ldots, F_n(x^0)\right)^t$, i.e., $F_n(x) <_{RM} F_n(x^0)$.

Definition 4.6: A feasible solution $x^0 = \left(x_1^0, \ldots, x_k^0\right)^t$ of a FMOLPP is the RM weakly efficient if there is no feasible solution: $x = \left(x_1, \ldots, x_k\right)^t$ such that $\left(F_1(x), \ldots, F_n(x)\right)^t \leq \left(F_1(x^0), \ldots, F_n(x^0)\right)^t$, i.e., $F_n(x) \leq_{RM} F_n(x^0)$.

13.5   Fuzzy weighted sum approach to solve a FMOLPP

In order to solve a FMOLPP, an attempt is being made to obtain a comparable crisp problem. The system formulation with multiobjective optimization problem and their solution procedure are shown in Figure 13.2.

This approach combines all the given objective functions by multiplying them with the certain weighting factor, w_i, to form a single function that is then minimized. The relative value of the weights generally reflects the relative importance of the objectives. The optimization problem is formulated as follows:

$$\min F(X) = w_1\left(f_1^L(x), f_1^N(x), f_1^R(x)\right) + w_2\left(f_2^L(x), f_2^N(x), f_2^R(x)\right)$$
$$+ \cdots + w_n\left(f_n^L(x), f_n^N(x), f_n^R(x)\right)$$

subject to

$$\sum_{j=1}^{k} [a_{tj}^L, a_{tj}^N, a_{tj}^R] x_j \leq [b_j^L, b_j^N, b_j^R]$$

$$x_j^L \leq x_j^N, x_j^N \leq x_j^R, x_j^L \geq 0,$$
$$t = 1, 2, \ldots, m, \ j = 1, 2, \ldots, k$$

(13.5)

where $\Sigma_{i=1}^{n} w_i = 1$ and $w_n \geq 0$.

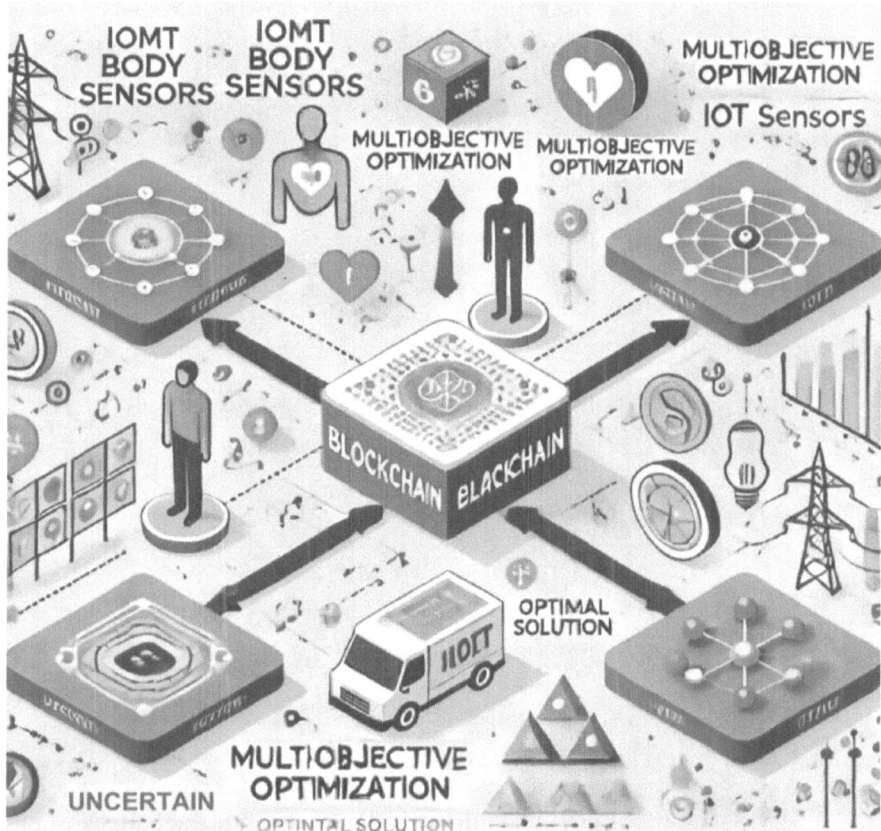

FIGURE 13.2 Proposed system formulation.

[Original (created by authors)]

To find the optimal solution by using the FMOLPP, one needs the left, center, and right computations. These computations are shown below.

The left computation is depicted through the following form, when $0 \leq \alpha < 1$.

$$\min F(x) = w_1 f_1^L(x) + w_2 f_2^L(x) + \cdots + w_n f_n^L(x)$$

subject to

$$\sum_{j=1}^{k} \left[a_{tj}^L \right] x_j \leq \left[b_j^L \right]$$

$$x_j^L \leq x_j^N, x_j^N \leq x_j^R, x_j^L \geq 0,$$

$$t = 1, 2, \ldots, m, \ j = 1, 2, \ldots, k$$

(13.6)

The center computation is depicted through the following form when $\alpha = 1$.

$$\min\ F(x) = w_1 f_1^N(x) + w_2 f_2^N(x) + \cdots + w_n f_n^N(x)$$

subject to

$$\sum_{j=1}^{k} \left[a_{tj}^N \right] x_j \leq \left[b_j^N \right] \tag{13.7}$$

$$x_j^L \leq x_j^N, x_j^N \leq x_j^R, x_j^L \geq 0,$$

$$t = 1, 2, \ldots, m,\ j = 1, 2, \ldots, k$$

The right computation is depicted through the following form when $0 \leq \alpha < 1$.

$$\min\ F(x) = w_1 f_1^R(x) + w_2 f_2^R(x) + \cdots + w_n f_n^R(x)$$

subject to

$$\sum_{j=1}^{k} \left[a_{tj}^R \right] x_j \leq \left[b_j^R \right] \tag{13.8}$$

$$x_j^L \leq x_j^N, x_j^N \leq x_j^R, x_j^L \geq 0,$$

$$t = 1, 2, \ldots, m,\ j = 1, 2, \ldots, k$$

The above computation will be discussed and solved through an example problem in the next section.

The discussed weights can be used in the following two ways:

1 The user may set w_i to reflect preferences.
2 The user may systematically change w_i to yield different Pareto optimal points.

Following are the advantages of the weighted sum method:

1 Easy to use.
2 If all of the weights are positive, the minimum of Eq. (13.5) is always Pareto optimal.
3 Weights can be used either to generate a single solution or multiple solutions.

The flow chart describes the procedure of the proposed fuzzy weighted sum method, which is shown in Figure 13.3.

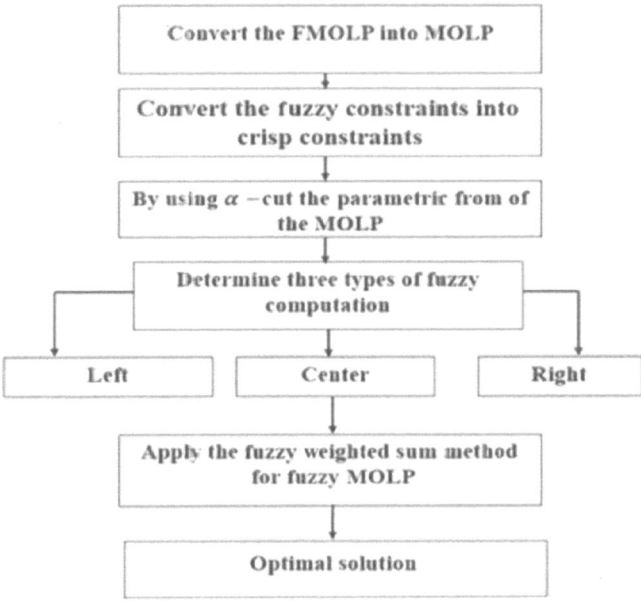

FIGURE 13.3 Flow chart of the fuzzy weighted sum method to solve a FMOLPP.
[Original (created by authors)]

Theorem 3: According to the order relation $>_{LM}$, any efficient solution to the problem with $\alpha \in [0,1]$ is an optimal solution to the FMOLPP.

Proof: Suppose $x^* = (x_1^*, \ldots, x_n^*)^t$ is an efficient solution to the FMOLPP with $\alpha -$ cut is zero. Assume that $\hat{x}$ is not an optimal solution to the problem according to the order relation $>_{LM}$. Therefore, there is a feasible solution, $x = (x_1, \ldots, x_n)^t$, of the FMOLPP such that

$$\sum_{i=1}^{n}\sum_{j=1}^{k}\left[w_i c_{ij}^L, w_i c_{ij}^R\right]x_j^* >_{LM} \sum_{i=1}^{n}\sum_{j=1}^{k}\left[w_i c_{ij}^L, w_i c_{ij}^R\right]x_j \qquad (13.9)$$

which is in contradiction to the efficiency of x^* for the problem with $\alpha = 0$.

Theorem 4: According to the order relation $<_{RM}$, any efficient solution to the problem with $\alpha \in [0,1]$ is an optimal solution to the FMOLPP.

Proof: Suppose $x^* = (x_1^*, \ldots, x_n^*)^t$ is an efficient solution to the problem when $\alpha -$ cut is zero. Assume that x^* is not an optimal solution to the problem according to the order relation $<_{RM}$. Therefore, there is a feasible solution, $x = (x_1, \ldots, x_n)^t$, of the FMOLPP such that

$$\sum_{i=1}^{n}\sum_{j=1}^{k}\left[w_ic_{ij}^L, w_ic_{ij}^R\right]x_j <_{RM} \sum_{i=1}^{n}\sum_{j=1}^{k}\left[w_ic_{ij}^L, w_ic_{ij}^R\right]x_j^* \qquad (13.10)$$

which is in contradiction to the efficiency of x^* for the FMOLPP with $\alpha = 0$.

Theorem 5: According to the order relation $<_N$, any efficient solution to the problem with $\alpha \in [0,1]$, is an optimal solution to the problem.

Proof: Suppose $x^* = (x_1^*, \ldots, x_n^*)^t$ is an efficient solution to the problem when $\alpha-$ cut is one. Assume that x^* is not an optimal solution to the problem according to the order relation $<_N$. Therefore, there is some feasible solution, $x = (x_1, \ldots, x_n)^t$, of the problem such that

$$\sum_{i=1}^{n}\sum_{j=1}^{k}\left[w_ic_{ij}^N\right]x_j <_N \sum_{i=1}^{n}\sum_{j=1}^{k}\left[w_ic_{ij}^N\right]x_j^* \qquad (13.11)$$

which is our contradiction to the efficiency of x^* for the FMOLPP with $\alpha = 1$ and the proof is completed.

Theorem 6: According to the order relation $\geq_{LM}$, any optimal solution to the problem with $w_k > 0, k = 1, \ldots, n$ is an LM-efficient solution to the FMOLPP.

Proof: Assume that $x^* = (x_1^*, \ldots, x_k^*)^t$ is an optimal solution to the weighting problem with a positive weight coefficient. According to the order relation $\geq_{LM}$, it is not a Pareto optimal solution to the existing problem. Therefore, by Theorem 1, there is a feasible solution, $x = (x_1, \ldots, x_l)^t$, of the MOLPP, such that

$$\left(f_1(x^*), \ldots, f_n(x^*)\right) \geq_{LM} \left(f_1(x), \ldots, f_n(x)\right) \qquad (13.12)$$

Since $w_k > 0$, $k = 1, \ldots, n$, we have $\sum_{i=1}^{n} w_if_i(x^*) >_{LM} \sum_{i=1}^{n} w_if_i(x)$; thus, it contradicts the assumption that x^* must be the optimal solution.

Theorem 7: According to the order relation $\geq_{LM}$, the unique optimal solution to the problem with $w_k \geq 0, k = 1, \ldots, n$ is an LM-efficient solution to the FMOLPP.

Proof: Assume that $x^* = \left(x_1^*,...,x_k^*\right)^t$ is a unique optimal solution to the weighting problem with a positive weight coefficient. Therefore, by Theorem 6, there is a feasible solution, $x = \left(x_1,...,x_l\right)^t$, of the MOLPP such that from Theorem 6, we can write as the following.

$$\left(f_1\left(x^*\right),...,f_n\left(x^*\right)\right) \geq_{LM} \left(f_1(x),...,f_n(x)\right) \tag{13.13}$$

and

$$\left(f_1\left(x^*\right),...,f_n\left(x^*\right)\right) >_{LM} \left(f_1(x),...,f_n(x)\right) \tag{13.14}$$

Since $w_k > 0, k = 1,...,n$, we have $\sum_{i=1}^n w_i f_i\left(x^*\right) >_{LM} \sum_{i=1}^n w_i f_i(x)$; thus, this contradicts the assumption that x^* must be the unique optimal solution.

Similarly, we can prove the order relation $\leq_{RM}$ is an optimal and unique optimal to the weighting problem as well as it is an efficient solution to the F MOLPP.

Theorem 8: Similar to the order relation $>_{LM}$, the solution to the weighting problem is properly optimal if all weighting coefficients are positive.

Proof: Assume that $x^* = \left(x_1^*,...,x_k^*\right)^t$ is an optimal solution to the weighting problem with a positive weight coefficient. By the Theorem 7, we have to express that the solution is optimal. We have to show that x^* is properly optimized. Assume that $\mathcal{M} = (n-1)\left(\dfrac{w_j}{w_i}\right)$.

Let us contradict the above. Assume x^* is not properly optimized for weighting problems. Then, from Theorem 7, $x^* = \left(x_1^*,...,x_k^*\right)^t$ and $\left(f_1\left(x^*\right),...,f_n\left(x^*\right)\right) >_{LM} \left(f_1(x),...,f_n(x)\right)$, we have

$$f_i\left(x^*\right) - f_i(x) >_{LM} \mathcal{M}\left(f_j(x) - f_j\left(x^*\right)\right) \tag{13.15}$$

where $i = 1,...,n; j = 1,...,m$.

For all j, $\left(f_1\left(x^*\right),...,f_m\left(x^*\right)\right) >_{LM} \left(f_1(x),...,f_m(x)\right)$

$$f_i\left(x^*\right) - f_i(x) >_{LM} (n-1)\left(\dfrac{w_j}{w_i}\right)\left(f_j(x) - f_j\left(x^*\right)\right) \tag{13.16}$$

Multiplying both sides with $\dfrac{w_i}{n-1} > 0$

$$\frac{w_i}{n-1} f_i\left(x^*\right) - f_i\left(x\right) >_{LM} w_j\left(f_j\left(x\right) - f_j\left(x^*\right)\right) \tag{13.17}$$

where $i \neq j$

$$w_i f_i\left(x^*\right) - f_i\left(x\right) >_{LM} \sum_{j=1}^{m}\left(w_j\left(f_j\left(x\right) - f_j\left(x^*\right)\right)\right) \tag{13.18}$$

that means

$$\sum_{j=1}^{m} w_j f_j\left(x^*\right) >_{LM} \sum_{j=1}^{m} w_j f_j\left(x\right) \tag{13.19}$$

$$w_j\left(f_1\left(x^*\right),\ldots,f_m\left(x^*\right)\right) >_{LM} w_j\left(f_1\left(x\right),\ldots,f_m\left(x\right)\right) \tag{13.20}$$

The contradiction principle of our assumption that x^* must be the solution to the weighting problem and that must be properly optimized.

Theorem 9: If $x^* = \left(\left(x_L^*\right),\left(x_N^*\right),\left(x_R^*\right)\right)$ is an optimal solution to the weighting problem, then it is an exact optimal solution to the FMOLPP.

Proof: By the contradiction, let $x^* = \left(\left(x_L^*\right),\left(x_N^*\right),\left(x_R^*\right)\right)$ be an optimal solution to a given FMOLPP, according to the order relation $>_{LM}$ and it is not the exact solution to the problem. There exists a feasible solution to the given problem.

Let $x^0 = \left(\left(x_L^0\right),\left(x_N^0\right),\left(x_R^0\right)\right) \neq x^*$, such that the minimization objective function of $\left(f\left(x^*\right)_L, f\left(x^*\right)_N, f\left(x^*\right)_R\right) >_{LM} \left(f\left(x^0\right)_L, f\left(x^0\right)_N, f\left(x^0\right)_R\right)$. By Theorem 7, we know that the weighting problem optimal solution is properly optimized. Regarding this, one of the prove can be center of TFN is getting the optimal solution to the weighting problem. Accordingly, we can prove that left and right also get optimal solutions to the FMOLPP by using the fuzzy weighted sum method.

Let the minimization problem of $\sum_{i=1}^{n} w_i\left(f_i^L\left(x_L^*\right) f_i^N\left(x_L^*\right) f_i^R\left(x_L^*\right)\right) >_{LM}$ $\sum_{i=1}^{n} w_i\left(f_i^L\left(x_L^0\right) f_i^N\left(x_L^0\right) f_i^R\left(x_L^0\right)\right)$. Also, assume we have $\left(Ax^0\right)_L = b_L$, $\left(Ax^0\right)_N = b_N, \left(Ax^0\right)_R = b_R$, and the objective function of left, center, and right are always greater than the objective value in $\left(x_L^*\right),\left(x_N^*\right),\left(x_R^*\right)$.

$$\left\{ \sum_{i=1}^{n} w_i f_i^R \left(x_R^* \right) >_{LM} \sum_{i=1}^{n} w_i f_i^R \left(x_R^0 \right) \right\} >_{LM}$$

$$\left\{ \sum_{i=1}^{n} w_i f_i^N \left(x_N^* \right) >_{LM} \sum_{i=1}^{r} w_i f_i^N \left(x_N^0 \right) \right\} >_{LM} \tag{13.21}$$

$$\left\{ \sum_{i=1}^{n} w_i f_i^L \left(x_L^* \right) >_{LM} \sum_{i=1}^{n} w_i f_i^L \left(x_L^0 \right) \right\}$$

By the contradiction principle, our assumption is that $\left(x_L^* \right), \left(x_N^* \right), \left(x_R^* \right)$ must be the solution to the FMOLPP and that must be the optimal solution.

13.6 Numerical example

In this section, we have employed the fuzzy weighted sum method to solve the given numerical example.

EXAMPLE 1

The problem [37] is formulated as a FMOLPP. Such as the objective function, coefficient constraint, decision variable, and right-hand side vector are taken as TFNs.

$$\min \left\{ F_1(x), F_2(x) \right\}$$

subject to

$$\left\{ \begin{array}{c} [1,2,4] x_1 + [2,8,10] x_2 = [3,22,36] \\ [2,3,6] x_1 + [4,10,15] x_2 = [6,29,54] \\ x_1, x_2 \in TFN \end{array} \right\} \tag{13.22}$$

where $F_1(x) = [7,10,11] x_1 + [8,10,13] x_2$, and $F_2(x) = [2,3,4] x_1 + [4,7,12] x_2$; $x = [x_1, x_2]^T = \left[\left[x_1^L, x_1^N, x_1^R \right], \left[x_2^L, x_2^N, x_2^R \right] \right]^T$

According to the given FMOLPP on TFNs, when we apply the fuzzy weighted sum method to find an optimal solution, it needs to perform left, center, and right computations of the FMOLPP. Therefore, FMOLP requirements to another parametric computation are the same. The crisp representation of TFNs possess two parameters (i.e., α and β). To find the efficient solution of the FMOLPP by using left, center, right, and parametric calculations, the weight value are taken from 0 to 1.

The obtained results are listed in Tables 13.1 and 13.2, whereas the final function values are listed in Table 13.3. The results are compared with [37]. Graphical representation of TFNs of [37] and a proposed method are shown in Figures 13.4 and 13.5. The objective function of the same are shown as Figures 13.4 and 13.5.

We calculate the left, center, and right computations from Eq. (13.22). An efficient solution by using the fuzzy weighted sum method with weights with values 0 to 1 with parameters are computed with the FMOLPP. Dealing with the parametric computation of the FMOLPP, we need to perform four types of computations: (i) $\alpha = 0$ and $\beta = 0$, (ii) $\alpha = 0$ and $\beta = 1$, (iii) $\alpha = 1$ and $\beta = 0$, (iv) $\alpha = 1$ and $\beta = 1$. These four types of solutions are represented in Tables 13.1 and 13.2.

The weight-wise solutions are given in Tables 13.1 and 13.2. At each value of the left, center, and right solutions and the uncertain solution lies in

TABLE 13.1 Solutions for component x_1 and its parametric computation

w	x_1^L	x_1^N	x_1^R	$x_{10,0}$	$x_{10,1}$	$x_{11,0}$	$x_{11,1}$
0	0	1	3	0.9964	9	3	6.0356
0.1	0	0	3	0	8.9996	3	6.0356
0.2	0	0	3	0	0	3	6.0356
0.3	0	0	3	0	0	3	6.0356
0.4	0	0	3	0	0	3	6.0356
0.5	0	0	3	0	0	3	6.0356
0.6	0	0	3	0	0	3	6.0356
0.7	0	0	3	0	0	3	6.0356
0.8	0	0	3	0	0	3	6.0356
0.9	0	0	3	0	0	3	6.0356

[Original (created by authors)]

TABLE 13.2 Optimal solutions for component x_2 and its parametric computation

w	x_2^L	x_2^N	x_2^R	$x_{20,0}$	$x_{20,1}$	$x_{21,0}$	$x_{21,1}$
0	1	2	3.6	1.0018	0	2	0.0001
0.1	1.5	2	3.6	1.5	0.0002	2	0.0001
0.2	1.5	2	3.6	1.5	3.6	2	0.0001
0.3	1.5	2	3.6	1.5	3.6	2	0.0001
0.4	1.5	2	3.6	1.5	3.6	2	0.0001
0.5	1.5	2	3.6	1.5	3.6	2	0.0001
0.6	1.5	2	3.6	1.5	3.6	2	0.0001
0.7	1.5	2	3.6	1.5	3.6	2	0.0001
0.8	1.5	2	3.6	1.5	3.6	2	0.0001
0.9	1.5	2	3.6	1.5	3.6	2	0.0001

[Original (created by authors)]

TABLE 13.3 Optimal solutions of objective function

w	F_L Value	F_N Value	F_R Value	$F_{0,0}$	$F_{0,1}$	$F_{1,0}$	$F_{1,1}$	Min
0	6	23	45	6	36	23	18.1074	6
0.1	6.6	25.7	45	5.7	42.3	25.3	22.3324	5.7
0.2	7.2	28.4	45	5.4	41.76	27.6	26.5573	5.4
0.3	7.8	31.1	45	5.1	41.04	29.9	30.7823	5.1
0.4	8.4	33.8	45	4.8	40.32	32.2	35.0073	4.8
0.5	9	36.5	45	4.5	39.6	34.5	39.2322	4.5
0.6	9.6	39.2	45	4.2	38.88	36.8	43.4572	4.2
0.7	10.2	41.9	45	3.9	38.16	39.1	47.6821	3.9
0.8	10.8	44.6	45	3.6	37.44	41.4	51.9071	3.6
0.9	11.4	47.3	45	3.3	36.72	43.7	56.1321	3.3

[Original (created by authors)]

between them. Further, to understand the effectiveness, the proposed method and obtained results are compared with [37].

The obtained TFNs given in Tables 13.1, 13.2, and 13.4 are shown in Figures 13.4, 13.5, 13.6, and 13.7 with a comparison to the existing method.

The width-wise solution of x_1 and x_2 are represented in Figure 13.8. From the above it can be mentioned that the proposed method possesses a good

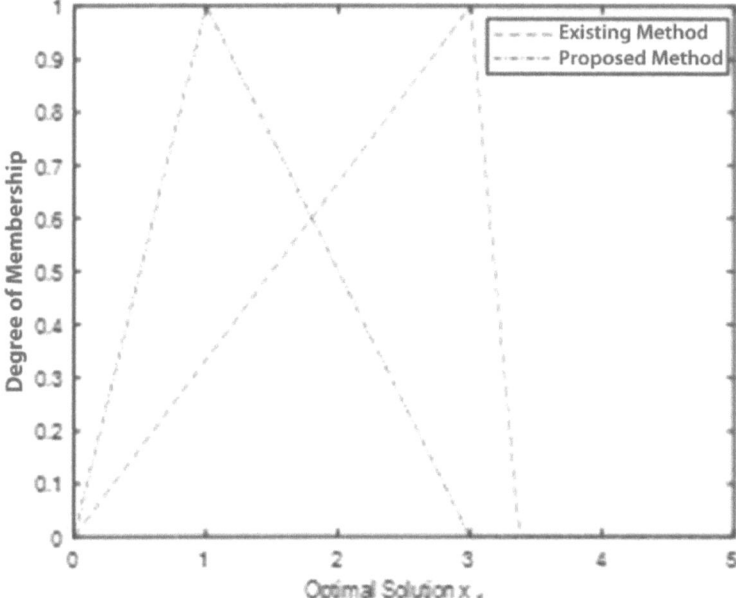

FIGURE 13.4 Comparison of fuzzy optimal solution of x_1.

[Original (created by authors)]

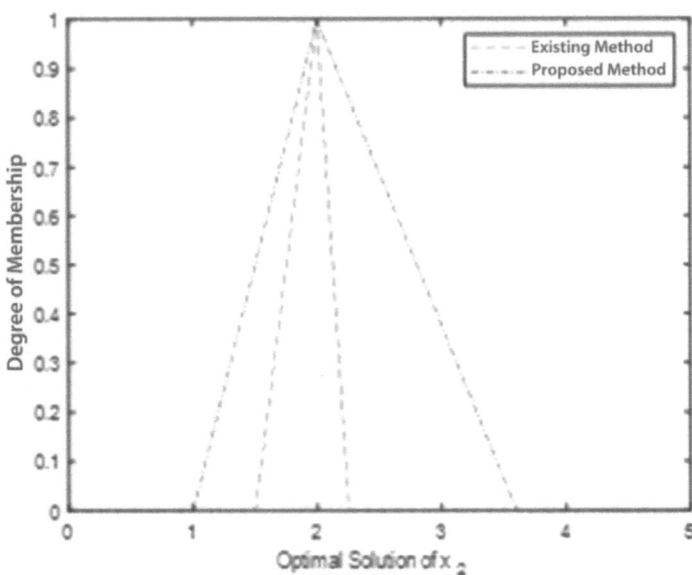

FIGURE 13.5 Comparison of fuzzy optimal solution of x_1.

[Original (created by authors)]

TABLE 13.4 Comparison of proposed method with [37]

Optimal solution	x_1	x_2	$F_1(x_1)$	$F_2(x_2)$
[37] Method	(0, 3.000, 3.3743)	(1.5, 2.000, 2.2503)	(12, 50, 66.3712)	(6, 23, 40.5008)
Proposed Method	(0, 1, 3)	(1, 2, 3.6)	(8, 30, 79.8)	(4, 17, 52.2)

[Original (created by authors)]

agreement with the results obtained in [37]. Finally, it can be noticed that the present method is easy to use, and it can be applicable for other FMOLPPs.

13.7 Conclusion

Here, a fuzzy-based approach is presented to solve a modeled optimization problem with blockchain technology. A novel solution approach based on a proper order relation of TFNs was proposed to deal with a FMOLPP. TFNs are taken as uncertainty in FMOLPPs. To show the efficiency of the proposed method, an example problem of a MOLPP in a fuzzy environment is demonstrated. The coefficient, objective function, and constraints are taken in TFNs. Using the proposed method, the same is solved and optimal solutions

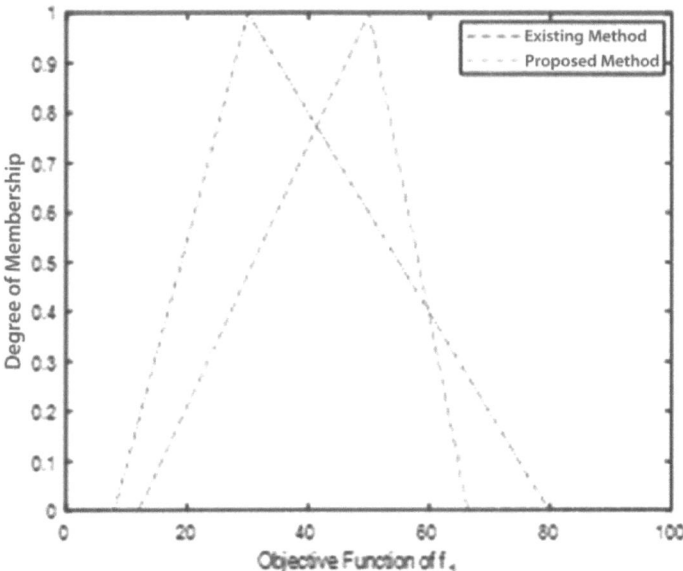

FIGURE 13.6 Optimal solution of fuzzy objective function f_1.

[Original (created by authors)]

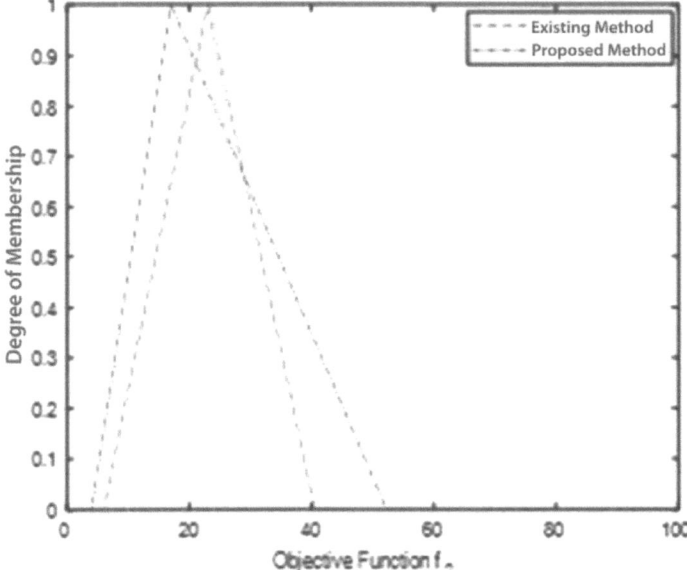

FIGURE 13.7 Optimal solution of fuzzy objective function f_2.

[Original (created by authors)]

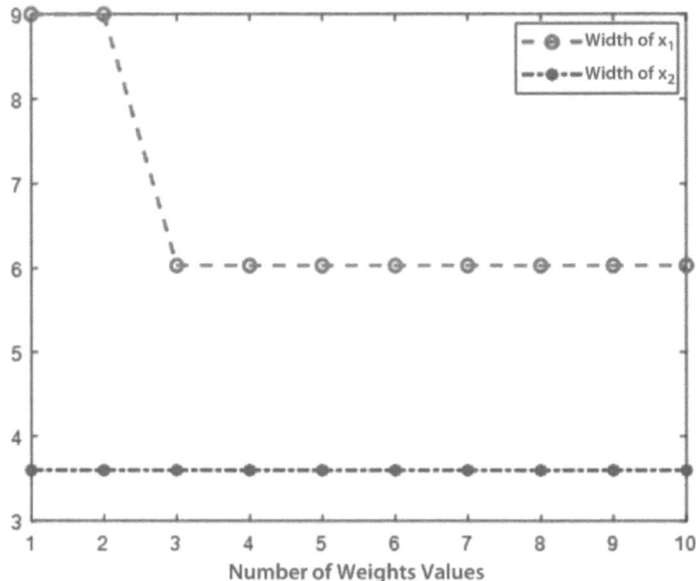

FIGURE 13.8   Width-wise optimal solution of x_1 and x_2.

[Original (created by authors)]

are reported. The obtained solutions are compared with other methods and were found to be in good agreement. It is also noted that the solution set produces a tight uncertain width. Finally, from the investigation, it is observed that the proposed approach may give promising results and a better fit for other FMOLPPs and blockchain technology-related models.

References

1. B. B. Gupta, K.-C. Li, V. C. Leung, K. E. Psannis and S. Yamaguchi, "Blockchain-assisted secure fine-grained searchable encryption for a cloud-based healthcare cyber-physical system," *IEEE/CAA Journal of Automatica Sinica*, vol. 8, no. 12, pp. 1877–1890, 2021.
2. R. Kumar and R. Tripathi, "DBTP2SF: A deep blockchain-based trustworthy privacy-preserving secured framework in industrial internet of things systems," *Transactions on Emerging Telecommunications Technologies*, vol. 32, no. 4, p. e4222, 2021.
3. L. Yan, S. Yin-He, Y. Qian, S. Zhi-Yu, W. Chun-Zi and L. Zi-Yun, "Method of reaching consensus on probability of food safety based on the integration of finite credible data on block chain," *IEEE access*, vol. 9, pp. 123764–123776, 2021.
4. A. Alagha, S. Singh, R. Mizouni, A. Ouali and H. Otrok, "Data-driven dynamic active node selection for event localization in IoT applications-a case study of radiation localization," *IEEE Access*, vol. 7, pp. 16168–16183, 2019.

5. Y. Xiao, X. Zuo, J. Huang, A. Konak and Y. Xu, "The continuous pollution routing problem," *Applied Mathematics and Computation*, vol. 387, p. 125072, 2020.

6. G. Sun, Y. Cong, Q. Wang, B. Zhong and Y. Fu, "Representative task self-selection for flexible clustered lifelong learning," *IEEE Transactions on Neural Networks and Learning Systems*, vol. 33, no. 4, pp. 1467–1481, 2020.

7. A. Shukla and S. Tripathi, "An effective relay node selection technique for energy efficient WSN-assisted IoT," *Wireless Personal Communications*, vol. 112, pp. 2611–2641, 2020.

8. R. E. Bellman and L. A. Zadeh, "Decision-making in a fuzzy environment," *Management Science*, vol. 17, no. 4, pp. B-141–B-164, 1970.

9. H. Tanaka, T. Okuda and K. Asai, "On fuzzy-mathematical programming," *Journal of Cybernetics*, vol. 3, no. 3, pp. 37–46, 1974.

10. H. J. Zimmermann, "Fuzzy programming and linear programming with several objective functions," *Fuzzy Sets and Systems*, vol. 1, no. 1, pp. 45–55, 1978.

11. S. M. Guua and Y.-K. Wu, "Two-phase approach for solving the fuzzy linear programming problems," *Fuzzy Sets and Systems*, vol. 107, no. 2, pp. 191–195, 1999.

12. M. Jiménez, M. Arenas, A. Bilbao and M. V. Rodrıguez, "Linear programming with fuzzy parameters: An interactive method resolution," *European Journal of Operational Research*, vol. 117, no. 3, pp. 1599–1609, 2007.

13. H. R. Maleki, M. Tata and M. Mashinchi, "Linear programming with fuzzy variables," *Fuzzy Sets and Systems*, vol. 109, no. 1, pp. 21–33, 2000.

14. J. J. Buckley and T. Feuring, "Evolutionary algorithm solution to fuzzy problems: Fuzzy linear programming," *Fuzzy Sets and Systems*, vol. 109, no. 1, pp. 35–53, 2000.

15. F. Lotfi, T. Allahviranloo, M. Jondabeh and L. Alizadeh, "Solving a full fuzzy linear programming using lexicography method and fuzzy approximate solution," *Applied Mathematical Modelling*, vol. 33, no. 7, pp. 3151–3156, 2009.

16. A. K. J. Kau and P. Singh, "A new method for solving fully fuzzy linear programming problems," *Applied Mathematical Modelling*, vol. 38, no. 17–18, pp. 817–823, 2011.

17. H. Cheng, W. Huang and J. Cai, "Solving a fully fuzzy linear programming problem through compromise programming," *Journal of Applied Mathematics*, vol. 2013, no. 726296, p. 10, 2013.

18. S. K. Das, T. Mandal and S. A. Edalatpanah, "A mathematical model for solving fully fuzzy linear programming problem with trapezoidal fuzzy numbers," *Applied Intelligence*, vol. 46, pp. 509–519, 2017.

19. Z. Gong, W. Zhao and K. Liu, "A straightforward approach for solving fully fuzzy linear programming problem with LR-type fuzzy numbers," *Journal of the Operations Research Society of Japan*, vol. 61, no. 2, pp. 172–185, 2018.

20. S. K. Das, "Modified method for solving fully fuzzy linear programming problem with triangular fuzzy numbers," *International Journal of Research in Industrial Engineering*, vol. 6, no. 4, pp. 293–311, 2017.

21. H. Najafi, S. A. Edalatpanah and H. Dutta, "A nonlinear model for fully fuzzy linear programming with fully unrestricted variables and parameters," *Alexandria Engineering Journal*, vol. 55, no. 3, pp. 2589–2595, 2016.

22. S. Chanas, "Fuzzy programming in multiobjective linear programming—A parametric approach," *Fuzzy Sets and Systems*, vol. 29, no. 3, pp. 303–313, 1989.

23. M. Jiménez and A. Bilbaob, "Pareto-optimal solutions in fuzzy multi-objective linear programming," *Fuzzy Sets and Systems*, vol. 160, no. 18, pp. 2714–2721, 2009.

24. M. K. Luhandjula and M. J. Rangoaga, "An approach for solving a fuzzy multiobjective programming problem," *European Journal of Operational Research*, vol. 232, no. 2, pp. 249–255, 2014.

25. H. F. Wang and M. L. Wang, "A fuzzy multiobjective linear programming," *Fuzzy Sets and Systems*, vol. 86, no. 1, pp. 61–72, 1997.
26. H. Nasseri, A. Baghban and I. Mahdavi, "A new approach for solving fuzzy multi-objective quadratic programming of water resource allocation problem," *Journal of Industrial Engineering and Management Studies*, vol. 6, no. 2, pp. 78–102, 2019.
27. A. Batamiz, M. Allahdadi and M. Hladík, "Obtaining efficient solutions of interval multi-objective linear programming problems," *International Journal of Fuzzy Systems*, vol. 3, p. 873–890, 2020.
28. S. Rivaz and Z. Saeidi, "Solving multiobjective linear programming problems with interval parameters," *Fuzzy Information and Engineering*, vol. 31, no. 4, pp. 497–504, 2021.
29. C. Li, "A fuzzy multi-objective linear programming with interval-typed triangular fuzzy numbers," *Open Mathematics*, vol. 17, no. 1, pp. 607–626, 2019.
30. S. Nayak and S. Chakraverty, "A new approach to solve fuzzy system of linear equations," *Journal of Mathematics and Computer Science*, vol. 7, no. 3, pp. 205–212, 2013.
31. P. K. Panigrahi and S. Nayak, "Numerical investigation of non-probabilistic systems using inner outer direct search optimization technique," *AIMS Mathematics*, vol. 8, no. 9, pp. 21329–21358, 2023.
32. P. K. Panigrahi and S. Nayak, "Numerical approach to solve imprecisely defined systems using inner outer direct search optimization technique," *Mathematics and Computers in Simulation*, vol. 215, pp. 578–606, 2024.
33. P. K. Panigrahi and S. Nayak, "Conjugate gradient with Armijo line search approach to investigate imprecisely defined unconstrained optimisation problem," *International Journal of Computational Science and Engineering*, vol. 27, no. 4, 2024.
34. S. Priyadarshini and S. Nayak, "A numerical approach to study heat and mass transfer in porous medium influenced by uncertain parameters," *International Communications in Heat and Mass Transfer*, vol. 139, p. 106411, 2022.
35. S. Priyadarshini and S. Nayak, "Effects of imprecisely defined parameters on heat and mass transfer in a vertical annular porous cylinder," *International Communications in Heat and Mass Transfer*, vol. 149, p. 107097, 2023.
36. S. Nayak, "Uncertain quantification of field variables involved in transient convection diffusion problems for imprecisely defined parameters," *International Communications in Heat and Mass Transfer*, vol. 119, p. 104894, 2020.
37. X.-P. Yang, B.-Y. Cao and H.-T. Lin, "Multi-objective fully fuzzy linear programming problems with triangular fuzzy numbers," in *International Conference on Fuzzy Systems and Knowledge Discovery*, Xiamen, China, 2014.

14

DECENTRALIZING HEALTH

The Future of Blockchain in Health Care

A. Thriveni, J. Balajee, and T. Vijaykumar

14.1 Introduction

In an era when technology breakthroughs are altering sectors, blockchain emerges as a transformative force in health care. "Decentralizing Health" digs into the convergence of blockchain technology and health care, examining its unparalleled potential to transform the way we handle, distribute, and safeguard health-related data. The traditional healthcare system has long struggled with issues including data fragmentation, security risks, and ineffective interoperability. Blockchain, known for its decentralized and secure nature, represents a paradigm change by delivering a transparent, tamperproof, and decentralized ledger. This ledger, also known as distributed ledger technology (DLT), shows promise in tackling the long-standing concerns of data silos and accessibility within the healthcare sector [1].

This research will delve into the complexities of how blockchain promotes a patient-centric approach. The decentralized structure of blockchain gives people more control over their health data, allowing for seamless exchange across healthcare providers while retaining privacy and security. This trend towards patient empowerment is expected to improve cooperation, treatment results, and the entire healthcare experience. Furthermore, the addition of smart contracts, which are programmable self-executing agreements, increases blockchain's transformational potential. Smart contracts enable the automatic and transparent implementation of preset rules, eliminating administrative hassles and inconsistencies in processes like insurance claims and billing [1].

As we traverse the changing world of health care, this investigation seeks to shed light on the unique applications of blockchain technology. From

DOI: 10.1201/9781003483113-14

interoperable electronic health records to pharmaceutical supply chain management, "Decentralizing Health" aims to peel back the layers of possibilities that blockchain brings to the forefront of healthcare innovation. Join us as we explore the future of health care, as decentralization provides the foundation for a more efficient, secure, and patient-centric ecosystem [2].

14.1.1 Background

Blockchain in health care has its roots in the industry's long-standing difficulties. Historically, health care has faced challenges such as fragmented and compartmentalized data, interoperability barriers, and worries about data security and privacy. Recognizing these flaws, the incorporation of blockchain technology emerged as a viable solution. Blockchain, which was originally designed as the underpinning technology for cryptocurrencies, gained popularity for its decentralized and tamper-resistant characteristics. This appealed to healthcare stakeholders who wanted a secure and transparent approach to manage health data. The opportunity to develop a single, interoperable system that spans corporate borders has fueled the investigation of blockchain applications in health care [3].

The notion gained traction as it became clear that blockchain might provide a strong foundation for securely storing and transmitting sensitive health information. As a decentralized ledger, it reduces the danger of data breaches while also ensuring the integrity of medical records. Over time, pilot initiatives and collaborations between digital entrepreneurs and healthcare institutions have proved the viability of blockchain applications, fueling the push for a decentralized and patient-centered future in health care [4].

14.1.2 Motivation for blockchain in health care

The impetus for using blockchain in health care derives from a strong desire to eliminate long-standing inefficiencies and weaknesses in the existing healthcare system. One of the key issues is the fragmentation of health data among several providers and systems, which results in disconnected patient records and impedes collaboration among healthcare professionals. Blockchain, with its decentralized and transparent nature, provides a solution for unifying this fragmented landscape. Concerns about data security and privacy have long persisted in health care. Blockchain's decentralized nature makes it a tamper-resistant and secure platform for storing sensitive health information. This trend toward better security is especially important considering the increasing frequency and sophistication of cyberattacks on healthcare databases. By implementing blockchain, the sector hopes to strengthen its defenses against data breaches and unwanted access, eventually protecting patient anonymity.

Furthermore, the impetus for blockchain in health care is profoundly entrenched in a desire to empower people. The existing system frequently restricts consumers' ownership over their health data, making it difficult to communicate information seamlessly across healthcare professionals. Blockchain's patient-centric approach enables patients to securely maintain and share their health information, promoting a more active and informed participation in their healthcare journey. Efficiency benefits are another appealing reason. Blockchain integration allows for more efficient procedures by utilizing smart contracts, which are self-executing agreements that automate previously stated actions. This automation alleviates administrative responsibilities, decreases mistakes, and guarantees that healthcare transactions, such as insurance claims and invoicing, are carried out clearly and effectively [5].

Collaboration within the healthcare ecosystem is critical to providing complete and coordinated treatment. Blockchain's capacity to construct a shared and interoperable ledger facilitates smooth information flow across many institutions, enabling a more collaborative and patient-centered healthcare environment. Finally, the impetus for blockchain in health care stems from its ability to alter a system riddled with inefficiencies, instability, and fragmentation, paving the way for a more interconnected, secure, and patient-centered future [6].

14.1.3   *Scope and objectives*

The scope and objectives of blockchain technology are multifaceted, aiming to revolutionize traditional systems across industries. At its core, blockchain seeks to decentralize networks, ensuring transparency and resilience while eliminating the need for intermediaries. Through immutable recordkeeping and cryptographic security measures, it promotes data integrity and trust among participants. Efficiency gains are achieved through automation and reduced administrative overhead, while interoperability fosters seamless communication between disparate systems. Blockchain's potential extends to enhancing privacy through user-controlled data access and facilitating smart contract execution for trustless agreements. Moreover, its application in supply chain management enables transparency and traceability, while decentralized identity management promises to transform digital identity verification. Overall, blockchain technology aspires to redefine paradigms, offering solutions that prioritize security, transparency, efficiency, and trust across a wide range of sectors. Table 14.1 describes the scope and objectives of blockchain technology.

TABLE 14.1 Scope and objectives of blockchain technology

Scope of blockchain	Objectives of blockchain
Interoperable Health Records: Facilitate the development of a single and interoperable health record system, allowing healthcare providers to share data seamlessly.	Enhance Data Interoperability: Improve health data interoperability, allowing for more efficient and secure information transmission among healthcare institutions.
Data Security and Integrity: Ensure the security and integrity of health data by leveraging blockchain's decentralized and tamper-resistant characteristics, reducing the danger of unwanted access and breaches.	Patient Empowerment: Empower patients by providing them more control over their health data, allowing them to securely manage and share information, and encouraging them to take an active part in making healthcare decisions.
Supply Chain Management: Improve the traceability and transparency of pharmaceutical supply chains, lowering the danger of counterfeit pharmaceuticals and maintaining the drug's integrity.	Administrative Efficiency: Smart contracts can help to streamline administrative procedures by automating tasks like insurance claims and billing, reducing mistakes and increasing efficiency.
Clinical Trials and Research: Allow for transparent and traceable management of clinical trial data, safeguarding the integrity of research results and advancing medical progress.	Credentialing and Verification: Simplify and secure healthcare professionals' credentialing processes, ensuring that qualifications are readily verified and eliminating administrative expenses.
Improved Decision-Making: Give healthcare workers access to extensive and accurate patient data, allowing them to make better decisions and provide more individualized treatment.	Collaborative Ecosystem: Encourage collaboration among healthcare stakeholders by establishing a common and secure platform for information sharing, resulting in a more coordinated and patient-centric healthcare system.

[Original (created by authors)]

14.2 Foundations of blockchain technology

Blockchain technology is fundamentally a decentralized and distributed ledger system that underpins a wide range of applications beyond its initial association with cryptocurrency. Blockchain's foundations are built on a number of essential ideas that together alter how data is stored, processed, and distributed.

- **Decentralization:** The elimination of a central authority lies at the heart of the blockchain concept. Unlike traditional databases, which are managed by a single entity, blockchains spread control over a network of nodes. Each network participant has a copy of the whole ledger, which eliminates the possibility of a single point of failure. Decentralization increases transparency, security, and resilience.

- **Distributed Ledger:** Blockchain runs on a distributed ledger, which is a digital record of transactions or information. This ledger is duplicated across the network to ensure that everyone has access to the same information. Changes to the ledger are stored in blocks and connected chronologically, resulting in an immutable chain of data.
- **Consensus Mechanism:** A consensus mechanism is used in blockchain networks to agree on transaction legitimacy and maintain a consistent ledger. This approach guarantees that all nodes in the network come to an agreement before adding a new block. Common consensus algorithms include proof-of-work (PoW; used in Bitcoin) and proof-of-stake (PoS), each with its unique method for confirming transactions.
- **Cryptographic Security:** Blockchain relies largely on cryptography methods to protect data and transactions. Hash functions, digital signatures, and encryption are critical for maintaining the integrity, validity, and secrecy of information recorded on the blockchain. Cryptography is a key component in making blockchain resistant to manipulation and fraud.
- **Smart Contracts:** Smart contracts are self-executing contracts in which the terms of the agreement are encoded directly into code. These contracts automate procedures and enforce regulations without the need of middlemen. Smart contracts improve productivity, eliminate mistakes, and streamline a wide range of procedures, from financial transactions to complicated corporate agreements.
- **Immutability:** Once a block is put to the blockchain, it is nearly difficult to change its contents. Immutability is achieved via cryptographic hashing and the consensus method, which ensures that historical documents are secure and unchangeable. This attribute increases trust in the stored data's integrity.

Blockchain technology's fundamentals, including decentralization, distributed ledgers, consensus processes, cryptographic security, smart contracts, and immutability, have opened the way for creative solutions in different industries, offering more transparency, security, and efficiency [7].

14.2.1 *Overview of blockchain*

Blockchain technology, which began as the underlying architecture for cryptocurrencies such as Bitcoin, has grown into a revolutionary force with far-reaching consequences across several sectors. Blockchain is fundamentally a decentralized and distributed ledger system that transforms data storage, validation, and sharing. Blockchain's primary characteristic is decentralization, which eliminates the need for a central authority and distributes control over a network of nodes. This decentralization improves transparency, security, and resilience by eliminating single points of failure. A blockchain's information is organized as a distributed ledger, or a chronological chain of blocks, with each network participant owning an identical copy [8].

Blockchain technology, which began as the basic architecture for cryptocurrencies like Bitcoin, has evolved into a transformative force with far-reaching implications across several industries. Blockchain is essentially a decentralized and distributed ledger system that revolutionizes data storage, validation, and sharing. Blockchain's main feature is decentralization, which eliminates the need for a central authority and distributes control over a network of nodes. This decentralization enhances transparency, security, and resilience by removing single points of failure. A blockchain's data is arranged as a distributed ledger, or a chronological chain of blocks, with each network participant possessing an identical copy [9].

Smart contracts, another important component, are self-executing agreements with terms expressed in code. These contracts automate procedures, enforce regulations, and eliminate the need for middlemen, therefore simplifying operations and lowering the risk of error. Immutability, a feature of blockchain, means that once data is entered into the ledger, it is virtually hard to change. This feature is provided by cryptographic hashing and the consensus method, which preserves the integrity of previous data while increasing confidence. Blockchain's adaptability goes beyond finance into fields such as health care, supply chain, and legal. Its decentralized design, along with cryptographic security, overcomes issues such as data fragmentation, inefficiencies, and security concerns that exist in traditional systems [10].

Blockchain technology is a decentralized, secure, and transparent system that has the ability to transform businesses by promoting trust, efficiency, and cooperation. As breakthroughs continue to emerge, blockchain's revolutionary capacity remains at the forefront of technological progress.

14.2.2 Key components and terminology

- Blockchain:
  - Definition: A distributed ledger composed of a series of blocks, each holding a list of transactions.
  - Significance: The fundamental framework that enables transparency, security, and immutability while recording transactions.

- Blocks:
  - Definition: The blockchain is made up of containers that retain a series of transactions connected chronologically to prior blocks.
  - Significance: Each block has a unique identifier (hash) and a reference to the preceding block, resulting in a tamper-resistant and verifiable chain.

- **Nodes:**
  - Definition: Participants in the blockchain network keep a copy of the whole ledger and validate transactions.
  - Significance: Decentralized nodes help to ensure the blockchain's security, resiliency, and integrity.

- **Cryptographic Hashing:**
  - Definition: A method that turns data into a fixed-length string of characters while maintaining data integrity and uniqueness.
  - Significance: Used to link blocks, protect transactions, and generate digital signatures, hence improving blockchain security.

- **Digital Signatures:**
  - Definition: Cryptographic procedures used to verify the origin, identity, and authenticity of a communication or transaction.
  - Significance: Ensures transaction security and nonrepudiation, hence increasing the blockchain's dependability.

- **Immutable Ledger:**
  - Definition: Once data is put to the blockchain, it is almost hard to change or erase.
  - Significance: Ensures the integrity and durability of recorded transactions, hence increasing trust in the ledger's correctness.

- **Mining:**
  - Definition: The process of confirming transactions and adding new blocks to the blockchain; frequently related with PoW consensus.
  - Significance: Maintains blockchain security and integrity while motivating participants with incentives.

Understanding these major components and terms sheds light on the fundamental ideas and methods that underpin blockchain technology, making it a safe, transparent, and decentralized solution with numerous uses.

14.2.3   Different types of blockchain platforms

There are several types of blockchain platforms, each designed with specific features and use cases. Here are some prominent types:

- **Public Blockchains:**
  - Characteristics: The consensus process is open to the public and decentralized, allowing anybody to join and contribute.
  - Examples: Bitcoin, Ethereum.

- **Private Blockchains:**
  - Characteristics: Restricted access, usually utilized inside a single organization and managed by a central body.
  - Examples: Hyperledger Fabric, Corda.

- **Consortium Blockchains:**
  - Characteristics: Shared by a coalition of enterprises, it provides a balance between public and private blockchains.
  - Example: R3 Corda (used by a consortium of banks).

- **Permissionless Blockchains:**
  - Characteristics: Open to anybody, there is no central authority, and participants stay anonymous.
  - Examples: Bitcoin, Ethereum.

- **Permissioned Blockchains:**
  - Characteristics: Access is restricted, participants are identified, and permission is frequently required to participate.
  - Examples: Hyperledger Fabric, Corda.

- **Hybrid Blockchains:**
  - Characteristics: Combines components of both public and private blockchains to maximize the benefits of both formats.
  - Example: Dragonchain.

- **Smart Contract Platforms:**
  - Characteristics: Focus on supporting and executing smart contracts, which are self-executing codes that enforce contract requirements.
  - Examples: Ethereum, Binance Smart Chain.

- **Enterprise Blockchain Platforms:**
  - Characteristics: Designed for enterprise-level applications, with improved scalability, privacy, and integration capabilities.
  - Examples: Hyperledger Fabric, Quorum.

- **Tokenization Platforms:**
  - Characteristics: Specialized in the creation and management of tokens, which reflect real-world assets on the blockchain.
  - Example: Ethereum (for creating ERC-20 tokens).

- **Scalable Blockchain Platforms:**
  - Characteristics: The emphasis is on scalability to accommodate a huge number of transactions per second.
  - Examples: Solana, Algorand.

14.2.4   Relevance to health care

Blockchain technology is extremely relevant in health care, providing answers to long-standing sector difficulties. Here are the primary areas where blockchain is having a big impact:

- **Interoperable Health Records:**

  - Challenge: Fragmented and noninteroperable health records impede the smooth exchange of patient information between healthcare providers.
  - Blockchain Solution: Creates a uniform, interoperable system in which patient records may be safely exchanged across many healthcare institutions, resulting in greater coordination and patient care.

- **Data Security and Privacy:**

  - Challenge: Traditional healthcare systems are prone to data breaches, which jeopardize patient confidentiality.
  - Blockchain Solution: Uses cryptographic security techniques to protect the integrity and confidentiality of health data, lowering the risk of unwanted access and improving overall data security.

- **Patient Empowerment:**

  - Challenge: Patients have limited control over their personal health data, and exchanging information with multiple healthcare providers is difficult.
  - Blockchain Solution: Gives people more control over their health data. Patients can provide access to certain providers, which increases data ownership and promotes patient-centered treatment.

- **Supply Chain Management:**

  - Challenge: Counterfeit medications and poor supply chain operations may jeopardize patient safety.
  - Blockchain Solution: Improves transparency and traceability in pharmaceutical supply chains, lowering the danger of counterfeit pharmaceuticals. The blockchain records each stage of the supply chain, assuring the process's integrity.

- **Clinical Trials and Research:**

  - Challenge: Lack of openness and data integrity concerns in clinical trials can have an influence on the credibility of study findings.
  - Blockchain Solution: Provides a transparent and immutable record of clinical trial data, ensuring the integrity of research results. This can accelerate the development of medical advancements and improve the credibility of research outcomes.

- **Credentialing and Verification:**

  - Challenge: Manual and time-consuming processes for verifying healthcare professionals' credentials.
  - Blockchain Solution: Streamlines credential verification by creating a secure, tamper-resistant record of professionals' qualifications. This reduces administrative burdens and enhances the efficiency of credentialing processes.

- **Administrative Efficiency:**

  - Challenge: Administrative processes, such as insurance claims and billing, can be prone to errors and inefficiencies.
  - Blockchain Solution: Smart contracts automate and enforce predefined rules in administrative processes, reducing errors, minimizing fraud, and improving the efficiency of insurance claims and billing.

- **Healthcare Data Monetization:**

  - Opportunity: Enables patients to share anonymized health data for research purposes, contributing to medical advancements.
  - Blockchain Solution: Facilitates secure and transparent data sharing, allowing patients to control and monetize their anonymized health data while maintaining privacy.

Blockchain's value in health care resides in its capacity to handle data security, interoperability, and efficiency concerns. By fostering trust, transparency, and patient empowerment, blockchain contributes to the transformation of the healthcare industry toward a more connected, secure, and patient-centric ecosystem.

14.3 Decentralization in health care

Decentralization, powered by blockchain technology, is reshaping the healthcare sector by revolutionizing the way data is stored, shared, and accessed. Traditional healthcare systems are often plagued by centralized databases, resulting in fragmented, inefficient, and less secure data management. Blockchain introduces a decentralized approach that addresses these challenges, fostering a more transparent, efficient, and patient-centric healthcare ecosystem. One key aspect of decentralization in health care is the creation of a distributed and interoperable health information system. Patient records are no longer confined to individual healthcare providers or institutions but are securely stored in a decentralized ledger accessible to authorized participants. This approach enhances data interoperability, allowing seamless sharing of patient information across different healthcare entities. As a result, healthcare professionals gain a comprehensive view of a patient's medical history, improving diagnostic accuracy and treatment outcomes [11].

Data security and privacy are critical in health care, and blockchain's decentralized nature contributes significantly to addressing these concerns. With traditional centralized databases, the risk of data breaches is heightened, exposing sensitive patient information. In a decentralized system, cryptographic techniques and consensus mechanisms ensure the integrity and security of health data. Patents have greater control over who accesses their information, promoting confidentiality and trust. Decentralization also empowers patients by granting them ownership of their health data. Through blockchain, individuals can control access to their medical records, share specific information with healthcare providers, and even contribute anonymized data for research purposes. This shift from provider-centric to patient-centric data management enhances patient engagement, fostering a more collaborative relationship between healthcare providers and individuals [12].

Moreover, the decentralized approach of blockchain mitigates the reliance on intermediaries in healthcare processes. Smart contracts, self-executing agreements embedded in the blockchain, automate and enforce predefined rules. This streamlines administrative tasks such as insurance claims, reducing costs and minimizing errors. In essence, decentralization in health care through blockchain technology promotes transparency, security, patient empowerment, and operational efficiency. As this transformative approach gains traction, it has the potential to redefine the healthcare landscape, making it more resilient, patient-focused, and technologically advanced.

14.3.1 Centralization challenges in traditional healthcare systems

Centralization poses significant challenges in traditional healthcare systems, manifesting in various aspects. One prominent issue is the concentration of patient data within centralized databases, making them lucrative targets for cyberattacks and data breaches. Moreover, centralization often leads to interoperability challenges between different healthcare providers and systems, hindering the seamless exchange of patient information critical for coordinated care. This lack of interoperability not only impedes medical decision-making but also contributes to inefficiencies and duplication of efforts. Additionally, centralized healthcare systems can be bureaucratic and slow to adapt to evolving patient needs and technological advancements. Patients may face difficulties accessing their own medical records or exercising control over their healthcare data due to centralized control mechanisms. Furthermore, the reliance on centralized authorities can result in disparities in healthcare access and quality, particularly in underserved or marginalized communities [13]. Overall, the centralization of healthcare systems presents formidable obstacles to achieving patient-centric, efficient, and resilient healthcare delivery models. Table 14.2 describes the centralization challenges with blockchain technology in traditional health care.

TABLE 14.2 Centralization challenges with blockchain technology in traditional health care

Centralization challenge	Solution with blockchain technology
Fragmented Health Records	Blockchain creates a unified and interoperable system for health records, securely storing patient data in a decentralized ledger accessible to authorized entities.
Interoperability Issues	Blockchain ensures seamless sharing and access to patient information among different healthcare providers by standardizing data formats and enabling secure data exchange across disparate systems.
Security Concerns	Blockchain's cryptographic features ensure the security and integrity of health data, with decentralized storage reducing the risk of data breaches and unauthorized access.
Administrative Inefficiencies	Smart contracts automate administrative processes such as insurance claims and billing, reducing errors, streamlining workflows, and minimizing the need for intermediaries.
Supply Chain Vulnerabilities	Blockchain enhances traceability and transparency in pharmaceutical supply chains, reducing the risk of counterfeit drugs and ensuring the integrity of medications.
Limited Patient Control	Blockchain empowers patients by giving them greater control over their health data, enabling them to manage access permissions and selectively share information with healthcare providers.

[Original (created by authors)]

By addressing these centralization challenges, blockchain technology revolutionizes data management, security, and patient care in traditional healthcare systems, fostering a more efficient, secure, and patient-centric ecosystem.

14.3.2 Advantages of decentralization

Decentralization using blockchain technology offers a range of advantages across various industries, and particularly in sectors like finance, health care, and supply chain. Here are the key advantages:

- **Enhanced Security:** Blockchain utilizes cryptographic techniques to secure transactions and data. Since the information is distributed across the network, there is no central point of failure, making it highly resistant to hacking and unauthorized access.

- **Improved Transparency:** The decentralized nature of blockchain ensures that all participants in the network have access to the same information. Transactions are visible to all parties involved, promoting transparency and reducing the risk of fraud.
- **Reduced Intermediaries:** Blockchain's smart contracts automate and enforce predefined rules, eliminating the need for intermediaries in various processes. This will speed up transactions, reduces costs, and minimizes the potential for errors.
- **Data Integrity:** Once information is recorded on the blockchain, it becomes practically impossible to alter. This immutability ensures the integrity of data, making it reliable and trustworthy for various applications, including supply chain management and digital identities.
- **Increased Efficiency:** Processes that traditionally involve multiple intermediaries and complex verification steps can be streamlined through decentralized blockchain networks. This results in faster and more efficient operations.
- **Empowered Individuals:** Decentralization often empowers individuals by giving them more control over their data. In blockchain-based systems, users can manage and control access to their information, contributing to enhanced privacy and user autonomy.
- **Global Accessibility:** Blockchain operates on a global network, allowing participants from different geographical locations to engage in transactions without the need for intermediaries. This fosters financial inclusion and global collaboration.
- **Interoperability:** Blockchain can facilitate interoperability between different systems and platforms. This is particularly beneficial in industries like health care, where seamless sharing of patient data among various providers can lead to improved healthcare outcomes.
- **Resilience to System Failures:** Traditional centralized systems are vulnerable to system failures or outages. In a decentralized blockchain network, the absence of a central point of control makes the system more resilient to such failures.
- **Incentivizing Network Participation:** Certain blockchain networks employ tokens or cryptocurrencies to encourage members for providing resources to the network, such as verifying transactions (e.g., PoS or PoW). This helps maintain a robust and secure network.

Decentralization through blockchain technology introduces a transformative approach to various industries, promoting trust, security, efficiency, and user empowerment. As technology advances, its impact on reshaping traditional centralized systems is likely to grow further.

14.3.3 Decentralized ledger technology in health care

Decentralized ledger technology (DLT), commonly exemplified by blockchain, is increasingly gaining prominence in the healthcare sector for its potential to address key challenges in data management, security, and interoperability. Here is an exploration of the application of DLT in health care:

- **Interoperable Health Records:** DLT enables the creation of a shared and interoperable system for health records. Patient data, securely stored in a decentralized ledger, can be seamlessly accessed and updated by authorized healthcare providers. This facilitates a comprehensive and real-time view of a patient's medical history.
- **Data Security and Integrity:** Blockchain's cryptographic features ensure the security and integrity of health data. The decentralized design of the ledger decreases the possibility of unauthorized access, manipulation, or data breaches, addressing one of the major issues in health care.
- **Patient-Centric Data Control:** DLT empowers patients by providing them greater control over their health data. Through private keys, individuals can manage access permissions and selectively share specific information with healthcare providers, promoting patient-centricity and data ownership.
- **Supply Chain Traceability:** Blockchain improves the traceability of drugs and medical supplies by documenting every transaction and movement on a ledger. This transparency decreases the possibility of counterfeit pharmaceuticals, protects supply chain integrity, and, ultimately, improves patient safety.
- **Clinical Trials and Research:** DLT protects the transparency and integrity of clinical trial data. By storing trial data on an irreversible ledger, the outcomes become more reliable, and the research process gains credibility, hastening medical progress.
- **Credentialing and Verification:** Blockchain streamlines and speeds up the certification process for healthcare professionals. Verified credentials are securely stored on the decentralized ledger, which reduces administrative overhead while providing efficient and trustworthy verification.
- **Streamlined Administrative Processes:** Smart contracts are self-executing agreements incorporated in the blockchain that automate administrative operations like insurance claims and billing. This lowers mistakes, increases efficiency, and decreases the need for intermediaries.
- **Data Monetization and Research Contributions:** DLT enables the secure and transparent sharing of anonymized health data for research purposes. Patients can contribute to medical research while retaining their privacy, and certain blockchain-based platforms enable them to monetize anonymized health data.

- **Immutable Audit Trails:** The immutability of the decentralized ledger guarantees an auditable and tamper-proof record of all transactions and modifications to health data. This feature improves accountability and creates a solid audit trail for compliance purposes.
- **Global Accessibility:** DLT operates on a decentralized global network, allowing healthcare information to be accessed and transacted across borders. This can be especially useful in emergency situations or for people who need medical attention while traveling.

As the healthcare sector investigates the possibilities of DLT, the use of DLT has the potential to transform data management, security, and cooperation, resulting in a more efficient, patient-centric, and integrated healthcare environment.

14.4   Applications of blockchain in health care

Blockchain technology is poised to revolutionize health care by addressing long-standing challenges and creating new opportunities for secure, efficient, and patient-centered care. One key area of impact lies in data management. Blockchain can securely store a patient's EHR in a distributed ledger, accessible only to authorized providers with the patient's consent. This not only fosters trust by empowering patients to control their data, but also creates a unified and traceable medical history for improved care coordination. Furthermore, blockchain's inherent immutability safeguards data integrity, preventing unauthorized alterations and ensuring the authenticity of medical records. This enhanced security extends to administrative processes as well. Blockchain can streamline tasks like insurance claim processing by eliminating paperwork and enabling secure, automated communication between providers, payers, and patients. Similarly, the technology can track the movement of pharmaceuticals and medical supplies throughout the supply chain, guaranteeing provenance and combating counterfeiting. Beyond administrative efficiency, blockchain empowers patients in other ways [14]. They can gain control over their data for clinical research purposes, while also facilitating seamless data sharing with different healthcare providers, eliminating redundant tests and fostering a more collaborative care approach. The potential applications extend even further, encompassing secure appointment scheduling and telemedicine consultations, as well as personalized medicine initiatives that leverage securely stored genomic data. While still an emerging technology in health care, blockchain's ability to enhance data security, streamline processes, and empower patients positions it as a transformative force for building a more efficient, transparent, and patient-centric healthcare system. Table 14.3 describes the major applications of blockchain technology in health care.

TABLE 14.3 Applications of blockchain technology in health care

Application	Description
Health Records Management	Blockchain technology offers a secure and interoperable platform for managing EHRs, assuring transparent and accessible patient data.
Supply Chain Traceability	Blockchain improves traceability in pharmaceutical supply chains by tracing medicine flow from producer to patient, eliminating counterfeit pharmaceuticals, and increasing patient safety.
Clinical Trials and Research	Blockchain provides clinical trial data openness and integrity, which boosts research credibility and accelerates medical discoveries.
Credentialing and Verification	Blockchain simplifies credential verification for healthcare professionals by securely recording validated credentials while lowering administrative constraints.
Insurance Claims and Billing	Smart contracts automate insurance claims and billing procedures, decreasing mistakes, fraud, and increasing administrative efficiency.
Telemedicine and Remote Health	Blockchain technology enables safe and transparent data exchange in telemedicine, ensuring privacy and integrity during remote healthcare consultations and testing.
Patient Data Ownership	Blockchain gives patients more control over their health data, allowing them to manage access rights and distribute information selectively.
Medical IoT and Wearables	Blockchain protects data from medical IoT devices and wearables, protecting the integrity and privacy of health information acquired by these devices.
Drug Authentication	Blockchain provides pharmaceutical authentication, which verifies medicine validity and reduces the circulation of counterfeit drugs.
Medical Research Collaboration	Blockchain promotes collaboration in medical research by offering a secure and transparent platform for exchanging data and conclusions across institutions.

[Original (created by authors)]

14.5 Patient-centric approach

14.5.1 *Patient empowerment through blockchain*

Blockchain technology gives patients more control over their health data, promoting openness, privacy, and autonomy in healthcare decision-making. Patients may use decentralized ledger technology to control access permissions, securely communicate information, and take a more active role in their treatment. Blockchain empowers patients by allowing them to own and control their health data. In conventional healthcare systems, patient data is frequently segregated and managed by healthcare practitioners or institutions. However, blockchain enables patients to securely keep their medical information on a decentralized ledger while maintaining ownership and control. This allows individuals to control who has access to their data, protecting privacy and confidentiality.

Furthermore, blockchain improves openness in healthcare transactions, giving patients a clear understanding of how their data is handled. Every contact with patient data is recorded on blockchain, resulting in an immutable audit trail. Patients can trace who has access to their information and for what purpose, which fosters confidence and accountability in the healthcare system. Blockchain also enables the safe and selective exchange of health information. Patients can use cryptographic methods to encrypt their data and provide access rights to select healthcare practitioners or researchers. This guarantees that sensitive information is safeguarded while allowing for cooperation and study. Furthermore, blockchain encourages patients to provide their data for research purposes. Patients may exchange anonymized health data on blockchain-based platforms, certain that their privacy is protected by encryption and decentralized storage. In exchange, patients may get remuneration or prizes for their efforts, resulting in a mutually beneficial environment for healthcare research [14].

Overall, blockchain technology empowers patients by providing ownership, transparency, and control over their health information. Patients may actively engage in their healthcare journey, make educated decisions, and contribute to medical research developments while keeping privacy and autonomy thanks to decentralized ledger technology. As blockchain evolves, its role in patient empowerment within the healthcare sector is set to grow even more.

14.5.2 *Privacy and security of patient records*

The privacy and security of patient records are paramount in health care, and blockchain technology offers innovative solutions to address these concerns. By leveraging cryptographic techniques and decentralized architecture, blockchain ensures the confidentiality, integrity, and accessibility of patient data. Patient records stored on the blockchain are encrypted and accessible only to authorized parties, enhancing privacy protection. Moreover, the immutable nature of blockchain transactions prevents unauthorized modifications or tampering with patient records, ensuring data integrity. Access controls and consent management mechanisms enable patients to control who can view their medical information, empowering them with greater privacy rights. Blockchain's distributed ledger eliminates single points of failure and reduces the risk of data breaches, as there is no central repository vulnerable to cyberattacks. Additionally, audit trails provided by blockchain enable

TABLE 14.4 Privacy and security measures of patient records in blockchain technology

Aspect	Description
Decentralization	Patient records kept on a decentralized blockchain network are spread across several nodes, eliminating the possibility of a single point of failure and illegal access.
Cryptographic Techniques	Blockchain secures patient data using cryptographic techniques such as encryption and hashing, guaranteeing that it stays secret and tamper-proof.
Immutable Ledger	Patient records that have been stored on the blockchain are immutable, which means they cannot be edited or removed. This function protects the integrity and validity of health data.
Access Control	Blockchain allows patients to manage access permissions to their health information using private keys, allowing them to give or deny access to certain people or institutions.
Transparency	Every transaction or access to patient information is publicly recorded on the blockchain, resulting in an auditable trail that increases responsibility and confidence in the system.
Data Ownership	Patients maintain ownership of their health data stored on the blockchain, providing them more choice over who may access, use, or share their information, hence improving privacy rights.

[Original (created by authors)]

transparent tracking of data access and modifications, enhancing accountability and compliance with privacy regulations such as Health Insurance Portability and Accountability Act (HIPAA). Overall, blockchain technology strengthens the privacy and security of patient records, fostering trust and confidence in healthcare systems while promoting patient autonomy and data sovereignty. Table 14.4 describes the privacy and security measures of patient records in blockchain technology.

14.5.3 Patient-controlled access to health data

Patient-controlled access to health data is a fundamental feature of blockchain technology, allowing individuals to own and control their own health information. Here is how blockchain allows patients to manage access to health data:

- **Decentralized Storage:** Blockchain technology enables decentralized storage of health data, with patient records held across a network of nodes rather than a single centralized database. This decentralization decreases the danger of data breaches and illegal access, offering patients greater assurance about the security of their information.

- **Private Keys and Access Permissions:** Patients are provided with private keys, which are cryptographic keys that permit access to their health data recorded on the blockchain. With these private keys, patients have control over who gets access to their information and under what conditions. They can provide or revoke access permissions for healthcare professionals, researchers, and other approved entities as needed.
- **Selective Data Sharing:** Blockchain technology allows people to choose to share particular bits of their health data with various parties. Patients can create rules for data sharing using smart contracts or other techniques, such as designating which healthcare providers have access to certain medical information or how the data can be utilized. This guarantees that people have control over their information and may safeguard their privacy while allowing for critical healthcare contacts.
- **Auditable Access Logs:** Every access or transaction involving patient health data is stored on the blockchain in a transparent and immutable format. This generates an auditable access log, which patients may inspect to see who accessed their information and for what purpose. This transparency increases responsibility and confidence in the system, allowing patients to monitor and verify how their data is used.
- **Enhanced Data Ownership:** Patients maintain ownership and control over their health data when it is stored on a blockchain. This changes the focus from healthcare professionals controlling patient data to patients owning and managing their own data. Patients have the capacity to control how their data is shared, utilized, and accessed, giving them more autonomy and privacy rights.

Overall, blockchain technology allows patients to regulate access to health data by enabling decentralized storage, private keys for access control, selective data sharing options, auditable access logs, and improved data ownership. This places patients at the heart of their healthcare experience, giving them the ability to control and secure their sensitive health information.

14.6 Smart contracts in health care

14.6.1 Understanding smart contracts

Smart contracts in health care are self-executing agreements based on blockchain technology that automatically enforce and execute preset norms and conditions without the need for middlemen. These digital contracts allow for safe, transparent, and efficient transactions across healthcare systems, transforming many areas of healthcare operations and patient care. Smart contracts in health care can improve patient–provider relations, expedite administrative procedures, and enable safe data exchange. Smart contracts, for example, can automate insurance claims processing by validating eligibility, establishing coverage, and processing payments according to established criteria. This saves administrative overhead, decreases mistakes, and speeds up reimbursement for healthcare providers.

Smart contracts can also help healthcare stakeholders share data securely and transparently. Patients, for example, might use smart contracts to provide access to their medical data to certain healthcare professionals or researchers, ensuring that sensitive health information is only accessed by authorized parties. This protects patient privacy and confidentiality while encouraging collaboration and information sharing in healthcare service and research. Furthermore, smart contracts enable the automation and enforcement of patient care guidelines and treatment regimens. For example, in clinical studies, smart contracts may automatically monitor and enforce adherence to research protocols, assuring compliance with set criteria and lowering the chance of protocol violations. This increases the dependability and integrity of clinical trial data, resulting in more accurate research findings and speedier drug development procedures [15].

Overall, smart contracts have the ability to alter several elements of healthcare operations, such as administrative procedures, data sharing, and patient care standards. Smart contracts use blockchain technology to enable safe, transparent, and efficient transactions in health care, thereby improving the quality, efficiency, and accessibility of healthcare services for both patients and providers. To fully reap the benefits of smart contracts in health care, it is necessary to overcome issues such as regulatory compliance, interoperability, and data protection.

14.6.2 Applications of smart contracts in health care

Leveraging the transformative power of blockchain technology, smart contracts are emerging as a disruptive force in health care, poised to streamline administrative processes and empower patients. By automating tasks like insurance claim adjudication based on predefined criteria within the contract, smart contracts can expedite claim processing, reduce errors, and ensure faster reimbursements for patients and healthcare providers alike. Furthermore, smart contracts can enhance supply chain efficiency and security by facilitating real-time provenance tracking of pharmaceuticals and medical supplies, preventing counterfeiting, and enabling targeted recalls if necessary [16]. Beyond these operational improvements, smart contracts empower patients by granting them greater control over their healthcare data. Patients can leverage smart contracts to manage consent for clinical trial participation and ensure secure data sharing for research purposes. Additionally, smart contracts can play a pivotal role in personalized medicine by enabling the secure storage and management of genomic data, paving the way for the development of individualized treatment plans. The inherent immutability and security offered by blockchain technology underpins these advancements, fostering trust and transparency within the healthcare ecosystem. While still under development, smart contracts hold immense potential to revolutionize healthcare delivery by automating processes, enhancing security, and empowering patients to take a more active role in their care [17]. Table 14.5 describes the major applications of smart contracts in health care.

TABLE 14.5 Applications of smart contracts in health care

Application	Description
Insurance Claims Processing	Smart contracts automate insurance claim processing by validating eligibility, calculating coverage, and executing payments using predetermined criteria. This simplifies administrative operations, lowers mistakes, and speeds up reimbursements.
Patient Data Sharing	Smart contracts allow healthcare providers and researchers to share patient data in a safe and transparent manner. Patients can allow access to their medical records to certain parties, protecting privacy and confidentiality while encouraging collaboration.
Clinical Trials Management	Smart contracts automate and enforce adherence to research procedures and treatment regimens during clinical trials. They monitor participant interactions, initiate payments, and check compliance with set criteria, thereby increasing the dependability of study findings.
Credential Verification	Smart contracts simplify the credential verification process for healthcare workers by securely capturing and confirming credentials. They automate the verification of credentials, licenses, and certificates, lowering administrative overhead while maintaining correctness.
Telemedicine and Remote Patient Monitoring	Smart contracts provide for safe and transparent transactions in telemedicine and remote patient monitoring. They automate payment processing, appointment scheduling, and data exchange to ensure privacy and efficiency during remote healthcare encounters.
Medical IoT Device Management	Smart contracts provide for safe data management and automation in medical Internet of Things (IoT) devices. They govern data collection, processing, and sharing, assuring the accuracy and privacy of health information obtained via linked devices.
Pharmaceutical Authentication	Smart contracts ensure the validity of pharmaceutical items by storing transaction information on a blockchain ledger. They ensure traceability, minimize counterfeit pharmaceuticals, and increase patient safety by checking medication authenticity across the supply chain.

[Original (created by authors)]

14.6.3 Streamlining transactions and workflows

Blockchain technology provides numerous options for streamlining healthcare transactions and workflows, transforming operations that have previously been hampered by middlemen, inefficiency, and security issues. Here is how blockchain may improve healthcare transactions and workflows:

- **Claims Processing and Billing:** Blockchain simplifies insurance claims processing by automating verification, adjudication, and payment procedures using smart contracts. This saves administrative overhead, decreases mistakes, and speeds up reimbursement for healthcare providers.
- **Credentialing and Verification:** Blockchain makes credential verification easier for healthcare workers by securely storing and confirming credentials on a decentralized ledger. This simplifies the verification process, eliminates administrative overhead, and guarantees credentialing is accurate and reliable.
- **Supply Chain Management:** Blockchain improves transparency and traceability in pharmaceutical supply chains by tracking the transfer of pharmaceuticals from producer to patient. This lowers the danger of counterfeit pharmaceuticals, ensures medication integrity, and increases patient safety.
- **Patient Data Sharing:** Blockchain technology facilitates the secure and transparent sharing of patient data between healthcare practitioners and researchers. Smart contracts allow patients to provide particular parties access to their medical information, protecting privacy and confidentiality while encouraging collaboration.
- **Clinical Trials Management:** Blockchain automates and enforces adherence to research procedures and treatment programs throughout clinical trials. Smart contracts track participant interactions, trigger rewards, and assure compliance with set criteria, which improves the trustworthiness of study findings.
- **Telemedicine and Remote Patient Monitoring:** Blockchain automates payment processing, appointment scheduling, and data exchange, making telemedicine and remote patient monitoring transactions more secure. This provides privacy and efficiency during remote healthcare encounters.
- **Drug Authentication:** Blockchain verifies the authenticity of pharmaceutical products by recording transactions. Blockchain validates the pharmaceutical items by storing transaction information on a blockchain ledger. This maintains traceability, minimizes counterfeit pharmaceuticals, and promotes patient safety by validating medication authenticity across the supply chain.
- **Administrative Processes:** Blockchain simplifies administrative procedures, including appointment scheduling, referrals, and medical record administration, by eliminating paperwork, increasing data accuracy, and reducing the need for intermediaries.

14.7 Case studies: Blockchain implementation in health care

14.7.1 Successful deployments in health care

Blockchain technology has sparked widespread interest in the healthcare industry because of its promise to transform data management, security, and interoperability. Several successful blockchain implementations in health care highlight the technology's capacity to address significant industry concerns while also improving patient outcomes. This case study looks at significant examples of successful blockchain installations in healthcare contexts.

14.7.1.1 Case study 1: MedRec

MedRec is a blockchain-based solution created by MIT researchers to solve fragmentation and interoperability issues in EHRs. The solution gives individuals complete control over their medical records, which are safely saved on the blockchain network. Smart contracts enable healthcare professionals to seek access to patient records while maintaining data privacy and transparency. MedRec has demonstrated encouraging outcomes in terms of data accessibility, administrative load reduction, and increased patient participation.

14.7.1.2 Case study 2: Guardtime

Guardtime, a cybersecurity company, worked with Estonia's e-Health Authority to utilize blockchain technology to protect patient health information. The KSI Blockchain technology maintains the integrity and immutability of health data by timestamping and hashing each blockchain record. This deployment greatly decreased the danger of data breaches and illegal access, boosting trust in Estonia's healthcare system.

14.7.1.3 Case study 3: Medicalchain

Medicalchain is a blockchain-based network that allows patients to securely store and exchange medical information with healthcare providers. The platform makes use of smart contracts to make transactions visible and auditable, guaranteeing that patient data stays private and tamper-proof. Medicalchain has been successfully applied in a variety of healthcare settings, including hospitals and clinics, to improve data accessibility and interoperability while protecting patient anonymity.

14.7.1.4 Case study 4: Solve.Care

Solve.Care is a blockchain-powered healthcare platform designed to reduce administrative operations and improve care coordination. The platform leverages smart contracts to manage healthcare payments, visits, and insurance claims, lowering administrative expenses and increasing efficiency. Solve. treatment has been implemented in a number of healthcare institutions globally, proving its potential to simplify workflows and improve patient access to excellent treatment.

These case studies illustrate successful blockchain implementations in health care, demonstrating the technology's ability to overcome long-standing difficulties and change healthcare delivery. By embracing blockchain's data security, transparency, and interoperability features, healthcare businesses may enhance patient outcomes, streamline workflows, and drive industry innovation. As blockchain use grows, it is likely to play a more important role in determining the future of health care.

14.7.2 Improved interoperability and transparency

Interoperability and transparency are key difficulties in health care since health data is scattered and healthcare systems are complicated. Blockchain technology is a viable option because it provides a secure, decentralized ledger that allows healthcare stakeholders to share data in a transparent and interoperable manner. This case study examines a successful blockchain application in health care that aims to improve interoperability and transparency. The Health Information Exchange (HIE) Consortium is a collaborative effort among several healthcare institutions, including hospitals, clinics, insurers, and government agencies, to improve the flow of health information throughout the healthcare ecosystem. Prior to deploying blockchain technology, the HIE Consortium experienced difficulties with data silos, interoperability, and data privacy and security [18].

The HIE Consortium developed a blockchain-based platform to solve these issues and promote interoperability and transparency in healthcare data sharing. The technology runs on a permissioned blockchain network, with member companies keeping a shared record of health data transactions. Smart contracts are used to provide the rules and rights for accessing and exchanging health information, providing openness and accountability.

Key Features:

- **Decentralized Data Sharing:** The blockchain technology facilitates decentralized data sharing among healthcare institutions, allowing for the frictionless transmission of health information while ensuring data integrity and security.
- **Immutable Audit Trail:** Every transaction on the blockchain is tamper-proof and unchangeable, giving a clear audit trail of data access and sharing actions. This improves responsibility and confidence among the involved organizations.
- **Patient-Centric Data Ownership:** Patients have greater control over access to their health information with digital identities and blockchain-based

permission processes. They can allow or remove access to their data while maintaining privacy and confidentiality.

• **Interoperability Standards Compliance:** The blockchain platform adheres to interoperability standards such as HL7 FHIR, assuring compatibility with existing healthcare systems and enabling easy data transmission across diverse platforms.

Results:

• **Improved Data Interoperability:** Blockchain technology has substantially enhanced data interoperability across healthcare companies, allowing for more efficient and effective care coordination and delivery.
• **Enhanced Transparency:** The transparency of the blockchain ledger has strengthened confidence and collaboration among participating companies, resulting in better data sharing and decision-making.
• **Strengthened Data Security:** The use of blockchain technology has improved data security and privacy, lowering the likelihood of data breaches and illegal access to critical health information.

The HIE Consortium's effective deployment of blockchain technology highlights how it might promote interoperability and transparency in healthcare data sharing. Healthcare firms may overcome current problems by utilizing blockchain's decentralized and immutable ledger to establish a more connected and efficient healthcare ecosystem. As blockchain use increases, it is likely to play an important role in driving innovation and revolution in healthcare data administration and exchange.

14.7.3   *Lessons learned from existing implementations*

As blockchain technology gains acceptance in the healthcare business, it is critical to review current deployments to find significant takeaways and best practices. This case study examines multiple blockchain applications in healthcare settings, highlighting the lessons learned from each. A healthcare company, XYZ Hospital, deployed a blockchain-based medical record management system to solve data security, interoperability, and patient access concerns. The system attempted to build a decentralized and transparent platform for securely storing and exchanging patient health information among healthcare providers.

XYZ Hospital cooperated with technology partners to create and launch a blockchain-based medical record management system. The system used a permissioned blockchain network in which participating healthcare providers kept a shared ledger of patient health information. Smart contracts were utilized to create access rights and data-sharing policies, which ensured privacy and security.

Key Features:

- **Decentralized Data Storage:** The blockchain-based approach enabled decentralized storage of patient health records, eliminating reliance on centralized systems and lowering the risk of data breaches.
- **Secure Data Sharing:** Smart contracts provided safe and auditable data sharing between healthcare providers, ensuring that only authorized parties had access to patient health information.
- **Patient-Controlled Access:** Patients were given authority over access to their health information via digital identities and blockchain-based permission processes, which improved privacy and openness.
- **Immutable Audit Trail:** Every transaction on the blockchain was tamper-proof and unchangeable, resulting in a clear audit trail of data access and sharing activities.

Lessons Learned:

- **Regulatory Compliance:** Compliance with healthcare standards, such as HIPAA in the United States, is critical for deploying blockchain systems in health care. Ensuring that the system meets regulatory criteria is critical to protecting patient privacy and data security.
- **User Education and Adoption:** Healthcare practitioners and patients need education and training to understand how to use blockchain-based solutions properly. User adoption can be difficult and continuous assistance and training are required to encourage uptake and utilization.
- **Interoperability with Existing Systems:** Integrating blockchain solutions into existing healthcare systems and technology might be challenging. Interoperability and compatibility with historical systems are critical for enabling seamless data interchange and workflow integration.
- **Scalability and Performance:** Scalability and performance are essential factors when deploying blockchain systems in health care, especially as the amount of health data increases. A successful deployment requires the blockchain network to be capable of handling massive quantities of transactions while maintaining performance.

The case study of XYZ Hospital's blockchain-based medical record management system emphasizes key lessons from previous healthcare implementations. Healthcare firms may maximize the benefits of blockchain technology while limiting possible problems by prioritizing regulatory compliance, user education, interoperability, scalability, and performance. Moving forward, applying these lessons will be critical for effective blockchain applications in health care.

14.8 Security and regulatory considerations

14.8.1 Addressing security concerns in blockchain

Blockchain technology has various benefits, including increased security, transparency, and decentralization. However, it, like all other technologies, is vulnerable to security threats. Addressing these issues is critical to ensuring the ongoing acceptance and success of blockchain solutions across a variety of industries, including health care, banking, supply chain, and others. We will look at some of the most common blockchain security challenges and how to address them.

- **51% Attacks:** A 51% assault happens when a single entity or group gets control of more than half of the computational power on a blockchain network, allowing them to influence transactions. To avoid this danger, blockchain networks use consensus techniques like PoW or PoS, which require a considerable amount of processing power or stake to carry out an attack. Furthermore, growing network involvement and diversity may make it more difficult for attackers to gain majority control.
- **Private Key Management:** Private keys are required for accessing and managing digital assets on a blockchain. A misplaced or compromised private key might result in unlawful access and asset theft. Secure key management measures, including the use of hardware wallets, multisignature wallets, and cold storage solutions, can help prevent private keys from being stolen or lost. Furthermore, using strong authentication methods and encryption protocols can improve the security of private key management.
- **Smart Contract Vulnerabilities:** Smart contracts, which are self-executing programs that operate on blockchain networks, are vulnerable and may be abused by attackers. Common vulnerabilities include reentrancy attacks, integer overflows/underflows, and unauthorized access to sensitive data. Conducting extensive code reviews, using established security standards like those defined in the OpenZeppelin library, and undertaking rigorous testing, such as fuzz testing and formal verification, may all help uncover and mitigate smart contract flaws.
- **Data Privacy and Confidentiality:** While blockchain enables openness and immutability, it also raises worries about data privacy and confidentiality, especially in areas like health care and finance that handle sensitive information. Implementing privacy-enhancing approaches such as zero-knowledge proofs, homomorphic encryption, and private/permissioned blockchain networks can help secure sensitive data while maximizing the benefits of blockchain technology.

- **Scalability and Performance:** As blockchain networks expand in size and popularity, scalability and performance become major problems. Increased transaction volume can cause network congestion, delays, and increased costs. Implementing scaling solutions such as sharding, layer-2 protocols (e.g., Lightning Network), and consensus algorithm modifications can assist enhance blockchain networks' throughput and speed while maintaining security.
- **Regulatory Compliance:** Blockchain technology operates in a complicated regulatory environment that differs by country and sector. Compliance with rules such as KYC (know your customer), AML (anti-money laundering), and GDPR (General Data Protection Regulation) is critical for ensuring legal and regulatory compliance. Collaborating with legal professionals and regulatory agencies, adopting compliance frameworks, and adhering to industry best practices may all help you handle regulatory difficulties successfully.

Addressing security risks in blockchain necessitates a multifaceted strategy that includes technological, organizational, and legislative safeguards. Blockchain stakeholders may reduce risks and enhance confidence in blockchain technology by employing strong security procedures, privacy-enhancing approaches, and maintaining compliance with relevant legislation. Continued research, cooperation, and innovation are crucial for staying ahead of new risks and maintaining blockchain's long-term security and sustainability.

14.8.2 Compliance with healthcare regulations

Compliance with healthcare legislation is an important factor when deploying blockchain technology in healthcare settings. Blockchain solutions must follow several standards to maintain patient privacy, data security, and legal compliance. The following are some important healthcare regulations that blockchain systems must address:

- **Health Insurance Portability and Accountability Act (HIPAA):** HIPAA establishes standards for the security of sensitive patient health information (PHI) and requires healthcare companies to employ measures to maintain PHI's confidentiality, integrity, and availability. To ensure patient privacy and security, healthcare blockchain systems must adhere to HIPAA laws by adopting strong encryption, access restrictions, and data management policies.
- **General Data Protection Regulation (GDPR):** GDPR is a European Union (EU) legislation governing the processing and protection of personal data. It applies to any entity that collects or processes personal data from EU citizens, regardless of its location. Blockchain systems that handle personal

data of EU individuals must adhere to GDPR regulations, which include getting express consent for data processing, implementing data protection measures, and safeguarding data subject rights such as the right to deletion and access.

- **Health Information Technology for Economic and Clinical Health (HITECH) Act:** The HITECH Act encourages the use of EHRs while strengthening HIPAA privacy and security standards. Blockchain solutions in health care must meet HITECH criteria, which include breach reporting, PHI encryption, and the deployment of access restrictions and audit trails.
- **21st Century Cures Act:** The 21st Century Cures Act seeks to expedite medical product development and innovation while protecting patient privacy and safety. Blockchain solutions for health care must adhere to the Cures Act's interoperability and information blocking rules, which encourage the smooth interchange of electronic health information among healthcare providers, patients, and other stakeholders.
- **Drug Supply Chain Security Act (DSCSA):** DSCSA specifies criteria for tracking and verifying prescription medications as they transit through the pharmaceutical supply chain. Blockchain technology can increase traceability and transparency in the medication supply chain by securely recording transactions and confirming the legitimacy of pharmaceuticals.

Healthcare firms that use blockchain technology should:

- Conduct a comprehensive regulatory investigation to identify the precise regulations that apply to their jurisdiction and use case.
- Implement technical and organizational safeguards to ensure patient privacy, data security, and confidentiality.
- Collaborate with legal experts, regulatory agencies, and industry stakeholders to ensure compliance with applicable legislation and standards.
- Continuously monitor changes in healthcare legislation and modify blockchain technologies to ensure compliance.

By proactively addressing regulatory constraints, healthcare firms may reap the benefits of blockchain technology while maintaining legal compliance and preserving patient rights and privacy.

14.8.3   *Legal and ethical implications*

The adoption of blockchain technology in health care raises various legal and ethical implications that require careful consideration. From a legal standpoint, compliance with existing regulations such as HIPAA and GDPR is essential to ensure patient privacy and data protection. However, the decentralized nature of blockchain poses challenges in terms of regulatory compliance, as jurisdictional issues and governance frameworks may be unclear. Moreover, the use of blockchain for health data management requires robust consent mechanisms and transparency to ensure patient autonomy and informed decision-making. Ethically, concerns arise regarding data ownership, as patients may not fully understand the implications of granting access to their medical information on a blockchain network. Additionally, the permanence of blockchain records raises questions about the right to be forgotten and data erasure, as individuals may seek to remove or modify sensitive health information. Furthermore, the potential for discrimination and stigmatization based on immutable health data underscores the importance of ethical considerations in blockchain implementation. Addressing these legal and ethical challenges requires collaboration between healthcare stakeholders, policymakers, and technologists to develop appropriate governance frameworks, standards, and guidelines that balance innovation with patient rights and welfare [19]. Table 14.6 describes the legal and ethical implications of blockchain technology.

TABLE 14.6 Legal and ethical implications of blockchain technology

Legal implications	Ethical implications
Compliance with Healthcare Regulations: Blockchain solutions in health care must adhere to HIPAA, GDPR, HITECH, and other standards to ensure patient privacy, data security, and legal compliance.	Patient Privacy and Consent: Blockchain implementations must emphasize patient privacy by obtaining express authorization for data sharing and processing. Patients should have control over their health data and be aware of how it is used and shared.
Liability and Accountability: Legal frameworks for blockchain-enabled healthcare systems must handle liability problems such as data breaches, mistakes, and misconduct. Clear norms and accountability procedures are critical for addressing legal issues and ensuring patient safety.	Data Integrity and Accuracy: Ensuring the integrity and quality of health data stored on the blockchain is critical for preserving confidence and transparency in healthcare transactions. Ethical concerns include avoiding manipulation, illegal access, and disinformation in the blockchain ledger.
Intellectual Property Rights: Legal frameworks should cover intellectual property rights associated with blockchain-based healthcare breakthroughs, such as patents, copyrights, and license agreements. Intellectual property protection is vital for encouraging innovation and investment in blockchain technology.	Equity and Access: Ethical issues include providing equal access to blockchain-enabled healthcare services and resolving gaps in healthcare delivery. Blockchain solutions should focus inclusion and accessibility in order to provide fair health outcomes for all people.

(Continued)

TABLE 14.6 (Continued)

Legal implications	Ethical implications
Jurisdictional and Cross-Border Issues: In blockchain-enabled healthcare systems, jurisdictional disparities and cross-border data transfers may present legal problems. To allow cross-border interoperability and data interchange, legislative frameworks must be harmonized and jurisdictional challenges addressed.	Transparency and Trust: Blockchain technology can improve transparency and trust in healthcare transactions by keeping an immutable record of data transfers. Promoting transparency, accountability, and trustworthiness in blockchain-enabled healthcare systems is an ethical aspect that may help patients and stakeholders feel more confident.

[Original (created by authors)]

14.9   Challenges and future directions

While blockchain technology offers a revolutionary vision for health care, with the potential to securely store and manage patient data, streamline administrative processes, and empower patients, several hurdles need to be addressed before it can reach its full potential. Scalability issues currently plague existing blockchain platforms, which are struggling to handle the massive amount of data generated in the healthcare system. Additionally, seamless data exchange between different blockchain systems, a crucial aspect of interoperability, remains a challenge.

Beyond the technical hurdles, navigating the legal and regulatory landscape surrounding blockchain in health care is paramount. Unclear regulations regarding data privacy, ownership in a decentralized ledger system, and the need for clear jurisdictional boundaries create uncertainty for implementation. Furthermore, the technical complexity of implementing and maintaining blockchain infrastructure can be a barrier for some healthcare organizations, requiring significant technical expertise. Finally, fostering user adoption hinges on building trust and awareness in this new technology. Both healthcare professionals and patients need to understand the benefits and potential risks associated with blockchain to drive wider acceptance.

However, the future of blockchain in health care is brimming with promise. Researchers are actively developing next-generation blockchain platforms specifically designed for health care, with improved scalability and transaction processing capabilities to handle the industry's data demands. Industry-wide collaboration is fostering efforts to establish clear standards and protocols for data exchange between different blockchain systems, ensuring seamless interoperability. On the regulatory front, governments and regulatory bodies are working with stakeholders to develop clear legal frameworks

TABLE 14.7 Challenges of blockchain technology

Challenge	Description
Regulatory Compliance	Adhering to sophisticated regulatory frameworks like HIPAA and GDPR is a huge task. Integrating blockchain while being compliant with existing rules necessitates careful navigation.
Interoperability	Creating seamless connectivity between diverse healthcare systems remains a challenge. Blockchain's ability to integrate data silos is hampered by the absence of common protocols and data formats throughout the healthcare environment.
Scalability	Scalability limits, especially in public blockchains, impede wider adoption. As transaction volumes rise, network congestion and longer processing times may limit blockchain's usefulness in managing healthcare data.
Data Privacy	Maintaining patient privacy while allowing for open data exchange is a tricky balance. Blockchain's intrinsic openness may collide with data privacy requirements, forcing novel privacy-preserving methods.

[Original (created by authors)]

that address data privacy, ownership, and security concerns within the context of blockchain in health care. Finally, user-friendly interfaces and educational programs are being developed to improve accessibility and bridge the knowledge gap for both healthcare professionals and patients.

By overcoming these challenges through ongoing research, collaboration between stakeholders, and a focus on responsible implementation, blockchain has the potential to revolutionize health care. This transformation could lead to a more efficient system that streamlines administrative tasks, a transparent system that fosters trust and accountability, and a patient-centric system that empowers individuals to take a more active role in managing their health data and care. Table 14.7 describes the challenges of blockchain technology.

Future directions:

- **Regulatory Alignment:** Collaboration between industry stakeholders and authorities is required to provide clear rules for blockchain use in health care. Creating regulatory sandboxes and frameworks for blockchain technology can encourage innovation while maintaining compliance.
- **Interoperability Standards:** Standardization initiatives to develop interoperable data formats and communication methods are critical. The widespread use of interoperability standards can promote smooth data interchange and improve patient care coordination.

- **Scalability Solutions:** Research and development initiatives to improve blockchain scalability are critical. Implementing layer-2 scaling solutions, such as sidechains and state channels, can reduce congestion and increase transaction throughput.
- **Privacy-Preserving Technologies:** Innovative privacy-preserving technologies, including as zero-knowledge proofs and secure multiparty computing, can solve privacy issues while using blockchain's transparency and auditability benefits.
- **Public-Private Collaborations:** Collaborations between public and private institutions can accelerate blockchain use in health care. Public sector initiatives to invest in blockchain infrastructure and encourage business engagement can help to expedite innovation and address common concerns.

Decentralizing health using blockchain in health care has tremendous promise, but it is accompanied by significant hurdles. By resolving regulatory, interoperability, scalability, and privacy problems, as well as adopting collaborative approaches, blockchain in health care can lead to greater data sharing, better patient outcomes, and a more decentralized and patient-centric healthcare ecosystem.

14.10 Blockchain's role in medical research

Blockchain technology shows great promise for transforming medical research by improving data integrity, security, and cooperation. Its decentralized and unchangeable ledger protects the integrity of research data by prohibiting tampering or manipulation. This builds confidence between researchers, institutions, and stakeholders. Furthermore, blockchain offers safe and transparent data sharing, allowing for collaboration beyond geographical borders. Researchers can access and verify data in real time, which simplifies the research process and speeds up scientific discoveries.

Smart contracts, or self-executing blockchain agreements, automate research agreements, funding distribution, and data-sharing protocols, lowering administrative overhead and assuring research protocol and regulatory compliance. Furthermore, blockchain-based platforms can incentivise data sharing via tokenization and incentive mechanisms, boosting participation and collaboration in research projects. Overall, blockchain's function in medical research goes beyond data management—it encourages openness, improves cooperation, and accelerates innovation, ultimately leading to a better knowledge of illnesses and patient outcomes.

14.10.1 Facilitating secure data sharing in clinical trials

Blockchain technology is a viable alternative for promoting safe data exchange in clinical trials, addressing issues such as data integrity, privacy, and cooperation. Here is how blockchain allows for safe data sharing in clinical trials:

- **Immutable Data Ledger:** Blockchain offers an immutable ledger that records data transactions in a tamper-proof way. Each transaction, whether data submission, access, or change, is cryptographically linked and timestamped to ensure the clinical trial data's integrity and transparency.
- **Enhanced Data Security:** Blockchain's decentralized architecture distributes data over a network of nodes, removing single points of failure and lowering the danger of data breaches or illegal access. Encryption methods help to secure sensitive data by ensuring that only authorized persons can access and read trial material.
- **Granular Access Control:** Smart contracts on the blockchain provide granular access control measures. Blockchain allows researchers, clinicians, and regulatory authorities to access, view, and modify data based on predefined criteria, ensuring compliance with data privacy regulations like HIPAA and GDPR.
- **Transparent Audit Trails:** Additionally, blockchain provides a transparent and auditable record of data transactions, providing a verifiable audit trail of access and sharing activities. This transparency increases responsibility and confidence among stakeholders, enabling real-time monitoring of data exchanges throughout the trial's duration.
- **Streamlined Collaboration:** Blockchain enables seamless cooperation among stakeholders in clinical trials, including researchers, sponsors, regulators, and participants. Data-sharing agreements and smart contracts automate cooperation methods, ensuring that all parties follow set data-sharing guidelines and schedules.
- **Data Tokenization and Incentives:** Blockchain-based platforms can tokenize clinical trial data, allowing participants to be rewarded with tokens or incentives for contributing data. This incentivizes data sharing and participation, encouraging broader involvement in clinical research while ensuring data privacy and security.

14.10.2 Accelerating research and development

Blockchain technology has the potential to greatly expedite R&D processes in a variety of industries, including health care, finance, and supply chain. Here is how blockchain speeds research and development:

- **Streamlined Collaboration:** Blockchain enables seamless cooperation among researchers, institutions, and stakeholders by offering a transparent and secure platform for data exchange and collaboration. Smart contracts automate cooperation agreements, guaranteeing that all parties follow set norms and standards, which accelerates research collaboration.

- **Enhanced Data Integrity and Trust:** The blockchain's unchangeable record preserves the integrity and transparency of research data, prohibiting tampering or manipulation. Researchers can trust the legitimacy of data stored on the blockchain, allowing for speedier decision-making and less time spent validating data integrity.
- **Efficient Intellectual Property Management:** Blockchain facilitates the transparent and secure administration of intellectual property (IP) rights, such as patents, copyrights, and licensing agreements. Smart contracts automate IP agreements and royalty payments, easing the IP management and licensing process and driving innovation by offering a clear and efficient framework for monetizing and safeguarding intellectual property.
- **Tokenization and Crowdfunding:** Blockchain-based systems can tokenize research initiatives, enabling academics to generate financing via token offers and crowdfunding campaigns. This democratizes access to finance and accelerates research by giving academics with new sources of cash and encourages collaboration between researchers and investors.
- **Decentralized Clinical Trials:** Blockchain facilitates decentralized clinical trials by securely recording patient data on the blockchain, ensuring data integrity, privacy, and transparency. Decentralized trials reduce the time and cost associated with traditional centralized trials, accelerate patient recruitment, and enable real-time monitoring of trial data, leading to faster insights and drug development.
- **Supply Chain Traceability:** In industries such as pharmaceuticals and food production, blockchain enhances supply chain traceability by recording the movement of goods from manufacturer to consumer. This transparency ensures product authenticity, reduces counterfeiting, and accelerates product development by enabling faster identification and resolution of supply chain issues.

Overall, blockchain technology accelerates research and development processes by streamlining collaboration, enhancing data integrity and trust, enabling efficient intellectual property management, facilitating crowdfunding, supporting decentralized clinical trials, and enhancing supply chain traceability. By leveraging blockchain's capabilities, organizations can unlock new opportunities for innovation, collaboration, and growth, leading to faster progress and advancements across various industries.

14.10.3 Collaborative opportunities

Blockchain technology presents numerous collaborative opportunities for medical research, fostering innovation, transparency, and efficiency across the research ecosystem. Here are some collaborative opportunities:

- **Data Sharing and Collaboration:** Blockchain enables secure and transparent data sharing among researchers, institutions, and stakeholders. Collaborative research initiatives can leverage blockchain platforms to securely share and access research data, accelerating scientific discovery and facilitating interdisciplinary collaborations.
- **Multi-Institutional Studies:** Blockchain facilitates multi-institutional studies by providing a decentralized and immutable ledger for securely recording and sharing research data. Researchers from different institutions can collaborate on large-scale studies, pooling resources and expertise to address complex research questions and advance medical knowledge.
- **Clinical Trial Collaboration:** Blockchain streamlines collaboration in clinical trials by providing a transparent and auditable record of trial data. Researchers, sponsors, regulators, and participants can collaborate more effectively, ensuring compliance with trial protocols, enhancing data integrity, and accelerating the pace of clinical research.
- **Intellectual Property Management:** Blockchain enhances collaboration in IP management by providing a transparent and secure platform for managing patents, copyrights, and licensing agreements. Researchers and institutions can collaborate on IP creation and commercialization, fostering innovation and maximizing the impact of research outcomes.
- **Crowdfunding and Funding Opportunities:** Blockchain-based platforms enable collaborative funding models such as token offerings and crowdfunding campaigns. Researchers can engage with a global community of investors and supporters, raising funds for research projects and accelerating the pace of innovation in medical research.
- **Decentralized Research Networks:** Blockchain enables the creation of decentralized research networks, in which scholars from across the world may cooperate on research projects without the need for centralized middlemen. Decentralized research networks encourage diversity, openness, and creativity while democratizing access to research opportunities and resources.
- **Supply Chain Collaboration:** Blockchain facilitates collaboration in supply chain management in industries such as pharmaceuticals and biotechnology by providing product visibility and traceability from start to end. Researchers, producers, distributors, and regulators may collaborate to ensure product authenticity, safety, and compliance across the supply chain.

Overall, blockchain technology opens up new opportunities for collaborative study in the medical field. By embracing blockchain capabilities, researchers and institutions may be able to collaborate more effectively, accelerate scientific discovery, and ultimately improve patient outcomes. Blockchain-driven collaborative efforts have the potential to transform medical research, resulting in breakthroughs in treatment, prevention, and healthcare delivery.

14.11 Conclusion

The future of blockchain in health care holds great promise for decentralizing health and revolutionizing business. Blockchain technology provides unparalleled opportunity to tackle long-standing issues including data fragmentation, interoperability, and patient privacy. Blockchain, by offering a secure, transparent, and irreversible platform for data management and collaboration, has the potential to transform healthcare delivery, research, and innovation. One of the primary advantages of blockchain in health care is its capacity to improve data integrity and security. The immutability of blockchain assures that health data is tamper-proof and reliable, lowering the danger of data breaches and illegal access. This increases confidence among patients, healthcare professionals, and other stakeholders, hence increasing openness and accountability in healthcare transactions.

Furthermore, blockchain facilitates seamless interoperability across diverse healthcare systems, allowing for the safe transmission of patient data across organizational borders. Blockchain promotes data sharing and cooperation by providing established protocols and data formats, allowing for more comprehensive and tailored medical care. Decentralized health using blockchain empowers people by providing them more control over their health data. Patients may securely keep and share their medical information, provide consent to data access, and engage in research projects, resulting in more patient-centric and participatory healthcare models.

Furthermore, blockchain speeds up medical research and innovation by easing cooperation, improving data integrity, and encouraging data exchange. Researchers may interact more efficiently, access greater data sets, and speed up scientific discovery, resulting in advances in treatment, prevention, and healthcare delivery. However, problems such as regulatory compliance, scalability, and privacy concerns must be overcome before blockchain can reach its full potential in health care. Collaboration among industry players, regulators, and politicians is required to provide clear norms, standards, and frameworks for blockchain use in health care. Blockchain has a promising future in health care, with dramatic prospects to decentralize health, enhance patient outcomes, and drive industry innovation. By adopting blockchain technology and addressing existing barriers, we can build a more integrated, transparent, and patient-centric healthcare ecosystem that benefits everyone.

References

1. Agbo, C. C., Mahmoud, Q. H., & Eklund, J. M. (2019). Blockchain technology in healthcare: A systematic review. Healthcare, 7(2), 56.
2. Azaria, A., Ekblaw, A., Vieira, T., & Lippman, A. (2016). MedRec: Using blockchain for medical data access and permission management. Proceedings of the 2nd International Conference on Open and Big Data, 25–30.
3. Benchoufi, M., & Ravaud, P. (2017). Blockchain technology for improving clinical research quality. Trials, 18(1), 335.
4. Dagher, G. G., Mohler, J., Milojkovic, M., & Marella, P. B. (2018). Ancile: Privacy-preserving framework for access control and interoperability of electronic health records using blockchain technology. Sustainable Cities and Society, 39, 283–297.
5. Dubovitskaya, A., Xu, Z., Ryu, S., & Schumacher, M. (2017). Secure and trustable electronic medical records sharing using blockchain. AMIA Annual Symposium Proceedings, 2017, 650.
6. Ekblaw, A., Azaria, A., Halamka, J. D., & Lippman, A. (2016). A case study for blockchain in healthcare: "MedRec" prototype for electronic health records and medical research data. Proceedings of IEEE Open & Big Data Conference, 228–231.
7. Fan, K., Wang, S., Ren, Y., Li, H., & Yang, Y. (2018). MedBlock: Efficient and secure medical data sharing via blockchain. Journal of Medical Systems, 42(8), 136.
8. Griggs, K. N., Ossipova, O., Kohlios, C. P., & Baccarini, A. N. (2018). A practical implementation of blockchain technology for secure electronic health records sharing across healthcare providers. AMIA Annual Symposium Proceedings, 2018, 729–738.
9. Hao, H., Liu, M., Gao, Y., Wang, Y., & Zhang, X. (2020). Blockchain-based electronic medical record system with access control. Journal of Medical Systems, 44(3), 71.
10. Hasan, M. R., & Yamamoto, G. (2019). Blockchain technology and healthcare: A comprehensive review and directions for future research. IEEE Access, 7, 194779–194797.
11. Krawiec, R. J. (2018). The future of healthcare: Decentralized and autonomous. Journal of Medical Internet Research, 20(10), e10518.
12. Kuo, T. T., Kim, H. E., & Ohno-Machado, L. (2017). Blockchain distributed ledger technologies for biomedical and health care applications. Journal of the American Medical Informatics Association, 24(6), 1211–1220.
13. Mense, A., Winkler, C., Janiesch, C., & Kolb, J. (2018). Securing patient data in the blockchain: A review of system architectures. IEEE Access, 6, 31577–31591.
14. Smith, K., & Nugent, T. (2019). Blockchain in healthcare: Decentralizing data to improve privacy, security, and interoperability. IEEE Transactions on Emerging Topics in Computing, 7(3), 442–451.
15. Yaqoob, I., Hashem, I. A. T., Ahmed, E., & Shuja, J. (2019). Blockchain in healthcare: Opportunities, challenges, and future directions. Journal of Network and Computer Applications, 135, 62–75.

16. Yuce, B., & Güneri, A. F. (2018). Use of blockchain in healthcare: A systematic literature review. Journal of Medical Systems, 42(7), 1–16.
17. Yue, X., Wang, H., Jin, D., Li, M., & Jiang, W. (2016). Healthcare data gateways: Found healthcare intelligence on blockchain with novel privacy risk control. Journal of Medical Systems, 40(10), 218.
18. Zheng, Z., Xie, S., Dai, H. N., Chen, X., & Wang, H. (2017). Blockchain challenges and opportunities: A survey. International Journal of Web and Grid Services, 14(4), 352–375.
19. Zheng, Z., Xie, S., Dai, H. N., Chen, X., & Wang, H. (2018). An overview of blockchain technology: Architecture, consensus, and future trends. IEEE International Congress on Big Data, 557–564.

15

THE ADOPTION OF BLOCKCHAIN TECHNOLOGY FOR RECRUITMENT PRACTICES IN HEALTHCARE INDUSTRIES

A Systematic Review

Rubee Singh, Kamalesh Ravesangar, Sivachandran Narayanan, and Mrinalini Choudhary

15.1 Introduction

"Blockchain" also known as distributed ledger technology (DLT), significantly plays an important role in financial services institutions. A blockchain is a decentralized collection of documents, known as "blocks," connected together by mining. This approach transforms pending transactions into mathematical puzzles. Miners (people) use computer systems to solve puzzles and generate unique hashes (letters and numbers) for each block [1]. Each block includes a cryptographic hash from the preceding block, a timestamp, and transaction data. It also holds information from earlier blocks and transactions, forming a network or chain. Changing the contents inside a block might cause a chain reaction, potentially freezing the entire blockchain. When the blockchain processes information, all computers in the network lock in at the same time, establishing a permanent and unchangeable digital record. Each blockchain system governs who may add new blocks to the chain and how the process is carried out. Blockchain's features include the ability to share data and transactions over an immutable network, leading to increased transparency and security [2].

The concept of blockchain is a decentralized transaction and data management technology introduced by Satoshi Nakamoto. It is a supporting mechanism, associated and mostly utilized for cryptocurrencies such as Bitcoin and financial transactions [3]. However, blockchain technology is gaining popularity in other areas over the last decade for government, energy, entertainment, manufacturing, and health care because of its increased security and privacy benefits [4]. Decentralization, privacy, and security are the key attributes of blockchain technology that offer significant advantages to healthcare applications. By leveraging blockchain, healthcare systems can guarantee

DOI: 10.1201/9781003483113-15

secure access to medical data for patients and all relevant stakeholders, including insurance companies, hospitals, and doctors. The ability to share healthcare data without the risk of jeopardizing users' privacy and data security is one essential step to make the healthcare system smarter and improve the quality of healthcare services and users' experiences [5]. Using blockchain technology, the notion of decentralization might be applied to large-scale data management in an electronic medical record (EMR) system, ensuring auditability, interoperability, and accessibility through a comprehensive log. Modern society requires new tools (e.g., distributed ledger and smart contracts) for sharing data among patients, doctors, and healthcare professionals by giving them control over the data and allowing smarter cooperation. In this situation, utilizing blockchain technology can resolve integrity, data privacy, security, and fraud issues; increase patient health autonomy; and provide access to better services [6]. Table 15.1 exhibits the benefits of blockchain to healthcare applications.

TABLE 15.1 Benefits of blockchain to healthcare applications

Decentralization	The decentralized nature of health care demands a decentralized management system. Blockchain can serve as the backbone for managing health data, providing controlled access to stakeholders without a central authority, fostering a collaborative and secure global health data environment.
Improved data security and privacy	Blockchain's immutability enhances the security of health data by preventing alteration or corruption. Data stored on the blockchain is encrypted, timestamped, and arranged chronologically. The use of cryptographic keys safeguards patient identity and privacy in the storage of health information.
Health data ownership	Patients should have ownership and control over their health data to prevent misuse. Blockchain, with robust cryptographic protocols and smart contracts, provides the necessary assurance and means for patients to detect and prevent unauthorized use of their health data by other stakeholders.
Availability/ robustness	Blockchain ensures the availability of health data by replicating records across multiple nodes. This robust and resilient system safeguards against data losses, corruption, and certain security attacks on data availability.
Transparency and trust	Blockchain's open and transparent nature fosters trust in distributed healthcare applications, encouraging acceptance among healthcare stakeholders.
Data verifiability	Blockchain allows verification of the integrity and validity of records without accessing the plaintext. This feature is particularly valuable in healthcare applications such as pharmaceutical supply chain management and insurance claim processing, where record verification is essential.

[Original (created by authors)]

On the other hand, blockchain technology also plays an important role in human resource (HR) management, particularly in the recruitment process. However, the empirical research specifically addressing the adoption of blockchain technology for recruitment practices in healthcare industries is limited. Yet the healthcare industry is facing several challenges in their recruitment and retention of potential candidates [6]. Therefore, it is vital to discuss the merit of blockchain's role and how it does significantly ease the recruitment process. The following sections will discuss the importance of blockchain in the recruitment process.

15.2 The evolution of blockchain technology

The blockchain technology holds the potential to completely transform the way businesses operate. Its impact can be felt across various sectors, including finance, manufacturing, and education. In 2009, Satoshi Nakamoto published a renowned white paper that outlined the capabilities of this technology. The paper highlighted how the decentralized nature of blockchain could enhance digital trust by eliminating the need for a central authority [7]. Since Nakamoto's departure, Bitcoin development has been taken over by other core application developers, leading to the evolution of DLT and the emergence of new blockchain applications. The growth of Bitcoin and other cryptocurrencies has garnered significant attention while also posing a threat to the foundations of the financial system. Nakamoto's original intention was to challenge the global financial crisis that severely impacted not only the United States but also the global economy, making it one of the most severe crises in history.

Blockchain, a technology that has revolutionized various industries, was actually invented in 1991. Its history can be traced back to the early 1990s when two researchers, Stuart Haber and W. Scott Stornetta, played significant roles in its development. Both Haber and Stornetta are recognized as coinventors of blockchain technology [8]. Stornetta's work particularly influenced several aspects of the Bitcoin blockchain architecture. They introduced the concept of a cryptographically secured network of blocks. The first mention of blockchain architecture can be found in a publication coauthored by Stornetta. This publication described a digital hierarchy system called a "block chain" that utilized digital timestamps to order transactions. Their aim was to create a chain of blocks that would be cryptographically secured, ensuring that no one could tamper with the timestamps of documents. In 1992, they further improved the block chain system by incorporating Merkle trees, which enhanced efficiency and allowed for the collection of more documents on a single block [9].

Furthermore, in 1998, Nick Szabo embarked on the development of a decentralized digital currency known as Bit Gold. However, it was not until

2009 that the first blockchain was implemented by developer Satoshi Nakamoto. Nakamoto is renowned for creating the world's first digital currency,
Bitcoin. Nakamoto represents a collective of developers who collaborated
to utilize blockchain technology in the creation of Bitcoin. Bitcoin utilized
the peer-to-peer network and blockchain technology as a ledger for all Bitcoin transactions. Nakamoto's identity remains shrouded in mystery, as it is
uncertain whether Nakamoto is an individual or a group of individuals who
worked on Bitcoin, which is widely recognized as the pioneering application
of DLT. Additionally, over time, blockchain technology has evolved to possess several crucial features. One such feature is its ability to facilitate a shift
from a centralized transactional model, which has traditionally prevailed,
to a decentralized one. This transition to a distributed system offers a more
robust and reliable solution compared to the conventional centralized authority's provision to its stakeholders, such as a government to its citizens
[10]. Figure 15.1 summarizes the distinctions between standard transactions
and blockchain transactions.

The three main advantages of a blockchain are transparency, authentication, and auditing abilities. The evolution of blockchain technology can be
divided into two phases. The first phase spans from 1991 to 2013. During
this period, the bankruptcy of Lehman Brothers in 2008 had a significant
impact on the United States, estimated to cost trillions of dollars. This event
triggered a series of events that led many countries into economic recession
or depression. In 2008, Bitcoin was introduced as the first application of
blockchain technology. One of the contributing factors to the crisis was the

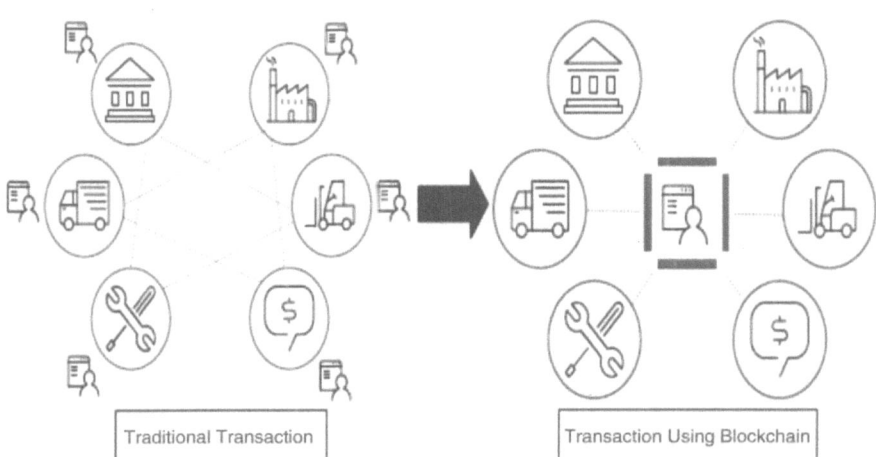

FIGURE 15.1   Standard versus blockchain-based transactional models.
[Original (created by authors)]

centralized payment and monetary system, which relied on clearinghouses as intermediaries between buyers and sellers, assuming the risk of defaults. Bitcoin, on the other hand, is an innovative technology that allows banks to settle accounts directly without the need for centralized entities. It operates on a global scale and is considered the first decentralized currency system, utilizing cryptographic proofs of work, digital signatures, and peer-to-peer networking to maintain a distributed ledger of transactions. Since the emergence of Bitcoin, numerous applications have been developed, all aiming to leverage the principles and capabilities of blockchain technology. As a result, the history of blockchain is filled with a wide range of applications that have emerged alongside the evolution of technology. The second phase of blockchain, known as Contracts, covers the years between 2013 and 2015. Ethereum, developed by Vitalik Buterin, was introduced during this phase as a new public blockchain with enhanced functionalities compared to Bitcoin. This development marked a pivotal moment in the timeline of blockchain evolution, as Ethereum allowed for the recording of other assets, such as contracts, on the blockchain. In 2015, the launch of the Ethereum blockchain marked a significant milestone in the development of cryptocurrency. With its innovative features, Ethereum not only served as a digital currency but also transformed into a robust platform for creating decentralized applications. This expansion of functionalities enabled the utilization of smart contracts, which facilitated the execution of diverse tasks. As a result, Ethereum emerged as one of the most prominent applications of blockchain technology [11].

15.3 Blockchain applications in health care and human resource management (HRM)

Blockchain's significance in health care lies in its ability to enhance data security and integrity. It offers promising solutions by exploring applications to improve the interoperability of patient health information across healthcare organizations. The focus is on maintaining data privacy and security in the process [12].

- **Electronic Medical Records (EMRs):** Blockchain technology has the potential to alter the way EMRs are managed and connected. While the words *EMRs* and *EHRs* are sometimes used interchangeably, their scopes differ, with EMRs focused on a single practice's medical and treatment history and EHRs offering a more comprehensive picture of a patient's entire health. Traditional paper-based medical records are inefficient, error-prone, and make it difficult to follow a patient's health over time. The emergence of EHRs via information technology has addressed these concerns. EHRs allow medical practices to improve treatment quality, illness management, and preventative care. The digital aspect of EHRs allows for improved decision support and encourages greater collaboration among healthcare practitioners. As a result, EHRs are rapidly being recognized for their critical role in enhancing patient care in the healthcare sector [13].

- **Supply Chain Management (SCM):** SCM in health care has problems as a result of scattered ordering environments and inherent hazards such as compromised supply chains and patient safety concerns. Counterfeit medications, incorrect dose, and packing mistakes all contribute to these issues. Blockchain technology appears as an important monitoring tool, giving a transparent and traceable record of medicine and medical goods movements. Each transaction recorded on the blockchain allows for quick verification of drug provenance, sellers, and distributors. The distributed ledger makes it easier to authenticate supplier credentials, giving healthcare practitioners a greater understanding of the supply chain and guaranteeing that legitimate pharmaceuticals reach their patients. Blockchain has the potential to develop a trusted vendor network, improve demand forecasting, ensure data provenance, avoid fraud, and increase overall transaction efficiency in healthcare SCM [14].

- **Pharmaceutical:** Pharmaceutical businesses endure a lengthy and complex process, from medical development to regulatory approval, which makes the sector vulnerable to drug recalls and counterfeiting. Blockchain technology can improve security and privacy throughout the pharmaceutical industry. A distributed ledger enables tamper-proof documentation of trial events, while private blockchains may enforce patent conformity via smart contracts, providing integrity, traceability, and transparency. A considerable number of pharmaceutical businesses are investigating or using blockchain, demonstrating its potential. Sylim et al. constructed a pharmacosurveillance blockchain system that illustrates the potential of using blockchain principles to improve medication traceability, with a focus on tackling the worldwide crisis of counterfeit pharmaceuticals in several Asian nations [15].

- **Internet of Medical Things (IoMT):** IoMT systems are crucial for advancing health and medical information systems by enabling real-time data gathering, processing, and sharing among healthcare devices. In the IoMT paradigm, patients serve as the primary data source, with IoMT devices generating significant volumes of data either through close attachment or remote monitoring. This data is then stored on blocks or on the cloud, and artificial intelligence (AI) assists blockchain in creating intelligent virtual agents, enhancing security for sensitive medical information. Healthcare providers, as end users, seek authorized access to this data to ensure safe and secure care delivery [16].

15.4 How blockchain technology is affecting the recruitment process

In order to mitigate the recruitment obstacles in the healthcare industry, the players can integrate blockchain to solve the problem. The following section will discuss the significance of blockchain technology in the recruitment process.

- **Streamlining the Hiring Process:** Blockchain technology can revolutionize HRM by improving recruiting, performance management, and training processes' transparency, security, and efficiency [17]. A study on the use of blockchain technology in recruitment found that blockchain-based recruitment systems enhance the recruitment processes by offering opportunities such as increasing the speed and efficiency of the hiring process.
- **Enhancing Data Security:** Blockchain's DLT provides a secure and transparent platform for storing and sharing candidate information, ensuring data integrity and protecting sensitive data from unauthorized access or alteration. This is particularly important in industries such as health care, where patient data must be protected by strict privacy regulations.
- **Improving Transparency:** Blockchain technology can provide a clear and verifiable record of candidate information, reducing the risk of fraud and boosting recruiter confidence in the authenticity of candidate data. This transparency can help recruiters make more informed decisions and select the best candidates for a particular role.
- **Automating Verification Processes:** Blockchain technology can be used to automate the verification of candidate information, such as academic qualifications, work history, and professional references. This can save time and resources for recruiters, allowing them to focus on other aspects of their job.

15.5 The recruitment practices in healthcare industries

Healthcare recruitment encompasses the entire process of finding, attracting, evaluating, employing, and integrating healthcare professionals into the workforce. This includes doctors, nurses, healthcare administrators, pharmacists, technicians, therapists, and other essential healthcare workers. It plays a vital role in ensuring the provision of high-quality patient care and the smooth functioning of healthcare facilities. In recent times, healthcare recruitment has become increasingly competitive and unpredictable, especially in the wake of the COVID-19 pandemic. Apart from the financial implications of replacing employees, high turnover rates can significantly impact patient care. Maintaining a low turnover rate not only improves the quality of care provided to patients but also contributes to the overall competence and effectiveness of the healthcare workforce. It is crucial to prioritize hiring and retaining skilled professionals to ensure the continued success of the healthcare industry.

- **Leverage AI for Talent Preselection:** The healthcare industry, in particular, is incorporating AI into its recruitment practices to expedite the time it takes to fill positions and address staff retention concerns. By swiftly scanning résumés, AI can identify key phrases, qualifications, and other relevant information. Consequently, an AI recruitment tool can promptly identify qualified candidates from a large pool of applicants. Moreover, AI technology can contribute to reducing bias in the sourcing process, thereby enhancing the candidate selection process. This enables organizations to engage with individuals who may not have passed traditional prescreening methods, ultimately fostering a more diverse talent pool. By replacing manual processes with an automated system that consistently applies the same screening rules to all candidates, organizations can cultivate a stronger brand image and make better hiring decisions [17].
- **Incorporate Behavioral Health Assessments into Regular Practice:** The American Medical Association has provided a definition for behavioral health care, which encompasses the prevention, diagnosis, and treatment of various mental health and substance use disorders, as well as addressing life stressors, crises, and stress-related physical symptoms. Considering the impact that these behavioral health concerns have on the management of chronic diseases, it is important to recognize the evidence supporting the integration of behavioral health care. It has been suggested that past behavior is a reliable indicator of future performance. By conducting behavioral health assessments, organizations can inquire about candidates' past responses to specific situations, ensuring that they are well suited for the organization. These assessments provide insights into the traits, temperament, and behavioral competencies necessary for the position and for working effectively in healthcare settings [18].
- **Embrace the Concept of Diversity and Inclusion:** In order to cultivate a team that encompasses a range of perspectives, it is crucial to implement an all-encompassing recruitment procedure. This entails thoroughly examining job descriptions, screening questions, and interview questions to identify any biases that may discourage diverse candidates from applying or being chosen for positions. It may be beneficial to establish a committee dedicated to diversity and inclusion to oversee the hiring process and ensure that it remains fair and inclusive. By recruiting healthcare professionals from diverse backgrounds, you not only expand your pool of talent but also encourage innovation and creativity through a multitude of viewpoints [19]. Additionally, this approach allows you to target diverse patient markets. Embracing diversity in your hiring

practices also fosters collaboration among team members. By actively seeking out candidates with diverse backgrounds, you demonstrate that your brand is inclusive, which can contribute to staff retention and the referral of new hires.

- **Sustain the Visibility of Brand:** Recruitment and maintaining a strong company profile are heavily influenced by branding, especially in a market where there is fierce competition for limited human resources [20]. Although the pandemic has limited traditional in-person channels like career fairs, there are still numerous digital and print options available to make a lasting impression on potential hires. Currently, virtual talent acquisition has become the standard practice. Therefore, it is crucial to establish yourself as a leader in this domain. Importantly, utilizing digital branding techniques such as advertisements, sponsoring virtual conferences, and leveraging social media platforms will ensure that your organization remains at the forefront of the minds of experienced healthcare professionals and prospective recruits who are active online. Furthermore, healthcare organizations should prioritize showcasing their unique selling points and highlighting the benefits they offer to employees. This can include providing competitive salaries and comprehensive benefits packages, emphasizing opportunities for professional growth, and promoting a positive work environment. Sharing success stories and testimonials from current employees can also significantly enhance the organization's reputation and attract top talent.

15.6 Implementation of blockchain technology as a recruitment tool in healthcare industries

In healthcare recruitment, blockchain technology disrupts the traditional process with a secure and transparent solution for both hospitals and medical professionals. Imagine a system where a doctor's licenses, certifications, and training are permanently stored on a tamper-proof digital ledger. This allows hospitals to instantly verify qualifications, streamlining the hiring process while guaranteeing patient safety by ensuring the authenticity of credentials. But the benefits extend beyond initial verification. The same secure system can eliminate repetitive checks for traveling doctors and locum tenens by creating a portable record of their qualifications. This not only simplifies the process for medical professionals but also allows them to connect with a wider range of healthcare institutions through secure talent networks built on blockchain. By fostering trust and transparency throughout the application process, from verification to communication, blockchain has the potential to revolutionize how healthcare institutions find and recruit top talent, ultimately leading to a more efficient and effective healthcare system.

15.6.1 The enrollment of potential healthcare staff

In the initial phase, individuals who wish to join the company are required to complete a registration process by submitting their curriculum vitae (CV) onto the company's blockchain [21]. To do so, prospective employees are directed to fill out a registration form and enter their data and CV on the company's blockchain website. Once the submission is made, the system will automatically generate a code for the prospective employee. The blockchain technology will then verify the accuracy of the provided data by comparing the codes. If any inconsistencies are detected, the blockchain will promptly deem the data as invalid. Hence, it is crucial for employees to ensure that the information they input aligns with their actual identity. This process significantly minimizes the risk of data manipulation and enhances the efficiency of data validation. Additionally, once the data has been submitted, prospective employees are unable to modify it unless both the employer and the healthcare industries reach a consensus.

15.6.2 Selection of prospective healthcare employees for administrative roles

Based on the 2018 HireRight employment screening benchmark report, it was found that 84% of applicants provided false information on their résumés. To address this issue, the implementation of blockchain-based credential verification systems can greatly benefit the recruitment process [22]. These systems can effectively reduce the time spent on background checks, minimize fraud, and enhance trust within the recruitment ecosystem. By utilizing blockchain technology, the information and documents of potential employees entering the system can be validated between healthcare industries and the respective agencies responsible for issuing certificates or files. This validation process can occur automatically, eliminating the need for healthcare industries to request verification from the certificate issuer. For instance, blockchain can be used to verify a prospective employee's college data, work experience, educational history, and self-identity.

15.6.3 Faster decision making

Blockchain technology streamlines and expedites the decision-making process within the selection and recruitment procedures. By utilizing advanced technology, it eliminates the need for third-party involvement in data retrieval from agencies, companies, and governments to verify the authenticity of prospective employees' information [23]. Employment contract details, including electronic signatures, payroll information, security access codes, performance reports, and even psychometrics/behavioral assessments, can be securely stored on the blockchain. The accuracy of this data is automatically verified through blockchain agencies, companies, and governments. The time taken to search for data using blockchain technology is approximately seven seconds, enabling immediate hiring and contract issuance, with payroll numbers assigned promptly.

15.6.4 Ensuring proper placement of healthcare employees in suitable positions and fields

According to a survey conducted by ResumeBuilder.com, it was discovered that 72% of individuals in the United States have provided false information on their résumés. This revelation may come as a surprise to the organization. However, with effective implementation of blockchain technology, the recruitment team now has the ability to instantly access accurate and comprehensive information about potential employees, including their work history [21]. The reliability of the data obtained through blockchain technology can serve as a valuable reference for placing employees in suitable positions. For instance, if prospective employee A is a graduate of a reputable university with a GPA of 3.90 and excels in healthcare-related courses, they can be considered for a professional position in healthcare industries. Healthcare industries can have confidence in the data obtained through the blockchain system, which can also aid in decision-making and ensure employees are placed in roles that align with their expertise.

15.7 Opportunities and challenges

Blockchain technology has the potential to revolutionize healthcare recruitment by offering a secure, efficient, and trustworthy system for both hospitals and medical professionals. Imagine a future where a doctor's licenses, certifications, and training are permanently stored on a tamper-proof digital ledger. This would allow for instant verification of qualifications by hospitals, significantly expediting the hiring process while guaranteeing patient safety through irrefutable proof of credentials. But the benefits go beyond streamlining initial verification. Blockchain can create portable records for traveling doctors and locum tenens, eliminating the need for repeated checks at each new facility. This not only simplifies the process for medical professionals but also allows them to connect with a wider range of healthcare institutions through secure talent networks built on blockchain. However, for widespread adoption to occur, some hurdles need to be addressed. Scalability is a key concern, as technology needs to adapt to handle the massive amount of data generated by healthcare institutions. Additionally, industry-wide standards for secure and consistent data exchange across different blockchain platforms are crucial for seamless integration. Despite these challenges, blockchain presents a promising future for healthcare recruitment, fostering trust and transparency throughout the entire process, from verification to communication, ultimately leading to a more efficient and effective healthcare system.

15.7.1 Opportunities

Blockchain is poised to revolutionize healthcare recruitment by offering a treasure trove of opportunities. Imagine a system where a doctor's credentials are instantly verified thanks to secure storage on a tamper-proof ledger. This not only expedites hiring but guarantees patient safety. The benefits extend beyond initial checks, as blockchain can create portable records for traveling medical professionals, eliminate repetitive verification, and connect them with a wider range of institutions through secure talent networks. Furthermore, by ensuring transparency and security throughout the application process, blockchain has the potential to significantly improve the candidate experience for medical professionals.

- **The Future of Blockchain Jobs:** As blockchain technology gains traction in various industries, the demand for professionals with blockchain skills is on the rise. Early adopters have successfully applied blockchain in business, prompting more organizations to seek talent in this field. The adoption and utilization of blockchain are viewed as disruptive innovations, further fueling the demand for skilled professionals. LinkedIn Learning identified blockchain as one of the most in-demand hard skills in 2020, highlighting a scarcity of talent in the labor market compared to the growing needs of businesses [22]. Scholars suggest that job opportunities in this area include blockchain developers, solution architects, project managers, User Experience (UX) designers, and quality specialists [23].
- **Building a Blockchain Team:** To build a successful blockchain team, a diverse set of skills is essential, encompassing programming, cryptography, legal expertise, and business acumen. Effective collaboration within cross-disciplinary teams is crucial, given the nature of blockchain projects requiring comprehensive solutions. Additionally, possessing industry knowledge is imperative to address specific needs and challenges, ensuring the development of relevant and effective blockchain solutions [24].
- **Identifying the Right Talent:** Identifying the right talent for blockchain opportunities involves seeking individuals with technical proficiency, including a strong background in computer science, cryptography, and relevant programming languages like Solidity. Additionally, candidates with strong analytical and problem-solving skills are valuable, as blockchain often presents complex challenges. Crucially, adaptability and a willingness for continuous learning are essential traits, given the dynamic and rapidly evolving nature of blockchain technology [25].

- **Upskilling and Continuous Learning:** Blockchain plays a pivotal role in enhancing corporate training centers by providing updated and secure information on workforce competencies from stakeholders. By deploying competencies on the blockchain, traceability information is strengthened, ensuring security. The proposed blockchain-IoT application for training material needs emphasizes lightweight and vaporized characteristics for enhanced system adaptability. Additionally, blockchain facilitates automatic modeling of training quality evaluation, including content, trainer, and satisfaction feedback. This results in more reliable monitoring of training content quality, reflecting actual effects from workforce activities in the workplace [26].

15.7.2 Challenges

Blockchain technology has several challenges that need to be addressed for its widespread adoption. These challenges include lack of awareness and understanding, technical expertise and skills gap, limited talent pool, and regulatory uncertainty.

- **Lack of Awareness and Understanding:** The primary environmental challenge in adopting blockchain technology is the lack of awareness and understanding among various sectors, particularly outside of the banking industry. The low awareness extends to a common misunderstanding of how blockchain can be implemented. The ever-evolving and complex nature of blockchain, with its intricate network structure, contributes to this lack of comprehension. A widespread lack of knowledge hampers the exploration of diverse applications for blockchain technology. Many individuals mistakenly associate blockchain solely with Bitcoin and remain unaware of its broader existence and potential uses [27].
- **Technical Expertise and Skills Gap:** Blockchain technology requires specialized technical expertise, and there is a significant skills gap in the industry, making it challenging for organizations to find professionals with the necessary knowledge and experience. The challenge in adopting blockchain technology is the lack of knowledge, skills, and abilities among practitioners. Many of the solutions offered by blockchain are new and technically demanding, creating a high demand for skilled employees. However, the complexity of blockchain makes it challenging for businesses to find qualified personnel who can comprehend its potential and its impact on business opportunities. HRM experts emphasize that learning blockchain is a difficult process. Consequently, some businesses choose not to embrace blockchain due to a lack of in-house capabilities, while others recognize the need for training to incorporate this emerging technology. Participants suggest that education is a key factor in overcoming

the shortage of knowledge, skills, and abilities in the realm of blockchain technology [27].

- **Limited Talent Pool:** There is a scarcity of professionals with expertise in blockchain technology. The limited talent pool can lead to increased competition among businesses for skilled individuals, making recruitment and team-building challenging. In their study [28], the European Union (EU) recognizes the critical role of blockchain in driving digital transformation, fostering societal and business benefits, and promoting sustainable growth. However, the competitiveness of blockchain development is hindered by a shortage of skilled professionals. The increasing demand for blockchain skills is not met adequately, posing challenges such as a talent shortage, global competition, and a lack of alignment between education and industry needs [29].

- **Regulatory Uncertainty:** Blockchain technology faces regulatory uncertainty, which poses a challenge for blockchain network operators and participants. Many national and regional regulators are adopting a wait-and-see approach, preferring to explore and understand blockchain's implications before moving forward with additional regulations. The lack of regulatory certainty and evolving legal and regulatory position is challenging for blockchain network participants, and it is necessary that they continually assess their participation in blockchain networks. According to [29], one of the key factors influencing the decisions of new technology-based firms (NTBFs) to adopt blockchain's core application—cryptocurrency—is regulatory uncertainty. Firms may hesitate to engage in blockchain networks, especially those involving cryptocurrencies, due to concerns over potential legal issues, such as the classification of digital assets, taxation, and compliance with anti-money laundering (AML) and know-your-customer (KYC) regulations. ccording to institutional theory, NTBFs are expected to delay technology adoption until regulatory uncertainty diminishes. In contrast, the resource-based view suggests that NTBFs may embrace technology during regulatory uncertainty to gain a competitive advantage in an unregulated space [30, 31].

15.8 Conclusion

In today's highly competitive business landscape, it is crucial for businesses to embrace advanced technologies and revamp their existing business models in order to achieve success. Among these technologies, digital advancements have emerged as the most significant breakthrough, offering valuable solutions. The field of HRM, particularly recruitment, is undergoing significant changes and advancements due to the widespread adoption of digital technology trends such as AI, machine learning, chatbots, big data, and blockchain. This study represents the initial effort to collectively discuss the opportunities, challenges, and blockchain-based recruitment practices. Consequently, it is deemed to make significant contributions in raising awareness and enhancing understanding among researchers and healthcare practitioners regarding the utilization of blockchain in recruitment. Furthermore, the scope of the study is restricted to recruitment practices among the healthcare industries exclusively. There are various untapped avenues for research in the field of HRM. In light of this, fresh investigations can be carried out to explore the potential applications of blockchain technology in areas such as training and development, career planning, performance appraisal, and compensation management.

References

1. Abu-Elezz, I., Hassan, A., Nazeemudeen, A., Househ, M., & Abd-Alrazaq, A. (2020). The benefits and threats of blockchain technology in healthcare: A scoping review. *International Journal of Medical Informatics, 142*, 104246.
2. Agbo, C. C., Mahmoud, Q. H., & Eklund, J. M. (2019). Blockchain technology in healthcare: A systematic review. *Healthcare, 7*(2), 56. https://doi.org/10.3390/healthcare7020056
3. AMA (2022). What is Behavioral Health? Available link https://www.ama-assn.org/delivering-care/public-health/what-behavioral-health?trk=article-ssr-frontend-pulse_little-text-block. Accessed 8 January 2024
4. Ateniese, G., Magri, B., Venturi, D., & Andrade, E. (2017). Redactable Blockchain – or – Rewriting History in Bitcoin and Friends. In *2nd IEEE European Symposium on Security and Privacy*—EuroS&P.
5. Attaran, M. (2020). Blockchain technology in healthcare: Challenges and opportunities. *International Journal of Healthcare Management*, 1–14. https://doi.org/10.1080/20479700.2020.1843887
6. Avdoshin, S., & Pesotskaya, E. (2019). Blockchain Revolution in the Healthcare Industry. In *Proceedings of the Future Technologies Conference (FTC) 2018*, Springer International Publishing, 1, 626–639.
7. Chen, Z. (2023). Revolutionising HRM practice with blockchain technology: Unleashing disruptive paradigms of work and overcoming management challenges. *Technology Analysis & Strategic Management*, 1–14. https://doi.org/10.1080/09537325.2023.2282083
8. Chillakuri, B., & Attili, V. S. P. (2021). Role of blockchain in HR's response to new-normal. *International Journal of Organizational Analysis, 30*(6), 1359–1378.
9. Chunmian, G. E., Haoyue, S. H. I., Jiang, J., & Xiaoying, X. U. (2021). Investigating the demand for blockchain talents in the recruitment market: Evidence from topic modeling analysis on job postings. *Information & Management, 59*(7), 103513. https://doi.org/10.1016/j.im.2021.103513.
10. Collomb, A., & Sok, K. (2016). Blockchain/distributed ledger technology (DLT) what impact on financial sector? *Digiworld Economic Journal, 103*, third quarter, 93.
11. Dutta, P., Choi, T. M., Somani, S., & Butala, R. (2020). Blockchain technology in supply chain operations: Applications, challenges and research opportunities. *Transportation Research Part E: Logistics and Transportation Review, 142*, 102067. https://doi.org/10.1016/j.tre.2020.102067
12. Fachrunnisa, O., & Hussain, F. K. (2020). Blockchain-based human resource management practices for mitigating skills and competencies gap in workforce.

International Journal of Engineering Business Management, 12, 1–11. https://doi. org/10.1177/1847979020966400

13. Frederiks, A. J., Costa, S., Hulst, B., & Groen, A. J. (2022). The early bird catches the worm: The role of regulatory uncertainty in early adoption of blockchain's cryptocurrency by fintech ventures. *Journal of Small Business Management*, 1–34. https://doi.org/10.1080/00472778.2022.2089355
14. Godsey, J., Perrott, B., & Hayes, T. (2020). Can brand theory help re-position the brand image of nursing? *Journal of Nursing Management.* https://onlinelibrary. wiley.com/doi/epdf/10.1111/jonm.13003 Published online while in press.
15. HireRight, Employment Screening Benchmark Report (2018)
16. Khezr, S., Moniruzzaman, M., Yassine, A., & Benlamri, R. (2019). Blockchain technology in healthcare: A comprehensive review and directions for future re-search. *Applied Sciences, 9*(9), 1736. https://doi.org/10.3390/app9091736
17. Kişi, N. (2022). Exploratory research on the use of blockchain technology in recruitment. *Sustainability, 14*(16), 10098. https://doi.org/10.3390/su141610098
18. Levis, D., Fontana, F., & Ughetto, E. (2021). A look into the future of block-chain technology. *PLoS One. 16*(11), e0258995. https://doi.org/10.1371/journal. pone.0258995
19. Mackey, T. K., Kuo, T. T., Gummadi, B., Clauson, K. A., Church, G., Grishin, D., Obbad, K., Barkovich, R., & Palombini, M. (2019). Fit-for-purpose? Chal-lenges and opportunities for applications of blockchain technology in the future of healthcare. *BMC Medicine. 17*(1), 1–17.
20. Newman, L. H. (2022, Jan 22). *Security News This Week: Crypto.com Finally Admits It Lost $30 Million in Hack.* Retrieved from Wired. https://www.wired. com/story/crypto-hack-nso-group-security-news/
21. Peisl, T., & Shah, B. (2019). The Impact of Blockchain Technologies on Re-cruitment Influencing the Employee Lifecycle. In Systems, Software and Services Process Improvement; Walker, A., O'Connor, R., Messnarz, R., Eds.; Springer: Cham, Switzerland; pp. 695–705.
22. Purohit, B., & Martineau, T. (2016). Issues and challenges in recruitment for government doctors in Gujarat, India. *Human Resources for Health, 14*, 1–14. https://doi.org/10.1186/s12960-016-0140-9
23. Radanović, I., & Likić, R. (2018). Opportunities for use of blockchain technol-ogy in medicine. *Applied Health Economics and Health Policy, 16*(5), 583–590.
24. Resume Builder (2023). 1 in 3 Americans have lied in the hiring process. Available link https://www.resumebuilder.com/1-in-3-have-lied-in-the-hiring-process/Accessed on 9th January 2024.
25. Rhemananda, H., Simbolon, D. R., & Fachrunnisa, O. (2021). Blockchain Tech-nology to Support Employee Recruitment and Selection in Industrial Revolution 4.0. In *Proceedings of the International Conference on Smart Computing and Cyber Security: Strategic Foresight, Security Challenges and Innovation*, Kosong, Korea, 28–29.
26. Salah, D., Ahmed, M. H., & ElDahshan, K. (2020). Blockchain Applications in Human Resources Management: Opportunities and Challenges. In *Proceedings of the Evaluation and Assessment in Software Engineering (EASE'20)*, Trond-heim, Norway, 15–17.
27. Seebacher, S., & Schüritz, R. (2017). Blockchain technology as an enabler of ser-vice systems: A structured literature review. *Springer Nature, 279*, 12–23.
28. Solomos, D., Tsianos, N., Ghodous, P., & Riel, A. (2021). The European Chaise Initiative to Shape the Future of Blockchain Skill Qualification and Certification. In *Systems, Software and Services Process Improvement: 28th European Con-ference, EuroSPI 2021, Krems, Austria, September 1–3, 2021, Proceedings 28* (pp. 640–650). Springer International Publishing.

29. Treweek, S., Pitkethly, M., Cook, J., Fraser, C., Mitchell, E., Sullivan, F., Jackson, C., Taskila, T. K., & Gardner, H. (2018). Strategies to improve recruitment to randomised trials. *Cochrane Database of Systematic Reviews*, MR000013. https://doi.org/10.1002/14651858.MR000013.pub6
30. Valeri, M., & Baggio, R. (2021). A critical reflection on the adoption of blockchain in tourism. *Information Technology & Tourism*, 23(2), 121–132.
31. Vujičić, D., Jagodić, D., & Ranđić, S. (2018). Blockchain Technology, Bitcoin, and Ethereum: A Brief Overview. In *17th International Symposium Infoteh-Jahorina (INFOTEH)*, IEEE, 1–6.

INDEX